NAP TIME

NAP TIME

...

Lisa Manshel

WILLIAM MORROW
AND COMPANY, INC.
NEW YORK

Copyright © 1990 by Lisa Manshel

Library of Congress Cataloging-in-Publication Data

Manshel, Lisa.
  Nap time / Lisa Manshel.
    p.   cm.
  ISBN 0-688-08763-9
  1. Child molesting—New Jersey—Essex County—Case studies.
2. Child molesting—New Jersey—Essex County—Investigation—Case
studies. 3. Day care centers—New Jersey—Essex County—Case studies. I.   Title.
HQ72.U53M27   1990
362.7'6—dc20   89-36625
                                                                                  CIP

Printed in the United States of America

First Edition

1 2 3 4 5 6 7 8 9 10

BOOK DESIGN BY RICHARD ORIOLO

Acknowledgments

From the moment I began research for this book, Peggy Foster has been a daily source of information and advice. Peggy first familiarized me with the facts of the ongoing *Michaels* case and then made introductions to many of the key figures in the investigation. Throughout the trial, she directed me to additional sources of information and pointed out alternative interpretations of the facts. Her allowing me to draw on her immense knowledge of the field of child sexual abuse has significantly increased the comprehensiveness of this book. Most of all, though, I have drawn on Peggy's intuitiveness—her keen empathy—that exemplifies, for me, the greatest of strength.

I would like to express my gratitude to the many people depicted in this book who were open about their experiences and feelings, for their willingness to share what they learned, both personally and professionally, during the *Michaels* case.

I would also like to thank Michaela Clavell and Helen Meyer for their patience and their sharp judgment; Roger Manshel, who opened my mind to sympathies; and both Lynn Manshel and Andy Kaplan, each of whom, word wise and tireless, immeasurably increased what I could have done alone. And for their guidance and professional wisdom: Eleanor Bergstein, Jeanne Bernkopf, Diane Curcio, Morton Farber, Trish de Gasperis, and Terri Harrison.

Finally, I am eager to thank my friends for their invaluable comments on the manuscript and their perceptions of the case: Jenna Gruen, Erika Hoffman, Deborah Rizzi, and Susan Thomas.

NAP TIME

Part

ONE

1

.·.

Jonathan Moore, naked, sprawled atop the examining table, maneuvering a jigsaw puzzle. He carefully considered a wedge shaped like something's paw.

The little boy wasn't himself these days. The four-year-old was aggressive, attacking his parents in sporadic, unprovoked fits, yelling, "I don't wanna go to school! I'm gonna have to take a nap!" His parents had decided he was outgrowing his nap. Sometimes, Jonathan was so disruptive at parties, kicking, spitting, biting, that his mother had to take him home. The Moores' friends had started whispering, "What's happened to Jonathan? What's the matter?"

He seemed to have an anger in him, an anger that was directed most often toward his mother, almost as if he'd had a bad dream in which Claudia played the toothy, devouring monster. Yet nothing more obvious was amiss. Then one morning Jonathan woke up with a pinkish rash all over his body, and so, on April 30, 1985, Jonathan's mother took him to the pediatrician.

The nurse came in to take Jonathan's measurements and background information. She had known him since he was three days old: He had become a forty-inch-tall preschooler weighing in at thirty-seven pounds. When she finished, Jonathan got a boost back onto the table, and the nurse let the puzzle entertain him while she took his temperature rectally. She eyed the second hand of her watch: ten, twenty, thirty. . . .

Jonathan flipped his head to the side and said, "That's what my teacher does to me at school."

"What does she do?" she asked, not really listening.

"Her takes my temperature." The boy turned back to the puzzle. The green piece didn't fit in anywhere; it was one of the tricky pieces without any insert knobs.

The nurse was almost positive schools were supposed to take temperatures by using plastic strips on the forehead. She asked Jonathan, "Which teacher?" trying to sound unalarmed.

"Kelly." He was still engrossed in the puzzle.

The nurse netted Claudia Moore's eye. She mouthed, "Who's Kelly?" Jonathan's mother shook her head blankly. She didn't know a Kelly at Wee Care.

The nurse turned away, lifted the thermometer, and read the number: normal. She wrote out some notes on her chart and left to get the doctor.

Claudia looked at her son, and her voice was soft. "Did anyone else have their temperature taken?"

"She does it to Sean."

When the doctor came in, Claudia didn't mention what had just happened—*what had just happened?* She didn't want to discuss this in front of Jonathan. This was completely out of her experience as a mother, and she didn't want to go at it in an impulsive way. The doctor carried out his examination, unaware of the outburst that throbbed within her.

.
. .

At about the same time, a new teacher was being welcomed at the Community Day Nursery in East Orange, New Jersey. The woman had left her job at Wee Care in Maplewood only days ago because, she said, this school was closer to her apartment in East Orange, only a mile's walk. The money was basically the same, only pennies more an hour, but this new school was airier and more spacious.

A tri-level brick building constructed specifically to house the school, the Community Day Nursery accommodated over one hundred families and maintained a long waiting list for new admittances. Checks and balances operated at this nursery: Teachers didn't spend time alone with the children. One of the new teacher's complaints about her old job was that the school's director had never been around. In her last few days at Wee Care, it had been no secret that she wanted to leave, and on her very last day a co-worker overheard her singing to herself with relief: "It's all over now, Baby Blue." She had finally told a former co-worker: "I just gotta go. I gotta get away."

If she was lucky, her new employment would be able to please her more. But as she began her tenure at the Community Day Nursery, the teachers who worked with her found the woman distant and nervous.

．
■ ■

At home, Claudia Moore made lunch for Jonathan while he played with some trucks on the kitchen floor, all the time thinking over what he'd said at the doctor's office. Glancing down, she asked her son, "Jonathan, who's Kelly?"

He didn't stop playing but answered, "She's the one—the teacher at nap."

After lunch, Claudia sent Jonathan up to his room to play and backed herself into a corner of the kitchen with the telephone and the phone book. The doctor had said that Jonathan's rash would disappear, so at least that was nothing to worry about.

Jonathan's doctor came on the line. His nurse had already filled him in about what Jonathan had said. The doctor didn't want to frighten Mrs. Moore, but he advised her to follow up on her son's allegation by calling New Jersey's child protective agency, the Division of Youth and Family Services.

Claudia Moore's call was referred to the Institutional Abuse Investigation Unit of DYFS. She gave a brief report to a DYFS worker, then contacted Arlene Spector, the director of her son's school, to let her know what had happened.

．
■ ■

On the morning of May 1, Lou Fonolleras of DYFS contacted Investigator George McGrath at the Essex County Prosecutor's Office and reported, as required by law, the new allegation of abuse. He wanted to know if he should interview the parties involved.

The Child Abuse Unit of the Prosecutor's Office, handling crimes against children under twelve, saw an average of one hundred cases a month, 55 percent of which involved sexual crimes against children. The unit operated with only one assistant prosecutor and two full-time investigators, George McGrath and Richard Mastrangelo. George put DYFS in a holding pattern and left the office to locate Assistant Prosecutor Sara Sencer.

.
. .

Kelly. Kelly.

The Moores didn't know a Kelly, not at the Wee Care Day Nursery, their son's school, or anywhere else. But Wee Care had, in fact, employed a young teacher by that name. In late September 1984, Kelly Michaels had started out at Wee Care as an aide, but when a preschool teacher had quit her job only a month into the academic year, Kelly had been drawn up through the thinned ranks and promoted to teacher. With no teaching experience or professional training, after only four weeks of cutting apples, dispensing toys, and monitoring trips to the bathroom, Kelly Michaels had taken charge of an abandoned class of three-year-olds. She also took on duties supervising four- and five-year-olds during lunch, nap, and the after-school play period.

Margaret Kelly Michaels was short and heavy, her dress stylish, funky: baggy jeans, penny loafers without the cent, and a man's jacket with the sleeves rolled up. Occasionally, she tied a twisted bandana around her neck. She could, it was said, look slovenly: her hair dirty, her clothes wrinkled (she wore the same jeans day after day). Sometimes she even smelled pungent. But Kelly herself was upbeat: She frequently had a smile on her face, even when a smile seemed inappropriate.

To her co-workers at Wee Care, Kelly was fun and funny, easy to talk to, but also somewhat aloof: She didn't socialize with them outside of school. And she didn't always seem to be with them: At times, Kelly would stare off into space, as if unplugged in the middle of a conversation, or she would just turn on her toes and ballet away, arms raised over her head.

Kelly helped out the other teachers and aides by volunteering to take children to the bathroom, despite the fact that that was an aide's responsibility. The children at Wee Care tended to like Kelly, in part because she could devise clever, fun games to play: monster games, in which she'd pretend to be a monster and chase the little ones on the playground; or the jail game, in which the children had to catch Kelly and pull her into a closet and pretend to lock her up.

For seven months, until her departure on April 26, Kelly Michaels worked at the Wee Care Day Nursery, and in that time the other employees never saw Kelly hit or yell at a child, but they reported that she wasn't very affectionate toward the children either. Even if a child was crying, Kelly could easily ignore the distress. When it came to the students at

Wee Care, Kelly betrayed no discernible emotional range, her responses not skewed toward cruelty or compassion.

.

. .

Assistant Prosecutor Sara Sencer, a woman in her mid-thirties, seemed ever frazzled: She was always racing, not walking, down courthouse corridors. And there was an electric intensity ever-present in her delicate features as she bore down on an idea. George McGrath ambled after her, casual with Styrofoam cup of coffee. As he spoke, Sara rocked nervously from foot to foot, then told him to have Rich Mastrangelo start an investigation into the little boy's allegation. George himself was tied up with a homicide investigation, his services having been temporarily lent out to another unit.

Sara had been the head of the Child Abuse Unit for less than a year, having only recently been transferred from general trial law (burglary, murder, robbery, rape) to child abuse. Although the unit had handled dozens of sexual abuse cases, most of those involved incest. An allegation of abuse in an institutional setting was something new, and Sara herself had as yet never worked with the institutional unit of DYFS. Reluctant to turn the investigation over to a bureau with which she was not familiar, Sara made it clear that DYFS was to be kept at bay until her own unit had had an opportunity to evaluate the case.

Rich informed Lou Fonolleras that the Prosecutor's Office was going to conduct the Wee Care investigation and promised to keep in touch and let him know when DYFS could get its own investigation under way. The Child Abuse Unit of the Essex County New Jersey Prosecutor's Office opened the file on 1985's case number 402. The year had only just dipped into May.

The Prosecutor's Office was a law-enforcement agency of the state of New Jersey, with the authority to prosecute criminal charges, and with units covering the gamut of crimes from child abuse to fraud to homicide. As enforcers of the law, prosecutors were in and out of court daily, so they had a prime office location: directly inside the courthouse building. On television, public defenders often wore the white hats, but in the courthouse, prosecuting attorneys were the home team.

Sara Sencer's unit operated out of a twelve- by eighteen-foot cubicle crammed with desks for two investigators and one secretary, a coatrack, refrigerator, sink, and coffee machine. As head of the unit, Sara had her own cubicle next door, a third of the size of the main one, her windows overlooking the twelve-story jailhouse adjacent to the court building. The back half of Sara's office was the wall of narrow windows, and the front wall where her desk rested was also glass, facing the hallway. The prosecutor had tried to convert the small office to a children's room, a mushroom field of midcalf tables and chairs. She had toys and games and books fashionable among preschoolers, as well as a massive dollhouse which served as the centerpiece to the room.

Sara first met Jonathan Moore as he walked down the hall of the Prosecutor's Office holding his mother's hand. The walls leading to Sara's office were lined with cartons labeled "Sex Files" from the Sex Crimes Unit next door which handled crimes against victims twelve and over.

Approaching from the opposite direction, Sara Sencer introduced herself: "Hi. I'm Sara. I'm your lawyer."

She reached out and handed Jonathan her card. The little boy held on to it loosely. Sara explained, "It's my job to protect children. It's my job to make sure that people who touch children never do it again."

Jonathan stared up at her.

Neither of the unit's rooms offered much space in which to interview; however, to avoid embarrassing Jonathan in the tight quarters, George and Sara kept the office cleared while he was there. Sara spoke to Jonathan first while his mother, Claudia, remained in the room as a witness. Sara didn't like to have too many adults around when she talked with a child, so Rich Mastrangelo and Sergeant John Noonan from the Maplewood police listened to Jonathan's interview from outside the door.

Jonathan Moore was shy, but not frightened as Sara chatted with him about his family, asking him comfortable questions about how many brothers and sisters he had. Slowly, naturally, she then introduced the subject of school into the conversation, making her voice astonishingly like a child's as she began: "Do you like school, Jonathan?"

"No." His head tipped down, white hair spreading out over the smooth forehead, so that his eyes were obscured for a moment.

Sara edged toward the allegation. "Do you like nap?"

"No!" Jonathan jumped off his chair and began to kick the bookshelves. His mother watched warily.

"Do you like Kelly?"

"No."

"Did Kelly touch you?"

Now he was kicking Sara's shin. "Yeah."

"How?" she asked, her voice tentative.

"Her takes my temperature."

Sara needed precision, clarity. She pointed to her lips and asked, "In your mouth?"

"No. You can't put 'gasoline' in your mouth."

"Well, where did she put it?"

His voice contorted, he screeched, "In my bum!" Then he added, "Her takes Sean's temperature too, and Evan's."

After the Moores had been sent home, Sara told Rich Mastrangelo to get on the phone and call in the two boys Jonathan had named, as well as the child's pediatrician and nurse.

Evan Connors came in that same day. When the second little boy entered Sara's fishbowl office, he became extremely self-conscious and withdrawn. His mother explained to Sara that during this whole school year, her son had had a persistent anal rash that they couldn't get rid of, but which had just now disappeared, the same week Kelly Michaels had left Wee Care. Yet, in the interview that followed, Evan denied all knowledge of wrongdoing at his school and would make no allegation. Sara sent Evan home and crossed him off her list but made an attempt to soften the effect of her office by putting balloons all over the walls. She called it the "Evan Connors Office."

The following day George McGrath interviewed Sean. The little boy was agitated, hostile, rushing around the room, almost trapped. His mother's presence in the room didn't soothe his anxiety. As he raced around, Sean knocked over the coatrack that was in the room: Several coats sloshed slowly to the floor; the metal crashed fast. Despite his obvious agitation, the five-year-old was able to tell the investigator that Kelly had touched him with her hand, on his penis.

. .
. .

The Moores had notified Arlene Spector, the director of Wee Care, about their son's allegations, bringing recent events to the attention of the members of the school board. One of the board members asked his son about the school. What Paul told his father about Wee Care, and what his father then reported to George McGrath, was astounding. Paul maintained that the teacher, Kelly, had fondled his penis with a spoon.

"A *spoon*?" Sara retorted.

George watched her with a calm smile.

She challenged, "Who the hell is ever going to believe a spoon? You want me to sell that to twenty-three jurors upstairs?" She paused for a minute, dumbfounded, then left the office.

. .
. .

On Sunday morning, Sara called George at home and asked if he would come down to the Maplewood police station. When he arrived, George found that the prosecutor had made arrangements to videotape an interview session with Sean, having borrowed a hand-held video camera from the police. They set up the equipment upstairs in an empty municipal courtroom, and George prepared to interview the child.

The little boy had a soup-bowl haircut which formed a golden helmet around his head. He sat poised facing George, who kept his body still and soft, so there would be nothing threatening in his posture. George didn't want to distract Sean or open himself up to accusations of cuing. Not even George's head moved, and his hands were clutched between his knees.

At first Sean was reticent and denied even knowing anybody named Kelly. He folded himself every which way in the chair, and when he finally came to rest, he was compacted into the seat's angled fold. Then Sean told George that Kelly punched him.

George asked quietly, "Why did she punch you?"

"'Cause," he said.

"Why?"

"'Cause I'm little."

George rounded forward to lean on his knees, and Sean leaned backward, elongating his skinny frame to vee backward in his chair. George peered forward and Sean poised in retreat, a grounded image of cat and mouse.

George asked, "Why are you afraid of Kelly?"

"'Cause I don't like her."

"Huh?"

"'Cause I'm bad," said Sean, slumped pitiably in the chair. He wiggled around, repacking himself into the seat's crease.

When the session was over, George warned Sara that they would most likely be unable to make use of the videotape for lack of playback equipment, but Sara warmed at the prospect of screening the incriminating video for Kelly Michaels herself.

．
．　．

On May 6, 1985, just after seven in the morning, Rich Mastrangelo and Maplewood's Sergeant John Noonan went to East Orange to bring in Margaret Kelly Michaels. Jonathan Moore had disclosed only a week ago: Things moved very quickly.

Kelly Michaels lived in an apartment just off the beaten path in East Orange, a tough town rivaling Newark for the highest crime rate in the county. Her apartment was in an old brick, elevator building, with small blue and white bathroom tiles decorating the front porch area. The lawn was yellow and dotted with blown garbage.

As the officers rang, Kelly was getting dressed for work at the Community Day Nursery. The two officers explained their business and asked if she would come down for questioning. She agreed.

When they arrived at the Prosecutor's Office, George McGrath stepped away from his homicide investigation to meet the Wee Care suspect. Kelly had thick bones, a belly, a wide head: Everything about her seemed overgrown, including her dense, dark hair, although her features, small and pretty, made her seem cute. Her body was hidden beneath baggy jeans pleated at the waist and a plaid oxford shirt. She was twenty-three years old.

Before an official statement could be taken from Michaels, the suspect had to be convinced to sign a *Miranda* waiver and relinquish her right to remain silent. George was known to be masterful at gaining the cooperation of suspects, and he now talked to Kelly simply, comfortingly, to make her understand that the questioning of a suspect was a routine part of operations. (As he had anticipated, the video of Sean was not usable.) When the two were finished talking, Kelly Michaels decided to sign the waiver and submit to questioning by the Prosecutor's Office: She insisted she had nothing to hide.

Rich Mastrangelo conducted the actual examination while George ambled in and out of the office whenever he had a minute free. In the course of the day, George decided that Kelly Michaels was one of three things: either the greatest liar he'd ever met, the craziest loon, or else just plain not guilty. And he believed the boys.

From the first moment of questioning, Kelly vehemently protested her innocence, wounded by the ill that was being thought of her: She was offended, she was shocked, she was angry, she was worn, she was indignant. One moment she would be crying, distraught, the next moment smiling, cavalier. Her personality shifts seemed drastic to Mastrangelo. During an intermission, Rich joked with a secretary: ''Go ask Kelly which one of her wants a cup of coffee.''

The questions the investigator asked were restricted to what the unit had learned from the boys: Rich basically just ran down the list of allegations. He began, ''Did you sexually assault Jonathan Moore during nap time or any other time while you were at Wee Care?''

''No.''

''Why would he say that you did?''

''I don't know, but I don't doubt that something happened to him. . . .''

''Did you ever touch or attempt to touch Sean sexually?''

''No.''

"Did you ever lock any of the pupils in a closet?"

"No."

So, Rich inquired, "Do you know why these students would state these allegations?"

Kelly shook her head. "Unless they've been frightened by someone else . . ." Her voice was low and thrumming: sexual. But the beseeching, lingering glances were those of a little girl.

Rich asked, "Did you ever touch Paul on his penis with a spoon?"

"NO."

"Are you sexually attracted to any of these pupils that we just talked about?"

"No."

Kelly Michaels insisted that she was never alone with her students. When she took children to the bathroom, she waited outside in the hallway. Furthermore, during her nap class, "parents were always coming and going."

In the onslaught of questions, Rich inserted one special question: "Are you willing to take a polygraph?" And in Kelly's eagerness to persuade him of her innocence, she answered yes.

He pressed on. "Is there any other teacher in the nursery school that may have sexually assaulted these children?"

The suspect's response baffled him. "I've never seen any sexual abuse, but I have seen strange behavior."

Rich pursued, "What do you mean by strange behavior?"

"Uh, playing games with the children by saying that she was me. She would say, 'I'm Kelly.' "

Was this an attempt to shelve her identity, blame an impostor? He would find out, but first Rich addressed this issue of strange behavior: "What else did you consider strange behavior?"

"That she would disappear for a long period of time . . . she was slow. Sometimes we would find her in the bathroom."

Now he asked, "*Who* would be in the bathroom?"

Kelly didn't seem to hear his question and just continued with her thoughts: "Sometimes she would go up to the bathroom with the children. She would be up there for a long period of time." Her hair seemed dank, heavy.

Rich asked again, "This teacher that you are speaking about, what's her name?"

Kelly named a teacher.

"Do you feel that she could have the potential to do these things to children?"

"Yes," said Kelly.

Rich had to follow through and ask, "Does she touch the kids often?"

Kelly's eyes were very serious, as if she were puzzling something out. "Yes. More than most teachers. She tickles them a lot."

Rich changed gears. "Did you ever have control of Jonathan, Paul, and Sean at the same time?"

Kelly played with her fingertips, molding and pinching the skin. "In a room with other children, and other *teachers*." Then she added confoundingly, "They should never be alone like that."

Before Kelly signed the report, Rich gave her an opportunity to adjust her statements. Kelly carefully added to the text: "After nap time, I was never"—then she crossed out *never*—"rarely responsible for bathroom. I am absolutely innocent."

By eleven o'clock that morning, Rich Mastrangelo had recorded two separate statements, each of which Margaret Kelly Michaels attested to with her signature, playful curlicues on the stems of her *m*'s. Taking precautions, George had instructed Rich to have Michaels sign a new *Miranda* waiver each time she gave a separate statement, although one would have sufficed, and Kelly signed yet another waiver before taking the polygraph. Her ready compliance convinced Sara's investigators that Kelly Michaels wanted desperately to clear herself.

Sara Sencer was not intrigued with Kelly Michaels. Earlier in the day, Sara had walked in on the questioning session and found Kelly pointing the finger at too many people: parents, another teacher, fabricating children. The young woman's immediate situation called for sadness, even pity, but Sara would not empathize with Kelly. Her job required her to think entirely of the children she was hired to protect. Kelly was an adult who had become what she would be.

After a lunch break, Kelly submitted to being hooked up to the polygraph machine because, as she later told her attorneys, she believed that if she passed the test, the Prosecutor's Office would suspend its investigation. Before she was released for the day, Kelly was taken over to the local police station in Maplewood and photographed. She waited awhile to be processed, sitting alone, crying silently.

When Kelly returned to her apartment, she called her parents. It was agreed: She had to stay and fight to clear her name. She then called the administrators of the Community Day Nursery in East Orange and told them what was being said about her. At first, the administrators replied that she still had a job: They were confident this was all a mistake and would blow over. But soon they placed their teacher of four and a half days on a permanent leave of absence.

Because Kelly had pointed a finger at another teacher, George McGrath now decided to make sure that the correct person had been named. Claudia Moore was asked to bring Jonathan to the Maplewood police department. There he was shown a collection of photographs of all the Wee Care teachers, including one of Kelly Michaels and one of the teacher Kelly had named under questioning.

Jonathan Moore identified Kelly Michaels as his assailant.

.
. .

The polygraph test would be inadmissible at a trial, but the state sought the results as an investigative tool. An initial reading indicated that Kelly had passed, but a second one, by an expert in the field, proved inconclusive.

Over the next few days, Sara met repeatedly in her own Newark office with Wee Care's director and its head teacher, Arlene Spector and Diane Costa. They both instructed her as to the various aides' and teachers' schedules, periods of employment, and duties in the school. Together the three drew charts of who would have been in the building at what times of the day and what times of the year.

In addition, statements were taken from the school's other employees, and Sara learned that early this past winter, almost every child in the school had abruptly stopped taking naps, and not only several boys in Kelly Michaels's nap room, but girls too. One of the teachers subsequently named the period "the Nap Rebellion." Yet, despite this mention of odd behavior among girls, Sara had no reason to believe that girls had been involved in the abuse: The boys hadn't named any girls. The accusations Sara had heard seemed confined to Kelly Michaels's nap class or the late-afternoon period when she had had occasion to supervise leftover children in the gym. So, the unit cordoned off the field of victims, excluding the girls.

.
. .

This was no time for a member of law enforcement to be involved in a day-care abuse case. Sara had recently attended a conference on sexual abuse in Chicago, and from what she had learned a child was popularly considered about as credible an eyewitness to a crime as a chimpanzee signing that he saw the whole thing. Young child victims had made claims of having seen people murdered, of having taken airplanes to sex parties, of having participated in sexual activities that were confused with the language of games. The children's often garbled allegations, mixtures of truth and pretense, suggested to the public that the allegations were untrue, and consequently, entire prosecutions were discredited and cases thrown away to appease public outcry.

In stretches of the country, allegations of sexual assault on children were being dismissed out of hand because children were considered truthless. Even many professionals felt that young children fantasize about sexual intercourse and that they cannot distinguish between fact and fantasy. And so, when a child alleged he had been abused, he was often seen to be a child who had *imagined* he had been abused, and then, becoming confused, had come to think that the episode had really happened.

In divorce cases, it was even becoming chic for one parent to encourage a child to accuse the other parent of improper sexual conduct. These occasional false allegations were also serving to discredit other child complainants. But Sara learned that most professionals agreed: Children as young as Jonathan rarely lied about sexual abuse. For one thing, their knowledge of sexual situations was extremely limited.

Multiple-victim day-care cases were relatively new territory for the courts and extremely difficult to prosecute. There existed a lack of professional guidelines about how to evaluate the state's witnesses for the strength of their accusations. Many prosecutors were unwilling to unleash their powers with nothing more to go on than the word of a child. And if a child at first said that nothing had happened, should the case then be tossed out?

And Sara had three victims of sexual abuse in a school setting alleging acts that defied popular disbelief and were likely to incur the local community's wrath for having shocked its naïveté. She settled in to wait for the accusations of overzealousness, witch-hunting, and opportunism.

▪
▪ ▪

The members of the board of Wee Care decided to provide some information to the parents while everyone was still calm enough to be attentive. Arlene Spector joined with the board in its deliberations over how to handle this developing crisis. It worked in the board's favor that most of the parents barely knew one another: At the moment, there wasn't much word of mouth about the incident at Jonathan's doctor's office.

On May 8, 1985, a letter was sent out to every Wee Care household:

Dear Parents,

There is currently an investigation being conducted by the Essex County Prosecutor's Office regarding serious allegations made by a child against a former employee of the Maplewood Center. We are cooperating with the Prosecutor's Office in this matter.

The Board has met to discuss these allegations and their implications for the children, their families and the school. While we are very concerned, it is important to emphasize that no formal charges have been made. The Board has discussed a variety of measures, and has appointed a committee to determine what actions need to be taken in this matter.

As we receive more information we will be communicating with you further.

The letter sparked immediate telephone mania, and parents by the dozen called Arlene, eager to be induced into unconcern.

Karen Steadman reached the director at her home. Arlene assured Karen that her daughter was safe because no girls were involved, and she implied that the boy who was saying all this "had problems."

Karen hung up the phone. The victims were all boys, someone else's children. Mentally, Karen paced out her own terrain, demarcating the universe of her loved ones and securing that area.

I'm fine, she thought, violently relieved, although she didn't exactly know what danger it was that she had eluded.

When Ellen Gardner received the board's letter, the ambiguous phrasing, "a former employee," suggested to her that whatever happened had happened years ago. Ellen threw the letter out, convinced that none of it had anything to do with her son. Joey was at an age when a little boy's mother was to him the sweetest thing on earth. She knew he would have told her anything.

Ellen went to her son for comfort. Joey was playing in the den. He had curly, light brown hair, a pointed chin, immense eyes.

"Joey, the school is closing because a teacher did bad things."

He sat still, barely listening.

"Joey, did anyone ever touch you, or did you ever see anything bad happen?"

He addressed the toy-strewn floor: "Well, I did see some things happen to me and Lewis, but it was only a dream." Joey jumped up and raced to his room and came back with a doll. He was shaking the doll violently, as if he were teaching it a lesson.

Ellen watched, sickened, as her son screamed over and over again: "I'll cut your head off!"

■
■ ■

The state was sealing up its investigation. The investigators had talked to the alleged victims as well as to the accused, and no more victims had come forward or been named. There was a consensus within the unit that it had achieved a true and satisfactory containment of the problem as Sara Sencer began to prepare the evidence to present to the Grand Jury. A sliver more than a week after "Her takes my temperature," the Prosecutor's Office concluded that the investigation was over.

Child Abuse investigation number 402 was concluded on May 8 with a total of three victims. They had contained the genie with only her head out of the bottle.

2

⋰

The members of the board had arranged an educational meeting at the school at which to inform the parents about child abuse while at the same time minimizing speculation. To conduct this meeting they chose Peg Foster, a social worker whose name had been given to Arlene Spector by several sources. Peg was co-director of the Sexual Assault Unit at United Hospitals Medical Center in Newark, New Jersey, a position she had held since 1975. Over the past ten years, Peg had seen over four thousand sexually abused children.

In the hectic week before Peg's scheduled appearance, Arlene Spector called her frequently, telling Peg that from what she was hearing from mothers, she feared that perhaps many more children were involved. On the night of May 15, Peg drove to Maplewood to St. George's Episcopal Church where Wee Care had been renting space for several years.

Maplewood tucked into the folds of the map in one of the loveliest, wealthiest sectors of northern New Jersey. Families were largely young and acquiring permanence in a town that offered a good environment for their children. The selection of private schools was wide, and the public schools were also commended. Local high schools sent the majority of graduates on to college, and a relatively high percentage entered Ivy League schools.

With women's entrance into the workplace, the demand for child-care services had far exceeded the available supply of reputable centers. Some communities had devised creative solutions, such as drawing senior citizens back into the work force to look after toddlers, but most large communities suffered from a shortage of good day care. New centers were sprouting everywhere, in basements, in homes, in storefronts, some of them no more than glorified baby-sitting factories. In Essex County, the Wee Care Day Nursery offered an expensive but well-respected alternative.

The parents who sent their children to Wee Care were the sort who thoroughly researched their choice, scouring an entire suburban region before consigning their baby to a facility. Word of mouth about the school was good, as was the plan of care. The school had instituted monthly educational themes, issued the children healthy snacks twice a day, had a playground for all students, and offered optional gym classes. And parents received accident reports whenever a child was injured. Of mixed financial backgrounds, some of the families were wealthy, others struggled to pay the expensive monthly fees, and still others sent their children to Wee Care on scholarship. Not every family lived in the school's immediate vicinity: A few children came from as far away as Irvington, New Jersey, a fifteen-minute drive.

St. George's Church, set in a deep lawn, aspired to an imposing height, but its stones appeared to weight it down in a pleasingly eerie crouch. The street it faced was a wide, tree-lined avenue known to be a speed trap. Children on bicycles rode along the sidewalk to the ice-cream shop or magazine store, gliding past the church, which stood embedded to its waist in the dip of the lawn. The colored slate of St. George's roof was barely above the level of traffic: The spacious, tiered, glassy houses across the street seemed to peer down on the church's wooden doors. Farther down the slope and to the left, the building spilled out into a stone corridor with a walkway which created a quiet garden enclosure.

Scanning the exterior of the church as she drove up, Peg Foster noticed a lot of walkways: railroad-tie paths leading to unused doors or a hulking, knotted bush. She entered the building from the rear parking lot into the school area.

Peg heard voices and wandered up to the third floor where the school board had gathered to dread communally the coming meeting. As Peg walked in, she saw a cluster of people whose eyes seemed to plead with her: "Don't create havoc. Don't ruin our world."

Arlene Spector approached and introduced herself, and as she and Peg looked at each other now for the first time, they realized immediately that decades ago they had gone to high school together: acquaintance friends. Their new last names had misinformed, temporarily muddling their identities. Peg remembered having always thought Arlene was a good person.

Arlene guided Peg over to a group of people who were talking nervously among themselves. The huddle was, individually, eight parents, who, together with Arlene, constituted the committee. Peg shook hands with eight extremely solemn individuals. She could sense that they were wary of her, understandably worried about what she intended to say, and she felt them sizing her up as they implored her to keep the parents calm, minimize the problem, and just deliver a very general talk on abuse.

Peg Foster was on the short side and, tan and athletic, looked like a tomboy, a tomboy dressed professionally in a pale gray suit with a silver lapel pin. Her thick brown hair was cut bluntly to circle her face. She appeared peaceably authoritative, as if she could handle the emotional nuances involved in the evening's events.

Just after eight, Peg was led to the gym through a series of tangled passageways. The building was like a network of gopher tunnels, complete with the dankness. The group emerged into a huge room, vaulting light and space, in which Peg encountered a blur of strange faces. About sixty-five parents were present: Almost every one of the school's sixty students was represented by one or both parents. Peg observed that they were casual, a lot of them dressed in jeans or sweats. The minister of St. George's was present too, formal in his clerical collar, but in the warmth of the crowded room, he was without a jacket. The night was humid, and the circulation in the basement parish hall, which served as the school's gym, was poor.

Peg stood facing her audience, impressed with its size; she hadn't expected the crowd. The room became quiet, as a spooked thoroughbred is quiet when soothed: The composure was a tenuous thing. Husbands and wives sat very close, except for a few couples who were stiff and coiled, as if they didn't want to touch each other. More than a few members of the audience contrived to be aloof, comporting themselves as mere spectators, as if here only out of idle curiosity.

No one had officially mentioned Kelly Michaels's name; however, since receiving the letter, a number of parents had guessed at the identity of the accused. Peg kept to the official knowledge, not mentioning Kelly, and opened by saying that she had been asked to address their meeting because there was a possibility that a child had been abused at Wee Care. She added that what they were talking about was a relatively benign example of abuse, an activity that by all appearances had been limited to the nap room of the school. However, despite the letter's limited account, there were rumors throughout the room tonight that other boys had been involved. Again, Peg Foster didn't confirm these suspicions.

To deal with the initial "How could it happen?" Peg started with statistics: "Because of underreporting, we don't have really good community data, but it seems to be that by the age of eighteen, one out of three people has had an inappropriate sexual experience."

Peg emphasized, "A third is a *lot*. Child sexual abuse is not unusual, and it is understandable that something could have happened at Wee Care. It's a very common problem. There are people in this room who have had an experience who've never told, who've never come to terms. But it's sitting there."

Everyone, very carefully, did not scan the room.

Peg went on: "Therefore, we're talking about a problem that's common, but upsetting because people still don't like to get into it." She encouraged the parents, subtly, to begin the process of identification with their children. "So many people have the experience, and yet they go on with their lives."

Peg's manner seemed to assume that the problem could be coped with and managed, and her attitude stamped out a lot of brush-fire despair, at least for now.

She was aware that many people expected the majority of sexual abuse victims to be girls, most likely because adult rape victims were pictured, incorrectly, as exclusively female, so she informed her audience that mental-health professionals estimated that almost half of all child victims were male. Peg encouraged the parents to take their children to their pediatricians to check for any physical injury as well as any physical evidence of abuse, hoping of course that nothing would be found. But repeatedly she drove into her audience the idea that, if something was, "It is not the end of one's life."

Having laid the groundwork of understanding, she distributed a list of some behavioral changes that could be clues to abuse, such as sleep difficulties, eating problems, fear of going to school or of separating from a parent, nightmares, soiling, constant crying, broad changes in personality, and the physical acting out of psychological disturbances: biting, spitting, masturbating a great deal, jumping on someone and trying to simulate intercourse. Peg stressed that it was *changes* in behavior that were significant and to which they, as parents, should be attuned. For instance, in a child who had always wet his bed, bed-wetting was not to be considered alarming, unless perhaps it had increased in frequency.

As her audience scrutinized the list, the parents became quiet in a new way, rigid.

She cautioned, "I want you to remember, these are symptoms that may be a sign, but they do not necessarily mean your child has been abused. They are reason for concern. I don't want you to leave frightened and then go home and interrogate your children. Just be good listeners, listen to anything they say, and *then* ask."

Peg told them that she believed Wee Care would be investigated fully, and she explained the legal and investigative process, adding that DYFS would have to be notified. Someone from the audience said it already had.

The name of the agency caused hesitancy among some parents, conjuring images of children torn out of home environments that were suspected of being abusive, images of reputations demolished by unfounded allegations phoned in anonymously. But Peg assured them that institutional abuse was an entirely different event, both legally and psychologically, from intrafamilial abuse, and that no one would try to take their children away from them.

After she had finished speaking, Peg fielded questions, hoping for a lot: She was much more comfortable with dialogue. Leaning on the podium, she opened up the floor, reassuring all of them: "There's nothing that we need to hold back. Don't be afraid to say anything. Say what you have to say."

Tonight, the questions were not slow to come. Hands were raised.

Peg stretched out her arm to point to a woman in the front, then dropped it and added, "We've perpetuated silence for generations. Not this one."

The woman in front wanted to know how it was possible, *if* anything had happened, that the boy had not come forward to tell his parents. Peg explained that a small child who has been abused often feels conflicting emotions about the perpetrator, because very often there has been a positive emotional relationship before the abuse began. The child can become emotionally attached to the perpetrator.

Peg elaborated, "They begin to identify with the aggressor, and that's terrible because they know that telling will get the abuser in trouble. But by not telling, it becomes a part of their lives." The process of disclosure involves overcoming great personal feelings of shame and responsibility.

Many more questions were asked, most of them prefaced with, "My daughter isn't involved, but . . ." or "I'm sure my son would have told me if anything had ever happened to him, but. . . ." The parents used denial to protect themselves. That's fine, thought Peg, as long as they absorb the information and go home with educated eyes.

For the most part, the men were silent partners, but one father spoke up, furious. He stood and shouted at Peg: "What're you gonna do about this?" His hostility ignited the audience which she had so carefully kept cool. "Yeah!" they seconded, roused. They weren't about to listen to some professional suggest that abuse could happen, then just nod and say okay.

Peg could only reiterate the investigative process. She explained yet again exactly who would conduct the inquiry: a special prosecutor and a very sensitive, caring group of detectives, often made up of officers who had volunteered or requested to join a sexual abuse unit. Peg spoke to the source of their anger and repeated that at no time had they had any control over this happening in their school, and she stressed over and over again that abuse was not a parent's fault.

But the behavior list had offered the parents a ruler with which to measure their new fears; now many of them spoke out about behaviors they had noticed in their own children and asked Peg what these behaviors meant. She explained that each symptom could mean any number of things, but sexual abuse had to be considered as one of the possible causes.

As she listened to mention after mention of fears and sleep disturbances and eating disorders, Peg was overwhelmed by a kinetic feeling of sudden conviction. Oh my God! she thought. They're all involved! But she saw clearly that not one of the parents believed his or her child could have been involved in any type of abuse, and she said nothing to encourage them to think otherwise, downplaying the severity of the little boy's allegation.

Karen Steadman thought the behavior list was a crock, and she challenged Peg: "What good is this list? My daughter isn't abused, but she has nightmares; she doesn't eat; she's afraid to leave the house or be alone in a part of the house; uh, she's become afraid of her grandmother who she used to be so close to; she has fears." The mother looked at Peg mockingly. "My daughter has every one of the things on this list." Karen held it on her fingertips, almost trying to give it back.

Peg stared at her, imprinting her with the gravity of her own insights. Then, nodding, Peg said, "Well, I guess you have a problem."

Karen calculated mentally, then told herself she didn't believe a word of it. She would have known. But Alison *did* manifest each of the symptoms on this list. Sexual behavior, like constantly sucking her fingers very slowly in and out. Well, a lot of times children went through phases, like when Alison insisted on wearing pajamas to school for four months, little red Dr. Dentons with the feet. Karen had had to put Allie in overalls every day because they were the only thing that would fit over her lurid body armor. But that wasn't symptomatic of anything. It was cute.

Karen Steadman began to wonder how much she could accept as normal. *How much?*

The meeting broke just before eleven. Dozens of parents drove in the sweet night air back to their comfortable homes. Most of them drove in silence, afraid that their spouse's denials would be weaker than, and thereby dilute, their own.

. .
. .

The next night, Karen Steadman went into her daughter's bedroom and asked her five-year-old a question to which she didn't want the answer. Her voice quavered. "Alison, did anyone ever touch you in a place you didn't like?" Karen reassured herself, She's going to say no with a silly voice, like mommy's being silly: no, no, no.

Allie, already suited up in her Superman pajamas, answered yes.

Trying not to show that she was reeling, Karen asked, "Oh, and who was that?"

"Kelly."

"Where did she touch you?"

"My privates," said her daughter.

Bedtime. Karen latched onto that thought and ended the conversation.

In the morning over cereal, Karen asked Alison: "Remember last night you said someone touched you in a place you didn't like? Where was that again? I forget what you said."

This time, Alison smiled and, pressing her forefinger to her cheek, twisted it there, marking out the innocuous spot. Karen immediately convinced herself that this was what Alison had meant all along.

In the next few days, the grapevine disseminated the fact that the teacher in question was Kelly Michaels. Karen told herself Kelly couldn't have done anything wrong, thinking: She's young. She wears a bandana around her throat. She carries a backpack!

If someone had lined up all the teachers at Wee Care and asked her to pick, Karen would have picked Kelly Michaels dead last, believing as she did that contact with the outside world kept people healthy.

Until now, Karen hadn't noticed that for the past several weeks, since the end of April, Allie had stopped asking for the note on her lunch bag. For three and a half months, every morning, Karen had etched onto the brown bag, "If Alison doesn't want to eat her lunch, she doesn't have to. If Alison doesn't want to take her nap, she doesn't have to." Alison was no longer asking for her talisman.

Karen began to realize that sexual abusers lived and breathed and moved and functioned in ordinary settings.

A few mornings later, when she dropped her daughter off at school, Karen hesitated, then parked the car. She found Arlene in her office and repeated in full everything she had elicited from Alison about being touched by Kelly, including the retraction. Karen prefaced her story with, "Personally, I don't think it happened."

And she didn't think such a thing had ever happened. In fact, the only thing that didn't add up was that at the end of April, exactly when Kelly Michaels had left Wee Care, Karen's daughter had stopped stuttering. Throughout the school year, Alison's stuttering had increased, until finally it was a constant impediment.

Karen asked Arlene to go down and talk to Alison's classroom teacher, Joan, and find out if Alison had ever said anything to her about Kelly. Then Karen left for work, leaving the matter in Arlene's hands.

Karen never heard back from the director, and that lack of information was, in itself, a relief. Somewhere in her mind she knew that it probably meant Arlene had never mentioned the discussion to Joan, but in these last days that were insulated by hope, Karen clung to any comfort she could find.

.
. .

For the majority of the parents living with uncertainty, no news was agony. Should they question their child and try to find out, or should they "enjoy" their ignorance? The terror was overwhelming because the truth was unknown, and thus its ramifications could be infinite. Their perfect children had been taken away from them. Physically, they were there in their same rooms with their same furniture and toys, but suddenly all meaning was corrupt, all interpretation unreliable. They no longer knew how they were, what had been done to them. The children were safely tucked in their beds, but even so missing, unknown, and their parents wondered how they had been changed.

Parents had gone home from Peg Foster's meeting insisting that if their child had been hurt, touched, or forced to do anything, they as parents would have known. After all, these children had been told that if they ever felt uncomfortable with something they were requested to do, they should tell their parents, and these children had been educated about good touch/bad touch.

Nina's mother asked her: "You would never let anyone touch you if you didn't want to be touched, would you, Nina?"

"No, Mommy."

"You'd tell Mommy?"

The child answered yes.

Nina's mother took away from the brief exchange all she wanted to know about what had happened at Wee Care.

Most of the parents' imaginations shut down. The kinds of things Peg Foster had discussed just didn't happen to people like them: educated, aware, open and conversational with their children, interested in their children's lives, and honest about sexuality. Urban crime didn't touch their area. Grade-schoolers walked home from school alone and rode bikes to friends' houses. Although security systems were chic, the idea of risk was surreal. The only anticipated crimes were emotional assaults: divorce, betrayal, disdain, indifference. People expected to steal from their own happiness.

Mitchell's father, in a stunning gesture of good faith and optimism, wrote a letter to Kelly pledging his support:

"Dear Kelly,

I was so sorry to hear about what's alleged to have been happening at Wee Care. No one has officially identified anyone, but, reading between the lines, it seems to me that these allegations probably involve you. From the first, I knew that Mitchell has not been abused. I cannot believe that you mistreated anyone. What an awful ordeal it must be for you to be going through. I feel especially bad because I know you worked very hard with the children, and you made a big, positive contribution to their education and welfare.

I enjoyed so much the day I came to class to read to the children. I want you to know that I would be happy to help you in any way I can; don't hesitate to write or call me. At the times in my life when I went through some very upsetting and difficult times . . . I didn't hesitate to get professional counseling, and it helped enormously. I hope you won't be offended when I suggest that it might be helpful for you. You have a lot going for you. You are young and bright and your life will be better if you can limit the damaging effects of what you're going through. Mitchell sends a big hello.

This man managed to dismiss his son's violently distorted behavior, even his son's regression to soiling himself. Mitchell was changed, very much a missing child, but his father pretended that he had his little boy right there beside him, the same as always.

The parents saw what they were able to see, and said and did what they had to do to keep their hearts alive.

▪
▪ ▪

Lucy's mother was sitting out on the lawn with a neighbor, her five-year-old playing nearby. She asked her little girl, "Do you know a teacher named Kelly?"

"Yes," answered Lucy.

Her mother quickly tried to think of a way to broach the subject innocuously. She asked, "Do you remember playing doctor with Kelly?"

Her daughter answered matter-of-factly: "Of course."

The woman then asked if they'd ever played any games.

"Well, we had to tiptoe up the stairs and be very quiet."

When Lucy's mother asked where they were going, her child responded, "I don't know what it is. The secret room."

A few days after Peg Foster's meeting, Sara Sencer was handed a phone message from a Wee Care mother who was concerned about her daughter. Sara read the message: "the secret room." It didn't mean anything to her, no allegation of abuse.

Sara threw out the scrap of paper.

▪
▪ ▪

The parents of the boys who had disclosed their abuse felt the crisis atmosphere growing dense around them: With secrecy broken, their sons' acting out intensified. In the chaotic home atmospheres that ensued, the parents required help to see through the panic and the confusion to what they needed to do, and some turned to Peg Foster.

Peg insisted that with time the boys' behaviors would subside as they gained confidence in their newfound safety, but at the moment they needed to be convinced that their parents could truly protect them. The support they offered their sons at home was going to be the most important component of their children's emotional and psychological recovery. And Peg advised them to share with their sons their own feelings of shame: "Look, there's never anything wrong with letting your children know you're not all that powerful."

Peg was also aware that guilt could readily lead a parent to become overly indulgent with a child, and so she warned: "Most importantly, maintain constancy in parenting. Don't give him three candy bars because you're thinking about what this poor child has been through. What the child craves is normal daily life. It's important to maintain whatever limits you used to maintain. Your child needs to be able to recognize his own life, the warm world that he felt safe in, loved in. This is what the child fears losing."

One mother had been giving her son whatever he wanted: TV all day, all the cookies in the world. She was advised to normalize her treatment of her son, but gradually. Because she had accustomed her child to complete lawlessness, she would have to wean him slowly, or else the sudden withdrawal of gifts and approval might make him feel as if he were being punished.

And Peg cautioned: "Be sure not to allow your child any aggressive treatment of you. It's very possible that your own guilt can lead you to permit this, because in a way you feel you deserve that treatment. But you have to know it's not good for you or your child. Do *not* let your child hit you."

The boys' parents were advised to concentrate on their sons' pain while not neglecting their own. In time, Peg promised, they would learn to cut their guilt down to size so as to measure their responsibility accurately, and not in the exaggerated proportions of self-recrimination.

▪
▪　▪

On May 22, Lou Fonolleras informed his statewide supervisor at the Division of Youth and Family Services that so far he had not been permitted to do anything on the Wee Care case. The Prosecutor's Office had held up DYFS almost three weeks while it was busy with its own inquiry, yet Lou still had his own mandate to fulfill, a legal obligation whenever he received a referral to set up an immediate interview with the victim. At the direction of his supervisor, Lou phoned the Child Abuse Unit and notified Rich Mastrangelo that, regardless of the prosecutor's earlier objections, the Division would have to become involved in the case.

That same day, Lou Fonolleras drove to Wee Care, having called Arlene Spector to advise her that he was on his way. Arriving in Maplewood early in the afternoon, he snooped leisurely outside St. George's, the green lawns and pre-summer trees camouflaging the church. Lou spotted some children playing on the lawn without any supervision and jotted the fact down on his notepad. Other children were playing on the jungle gym around back, accompanied by two teachers who greeted him as he walked by. The preschoolers' childlike behavior, oblivious behavior, made him tense.

Inside the building, several children were running up and down the stairwell, also unsupervised. Lou headed up the stairs to Arlene's office. She'd said the third floor. Lou noted the general layout: Three of the classrooms were located down in the basement, but the bathrooms were upstairs on the second and third floors. Arlene was on the phone when he looked in, so he explored the third floor.

It was not as well lit as the lower level, but the kindergarten room was up here, a large room dotted with books and toys and tiny furniture. Lou meandered on through the corridor. Several adults walked past him and said hello, but no one questioned who he was or what he was doing there. He went into the men's room on the third floor, and three little girls strolled in, unescorted: "Hi, mister!" Lou, mortified, said hello and hurried out.

Lou and the school's director talked for half an hour, Lou explaining DYFS's authority to conduct its own investigation and generally setting the director's mind at ease about his intentions. Arlene was extremely accommodating: She gave Lou a room to work in and helped him by making the phone introductions, calling Evan Connors's mother for permission to have her child interviewed. Lou wanted to speak with the boy who had steadfastly denied involvement and had consequently been dropped from Sara Sencer's list of witnesses.

Lou Fonolleras was a big, tall, round-faced man, with dark, caring eyes, eyes that could hear, and children confided in him. Unlike police officers, Lou didn't carry a gun: It was not that kind of relationship. Though he'd had extensive training, talking to children was something Lou had learned by doing. A lot of it was intuitive. He was particularly attentive to eyes, feet, body language. Lou asked Evan if he would draw some pictures, maybe of his family, and he watched while Evan casually colored the members of his family. When Lou then asked the little boy to draw a picture of Kelly, Evan depicted her with a mouth stretched open, filled with dagger teeth. Lou had to lean in closer to make certain of what he was hearing. . . . Evan was growling.

The boy had been gregarious with Lou at first, even playful, but as soon as the subject of Kelly came up and Lou mentioned Jonathan Moore, Evan became taut and agitated. Still, the child would not admit personal contact.

Lou accompanied Evan back to his classroom and, just to be thorough, chose another little boy, one who was also in Evan's class. Robert had a tiny face crowded with expressiveness. When Lou asked him to draw a picture of Kelly, Robert crayoned in a sizable cylindrical appendage between her legs. Lou asked him what it was.

"Vagina," said Robert.

Robert, though visibly upset and angry at being questioned, denied any knowledge of harm.

Lou didn't see Jonathan, Paul, or Sean, feeling that they had been fully interviewed by law enforcement, and by all appearances, they had come to full disclosure. It wasn't necessary to reinterview them.

Based on his one-day probe, Lou Fonolleras submitted a report to his DYFS supervisor outlining his assessment of the Wee Care facility. He didn't approve of having been allowed to walk all around the school without being challenged. Furthermore, he was concerned about the children he'd seen playing outside, wandering up and down the stairwell, and ambling into the bathroom without a teacher or aide. And finally, Lou was disturbed by the distance of the bathroom from the classes. He recommended modifications on the site or, better yet, that Wee Care relocate to a new facility. St. George's was a lovely old church, but as presently set up, it wasn't suited to doubling as a school.

.
. .

The Wee Care case was prepared to go to Grand Jury with the complaints of the three male victims. Only Jonathan, Sean, and Paul were to appear at Grand Jury: Evan would not be there, as he would not testify to personal victimization. The state was requesting a formal indictment against Margaret Kelly Michaels based on a skeletal presentation of the prosecution's case. Sara simply had to demonstrate that a crime had been committed and that Kelly Michaels had committed it. These crimes Kelly Michaels stood accused of having committed at Wee Care fell under the headings of first- and second-degree sexual assault and third-degree endangering the welfare of a minor.

Aggravated sexual assault was a crime in the first degree that involved penetration by an object or a body part, including vaginal and anal penetration and oral contact (treated by law as a penetration). Assaulting children by performing on them or forcing them to perform cunnilingus or fellatio was a crime in the first degree. Assault by sexual contact was a crime in the second degree that entailed touching of the intimate parts, legally defined as the sex organs, anal area, groin, buttocks, breast, inner thighs, and genital area. Endangering the welfare of a child was a crime in the third degree, including performing a sex act on someone else in front of a child, forcing the child to perform a sex act on another child, and also physical abuse.

Sara knew how hard the court appearance was going to be on these preschoolers because they were going to be questioned openly while the emotional chaos of their disclosure was still excruciatingly recent. In addition, their parents wouldn't be allowed into the courtroom with them. So, Sara invited the three boys to the courthouse and took each of them up to the Grand Jury room to explore the landscape, letting them test-sit all the different chairs in the room and feel what it was like to be in everybody's position. Sara promised them that Kelly wouldn't be there when they talked.

On May 24, 1985, a Grand Jury panel of twenty-three members heard the evidence presented by Assistant Prosecutor Sara Sencer. The defense had no part in a Grand Jury proceeding unless the prosecution invited the defendant to testify. Kelly wasn't invited.

The three little boys waited, playing together outside the Grand Jury room. They were agitated, racing around, screaming and wild, until finally they had to be removed from the waiting room and taken to another courtroom upstairs where they wouldn't cause a disturbance.

No special concessions were made for the witnesses' youth. The boys sat at a table in a courtroom full of strangers, while Sara drew from each one a repetition of the allegations they had made to her officers, including the—to her—preposterous allegation about silverware. Standing in front of the jury box, Sara asked Paul about the spoon. She said the words without having any confidence in them, just eliciting the allegation to allow the panelists to make of it what they would.

The first indictment was returned against Margaret Kelly Michaels authorizing six charges: one first-degree sexual assault by anal penetration (taking Jonathan's temperature); one second-degree sexual assault by sexual contact (fondling Sean's genitals); one second-degree sexual assault by sexual contact (fondling Paul's genitals with a spoon); and three counts of endangering the welfare of a child.

In a couple of weeks, the indictment was scheduled to be handed down at an arraignment. Technically, the state had had enough evidence in the victims' complaints of the three boys to arrest Kelly, but the Essex County Prosecutor had instructed Sara that this case was to be handled as an original complaint, meaning that the defendant was not to be arrested until the Grand Jury had officially handed down its own complaint. Until the arraignment, then, the defendant was to remain at large.

3

∴

Somewhere in the back of his mind where he couldn't get to it, Lou Fonolleras had the sense that the Wee Care case was heating up. After filing his report on Wee Care, Lou had turned his attention to other matters: a single-victim incident in a Boy Scout troop, an allegation against a priest. The Wee Care case simmered. Then, on June 6, Evan Connors's mother called DYFS.

She reported to Lou that since Evan had been interviewed two weeks ago, his behavior had worsened. He couldn't sleep through a night without some horrifying terror wrenching him out of bed. As Lou had suggested, Mrs. Connors read her son the children's book *No More Secrets for Me* at bedtime to encourage him to unburden himself. But Evan treasured his silence, and he continued to be angry and fearful, despite his mother's steady assurances of love and the nighttime invitation to slough secrets. Then one day, Evan's resistance ended and he told his mother that Kelly had sucked his penis (''a lot, a lot'') and scraped the boys' nipples with a fork.

Lou refused to jump to any conclusions, but at Mrs. Connors's request, he returned that day to Wee Care to reinterview Evan and withstood a flood of information: Evan had had to fondle Kelly's pubic hair; she had beat him about his naked body with a wooden spoon; she had sucked all the boys' penises. Evan confirmed everything he had told his mother and also corroborated Paul's statement about the spoon. In fact, Kelly had inserted all kinds of flatware in his private parts: forks and knives and spoons. He reported what she'd said: "Let's play nurse. I'll take your temperature. You feel warm."

Lou asked Evan where he was when this had happened to him, and Evan replied, "The music room." Lou had never heard of this place, so he asked the little boy to take him there. Evan, holding Lou's hand, barely coming to midthigh on him, walked Lou from the third-floor living room (Lou's "office"), past the kindergarten room, and down the hallway to a thick wooden door with a small window set up high. Lou glanced at Evan then pushed it open.

Lou saw two pews, a row of tall, small-paned windows along the right wall, leaking pale light onto the floor, a rack of choir robes in a cabinet to the left, and numerous crucifixes on stands around the room. It almost looked like a storeroom for icons. As soon as they stepped into the room, Lou could tell that Evan was sorry he'd volunteered: The little boy was very upset and clearly frightened. Lou stood, stunned, not knowing what to make of this.

As far as Lou knew, the church rooms were off limits to all school personnel, and this was clearly the church choir room. Teachers, students, Arlene herself, supposedly never entered this room. There was no way Lou could think of that Evan would have known about this room unless a teacher had brought him. He guessed that the lacquered baby grand to the left of the door was what made it "the music room." Lou noticed two small bathrooms set into the left wall opposite the windows.

Evan told Lou that Kelly had made the children undress in the choir room and pile on top of one another's bodies, himself included. The "pileup game" they'd called it. Evan pointed out the benches on top of which they'd sometimes lain. The new allegation of naked pileups, involving anywhere from two to six children judging by the names Evan gave, radically altered the scope of this case.

Over the next few days, Lou began to interview the children Evan had named as being in the pileup, realizing that he would have to see all the children who could possibly have come to harm, as well as all the children who were Evan's playmates.

Lou borrowed some utensils from the school's kitchen and added them to the pile of crayons and toys that littered the interview room. With these utensils, several children demonstrated on a doll exactly what Kelly had done to them with a knife. The rag dolls had sexual characteristics, including genital orifices, and they were used widely by professionals to provide an alternative way for children to communicate intimidating things. No diagnosis was to be based on the dolls, but the child's reactions to the dolls' sexual features were often revealing, and Lou was on the lookout for any peculiarities.

Arlene worked with him, functioning as his secretary. She called parents and secured permission to take their children out of class to be interviewed or, if the children were no longer attending the school, set up appointments with Lou. He sensed that this was difficult for her, that Arlene was frightened both personally and for her center.

This time, Lou's inquiries extended even to the children of parents who had not yet come to terms with the possibility of abuse, so when Arlene made her calls, many initially resisted Lou's request, denying that anything was wrong with the child. Arlene had to scale their walls of defense. It had to be one of the hardest things she'd ever done, convincing parents to believe that while under her care and while in her school, their children might have been hurt. Arlene convinced the reluctant parents that Lou Fonolleras would handle the children with compassion and competence.

With each child he interviewed, Lou received a slightly different tally of children who had been involved, and he added any new names to his interview list. Arlene kept apprised of Lou's findings and called Peg Foster periodically to tell her how big the whole thing could be. Peg would try to talk Arlene back into calmer regions, but Peg wasn't convinced herself, and she approached Assistant Prosecutor Sara Sencer to warn her that the Wee Care case could well be immense.

Paul's mother also called to warn Sara, "There's an awful lot he's not telling you. He's not telling you the half of it."

At the school, the teachers ranged from skeptical about the allegations to disbelieving. They knew that Kelly was the accused, and most of them had liked her. Their students didn't talk much about the interviewing, although sometimes the teachers overheard the kids whispering, "Did you see the dolls?" But that was all. The children were hushed about what was stirring in the school, and the teachers stayed apart from the big man who walked in in the mornings with a bundle of soft dolls in his arms.

The instant that Lou saw the face of the first girl, momentum happened.

She was Jessica Howe, who had been named by Robert in another interview. Robert had told Lou that he and Jessica had had to suck each other's private parts. And Jessica was the very first child to tell Lou Fonolleras that Kelly had played "Jingle Bells" on the piano, without wearing any of her clothes. Up to this point, the children's allegations had all been of ordinary sexual acts, if somewhat confused by the language of temperature taking. Naked "Jingle Bells" introduced the concept of more unusual abuse.

Five weeks after Jonathan Moore's breakthrough disclosure, the assumption that Kelly had abused only boys was demolished. The second little girl Lou talked to, Nina Anderson, corroborated every type of abuse the boys had related and confirmed that Kelly had made all the children take off their clothes and play the pileup game. Lou usually had to work twice as hard to get little ones to trust him (he was imposingly large), but Nina didn't seem intimidated by him. She related a different variation of the game: They all lay on top of one another, the girls with the boys; but first, Kelly put knives, forks, and spoons on the floor, and then they had to lie naked on top of the metal.

By this time, Lou acknowledged to himself that he would have to see everyone, all sixty students, and for the next six weeks Lou Fonolleras was at Wee Care almost daily, but June wasn't halfway over when he called the Prosecutor's Office. He suggested that the Child Abuse Unit might be interested in reinvestigating the Wee Care case.

During the past three weeks, many parents had been calling Sara's office with their children's statements about abuse, and Sara had already been leaning toward reopening the investigation. Now she agreed with Lou that her investigators would have to get back into the school and interview the additional victims that DYFS was uncovering.

Lou wasn't gathering evidence for a criminal case: That was the prosecutor's job. Every governmental agency cut into the situation at a different strata, the Prosecutor's Office taking the deepest cut. Lou's findings would impact only on civil issues, such as licensing. DYFS approached the school as a going concern and assessed it in terms of its continued operations or an improved format. If Lou were to find that a "preponderance of the evidence" warranted a more complete investigation, he could recommend that course of action.

It was up to the Prosecutor's Office, however, to determine whether the density of evidence warranted a criminal prosecution "beyond a reasonable doubt." With Lou successfully getting statements, Sara's office would reduce duplication and spare the children repetitious interviews. The two state offices, the Prosecutor's Office and the Division of Youth and Family Services, agreed to launch a joint investigation of the day-care abuse case. Only occasionally did Sara's unit actually take a case through trial: After indictment, most cases were handed over to the Trial Division. These conversations with the children were to gather evidence for further Grand Juries.

The three- to five-year-old victims of Kelly Michaels kept looming into focus, and the body count continued to rise. Lou Fonolleras and the state's investigators prepared to enter the school as a team.

▪
▪　▪

Peg Foster, aware of the joint effort, called Sara Sencer and told her that the three-man unit couldn't handle this investigation alone, and she offered her services. Given that Peg was employed by United Hospitals, and the Prosecutor's Office frequently liaisoned with United for social and medical services because the hospital housed the Essex County Sexual Assault Unit, she was already in place to contribute to a state's case. Sara gratefully accepted.

Sara's office had sufficed (after emergency decorative modifications) for questioning a handful of boys, but for a joint investigation of any number of children, a twelve-by-eighteen office no longer measured up. Sara didn't want to force the children to return to the scene of the crime, and yet the school seemed the only logical place to conduct the investigation.

Although the school gamely remained open, many parents had withdrawn their children. One mother allowed her daughter to attend because the little girl was so determined to go to school, but the mother herself waited in the building at all times, an escape.

Ellen Gardner was uncomfortable about the school, and she would have been more than willing to keep Joey home, but he insisted on going. This was his second year there: Joey attended Wee Care nine-to-five, four days a week, and he was fiercely attached. It was his life. Ellen didn't want to keep him home just to feel that she was able to do something for him. After all, Kelly was gone, and Joey wanted to be in school.

Still, all in all, only a handful of students remained, a chicken pox epidemic further decreasing the ranks in the season's last days. The children who continued to attend the school seemed startlingly comfortable in their surroundings, not visibly disturbed to be in the school's grip. The investigators, conversely, were just beginning to live the experience that the children had endured for months. For these adults, being in the school was freshly painful, the atmosphere textured with dread.

The team held a breakfast meeting to coordinate plans and synchronize watches. Lou filled in George, Rich, and Peg on the nine or so children he had talked to so far. Not every child had admitted personal involvement, but from the mothers' histories of their children's behavioral problems and from the children's body language and reactions to questions, Lou suspected that even some of the deniers were victims. Every child he had spoken to had had something to add or seemingly something to hide.

George McGrath reviewed the interview procedure with Lou, and they agreed on basic principles, including the need to have different interviewers take turns with a child. While free recall, or out-of-the-blue statements would in theory be the most reliable type of allegation, the entire team was aware that most of the time a child would not just volunteer information: He or she had to be asked questions. For the sake of the criminal prosecution, Lou agreed to avoid leading questions whenever possible. Lou was going to have to see every child who had attended the school, but George and Rich were not compelled to talk to each one, and Peg had no pre-set course of action. She was more or less screening, but was of course willing to interview any child whose parent requested it. Lou set the pace.

None of the team set out to be alone with one of these children during an official interview. Each wanted a witness, and each wanted emotional support, so they always started an interview with one other person in the room. Usually, the interview pair was Lou and another investigator. The lead interviewer would offer to clear the room if it would make the child more comfortable. Parents generally were not permitted to accompany the child. As shame was a major cause for the child's reluctance to disclose, the standard interview procedure directed that every child be interviewed with as much privacy as possible: That meant no parents and no superfluous professionals.

.   .
.   .

Routinely, the investigators would arrive at nine o'clock and unwind over breakfast together. Someone would stop and pick up fresh bagels on the way to the school. Rich was chronically late, if only by twenty minutes or half an hour, because he had to drop off his cleaning or run by the bank, and Sara, who called in what seemed like every half hour emitting questions ("What're you doin' now? What's goin' on? Why's Rich late?"), always caught him and yelled. As Rich rushed into the church in the morning, the first thing from his lips was, "Did she call?"

By a natural development of concern and anger, Wee Care had become a unit priority, and Sara, who thought about the case constantly, was increasingly dissatisfied to be at arm's length. However, the County Prosecutor believed that prosecuting attorneys should not perform their own investigations: they could not testify in their own cases, and so it was wiser to have statements taken by investigators who could later take the stand at trial.

In light of what Sara had learned at the Chicago conference, she had decided not to be present at the school at all: A prosecutor from Minnesota had been severely criticized for conducting her own investigation, for tainting the results with her alleged overzealousness. Circumspect, Sara remained at the office and ran the unit: answering phones, working with DYFS, and presenting cases to the Grand Jury each Friday. But from her far-off command post, Sara kept warning: "Don't screw this thing up."

Word of Lou's tenderness had been passed along from mother to mother, and many parents wanted no one but Lou Fonolleras to interview their children. For the parents, anyone who was going to reach into their child's psyche was a dangerous stranger, even Lou; however, thanks to his reputation, he at least seemed to be a known quantity. Yet, some parents, after having placed their own fears on the block, were disappointed by an empty return. Lou would pull over a doll to go through body part identification with their child. Then he would ask the child if it was okay to take off the doll's clothes, and if the child said no, that was the end of that: Everybody went home. One little boy said nothing but trashed the lounge, taking dolls and hurtling them across the room. Successfully acquiring an interview appointment with Mr. Fonolleras was sometimes, therefore, no more than a false start, as the children were going to talk only when they were ready.

First thing in the morning, parents crowded in the school hallways waiting to be taken care of, one day eight of them simultaneously demanding information, demanding their children be seen, but the team made them wait until breakfast was finished. The investigators needed a calm start-up in the morning to secure their own sanity. As they spread cream cheese on a second bagel, they were preparing for the day by asserting some small control over their lives.

Wildness throbbed around the edges of order, but every morning as the investigators relaxed over breakfast, they talked and puzzled over how the abuse could have gone on for so long, and when and how Kelly had gained access to the various children. They would shout to one another across the breakfast table, "Nah, that couldn't happen!" but then as soon as they had finished eating and went one-on-one with a child, the investigators respectfully accepted whatever the child said and left it for Sara Sencer to corroborate the statements.

Professionals, to do their job well, thought with their feelings. Empathizing with these children was excruciating, but that was how to listen and to understand. The investigators all supported one another in the work. Lou had been feeling a little wilted when his co-investigators showed up, and now he found comfort in all the humanity around him. By the end of a day, the investigators needed each other.

▪
▪ ▪

The indictment was handed down approximately ten days after the Grand Jury had convened, and midmorning on June 12, 1985, George McGrath, Rich Mastrangelo, and John Noonan set out for East Orange. Central Avenue, off which Kelly Michaels lived, set the tone for the middle-urban neighborhood: dozens of local-brand gas stations, car lots, auto repair shops, car washes, car culture. The avenue was cramped with check-cashing establishments, fast-food restaurants, "odd lots" clothing stores, fortress-style banks. Commercial points were made with neon and lit plastic: "We fix anything," "We accept food stamps."

Kelly's roommate came to the door, and when George asked if Kelly was there, the woman answered no. But George, arrest warrant in hand, heard Kelly in the background asking, "Who's at the door?"

Kelly came forward. She was wearing pajamas. The apartment was seedy: one room with clothes and cartons tossed into a near corner, a double mattress on the dirty floor of the far corner, rumpled sheets shoved over onto the floor. George didn't see any furniture. Noonan checked the bathroom for concealed weapons. Since they hadn't brought a female officer with them, George permitted Kelly to get dressed in private, but as she headed toward the bathroom he recommended sarcastically, "Dress warm, 'cause it's very cold in jail."

The two officers didn't search the apartment: Their warrant was only for her arrest. As Rich cuffed her, Kelly kept muttering, "I don't believe this!" so Rich told her, "Well, believe it for now." George and Rich pulled Kelly out of the apartment while her girlfriend repeated over and over again, "You can't do this!" Kelly cried and prayed and quoted Jesus, but she was utterly compliant.

George McGrath got visceral satisfaction out of working to take sex offenders off the street. Since his assignment to the Child Abuse Unit early in 1984, George had placed himself on call twenty-four hours a day. He would go out on a call in the middle of the night if a father was bashing his child or if an assault victim appeared at an emergency room. He found personal gratification in making arrests. George felt great arresting Kelly.

He had had strong feelings about Kelly from that day in May when she was brought in for questioning. She had fascinated him then, mainly because she was an unexplained phenomenon. Even now, whenever the name of Margaret Kelly Michaels came up, George McGrath would glower and warn, "Never underestimate Kelly Michaels."

The officers had radioed in their location before leaving Kelly's apartment, and they radioed in again when they arrived back at the Prosecutor's Office: They were extremely careful to document their journey so that Michaels couldn't later claim to have been taken for a ride. She was booked at the Prosecutor's Office. In the mug shot they took, her eyebrows were uptilting strike marks, thin and high, together somehow shaped like a shrug. Kelly's mouth pinched self-consciously at the corners, and the flattish bulge under her jaw hinted at a double chin. Her eyes, hard and forlorn, seemed to be staring up out of a puddle of flesh. They looked like the only thing alive about her.

Kelly was then taken to the county jail annex in Caldwell and confined in protective custody. Soon after, Kelly agreed to be tested for venereal disease: Her tests came back negative.

Michaels was cloistered out of the general prison population where the average child abuser would find many enemies: Rapists of children were about as popular in prison as they were on the outside. She had her own private jail guard and, for the first forty-eight hours of incarceration, was placed on suicide watch. This was in compliance with routine, and not because Kelly had in any way indicated a suicide wish. On the contrary, Kelly was withdrawn but pleasant to the inmates who managed to converse with her, and she began to exercise to keep in shape in her lonely cell, a cell with inexplicably appropriate rose-colored walls.

Kelly was an unlikely inhabitant of a prison. George McGrath's background research had shown her to be a sweet, wholesome child who had attended Pittsburgh's St. Benedict Academy, a Catholic school for girls. She had collected Bible missals and pictures of Jesus, and in her circle of friends, girls became nuns as routinely as girls in other spheres became cheerleaders. Kelly had moved on to Seton Hill College, a Catholic school near Pittsburgh, where she had majored in theater. She had no criminal record in either Pennsylvania or New Jersey.

The Michaels family lived in Pittsburgh, Pennsylvania, with a German shepherd and several cats. Margaret, called Kelly, Michaels had studied piano for twelve years, she said, practicing on a piano handed down by a friend of the family. She had baby-sat for her younger brothers and sisters from the time she was thirteen, earning extra money by doing the same for other little children in the neighborhood. Her mother, Marilyn, worked as a nurse, providing in-house health care, sometimes for traumatized or abused children. Her father, John, was an insurance representative.

Kelly Michaels was a somewhat attractive, white, middle-class, educated young woman who violated every common preconception about the nature of a sex offender. Predictably, people surrounding her case had one reaction: "She doesn't look it." Even the investigators agreed that she was the "nice girl" on the bus with whom they'd be likely to strike up a conversation.

Over the course of her stay in Caldwell, the sweet schoolgirl gave away cigarettes, stamps, and leftover food, adept at the maneuvers of ingratiation.

▪
▪ ▪

Sara Sencer had requested a $500,000 bail bond for Kelly Michaels. The existing indictment charged only six counts, but dozens of additional counts were pending on complaints already accumulated in the joint investigation's interviews. A judge declined the state's recommendation and set bail at $150,000 bond with a $25,000 cash alternative. For a crime that was not a capital offense, the Constitution guaranteed meetable bail standards, and a bail bond of $500,000 would be equivalent to denying the defendant bail.

However, even at the lower figure, Kelly Michaels and her family were unable to make bail. In fact, they appeared to be unable to continue paying Kelly's attorney. Since the time of the initial complaints, Kelly Michaels had been represented by a number of private attorneys, with each of whom she had come to a parting of the ways. Her most recent lawyer had left the case because she didn't believe the Michaelses could continue to pay her. Kelly then applied for a public defender, and the Office of the Public Defender made a determination of indigency, finding her eligible for free legal counsel.

The PD Office was by statute considered to be the legal guardian of children, and so to avoid a conflict of interest with DYFS which was mandated to protect children, office policy required that all child sexual abuse cases be listed as pool cases. Pool cases were those public defense cases handled by private attorneys picking up some extra work. While Kelly's friends and family tried to get together bail money, her file waited among the other pool cases to be picked up by an interested attorney.

Immediately after Kelly was arrested, local newspaper coverage reported her East Orange address. While Kelly lingered in jail, notes of outrage were placed outside her apartment door: "MOVE!" "GET OUT!" One day, there even appeared a gruesome threat in the form of a dead cat. Several weeks passed, until finally an old girlfriend of Kelly's posted the required twenty-five thousand dollars cash, and Kelly, free on bail, went to Pittsburgh in her parents' custody.

Most of the children in the case weren't told Kelly was at large: They continued to believe she was in jail where she couldn't carry out her threats to kill them or their parents. The parents for their part were terrified that Kelly would turn up in Maplewood. If any of the children were to see her, they could lose whatever tenuous sense of security had been recovered. To prevent just such a scene, one of the provisions of her bail required that she stay out of Essex County except when on official business to her lawyer's office or for a court appearance. While out on bail, Kelly was also to stay away from young children.

When the investigators had first encountered the Wee Care children's fear of reprisals, they had arranged for those who wanted to visit the jail at the Maplewood police department in the hope that the children would feel safer once they'd seen how impregnable it was. But in many instances, those visits to the jail had backfired by reinforcing yet another of the children's fears: that they, themselves, were going to be incarcerated for their part in the sexual activity.

And some of the children didn't believe that anything, even jail, would be able to keep them safe from Kelly. One little girl, Julie, made her mother walk through their house every night checking the locks on all the doors and windows. When her mother explained that the locks would definitely keep Kelly out, Julie put it plainly: "She can change into other things."

.
. .

Even with Kelly gone, the children were very suspicious of adults, or sometimes only of women or strangers. Trust no longer came naturally to them. All the investigators expected denials, especially in the first passes at the underlying trauma, but they hoped eventually to identify every victim. They were convinced that—with the pressure of a massive headache—these children pounded with things they needed to tell. The investigators could see in the agitation, the tears, the fearful tensed eyes, the massive thing in their brains.

The children were more likely to disclose their involvement to an investigator than to a parent, in part because the investigators asked direct

questions. Furthermore, the children had no need to protect the investigators from the ugly truth, as they thought they did with their own parents.
Nor did the children fear the investigators' being furious or disgusted,
because these strangers had never occupied a punishing role in their lives.

Most of the Wee Care employees remained aloof, smirking and whispering among themselves when the investigators walked by. It was dangerous to be a teacher working in a center amid allegations of sexual
abuse: Reputations could easily be smudged by association. The younger
staff members could not believe that anything so devastating could have
happened under their noses.

Arlene's attitude was different. She instructed her staff to tell the
children that Kelly was never ever coming back to school, and they would
never see her again.

Belatedly, but at last, the children were safe in her school, and they
deserved to be told so.

▪
▪ ▪

Peg's first appointment of the June day was for ten-thirty. She was using
one of the downstairs classrooms that was empty. The girl she was talking
to had a cubic face, with squared-off cheeks, jaw, and mouth; even her
eyes appeared rectilinear. Peg asked the child her name, but the girl
refused to answer, just flattened her lips together and sucked them inward.
When Peg dragged over one of the dolls to ask the child if she could
name the body parts, the little girl looked blank, stunned, as if Peg had
blasted her with a ray gun.

During the entire ten minutes they spent together, the child was mute.
Peg wanted many times to stop the interview and let her go, but she felt
compelled at least to ask the questions: Unshared pain was much uglier
than spoken pain, and here was the child's chance to unburden herself.
Peg dragged herself through the motions, starting unsuccessfully with
body part identification, then moving to the events at the school. The
child was grave, sitting through the brief interview session petrified,
stalled, as if she'd lost the momentum of her childhood.

Another little girl, arriving at the school for her interview, refused,
without a rebellious word, to leave her mother's car. The child just
stiffened into the seat's curve and refused to be pried away from it. She
had a sad, pouty little face with downcast eyes, and thick, ash-blond hair
that looked almost too heavy to bear. She sat rigid under her blanket in
the large passenger seat, sucking her thumb, her forefinger a sheepish
question mark hooked over her nose.

An investigator from the Prosecutor's Office helping out for the day emerged from the school and, leaning down into the window of the car, tried some gentle coaxing. The little girl, her thumb still stopping up her speech, didn't answer except to shake her head and stare at the woman with stark eyes.

With finality, the little girl raised the blanket off her lap, opened it out to its full span, and draped it again over her torso. Then she folded her arms across her chest and hugged the blanket into armor. The investigator's knees were beginning to ache from her half-crouched position. She left, and the little girl and her mother backed out of the driveway and returned home.

Interviewing was extraordinarily frustrating at times: The children were hesitant and difficult. But the pain was clear in their faces and behavior. The investigators knew they had to be patient and take what came without pushing for more. Intuitively, they respected each child's internal timing.

. .

Ellen Gardner, Joey's mother, waited in Arlene's office. She knew that she wasn't qualified to be the one to extract this pain from her son, but sitting here in this office while Joey was down the hall talking to Lou, she felt helpless, completely in the dark. What she wanted now was for the truth not to be true.

Lou watched Joey seemingly unravel, telling about all kinds of abuse: The little boy's skin was translucent, vulnerable, as he told of Kelly's poking him about his naked body with a fork, taking his penis in her mouth, kissing his penis, and pushing a knife and then a wooden spoon into his rectum. Then Joey admitted to Lou that he had played with Kelly's breasts, perpetrating—himself—a sexual act.

When Joey was excused and sent back to his classroom, Lou had to take a moment to wipe his eyes and collect himself before seeing Joey's mother. He repeated to Ellen what Joey had told him, but Lou soft-played the details of her son's agonizing delivery. Joey had been off-the-wall, completely flailing, and Mrs. Gardner didn't need to be tested with that knowledge.

Ellen Gardner turned ashen, but she wouldn't allow herself to cry. She knew, vaguely, that she believed what Joey had told Lou: That was obvious to her in the accepting way that she was now moving along to subsequent thoughts. And oddly, perversely, her first reaction was to feel sorry for Kelly. What horrible, gruesome things must have happened to her in her own childhood for her to do these things, she thought.

Lou warned Ellen that her son's recovery would hinge in large part on his mother's and his father's reactions to what he had disclosed. He cautioned her: "If you want to vent anger, or you're upset, try to do it when Joey isn't there. When you talk to him, go easy, and don't pressure him, whatever you do. If you want, you can say that other kids have told and ask, 'Is there anything you want to tell me?' But don't mine for answers, and don't register shock or horror at what he discloses."

Some parents cried when Lou told them what their child had said, some laughed nervously, some were violent, saying that Lou had no idea what he was doing, accusing him of planting ideas in the child's mind. Some took in the information and went into shutdown, didn't deal with it. Ellen was calm, resigned.

That night Joey literally bounced off the walls. When Ellen took him up to bed, he said, "She played the piano. 'Jingle Bells.' "

"Oh yeah? What else?" she asked.

"She took her clothes off."

"She did?" said Ellen matter-of-factly. "When?"

"Playing 'Jingle Bells.' " Then Joey started to yell: "She said she'd turn me into a mouse! She said she'd turn me into a Transformer!"

Ellen, almost stiff with self-control, tried desperately to act natural. "You know, nobody has the power to turn you into anything."

"Well, Kelly had the power to turn herself into a monster, so why couldn't she turn me into a mouse?"

Ellen reasoned, weakly, "She won't *know* you told."

"But she thinks she knows everything," he said.

Joey asked repeatedly if Kelly was in jail and if he also would go to jail. He insisted that he'd done the same things as Kelly had, so he was going to get arrested too. Ellen explained to him that children don't get blamed for things grown-ups do, that grown-ups should know better. Grown-ups were supposed to take care of little children, not hurt them.

She paused, imagining Joey was at that moment thinking of her own guilt, just as she was. Ellen looked down. It wasn't easy being the parent with the answers, giving comfort.

▪
▪ ▪

George McGrath's daughter was having a birthday in a few days, and George wanted to finish off the back stairs in time for the party. It was three in the morning, and he had been working out back cutting tiles ever since nine o'clock. Now, nearing the end of the job, George accidentally sliced off the tip of his finger. His wife and the two babies were upstairs asleep, and he didn't want to wake them, so he just picked the fingertip up off the tile, wrapped it in ice, and drove one-handed to the emergency room, stanching the flow of blood by bending his fingers backward against the towel. At the hospital, the fingertip was sewn back on with micro-surgery.

George went to Wee Care later that morning, in a great deal of pain which he wouldn't acknowledge to Peg or Rich. George hadn't even considered not reporting to work, and once he was at Wee Care, he didn't really think much about the pain in his finger. He was committed to these children with a fierceness, a love for them, that nothing could attenuate. George would protect any of the children, no matter what.

By a standard rule, officers never announced to children that they were cops, lest an abuser had threatened that if they told anyone what had happened the cops would come and take them away from their mommy and daddy. Instead, officers explained that their job was to protect children. However, if a child ever *asked* to see his badge, George showed it and talked cop stuff with them to make them feel safe. He wanted the children to trust him and to know that he would take care of them.

Angie McMahon was in the school for her second interview. She was talking, but she was giddy with fear as she demonstrated what Kelly did to her by licking the genitals on a doll. With every note, her voice, almost hysterical, sounded about to take off. Toward the end of the interview, Angie asked George to take a walk and led him by the hand to the choir room.

"Can you play the piano?" she asked, glancing at the baby grand.

"Yes," he said.

She asked him to play "Jingle Bells," and George played the song.

"Put on one of those," she then ordered, pointing to the choir robes. He did.

Angie insisted that the two of them go find her parents because she wanted them to see George in the black robe. Angie was suddenly standing away from him, maintaining a margin. As they ambled down the hallway, he asked her why they were going to see her parents, and she answered that she wanted to show them what Kelly had looked like.

After they had shown Angie's parents the robe and returned to the choir room, Angie told George to take off the robe.

"Why?" he asked, flipping his chin up defiantly.

She answered straight: "Because you're a friend."

As they left the choir room, Angie again clasped George's hand.

■
■ ■

Before each interview with a child, Lou spoke briefly and privately with the child's mother to find out what, if anything, the child had already disclosed to her. That gave him a direction to go in. It was nearly impossible to question a child without at least steering the child toward the subject matter. Ordinarily, Lou used the information from the mother to try to reintroduce whatever the child had disclosed at home, then move forward from there.

Both Heather and her older brother, Kevin, had attended Wee Care. Heather was only four now, but she was much more outgoing than her five-year-old big brother, who was quite shy. Kevin seemed to have taken some relief from disclosure, while Heather's fears had escalated after she told: One felt more secure after telling; the other felt jeopardized.

Hovering in the hallway now, Heather refused to come into the room without her big brother, so this immediately became a joint interview. Lou had already seen each of them once before, so he greeted them easily with "Okay, guys, I hear that you want to help me investigate and crack this case wide open." He contorted himself to set them at ease. "Come on, you were so brave last time."

He knew the children were soft and could easily be dented and grow misshapen around that dent, so Lou was extra tender. The two siblings stared at him with sleepy eyes, blanking out, their attention going elsewhere. Lou poked at them: "Come on, did you guys sleep last night?"

Heather piped, "My mom is stronger than Kelly."

Kevin worried, "I know my mom's listening through the door."

Lou repeated a monster story these two had said Kelly had once told them, a story their mother had reported was still frightening them. Then Lou spent a good deal of time explaining that Kelly had told them that only to scare them, and that none of it was really true: Nobody had special, superhuman powers.

"You know that?" asked Lou, checking their attention.

"Yes."

"Yes."

Then Kevin said shyly, "She floats through walls."

Lou felt all his progress batted away. He was up against Kelly Michaels's hold over these children. Daily, for almost seven months, Kelly had been in control of their minds, their bodies, and their emotions. When Sara heard about the interview, she explained it: "In their minds, Kelly was all-powerful. Each time she touched these children or one of their friends, she demonstrated her power over them. She was the most powerful person they had ever met."

By this time, Heather had had enough of the interview, and she withdrew to the door, ready to leave, but she lingered, curious about what Kevin might say.

Lou asked Kevin, "How'd it feel when she hit you on the penis?"

Heather opened the door and went out.

"I can't hear ya, buddy."

"Bad," the boy squeaked.

Lou asked, "You feel better now that you started talking, it's not a big secret anymore?"

"Yeah."

Lou asked, "Did Kelly ever kiss anybody's penis?"

"Yes," said Kevin.

"Whose?"

"Heather's"

Lou started. "But Heather doesn't have a penis. She has a—"

"Vagina."

"Is that what you mean?" asked Lou.

"Yes," said Kevin. He cringed, and Lou sensed his anger over Kelly having hurt his little sister.

"Boy. You've been really helpful, a real investigator. I thank you. How you feelin'?" Lou asked, looking down at Kevin.

"Good." But Kevin's voice was threadbare.

Lou's heart went out to him, so timid and tender. "I promise you'll feel better," he said.

.   .
.

George McGrath called the office and informed Sara that they were finding things all over the place. That update didn't fit with the theory that the abuse had been restricted to the nap room. Kelly obviously would have had access to children during her nap class, but how could she get to them in the gym, the bathroom, a choir room?

Sara said, "I'm coming over to see what we're talking about!" She hung up the phone immediately and rushed to her car.

The school was a knot of interwoven passageways and staircases. The choir room was quite remote and private: at the end of a long hallway and separated from the trafficked area of the third floor by two bathrooms, the church lounge, and then more hallway. Sara gave herself a complete tour of the school and church, examined the layout, and compared it to what Arlene Spector and Diane Costa had drawn for her.

When Sara returned to her office, she no longer had any doubts.

▪
▪ ▪

The team uncovered more and more boys and girls who admitted the abuse, more allegations of the naked pileup, ''Jingle Bells,'' nudity, and the anal and vaginal insertion of utensils. In addition, the children were discussing new allegations of having played duck, duck, goose while naked, and of animal licking games played to the tunes of ''Old MacDonald'' and ''Bingo.'' Even among consenting adults the acts that were disclosed were considered foul and degrading. The team was horrified by the carnage.

Yet, the job demanded that the investigators be cheerful in front of the children and cool and professional in front of the parents. At the end of a day, when the investigators were nauseated with tension and shuddering on the verge of tears, someone would crack a joke, and they would release all the sickness in laughter. Naked ''Jingle Bells'' seemed screamingly funny at times.

But the investigators' colds dug in and stayed, and they suffered persistent headaches. Lou had muscle spasms. After work, the team members frequently convoyed to a bar for a few beers, ostensibly to unwind, but in reality, just to make sure that everybody was okay before they all drove home alone. The investigators hadn't been together for long, but they were very protective of one another.

▪
▪ ▪

Peg dropped into Arlene's office to chat. The director was distraught: She felt terrible for the children, but, as usual, she queried, ''Do you really believe it happened?''

Peg was soothing, but very firm. ''Yes, Arlene. I do believe it happened. It did happen.''

Although this was the most bizarre, repulsive thing she'd ever seen, Peg had no doubts. She knew that preschoolers didn't lie about such things. If anyone lied or misunderstood, it was usually the parents. Peg repeated, ''It happened.''

Arlene pushed on. ''Do you think *all* the kids?''

Peg paused. They had all tried to avoid this question. ''At this point, I guess so. It's hard to say, but it seems like everyone we interview has some kind of something to say.''

Peg felt sorry for Arlene, but no one could protect Arlene from the truth about herself: Responsibility meant more than a name on the letterhead.

■
■   ■

Several weeks into the investigation, Karen brought Alison to Lou first thing in the morning. She had steeled herself to have her daughter interviewed. Now she just wanted to get this over with, to sever the suspense once and for all.

While Lou questioned Alison in a room adjacent to Arlene's office, Karen waited across the hall. From where she sat, she could watch Arlene in her office talking to Diane Costa, the school's head teacher. Karen's eyes vaguely took in their interaction, as she felt what seemed to be a heavy bar lowering from the sky, and she realized abruptly: The line has been drawn. Arlene's the enemy.

Alison told Lou Fonolleras about the abuse, and this time she didn't take it back with the twirl of a finger on her cheek.

■
■   ■

In one sense, the investigation proceeded without method. Children were brought in as they were named by other children or as their parents brought them in, and occasionally a child would be taken from class to follow up on an allegation that was puzzling an investigator. The body of information was amassed haphazardly. In another sense, though, the investigation was well ordered and methodical. The parents were asked to take their children, at their own convenience, to the Maplewood police department, where the children faced a photo line-up of the Wee Care teachers.

Sara Sencer knew that the abuser was Kelly Michaels—too many children had accused her for them to be mistaken—but she was exceedingly cautious. Most of the resources of the Child Abuse Unit for all of Essex County were presently being fed into and eaten away by this case. Sara had to be more than positive that she was investigating the correct person. Each child was presented with an array of photographs and asked to pick out the person who had hurt him or her. Without fail, every single child pointed out Margaret Kelly Michaels. No child even hesitated over the photograph of the other teacher that Kelly Michaels had named as the possible perpetrator of these crimes.

No one involved wanted to make a mistake. They acknowledged that the slightest misinformation could lead them into a morass of allegations of falsehood that would be destructive to the case and devastating to the children. Sara had, scattered across her jumbled desk, the time cards of all the school's teachers. She wanted to see if they contained anything that would illuminate what had gone on in that school daily while parents thought their children were being well supervised. Her constant intention was to check out the feasibility of each specific allegation in terms of access and opportunity.

Apparently, in the late summer of 1984, Wee Care had lost a lot of staff at the last minute, and Arlene Spector had had to scramble to fill positions. The school was still understaffed when it began its fall session, and throughout the year, employees came and went, so that each class of preschoolers was taught by various teachers at different times. Whenever one teacher was absent, the remaining staff would encompass the extra class load in their own rooms, so the children were always shifted around.

For the after-lunch nap period, the three preschool classes were split up into two rooms. Generally, there was one teacher assigned to each nap room, but occasionally only one teacher was available for both preschool nap classes. As the two rooms used for nap were separated only by an accordion door, the one remaining nap teacher could simply unzip the divider and supervise both rooms at once. On occasion, that teacher would have been Kelly Michaels.

Sara was told by the teachers and mothers that Arlene Spector often left the premises at two-thirty, didn't work on Fridays, and that when she did work she spent considerable time on the phone in her remote office. An aide stated, "I rarely saw her. I *barely* saw her." Arlene had even been spotted en route to Manhattan to shop for her daughter's prom dress when, purportedly, she was at the school. One mother commented that whenever she ran into Arlene, they didn't discuss her child or her classwork: they talked about diets. Diane Costa, the administrative head teacher, had in the spring reportedly spent her days up on the third floor, preparing projects and games for the children rather than checking the downstairs classrooms.

Wee Care, in truth, ran in a very different fashion from how it ran on paper.

For most of the 1984–85 year, the classrooms were poorly supervised, and teachers or aides were left alone with their children for long expanses of time. When Kelly had first arrived at Wee Care in the capacity of aide, she was the only aide serving the entire school, including all three preschool classrooms and the kindergarten upstairs. When a month later she became a full teacher for a class of three-year-olds, again there was only one aide in the school: the woman who had replaced her. As the school's employment records showed, the names and faces shifted kaleidoscopically, dizzyingly. A teacher complained, "Nothing was the same any two days in a row."

. .

Since the first days of the joint investigation, George had become able to control the parents so that they arrived only on the days they had appointments. Arlene no longer handled the scheduling: George made the arrangements. Thanks to him, the team was finally able to do its awful work in relative peace.

After an interview, the investigator tried to downplay a child's disclosure, offering compassion and emphasizing constructive ways for the parent to make the situation better. With each parent the investigator recommended that the child be taken to a pediatrician if that had not been done already, and that the parents perhaps seek guidance from a therapist, for themselves and/or for their child.

The investigators were sharply conscious of the guilt the parents felt for not having prevented the abuse. Some of the mothers had placed their children in day care even though they themselves didn't work. These women often manifested the strongest remorse, as if they had frivolously put their children aside. When Peg encountered a mother in this position, she would try to tell her that going to school was a part of growing up and that preschool was important in teaching children socialization skills.

Most parents would want to take on their babies' pain for them, and in a way, by castigating themselves, these parents tried to take on their children's suffering even now. They were learning all sorts of nightmarish clinical phrases: "frank bleeding," "severity of insertion," "simple touching." The most forthright word, "rape," was put off, denied, resisted by a good number of them for its blatancy, its hardness. The things that had happened to their children were repulsive, and the parents blamed themselves for not seeing and thus averting the tragedy. Generally, a parent's self-esteem plummeted with the child's.

As much as possible, the investigators avoided talking about the ways the parents were to blame: None of the team wanted to reinforce the guilt. But they did help the parents to define the entangled, complicated emotion so that the parents could begin to see their pain in perspective. Some who had not yet named their guilt were angry at the world and lashed out in random anger. These particular parents radiated fury so as to insulate themselves from inner anger, and it was stressful for the investigators to tiptoe around their bruising defensiveness day in and day out.

Kelly Michaels, the true object of their rage, was out of reach, so their tension was intact and viable when they arrived at the school accompanying their child. Then they had to sit peaceably, if possible, in another room, while their baby was grilled about the most painful and unfortunate experience in his or her existence. They were called upon to be calm and reasonable while the interviewer, who to them could never seem innocuous enough, related to them the filth that had come from the child's mouth—and then be able to accept it and believe it, purely on faith in their child's ability to perceive.

4

∴

Lately, Lou had been hearing a lot about group games, but he didn't have a good understanding of them. Evan's mother had told him over the phone about something mysterious called the "Buffalo Bill" game, something her son had been babbling about. All she knew was that Kelly had contrived to have the children sing the words, but Lou wondered what else the performance had entailed. Both Evan and his friend Robert seemed to know about the game, so Lou got them together for a joint interview and asked them to sing the Buffalo Bill song.

The boys started to hum, then laughed and changed the subject, then sang the name, then petered out. Lou tried to jolly them along: "Come on guys. Aren't you gonna sing the song for me?"

Robert and Evan giggled and sang weakly, "Buff-alo Bill . . ."

All of a sudden, through the window, the two boys noticed a black child coming toward the school. "There's Lewis!" they shouted. Lewis Dixon was smaller than his reputation, but he was known as the school tough guy, the funny man who had become a bully as the Wee Care year progressed, but whom the other kids still loved and revered. Robert and Evan stood by the windowpane, excited by Lewis's approach. Everyone was compelled to stare when they brought the big man down.

Lou drew them back from the window and asked them to tell him about the thing Kelly had pulled out of her vagina. Robert fluttered, a little breathless, trying to describe the thing. "It looked like little tiny meats." Robert pulled his hands apart and made a ripping noise.

"Do you know what a tampon is?" Lou asked, a note of wonder in his voice. He was pretty certain neither boy had the word in his vocabulary. As he expected, the boys looked at him blankly. The mystery of the Buffalo Bill game remained, for the moment, unsolved.

Lou walked the two boys back to their classroom as Rich Mastrangelo went downstairs to get Lewis Dixon.

Rich greeted the boy and sat down opposite him at a tiny table. Rich took off his tie and rolled up his sleeves while he introduced himself: "My name is Rich Mastrangelo, but you can call me Rich, because it's a lot easier to remember. I've been talking to all your buddies, and you know what we've been talking about?"

"What?" asked Lewis.

"We've been talking about some stuff that's not so nice that's been happening at school with Kelly."

Lewis listened, not tipping his hand. Rich pulled a doll across the floor and undressed it. He pointed to a body part, and Lewis named it for him. Rich worked down the body, and Lewis stared, a beautiful, chestnut boy, glowing with vitality. Rich pointed to the penis. "What's that?" he asked.

Lewis answered, "Blood."

■
■ ■

The investigators were becoming more and more certain that they didn't have the first idea what these children had endured. When the professionals met to share their findings, they noticed that their interviews were turning up the same allegations. Statements that they had hoped were simply an error on the part of the child they later saw were, in fact, widely corroborated.

This time, Rich told the team about the blood. No one else had heard anything of the sort, and none of them had any idea what this blood development signified. For now, they set aside the mention and struggled to interpret some of the other allegations.

They were choked with information, imponderable statements that at times made no logical sense, at least not by an adult's logic, but as they learned more and more, they started to decode what the children were saying. Kelly's earliest activities seemed to have been engaging to the children and only mildly sexualized, just titillating enough to draw the children gradually into her own sexuality. She had cajoled them with promises to be their best friend, had set them at ease by pretending to be a nurse: taking temperatures, applying Band-Aids, making them "feel better."

The pileup game was an early trick to condition the children to expose themselves and to accustom them to the touch of one another's bodies. Licking games, pretending they were dogs and cats, had facilitated oral sex. A game simulating a thermometer in the rectum had eventually led to undisguised penetration. Naked duck, duck, goose gave the premise of an acceptable game for nudity and touching. The use of "Jingle Bells" had been an early accompaniment to nudity so that the children would be made to feel they were involved in something familiar and fun. "Bingo" and "Old MacDonald" had been the background song to animal games in which the children, pretending to be animals, had pursued and licked one another.

None of these investigators had ever encountered such human damage. The out-and-out sexual activity was like a piggyback virus stealing into the children's systems with the games, songs, and make-believe ruses. In institutional cases, there was the gruesome possibility that the victims would include, say, a troop of Cub Scouts or a complete Confirmation class, or maybe even an entire preschool class. But in the Wee Care case it was almost as if, territorially, Kelly had set out to touch and torment every child in the entire school. To the investigators, it seemed unbelievable that one person could have done all this.

DYFS was too short of personnel to send reinforcements, and Lou felt overloaded. He was working with all sixty children, interviewing most of them two or more times. The other investigators, George, Rich, Peg, were there to help, and they did; but, bottom line, it was Lou's responsibility to see every child, personally. And the responsibility was bearing down and crushing him.

．
．　．

Ellen and her husband had talked it through, and they weren't satisfied. They couldn't get their minds around the idea that all this could have happened without anyone noticing, and so Ellen Gardner called Arlene.

In her most basic voice, Ellen asked, "Arlene, I don't understand any of this. When could Kelly possibly have had the opportunity to do these things?"

Arlene answered, "Oh, she had lots of opportunity," and the school's director proceeded to enumerate all the times Kelly had been alone with Ellen's child and others. She gave as an example the time when the children were in the gym in the afternoon, at which time Kelly could have taken them to the bathroom or anywhere she wanted.

Ellen hung up the phone, unsaved. She thought, God, I dressed Joey in elastic-waist pants and a pullover top. I made it easy.

Joey was out on the sidewalk, his feet over the curb as he watched the cars drive by. Ellen joined him there.

He carried a big stick, and as a car nosed into the street, he smashed the stick into the gravel, shouting, "Stop!" at the invading automobile. Ellen figured he was guarding his turf.

While he sat there, Joey began telling Ellen all about Kelly. Lou had prepared her for this. She knew that she could expect a gradual release of the things that were haunting him. Joey showed her how Kelly had put her hand inside his pants and on his penis, and he told her it had gotten big, and very uncomfortable.

Ellen tried to ignore her nausea. "Did you say anything to her?" she asked.

"I said, 'Don't do that.' " The way he said it it was an order.

"What'd she say?"

" 'Yes! I'm going to!' " Joey slashed the street with the stick. Ellen dutifully watched the impact, but her eyes were burning wet holes into her sinuses.

"Stop! Stop! Stop!" he yelled after a car.

Joey was lurching up and sitting down. " 'Take off your clothes and I'll hit you anywhere you want!' "

Ellen looked at her son. The makeshift hatchet he was using for chopping up the road had now lost enough chunks off its end to be only a stub. She wished she could walk away from it, just leave him sitting there at the curb. Nothing would ever make her feel up to this.

■
■ ■

The Wee Care parents had expressed a desire to meet with the Prosecutor's Office, but Sara Sencer's first instinct was not to see them. The investigators were still unclear as to how many children were actually involved, and Sara didn't know how to handle the dozens of parents whose children were coming forward. Still, Peg Foster insisted that it was important for the parents to meet with Sara and to become involved in the legal process. The parents greatly needed direction from someone in authority.

As Peg put it, "You really have no choice. You're such an integral part of this process. The parents have to meet you and they have to have confidence in you, because you represent the law. And if they don't have confidence in that, it'll all fall apart. They really need you.'' And Sara accepted that she needed the parents in order to have witnesses, in order to prosecute Kelly Michaels.

The meeting took place in the third-floor lounge at St. George's. Peg Foster accompanied Sara. To Peg, the ideal nursery school would be one schoolroom and two teachers, a very old-fashioned, self-contained institution without a lot of roaming about. Peg looked at Wee Care and saw a poorly lit school with no bathrooms on the classroom floor, winding hallways, and rambling basement rooms. This school did not fulfill her dreams.

The church living room was packed with bright, articulate adults, and Sara was uncertain as to how to handle their fears and their questions. She explained to her audience why it was important that they be careful how they talked about what had happened and be scrupulous about not tainting or confusing one another's testimony. Certainly, everyone was free to seek private therapy, and she understood that the mothers wanted to meet in support groups. That was fine, as long as they didn't trade allegations. By destroying the purity of the evidence, they could well doom the prosecution.

Sara's deep-set, darkly hooded eyes were serious and intelligent as she spoke. She wrapped the parents into her orderly proposals of what to do next and methodically went through the procedures for accumulating evidence, presenting to the Grand Jury, preparation for trial—the entire hopeful mechanism of the justice system.

A number of parents reeled with angry words, but Sara dissuaded them from making any comment to the press just yet. She assured them they would have their say, but asked them to tough it out until after the trial was over. If they spoke too soon, she warned them, their comments would be premature, and inevitably, as world events unfolded, their story would lose its newsworthiness before they were truly ready to rise to their platform.

Sara was convinced the press could ruin this case. She pointed out that across the country day-care abuse cases were being wrecked by media derision and public disbelief. Sara was prepared to face accusations of a witch-hunt somewhere along the way—that was pretty standard in a big case like this—but if it appeared that the prosecution was out for publicity, the witch-hunt response would be triggered immediately. Furthermore, when the material was as private as this was, any media interest could embarrass other parents and thereby scare away potential witnesses.

These people Sara was addressing were not a homogeneous group. There were married couples and unmarried couples, single mothers, mixed marriages, and extended families . . . lawyers, construction workers, engineers, landscapers, policemen, housewives, teachers, social workers, speech therapists, clerks, students, businessmen . . . parents of white children, black children, Oriental children . . . Jews, Catholics, atheists, Protestants . . . wealthy families and poor families. For the most part, the only thing these families had in common was Margaret Kelly Michaels.

Most of the Wee Care parents didn't know one another except to share a tragedy, but Sara Sencer now united them in the prosecutorial effort. They pulled together in an agreement not to exchange allegations and in a determination to support Sara in the prosecution of Kelly Michaels. Some acted out of a commitment to pursue legal revenge, some to attain justice, but all to make certain that nothing like this ever happened again.

When the evening was over and they were leaving the building, Sara said bluntly to Peg, "I'm gonna try this case." And later, when her boss, the County Prosecutor, wanted to know how Sara was going to take the Wee Care case to trial and still be able to run her unit, Sara's impassive, patient eyes glittered with edge, as she repeated, "*I'm* trying this case."

▪
▪ ▪

Peg wasn't getting anything from Melissa. She was certain the child had something to say because she had made statements to her mother the night before. Peg was working out of the church living room, and it occurred to her that maybe Melissa's reticence had something to do with the setting. The choir room was just down the hall. On an impulse, Peg decided to take her back to what might be the scene of the crime. They walked down the hallway into what was variously referred to by the children as the "piano room" and the "music room."

Peg was right: The empty room stirred something in Melissa. The pretty, dark girl said she had been in the room with Kelly and some other children. Her sentences were convoluted and garbled as she showed Peg where they had sat. Then Melissa explained that Kelly took off their clothes and they all played a game where they put peanut butter on one another, a sucking game.

Peg asked, "What'd you do with the peanut butter?"

Melissa answered, "We licked it off."

Peg's imagination spasmed. She didn't want to believe this.

The next morning, Peg announced the peanut butter disclosure to the rest of the team, and they batted the notion around in an interval of raw shock. Then the banter began. "Come on! Could it be? Nah! That can't possibly be what she meant." They joked about "peanut butter and Kelly," laughing, wishing they could really feel amused.

Peg had given her interview with Melissa a restless night's consideration: Peanut butter could well have been another engagement mechanism, a way to use a food the children liked in order to slowly introduce them to oral sex. Peg now checked the faces around the table, then said, "If they could do peanut butter and jelly, then they could do urination and defecation."

Someone snorted. But Peg insisted that they had to appreciate that this might be the first significant lead to sex acts that were about something other than sex: degradation.

There was a general rumbling, "Oh, no. It can't be." The others laughed nervously, and someone called over, "What'd you do to that girl, Peggy?"

Then someone interjected, "My kid mentioned jelly yesterday." Lou looked up: he too was getting jelly.

Sickened, they all played at being mock-annoyed with Peg, but each of them left the room devastated.

Later in the morning, Peg rummaged through the school kitchen searching for the peanut butter. She found several already opened jars, and though she knew the teachers had used peanut butter for snacks, disgust overwhelmed her. She thought, Oh God, it's really here. I really found it!

Peg was surprised at herself for not having expected success, stunned, even after all she had heard, to be reminded that the sexual activity had actually happened, not in theory, but in time.

The team of investigators began to incorporate peanut butter questions into their interviews. And only days after Melissa's disclosure, the investigators were told by a little girl that Kelly had urinated into a spoon. Now as interviews continued, the occurrence of urination games became a reality. Some children alleged having peed into a "piss pot," although the investigators had no idea what that could be. In due course, they learned that the Buffalo Bill game had in fact entailed peeing on paper towels and then throwing the towels away, although they never learned anything more about the Buffalo Bill song.

Insertion of utensils Lou could handle, but bodily fluids? Lewis Dixon had called the penis *blood*: Kelly had shown them her blood, that much was clear. But when Lou realized that the blood Lewis Dixon had mentioned previously might, in fact, be the *jelly* that numerous children were talking about, and when he learned that urine was widely used by Kelly

in the abuse, Lou was ready to leave the case. He begged his supervisor:
"Replace me."

▪
▪ ▪

The prosecutor felt inundated. This was a much broader investigation
than she had ever anticipated: Sara had taken to dividing the case's phases
into "little Wee Care" and "big Wee Care," so clearly were the two
investigations delineated. To keep all this new information straight, Sara
decided the investigators should start to audio-tape the interview sessions
and create some kind of contemporaneous record.

Lou didn't love the idea. DYFS policy was never to tape, and Lou
himself felt uncomfortable interviewing with a recorder running. He noticed the children, too, were self-conscious about the machine. But trial
evidence was the prosecutor's business, and Sara insisted on having
audiotapes, so Lou went along with it. The team began to record those
children who as yet still hadn't completed their disclosures.

Sara received the tapes when George brought them down to the Prosecutor's Office, and she listened to them critically, hypersensitive to the
slightest note of suggestion by the interviewers. Because Lou conducted
most of the interviews, he took most of the heat, with Sara harping on
her standards: "No leading questions! No verbal pressure!" And she
picked at all her investigators with skepticism: "Did she really do it?
How could she really do this? Are we sure?"

Peg watched Sara struggle with the conflicting feelings of conviction
and ambivalence. The stronger Sara's belief became, the more forceful
her bouts with skepticism seemed to become and the more abrasive Sara
certainly became, wary of the evidence that was amassing before her,
readying to bury both herself and her unit in a scandal.

By pretending that she doubted the charges, Sara got what she wanted:
She got to be convinced. "This didn't happen," Sara would challenge.

Peg would smile. "It happened." Peg stared her down. "Look, Sara,
the occasional teenager might lie about an incident, but there is practically
no incidence of preschoolers making up these things."

Sara was sure that Kelly Michaels was guilty, but she couldn't risk
even a small mistake. Her office's credibility in prosecuting child sexual
abuse was tied to the integrity of this large, soon-to-be high-profile case.
Sara had a real concern for the law and for her own power, and she was
scrupulous not to falsely accuse, so that everyone on the team appreciated
her uncertainty. Of course Sara was going to have doubts, and of course
she was going to be slow and uncertain. She was a *prosecutor*.

If Sara heard an audiotape and called up sniping, "This is terrible," the investigators accepted her critique, but they also knew among themselves that they had done what they had to do. Those who were in the school every day realized that there were no unbreakable rules.

They couldn't conduct an interview with both eyes on the purity of the case: Part of them always had to be there in the present experience with the child, feeling with the child. Lou greatly identified with the victims. The Wee Care parents loved him, and so did the children, because he didn't just interview the children, he empathized with them, and each child sensed his sweetness. Emotionally, the children responded to him, and as a result they entrusted him with their experience of abuse.

.
. .

Karen Steadman was just stepping out of the shower when Alison came into the bathroom. Karen started to towel off while her daughter watched.

She barely noticed she had company. Then Allie lunged at her, clutching her from behind.

"Pee on me!" her daughter said.

.
. .

Ellen Gardner sat in her bedroom. Her son's life-size self-portrait from Wee Care presided over the wall above the dresser.

Joey came into the room, crawled under Ellen's desk, and folded himself into an angular ball. He informed his mother that Kelly had made him stuff knives into her body, and he was terrified that he had hurt Kelly. Ellen fixed on that image, imagined Kelly in pain.

She talked to her son about how brave he had been to talk to Lou, how he didn't have to keep secrets from Mommy, and how nobody was angry with him. And she told him once again that he would never have to go to jail: He hadn't done anything wrong; only Kelly had.

"I made her bleed," Joey said. He roiled around on the floor.

"Do you think maybe she got cut?" Ellen asked. She used knives, Ellen thought. A phallic utensil for a girl who wanted to enter in?

Joey said, "That isn't it. It wasn't the knives. She was bouncing me."

His voice was so babyish, so faint and filmy. A mature voice should go with this knowledge. The discrepancy was grotesque.

Slowly, Ellen learned that what her child called "bouncing in the blood" was Kelly lying on the floor without any clothes on and Joey on top of her.

"That's how I made her bleed," he said.

Don't visualize, she shouted at herself. That'll kill you. This day was

5

⸫

Peg and George were getting nothing out of Freddie Mercer. Anne, a young graduate student of clinical psychology, was observing the interview. Peg used a doll to help him identify body parts, but Freddie just took the doll and whacked it with a wooden spoon he lifted from the clutter of books and toys and dolls around the tape recorder.

Freddie was a baby, only about to turn four, and so far he was extremely unresponsive to them. It wasn't that he was inarticulate: For a three-year-old, his verbal skills were outstanding. When Peg told him that they were here to talk about things that happened at the school, Freddie retorted, "You're aggravating me."

George left the room and Peg continued to try to talk to the little boy, but Freddie was giggling and muttering and barely even listening to what she was asking. Finally, at the moment too frustrated to continue, Peg turned off the tape recorder and left Anne with Freddie. She didn't expect any disclosure but suggested maybe a new voice would help.

Anne pulled over some crayons and paper, and Freddie began to scribble, peering over at Anne every few moments, then ducking down to his work. Quickly then, he walked over to Anne and shoved his hand down the front of her scoop-necked blouse. Anne pushed him off her and asked him where he had learned to do that, but Freddie didn't answer.

"Who did you do that to?"

"You," he said, smiling.

"All right. Did you touch anyone else like that?"

"You know who."

Anne understood. She had to play a guessing game with Freddie: Gerald? No. Amy? No. Clifford? No. Kelly? Yes.

Anne asked, "Was Kelly dressed like this?"

"No."

"What did she have on?"

"Nothing." This statement reminded him of something. Freddie ordered Anne: "Take your clothes off!"

"No, I can't do that."

Anne was sitting cross-legged on the floor. Freddie reached over with his thin arms and tried to undo her belt. She pushed him away. In a rush of endeavor, he tugged at her shoes and the bottom of her pants, demanding repeatedly, "Take your clothes off!"

Anne couldn't tell how many hands were touching her or where, she was so overwhelmed. Flustered and alarmed, she managed to hold him back.

There was some noise out in the hallway. Freddie stopped in a stone panic. Then he slipped free of her grasp and lunged for her crotch and tried to lick her. Freddie was just a three-year-old boy. Anne couldn't react as she wanted to, yet he was assaulting her. Warding him off with the palm of her hand, she said, "Look, there're dolls over there!"

Freddie glanced over and grabbed a boy doll and yanked its outfit off, snagging, in his haste, the pants. Anne helped him with them. Freddie picked up the girl doll and undressed that one too. While Freddie's attention was diverted, Anne leaned around and pushed the tape recorder back on. When she turned back, she saw that Freddie was holding the girl doll upside down by the ankles.

He opened up the legs. "It's wet."

"Who's wet?" asked Anne.

"Look at her!" he ordered, and looked, himself, at the doll. Then he licked it between the legs. He was like a lecherous old man with a kiddie face.

Anne lowered her voice into neutral. "Oh, you licked her booty? Who'd you do that to?"

"You!"

It was as if all his earlier resistance had given way and now he was acting out everything that was in his head. He refrained, "Come here and take your clothes off."

Anne countered. "Why should I?"

"Because I want you to."

"Why?"

Because. Why. Because.

"Who did you ever do that to before?" she asked again.

He ignored her and tried to lick her again, said, "Now you're wet."

"Can I guess who?" Anne offered.

"Guess, and take your clothes off." Freddie ran on slim legs to close the cracked door to the room.

"Take your clothes off!"

Freddie crumpled at her feet and struggled with her shoes. She helped him take one off, though she didn't know why she did. Anne certainly didn't want to encourage him, but she felt sorry for the little boy, sick at seeing him scrambling around pitiable and frustrated and broken.

"Take off your socks," he ordered.

"Who did this?"

"I'll take off your socks."

The door opened, and Peg walked in. Freddie spun around, flailing, overwrought. Catching sight of Peg, he shrieked at her, "Take your clothes off!"

"Why would you ask such a thing?" said Peg.

Freddie was unresponsive again, sitting on the floor, grinning.

Peg was firm. "I'm not going to take my clothes off."

"Then *be quiet*," he ordered.

Anne stood up and Freddie told her to take off her clothes in the closet, and Peg wondered momentarily whether that was where Kelly had undressed, in the choir room closet where the black robes had hung.

When Anne didn't move toward the closet, Freddie shimmied up the grad student's leg. Anne peeled him away and tried one last time to find out where he had learned this behavior, but all he'd say was, "You know," with a big, smirky grin on his face, and then he looked at the tape recorder and smiled: "You tell me."

In Peg's opinion, Freddie was desperate for someone to set limits on his sexual behavior. Children who had had everything done to them often knew no boundaries of right from wrong and had no sense of demarcation: what was theirs, what was everyone's. To anyone, but particularly to a child this young, this free-for-all attitude was overwhelmingly confusing, even terrifying, because it stood to reason that if Freddie was at liberty to be with absolutely anyone, then conversely, anyone was at liberty to be with him and to use his body in any way they wanted. Freddie needed someone to say, "No. This will not be done."

Peg took Freddie and deposited him with George in another room, then went to get his parents. Anne was shaking as she flipped the recorder back on and quickly started to describe what had happened before she had been able to restart the tape. *It's wet*. Anne wanted to document the incident so there wouldn't be even a chink in the chain of evidence.

Freddie hadn't mentioned the pileup game, kitchen utensils, oral sex, or kissing. In fact, he'd said very little, but he had acted out every one of those things on Anne or on the dolls. Normally, even the most disturbed child limited his sexual acting out to inanimate objects, rarely making the crossover into the world of the living. This little boy was broken, just as if Kelly had thrown wreckage into his mechanism. She had made of him a mini would-be rapist, or so Anne felt.

Peg joined Freddie's parents in St. George's living room, where they waited on a couch. The Mercers had brought to Peg a problem they were having with their son: He was obsessed with female anatomy, kept trying to fondle his mother's breasts. Before his disclosure, when he had tried to do this, his mother had shoved him away, repulsed and irritated. Since his disclosure, though, Valerie Mercer felt guilty, and because she didn't want to embarrass or hurt her little boy, she was now letting him do what he wanted.

Peg told Valerie that she understood her reluctance to criticize this behavior, but Peg was clear that Valerie's allowing herself to be incestuously abused was not the answer. Mrs. Mercer was only going to bring more harm to her son if she refused to set the limits he craved. By touching her in that way, Peg said, Freddie was challenging limits. He was asking her, "What are my boundaries?" Peg advised Valerie to tell her son that she understood, and that it wasn't his fault how he was feeling, it was okay to feel that way. But, Peg insisted, "Tell him he isn't allowed to touch."

George brought Freddie into the living room. The three-year-old ran to his mother's side and fitted his small, round head into her waist. Valerie curved her arm around his shoulder.

Returning to the interview room, Peg tried to calm Anne down, but she worried about what was going to become of this boy. Would psychological counseling be able to defuse the damage and place Freddie back on a healthy developmental path?

a fetal position, this time on top of the table where Lou and the tape recorder sat.

Lou tried to reassure him. "We talked to a few more of your buddies. We talked to everybody now. . . . And everyone told me about the nap room stuff and the bathroom stuff and the music room stuff and the peanut butter stuff and the pee stuff and everything." The list was offered as a soothing acknowledgment of all Joey's most formidable fears: Lou wanted this child to know that he had heard them all and he was still Joey's buddy.

Lou added, "So nothing surprises me anymore."

Joey's voice teased, "I hate you."

"No you don't." "Yes I do." "No you don't." "Yes I do."

"You just don't like talking about this, but you don't hate me."

Joey punched Lou on the face, gently but repeatedly.

". . . Did Kelly ever tell you that she could turn you into a mouse?"

"Yeah."

"She did . . . ?"

"Yeah."

"And what did she say she would turn into?"

"A monster."

"Did she say she would turn you into a—"

"Yike!"

"—monster?"

"Yeah."

"You didn't believe that stuff, did you?"

"No."

"But it scared you a little bit?"

"Yep."

"Yeah, it scared me too," Lou agreed.

"Bluh. I'm big," imparted Joey. Lou followed his lead and concurred, letting the conversation incline that way.

"Ha ha, I'm almost five," Joey sang.

"When are you gonna be five? When's your birthday?"

"In the fall."

"In the fall? Oh come on, you gonna help us out?" Lou pleaded, contorting his voice into a little boy's.

"Yeah."

"Do you want to help us keep her in jail longer? Huh? Do ya, huh?"

Joey huffed. "Uh, ooh." He rolled his body around the edge of the table.

"Do you want to help us keep her in jail longer?"

"Ugh." Joey fell down on the tabletop, played dead.

"I'm not going to be there when you fall," Lou warned. "Do you? Why not?"

Joey lunged for Lou, groping to get a hold so they could wrestle.

Lou started, "Don't mess up my, ooh, there you go. I got him. He's on his butt, he's on his butt." Joey laughed hysterically.

"Okay. Now tell me everything you know."

"No," laughed Joey. He was beating on Lou from his vantage point on the table.

Rich intervened: "No, no. That's not nice."

Joey hopped on and off Lou's lap, back and forth to his perch on the table.

Lou wrestled him into a headlock from within which Joey kicked him. "Tell me what happened."

Joey did some thick monster breathing.

"Come on," said Lou. Letting Joey slip away, Lou slid two dolls over to him. "You told us everything once before. Do you want to undress the doll? Let's do it."

"Hold it. Hold it," said Joey. His voice became a whine as he tried to slow things down.

"Why don't you take Kelly and I'll take this one."

"I'm taking Kelly. Oh no! I'm gonna chop her head off!"

Lou ran through identification of body parts, starting with the identification of the sexes, then the genitals. As he drew out answers, Joey's restlessness intensified. He twirled on the tabletop.

"Sit down. Sit down. Stop now, that's dangerous stuff. Sit down just a coupla more minutes."

Joey chimed in, "Do you want me to chop your head off?"

"Not yet, later on," Lou deflected.

"I got a knife."

"You do?"

"Yep."

"Where?"

"That many knives," said Joey, holding up a few fingers.

"I don't see a knife."

"I got a knife at home." Still atop the table, Joey sprawled on his belly and splayed his arms and legs.

"Look, Joey. You're flying." Lou maneuvered: "Did you ever see Kelly play 'Jingle Bells' on the piano?"

Joey muttered something.

"I can't hear you. Did you? Did ya?"

Joey nodded.

"And was she wearing any clothes?"

"No."

"No?" Lou repeated the answer out of reflex, as if checking his own hearing.

"I saw her penis, too."

"You saw her penis? You mean, like, show me on the Kelly doll."

Joey lifted the doll by the crotch and held it forward.

"You saw that? Oh."

"She doodied on me," Joey said, softly now.

"She doodied on you?"

"She peed on us." He giggled nervously.

"She peed on you?"

"Yeah."

"And where were you? Were you lying on the floor or something?"

"No." Then Joey let it out, just opened up on the word. "She peed on me and just peeeeed!"

"Where were you?"

"Next door." It didn't occur to Lou at the moment that the choir room was right down the hall.

Lou inquired about bleeding.

Extremely agitated, Joey said, "She."

"She?"

"Was."

"What?" Lou prompted.

"Bleeding."

"Bleeding," Lou echoed automatically. Ellen had already told him about the self-portrait. Lou prompted, "She was bleeding in her penis?"

"Yeah. Ugh."

"Did you have to put your penis in her penis?" asked Lou, adopting Joey's confused terminology.

"Yes."

"You did?"

"And I peed in her own pee pee."

Lou repeated, "You peed in her penis. Ooh, what was that like? What did that feel like?"

"Like a lightning—a shot."

Lou was astonished. Lightning, yes.

As Joey spoke, he manipulated the dolls, approximating intercourse.

Lou repeated, "Like a shot? Boy. Did Robert have to put his penis in her penis, too?"

"At the same time."

"At the same time? How did you do that?" Lou asked, counting on making nonsense or sense out of this material later.

"We chopped our penises off."

"Aw, so she was bleeding in her penis, and you had to put your penis and Robert's penis inside her penis?"

"At the same time," he said, again confoundingly.

"At the same time? And that's how you got the blood on it?"

"Yes."

"Wow."

"Ugh . . ."

"Did anybody else have to put their penis in her penis?" asked Lou. Joey yowled, "No! No! You better not eat my shirt."

"How about—"

"You better not eat my new shirt. If you eat my new shirt, you chump, I'll chop your head off. . . ."

Lou tried to get Joey back to the subject. Joey spoke inaudibly.

Lou nudged, "Huh?"

"I'm just talkin' to myself," Joey said.

"Did you have to do any pee stuff in the nap room too? Or was that just in the music room?"

"Yep, pee," he sang.

"Pee in the mouth?" Lou asked, remembering something Ellen Gardner had mentioned.

Now Joey laughed hysterically.

"Did anybody drink anybody's pee?"

"Yes."

"Who did?"

"Jessica."

"Jessica had to drink whose pee?"

"Kelly's peeeee!"

The door to the room opened. As Lou turned to see who had just walked in, Joey stood up on the tabletop and unzipped his fly. When Lou turned around, there he was, penis in hand, pressing it forward toward Lou's mouth. Lou pressed his palm against Joey's forehead and pushed him back.

"Why are you putting Joey's penis in my mouth? Who put their mouth on Joey's penis?"

"Peeeeee!" Joey lifted the Joey doll and directed the exposed penis toward Lou's face.

"Whose mouth did you have to put your penis in?"

"In little mouth."

"Whose mouth did you have to put your penis in," Lou repeated.

"Nobody's. Peeeeee." Joey sang.

"Nobody's what?"

Rich interjected, "Who put their mouth on yours?"

"NO!"

"Did anybody kiss your penis? Kelly didn't?" Lou already knew from the last interview that she had.

"No . . ."

"Now, how about the knives and stuff? Did she put the knife in your bottom?"

"Yes . . . I said I want to go home." Joey assumed the fetal position on Lou's lap now.

"You want to go home?" Lou looked down at the child curled in his lap. "Did Kelly say anything to you about people becoming dogs?"

"No. I'm going to shoot you, then you'll be dead. . . ."

"Let me ask you some questions. Did she make everybody take off their clothes in the music room?"

"Meow, meow."

"Did she?"

"Meow."

"Did she make everybody lay on top of each other?"

"Meow, meow." Joey convulsed, giggling.

"I thought that you were going to help me."

"No. Bad me."

Lou tried to get Joey to pay attention, but it was almost as if Lou wasn't even in the room.

"Meow, meow, meow. You're sad."

"Did she hurt you in the bathroom?"

"Meow, meow. No, baby." Joey's voice held a hideous, rotting tenderness.

"What did she do to you in the nap room."

"Nothing, baby. She just peed on the floor."

"She peed on the floor in the nap room?" Lou's voice wasn't skeptical, just asking for confirmation.

"Yep."

"Who had to clean that up?"

"Nobody."

"Nobody?" Lou echoed. "Did she hurt your heinie in the nap room?"

Joey laughed, elfin. "Meow, meow."

"Did she hurt your penis in the nap room?"

"Meow, meow."

"Who did she hurt in that nap room?" Lou continued to strive for answers.

"Only."

"Only who?"

"Jessica." Then Joey said, "She pinched her."

"Pinched her where? Where did she pinch her?"

Suddenly, Joey announced, "Toys, toys, toys. Everybody needs a toy," and he grabbed a doll and pinched its cloth flesh, hard.

▪

▪   ▪

The thirty-five minutes he shared with Joey Gardner were the most disturbing in Lou Fonolleras's professional life: Joey had been extremely physical with Lou, had even grabbed at Lou's penis with a latex pig puppet that the investigators had found in one of the classrooms. Lou had walked out of the interview thinking of *The Exorcist*: This beautiful little boy (Joey had pale brown ringlets surrounding an extremely clear face) had seemed almost possessed, had turned into an ugly, violent creature. Every time Joey demonstrated a sexual act on a doll, it was a violent sexual act: He would jab the knife into the doll.

Lou was brokenhearted, and appalled. Vaginal intercourse at the age of four? Lou inferred that "chopping off heads" meant sexual intercourse. From the little boy's perspective, his penis had disappeared into Kelly as if it had been chopped off. Maybe Kelly had even named the thing herself.

And—blood. The investigators were already resigned to the fact that the children had seen blood, but Joey Gardner had just clearly identified what he'd seen as being not just blood, but vaginal blood. Not only that: It now appeared that the children hadn't just looked at the blood—Kelly had had intercourse with the boys while she was menstruating.

Drinking urine? Ellen Gardner had forewarned Lou, but Lou was nevertheless stunned. Kelly had urinated on the floor in front of the children, she had made them pee on one another, but no child had ever before mentioned anything about *drinking* urine. Peg had been right. If it hadn't already been clear that degradation was part of her motive, now it seemed irrefutable that Kelly had intended to dominate and degrade.

The morning after seeing Joey, Lou unburdened himself at the breakfast meeting. The same old story: Before the morning meeting was half over, Lou had the others convulsed with heaving laughter. Then, in the aftermath, having by laughter made room in his soul, Lou told them how he felt.

▪
▪ ▪

Dr. Susan Esquilin, a consulting psychologist to the United Hospitals Sexual Assault Unit, had seen a number of the Wee Care children for evaluation, called in by several parents who desired confirmation of the abuse. The children she had seen displayed tremendous guilt about having hurt one another, and Dr. Esquilin felt strongly that they should all be brought together to see with their own eyes that their friends were safe and well, even after having told on Kelly. In addition, because much of the abuse had occurred in groups of children, Dr. Esquilin wanted to re-create the group setting, this time for a positive experience. Therefore, as the investigation was finishing up, Susan approached the Prosecutor's Office with a proposal to organize group therapy sessions for the Wee Care children.

When Susan told Sara Sencer what she wanted, Sara at first refused. She had visions of the case being pulverized by defense attorneys after they learned that the children had been "getting together to compare notes."

Sara insisted: "It'd destroy the case." But Susan didn't let the idea drop.

Only after Sara's supervisor instructed her, "What's best for the children is best for the case," did Sara agree to allow the groups, but under some conditions. The group meetings were not to begin until every single child had been interviewed at least twice by the investigators. Furthermore, Susan was not to raise issues of Wee Care directly. Sara didn't want the children discussing either Kelly or the school in one another's presence because that would surely fuel the defense's inevitable accusations of group contamination.

Susan agreed entirely. For therapeutic reasons alone, she felt that extensive talk about Wee Care should not be forced on children who were not able or ready to deal with it. Her intention was to address the underlying psychological issues.

When these terms were settled, Dr. Esquilin moved forward, dividing the children into several groups that would meet together for each session, the groups arranged roughly according to which children had been friends or classmates. Parents were to join in these sessions in case their child needed comfort and also to learn about their child's fears.

The first session was held on the fifth of July at the home of one of the children. All the participants sat on the floor. Susan told them: "We're here today because of things that happened at Wee Care, some things involving Kelly.'' Then she moved immediately away from that subject, and although in the course of the subsequent five sessions over the ensuing month and a half, children at times mentioned Kelly or Wee Care, those things were never again brought up for discussion.

With all the talk about ''bad Kelly'' and ''the bad things'' (the investigators suspected that that terminology had been a mistake, because it implicated the children too for the things they had done), the children's ability to judge the goodness of people they met had become confused. Dr. Esquilin wanted to help them form a more integrated view of people so that their view of good and bad wouldn't split. When the groups got together, the children talked about good and bad people they knew and about how everybody had in them some good and some bad.

They drew self-portraits, discussing the body's uses and their fears about bodily integrity, then they drew pictures of things that scared them and talked about how to control the monsters in their dreams. Susan read them Maurice Sendak's *Where the Wild Things Are*, and the children practiced staring at the monsters like Max did, practiced making the monsters do what they said. Susan led them in a game in which someone (chosen by a child, usually a big person: Susan or a parent) pretended to be a monster, and all the rest of the group, both children and parents, protected one of the children from the attacking monster. This game was designed to teach them that there were people who were ready and able to protect them.

Dr. Esquilin also read the children a book called *A Horse Grows Up*, a story about a baby horse that becomes separated from its mother. The book addressed these children's anxiety about having their mothers taken away from them and their difficulties separating. And she read *Making Babies*, a preschool sex education book, intended to inform the children about their bodies on a level they could understand. Some of the children seemed unimpressed by the information about sexual intercourse, while others reacted to that information as if it was new and startling material.

Then, because the abuse had often been enacted in the context of normal children's games, at the end of every group meeting, the children sang songs and played games, some of them the same ones that Kelly had corrupted, such as ''Jingle Bells'' and ''Bingo.'' Dr. Esquilin wanted them to repeat these experiences then and there to detoxify the songs and games. The children would all be returning to school in the fall, and the doctor was hopeful that they would be able to play games with the other children and hear songs and stories without anxiety, without constantly being stopped by something that reminded them of Kelly.

▪
▪ ▪

Each of the children's parents had signed waivers releasing confidential medical information, so that Sara now had in her possession dozens of doctor's reports. A few of the children had been taken to see Dr. Anna Haroutunian, a pediatrician who was the co-director with Peg Foster of the Sexual Assault Unit of United Hospitals. In her dealings with the parents, Sara had emphatically recommended Dr. Haroutunian because of her expertise in examining children for physical indications of abuse. However, most parents had used their regular pediatricians, and to Sara's amazement, only a few of the children's doctors had conducted a proper examination.

Claudia Moore took Jonathan back to his pediatrician specifically to be examined for indications of sexual abuse, but the doctor rationalized that since Jonathan was not complaining of rectal pain, there was no need to examine the genital area. Julie Danvers's doctor took only a bird's-eye view of the little girl's genitals. As she settled down onto the examining table and spread apart her legs, she asked, "Are you going to bite me?" And yet, even faced with that reminder of why he was there examining this child, the doctor simply peered down at her crotch from a distance and recorded negative genital findings.

The investigative team hadn't expected universal physical findings in this case, largely because the victims hadn't seen their doctors until at least two weeks after Kelly had left Wee Care, long enough for indications to start healing. Even a dilated hymen could revert to perfectly normal closure if given enough time. And in the case of lacerations, the genital area had the ability to heal very rapidly, sometimes even without scarring.

Many sexual acts perpetrated on children caused only redness. Acts such as oral sex, fondling, and fingering of genitalia all fell into the legal category of sexual assault, and all had devastating long-term effects on the victim, but none left an outward marking. The examiner might have noted a bruise, but then, what toddler didn't have a bruise on his shin? Softer indications were often overlooked by doctors, and if a child had genital redness or discomfort, the first thought was that it was vaginitis or a reaction to bubble bath. Medical literature constantly sought to educate doctors that child sexual abuse exists, but often the diagnosis of abuse wasn't even considered by an examining doctor seeking to explain symptoms such as redness or irritation.

Dr. Haroutunian explained to the prosecutor that unless doctors had special training in this area they rarely knew how to evaluate allegations of sexual abuse, and many were hampered by a visceral disinclination to do a genital exam on a little child. Even when a child's visit to the doctor was specifically fomented by allegations of abuse, the doctor frequently didn't perform a genital examination. Jonathan's pediatrician was a case in point. With professionals, as with everyone else, allegations of child sexual abuse were met with a great deal of denial: Professionals tried to avoid the issue. Medical conferences revealed that a large number of otherwise good pediatricians didn't know that the size of a normal hymenal opening was anything from totally closed up to five millimeters in diameter, seven millimeters at most. Numerous pediatricians believed that an opening of even ten millimeters was normal. If such a doctor had seen a girl with a broken hymen, he could improperly conclude that everything was normal.

Elizabeth Kelsey was seen by her family pediatrician, but she became hysterical, screaming, crying, kicking, and clawing, and her mother had to restrain her. As a result, the doctor conducted only an incomplete examination and noted no signs of abuse. Jackie Kelsey brought Elizabeth in for further examination by Anna Haroutunian on the agreed-upon pretext that Elizabeth was having a routine exam for camp, just getting her summer checkup like every other child. Once Dr. Haroutunian explained to her that there would be no needles, she and Elizabeth had a nice rapport. Elizabeth was sweet and cooperative and, despite her obvious anxiety, not at all hyperactive. And the doctor explained, step by step, exactly what she was going to do.

In girls, Dr. Haroutunian always checked for an abnormal hymenal opening. She examined Elizabeth in the frog-leg position, using only her hands, as instruments had the potential to traumatize a child who might not be able to differentiate between a victimization and a professional intrusion.

Elizabeth's genitals were borderline, but still within the normal five millimeter range. Her rectum was normal. Elizabeth, however, had two notches on her hymen set apart by 180 degrees. These notches could be the remnants of healed lacerations caused by the insertion of a knife, or they could reflect a developmental variation. Variations that were symmetrical often occurred naturally as a child's body grew, and these two marks were indeed placed evenly along the hymenal ring. The doctor assured the little girl that she was fine, but she told her mother that, although inconclusive, her findings did not rule out sexual abuse.

Angie McMahon's mother had been taking her to the pediatrician throughout the Wee Care school year because she was concerned about Angie's persistent bed-wetting. The pediatrician had noted a red vulva at the time, concurrent with the alleged sexual activity. Following the disclosure of abuse, her mother returned to the pediatrician, who at that time put off doing a genital examination on Angie. Therefore, Angie's mother brought her down to United Hospitals to be seen by Anna Haroutunian.

Dr. Haroutunian found Angie's hymenal opening to be over one centimeter in diameter, clearly wider than that of a normal girl her age, and Dr. Haroutunian concluded that Angie had abnormal genitals, most likely secondary to sexual abuse. Before she spoke to Angie's mother privately, she reassured the child that she was going to grow up to be a healthy woman able to bear children, and that despite the fact that something physical had happened to her, there would be no permanent damage from it. The doctor was sweetly firm.

Angie's mother, grasping for an alternative to the truth, suggested that Angie roughhoused a lot, and maybe her daughter's hymen broke while she was riding a bike or something. Dr. Haroutunian was adamant that girls did not break their hymens that way: The horseback riding cliché was a myth. The hymen was set back into the vagina, anywhere up to an inch inside the opening. A perpetrator could conceivably insert something into the child and still not disturb the anatomy of the hymen. In addition, the hymen was somewhat protected front and back by protruding bones, the pelvic bone in front and the buttocks and tailbone in back. Unless a female fell, legs astride, upon some penetrating object, the soft tissues to which the hymen was attached would give, and the bones jutting protectively before and behind could prevent rupture.

While she was at it, Dr. Haroutunian clarified that it would be very unlikely for a girl to stretch that orifice while masturbating, for the simple reason that it would be painful. And she pointed out that it was unheard of to have a girl born without a hymen if the genitalia were in all other ways normal. Hymens clearly developed in a variety of shapes, but a finding like Angie's could not be explained away by claiming that some girls were born without them. She cited a study of eleven hundred infant girls, not one of whom was born without a hymen. Statistically, that occurrence was simply too extraordinary to explain this finding of a one-centimeter opening.

Sara Sencer wished fervently that all the children had been taken to see Dr. Haroutunian right off. Then maybe she could have presented to a jury an overall percentage of abnormal genitals in the group to compare to national averages. She could have argued statistically that the disproportionate number of girls with an enlarged hymen was a positive indication that the allegations were truthful. However, most of the children had been seen by their regular doctors who had not done a proper genital examination.

All Sara had was a handful of isolated physical findings as reported by pediatricians and the children's parents. In addition to Anna Haroutunian's reports, she had two other girls with virtually no hymens, as well as Evan's anal rash, one boy's impetigo, two black eyes, and numerous children with shin bruises, four with paired circular bruises on the small of the back (the children said Kelly had pounded them with the handle of a wooden spoon), scratch marks, and complaints of anal and genital soreness and genital redness. None of the children had venereal disease.

Unfortunately, some of the best physical evidence Sara had was from children who weren't communicating and therefore would most likely not be testifying. One little boy had been examined by his father, a physician, when he complained of rectal pain, and the father had found anal lacerations. This had occurred early in the 1984–85 academic year, contemporaneous with the alleged abuse. The father had explained away the finding as being the result of constipation, never considering the possibility of sexual abuse. That physical finding, made by a doctor during the time of Kelly's tenure, could have been tremendously persuasive to a jury, but it would never make it into the trial.

. .
.

In the first week of July, the joint investigation was concluded. Of Wee Care's sixty students, Lou Fonolleras on behalf of DYFS determined that fifty-one of them had endured Kelly. The nine children who were overlooked had either begun school in May—after Kelly had already left the school—or had attended only briefly and part-time. Some of the nine had been mute in interviews, so that their involvement could not be determined. The results of the joint investigation made it clear to the investigative team that Kelly Michaels had deliberately and methodically assaulted every child she could get her hands on.

The Wee Care children had suffered identical agonies and indignities, and now they manifested identical symptoms: fears, sleeping problems, eating problems, sexual distortions, regressive behaviors. All fifty-one children fit into one diagnostic category, and yet they were individual little people. Each child's pain was unique.

Lewis Dixon, for example, had been one of Kelly's special helpers: That's what Kelly had named the little boys (she had pulled their names out of a confiscated baseball cap) who had helped her with cleanup and crowd control, making the other children behave and catching the run-aways on their way out of the room. Lewis had acted out his own trau-matization by bullying the other little children, even his best friend, Joey Gardner.

Another little boy had developed a seizure disorder following disclo-sure, and yet another had responded to the stress of disclosure by acting out in violence against his baby brother, who had become severely with-drawn as a result. This little boy's parents weren't going to allow him to testify for fear that he might start to pick on his brother again and push the infant further into seclusion.

Mitchell, whose father had written the words of encouragement to Kelly, had to live with the knowledge that after he disclosed the abuse, his mother was diagnosed with cancer. Mitchell believed that Kelly had made this happen because he had told on her, and he was sure his mother's cancer was all his fault, that by his own choices and actions he had given it to her.

Kevin and Heather Brennan had witnessed each other's violation. The brother and sister had lived with the guilt of not being able to prevent each other's unhappiness, and now they lived with the confusion of having shared sexual relations. Their mother found them, long after they'd dis-closed, attempting to have intercourse on her bed.

▪
▪ ▪

None of the investigators knew exactly when this abuse at Wee Care had started: They were thrown off by the children's inexact senses of time, weather, season. But from the onset of the behavioral symptoms, Sara deduced that it must have begun no later than October or November 1984, soon after Kelly Michaels had been given her own class of preschoolers. It might have occurred daily, but possibly only sporadically. The games could have entailed three naked children or seven. The jelly could have been jelly or blood; the peanut butter could have been peanut butter or feces. As Paul's mother had said, there was bound to be a lot more that had happened that the children weren't talking about, and ultimately only the children and Kelly would ever know for sure.

Meanwhile, the investigative team disbanded. George McGrath and Rich Mastrangelo returned to the Prosecutor's Office to tackle the rest of the unit's case load. Peg Foster returned to the United Hospitals Sexual Assault Unit. Lou Fonolleras returned to the DYFS office and endeavored to distance himself from the case and the pain.

Part

TWO

6

.ˑ.

The parents urged Sara Sencer to push for a December 1985 trial date. When Sara insisted that she couldn't possibly deliver such an early court date, some of them were angry: They felt their lives were tethered to the slow buildup of this case, and they wanted to have their pain and move on.

.ˑ.

So far, despite the vast body of evidence compiled against Kelly Michaels, the only crimes she had been charged with were the six counts handed down by the first Grand Jury back in May. As the investigators were winding up their final interviews, Sara Sencer had set out to organize and present a new indictment that would take into account the voluminous additional information the joint investigation had uncovered. But determining just how to phrase criminal charges in a case like this was complex and uncertain.

The state had a Constitutional obligation to charge a defendant with specific crimes. If any count in an indictment was ambiguous or referred conceivably to more than one criminal event, then the defendant could have difficulty answering the accusation, unable to know which facts to address. The state's charges had to be precise enough to allow Kelly Michaels to prepare an adequate defense, and also to prevent her from perhaps being charged at a later date with the same crime on slightly different specifics.

If Sara charged one count of anal penetration by Kelly Michaels on, say, Lewis Dixon, Lewis might ultimately testify that Kelly had inserted both a knife and a fork in him. He would thereby introduce a potential confusion by dividing the penetration count into two incidents of abuse, each of which constituted one penetration. In coming to their verdict, if half the jurors were persuaded by the evidence that the knife incident had happened, and the other half were persuaded that the fork incident had happened, then by law, they could not convict the defendant on that count of penetration, despite the fact that they agreed unanimously that some type of penetration had occurred. The law required that the state prove one underlying criminal act for every count in the indictment. The jurors would be required to agree unanimously that Kelly Michaels had penetrated Lewis either with a fork or with a knife.

The appellate section of the Prosecutor's Office instructed Sara to charge the first-degree crimes by the instrument. Instead of charging one count of vaginal penetration and one count of anal penetration for each girl, Sara was to charge up to three separate counts for vaginal penetration (fork, knife, and spoon) and up to three separate counts for anal penetration (fork, knife, and spoon). If she charged the penetrations by the orifice alone, the variety of instruments that might be mentioned in testimony could confuse the jury or cause appellate problems down the road.

The information on threats, a third-degree offense, was also confusing. One child had said that Kelly had a spider on a string that she'd used to tickle the children or to scare them with until they cried. Another had said that Kelly scared her by crossing her eyes and by making them all white by inverting her eyelids. The Child Abuse Unit had never before charged terroristic threats. Prior to this case, Sara's unit had never even inquired of victims if they had been threatened. Sara decided to charge terroristic threats specifically as threats against the child himself or herself.

∎ ∎

Joey Gardner testified before the Grand Jury in July. Sara fed him simple, straightforward questions so that he could finish quickly and be released. At first, it seemed to be going all right. Joey was, blessedly, answering her questions, even if from underneath the table in the Grand Jury room. Joey had withdrawn to the safety of that space, away from all the unfamiliar eyes.

Sara was well into her list of questions when she realized that she'd forgotten to qualify him to testify. In New Jersey, child witnesses were required to undergo a voir dire, or qualification procedure, to demonstrate their understanding of the difference between the truth and a lie, their willingness to tell the truth, and an appreciation of the punishment that could follow if they were to lie. Sara switched over and ran through the qualification, confronting Joey with a series of questions.

Finishing up, she asked, "Do you promise to tell the truth?"

Joey promised, his voice becoming shrill as it wafted up from the floor.

Then, concerned about the statements he had already made, Sara asked, "Was everything you told us before the truth?"

Joey screamed, "Lies! Lies! Lies!" suddenly wild.

"What you said before, that wasn't the truth?"

"Lies! Lies! Lies!"

Sara changed tacks. "Okay. Then what *did* Kelly do?"

Joey was quiet for a moment, and then he answered softly in an uncontorted voice, "No. It's the truth."

■
■ ■

The result of the second Grand Jury was a 174-count indictment which might well have caused a sensation if the Grand Jury had not been a closed proceeding, the facts of the indictment shielded from the press as they had been back in May. Sara didn't want the press to go crazy with the Wee Care story and possibly frighten away her witnesses. A lot of the material that had emerged in the investigation still had to be presented for indictment, so an arraignment of the defendant was postponed until all the indictments could be unsealed at the same time.

Immediately following the July Grand Jury, Sara left the United States with her boyfriend, Kevin McArdle, on a six-week leave to visit his family in England. Sara leaned on Kevin for legal consultation, talking over the evidence gathered in the Wee Care investigation and checking her proposed tactics with him. Kevin McArdle was also an assistant prosecutor in the Essex County Prosecutor's Office. Although this trip was slated as a vacation, Sara couldn't put the Wee Care case out of her mind, and they had a terrible vacation: Sara was jumpy for six weeks running.

When they returned to the United States, she and Kevin were engaged to be married the following summer, and Sara became temporarily immersed in wedding plans. But by late September, she had to resume work on Wee Care to prepare for the final Grand Jury. Through October, Sara met with each child who was scheduled to appear, each parent, therapist, and investigator, and she reviewed over and over again the interview tapes made during the joint investigation. The late-summer season was withering, but Sara hardly noticed: She lived less and less in the calendar and more in the clock.

The audiotapes contained some disturbing statements that had caused the investigators some distress. A number of children had told their parents or interviewers that someone other than Kelly Michaels had known about or been present during the abuse. Alison Steadman had told her mother that early in the school year she'd told her classroom teacher, Joan, what Kelly was doing. Another girl claimed that Diane Costa, Wee Care's administrative head teacher, had walked in on Kelly as she was penetrating the children with utensils and had taken the silverware and put it in her briefcase. One boy claimed that Diane had cleaned up blood. Freddie Mercer, in his reinterview, told Lou Fonolleras that Brenda, an aide, had actually participated in the abuse, although his answers were scattered and contradictory.

Lou had been very careful to keep his eyes and ears open when anyone other than Kelly Michaels was mentioned, but he had asked the children, "Did that really happen, or did you wish it happened?" A lot of times they would answer, "What I wished," though others would fantasize outrageously about rescuers. Several children, mostly boys, had said that they themselves became specially empowered and defeated Kelly, saving all the children. Lewis Dixon attested to the fact that he himself had beaten up Kelly and then thrown her out the window.

For Sara Sencer, the trigger point was when she learned that some children were naming their parents as having been present during the abuse: Faced with that impossibility, she then realized that she would have to rethink what it meant when a child said an adult had been there. Sara discovered that these could be rescue fantasies: A child thought back and described a traumatic event, and then added to that mental picture a safe, reassuring face. It was a coping mechanism, changing the ending of the story to one that was emotionally easier to handle. Sara noticed that the several black children who had rescue fantasies most commonly named Brenda, a black staff member, as the other adult involved, and she considered that personal identification to be consistent with fantasy. After all, the children were picking only one person out of the photographic line-up: Kelly Michaels.

Actually, the children's allegations held together, displaying a great deal of internal consistency when compared. For instance, allegations of the use of peanut butter came mostly out of Kelly's morning classroom, while allegations of naked duck, duck, goose came mostly out of Kelly's after-school supervision period. Apparently, the children remembered accurately the actual incidents of abuse because their accounts were consistent. The children, then, knew the difference between what had really happened and their rescue fantasies.

The November Grand Jury handed down an indictment charging Margaret Kelly Michaels with assorted acts of first- and second-degree sexual assault and third-degree endangerment. The unbelievable statements involving rescue fantasy had not prevented the majority of jurors from believing the children's statements and recommending that the state proceed with prosecution.

The formal unsealing of the results of this Grand Jury, along with the July results, was scheduled to take place at an arraignment sometime in early December.

. .
■ ■

From the perspective of a defense attorney, the Kelly Michaels case had more than one drawback. For starters, the grandfather of one of the victims was an area judge, and to take on the defense of his grandchild's alleged rapist wasn't quite the direct approach to currying favor. More importantly, Assistant Prosecutor Sara Sencer had amassed evidence that could crush a defendant. Twenty-two children had appeared before the Grand Jury, and nine more were included in the indictment as a result of their parents' testimony. Even with some attrition, the testimonial evidence of the state appeared mighty.

Pool attorneys weren't salaried employees of the Office of the Public Defender, so they could pick and choose among the available cases. The Michaels case was passed over by many of these lawyers for a variety of reasons, including the great amount of time such a large case would consume.

The case had been unassigned for four months when finally Jed-Mathew Philwin agreed to handle it. Jed, a transplanted Arizona cowboy, who wore a Stetson in all seasons, even inside the Newark courthouse, and occasionally a black string tie with a turquoise bolt, handled a lot of sexual abuse cases or, as he called it, "kiddie rape." He had no qualms about defending Kelly Michaels: he could use the work, and he knew he would earn favor with the PD Office for helping it unload the case. He also knew the publicity potential was tremendous. Jed Philwin knew this could be the largest child sexual abuse case ever prosecuted in the United

States against any single female defendant, but he insisted he took the case primarily because the potential legal issues would be challenging.

To join him for the defense, Jed drew in his office mate, Robert B. Clark, and an acquaintance who also took pool work, Harvey Meltzer. This case could be a year in preparation, and it was going to take three attorneys to ready it if they were to be able to sustain their private practices as well.

While Bob and Harvey went about their other business, Jed Philwin assumed himself lead attorney of the case and began to generate a game plan. If Kelly were to plead not guilty, Philwin felt that the theory of suggestibility would offer a viable defense. A suggestibility defense involved an attempt to show that the investigators had influenced the children's responses. However, Jed himself was more attracted to the alternative of pleading Kelly's diminished capacity.

Diminished capacity was similar to an insanity plea, but different in that it did not argue pathological mental disorder. The application of the statute was not clearly established in case law, but Jed believed he could maintain that for some reason this defendant lacked the ability to distinguish right from wrong in the particular area of the alleged criminal behavior. For example, if they could show that Kelly had herself been the victim of extensive sexual abuse, her attorneys could then argue that she had a diminished capacity to determine that assault was a crime that would harm the children.

Although the plea required an implicit admission, its attraction was that if Kelly Michaels were indeed found to be of diminished capacity, then, according to Jed's own reading of the statute, she might just walk out the back door and not have to do time.

The more Jed thought about it, the more optimal the strategy seemed. He felt sure he would have no trouble getting the children to testify at length to all the weirdest things in the allegations. After they were finished describing how Kelly had said she'd turn them into mice, had worn a choir robe, thought she could float through walls, had made them drink urine and suck peanut butter off her naked flesh, Jed imagined the jury would be ready to find her mentally incompetent to distinguish right from wrong. Then they could go home happy. For all its murkiness, mental disorder was easier to understand than suggestibility because it didn't require an intimacy with ghastly specifics. However, Jed still kept open the idea of a straight suggestibility defense to discredit the testimony of the children and the investigators.

Jed Philwin had not, though, taken into account the fact that Harvey Meltzer and Bob Clark did not concur with his assessment of the case.

As far as Bob was concerned, "She says she's innocent. Diminished capacity is inconsistent." And Kelly herself had no intention of authorizing such a plea. At the outset, a schism opened among the members of the defense team.

▪
▪ ▪

Ellen bathed Joey in the evenings. Tonight, he was playing with a turkey baster, filling it with water and then squirting it around.

Joey looked at his mother and said, "Do you want me to put this in your tushy so you can be healthy?"

Without missing a beat, she asked, "Is that what she told you?"

"Well, yeah."

He splashed around some more, then popped the bulb off the baster and stuffed it over his penis.

Ellen had begun to keep a diary of the things Joey told her. Some things she knew she would never forget, like bouncing in the blood. This was an incident she didn't think she would forget either, but after putting Joey to bed, Ellen noted, "bathtub enema," as a reminder of this encounter.

Six months after his disclosure, her son was still terrified of being hauled away to jail. Joey was convinced that he was going to share Kelly's fate, and deserve it.

Every time these feelings of culpability would arise, Ellen would try to clarify for her son the issues of blame and explain to him why he had nothing to fear. Finally, she determined to set him straight once and for all. She said, slowly, thoughtfully, "You were only four. Kelly was an adult. She knew you don't do that with children!"

But Joey looked at her and said, "Mommy, I *knew* what we were doing was wrong."

His eyes seemed older than her own, and more frightening.

▪
▪ ▪

The December arraignment was to present to the defendant the compilation of all the indictments, a stupefying total of 235 counts naming thirty-one children, ages three to six. The total indictment measured two inches thick when squeezed shut. A local television station had received a copy in advance so the reporters could familiarize themselves with the pending story. Even callous journalists were stunned, scandalized by the nature of the counts, the grotesqueness of the allegations. And yet, there was not one of them who exclaimed that the charges were ludicrous.

Kelly Michaels returned to Newark from Pittsburgh to make the appearance, and the night before her arraignment, Jed Philwin met his client for the first time. He was taken aback by Kelly's looks. She was the last type of person he would expect to have been accused of such a massive crime, and Jed immediately felt sympathy: He knew that even if the allegations proved to be ungrounded, the mere fact that they had been leveled against her could destroy her life.

In the courthouse the following morning, while waiting for the arraignment, Bob Clark had his own first face-to-face with his client. Bob was a spiritual, churchgoing man who believed that he possessed "gifts of the spirit," and when he set out to meet Kelly Michaels, he felt confident that if she was indeed guilty of what she was charged with, he would know that he was in the presence of evil.

What Bob found when he met Kelly was a very strong, spiritual person with a deep and abiding faith in God. The two of them passed the time talking of their faith and praying together. Bob felt that Kelly had a deep inner calm. From this moment on, Bob was unshakable in his belief in her innocence, and he commented to Jed, "This is an innocent girl. God has sent her to us for a reason."

The arraignment had been scheduled for two o'clock the afternoon of December 6, 1985. The members of the press were there en masse hours early, and dozens of Wee Care parents were in attendance. Although the press was going to be allowed to cover the story, they were restricted by the judge's order that the identities of the children and their parents be concealed (as he put it, "Because you can't unbreak an egg"). The viewing gallery was composed of four rows of wooden benches divided up the middle by a central aisle. This gallery was separated from open court by the bar, a waist-high wall with swinging doors at the end of the aisle. The gallery was crammed with viewers who mashed toward that middle aisle, eager to lay eyes on the defendant. Reporters filled not only the best rows of the gallery but even the unused jury box stretching along the left wall.

After repeated delays, two guards finally escorted Kelly Michaels from chambers, spiraling through the corridors to the back door of the courtroom. The four attorneys (Sara Sencer and the three-man defense team) entered the courtroom, followed by the defendant.

Kelly's face was extremely pale, more than white. She appeared petite, though she was still well overweight, wearing a flowered cotton blouse, white at the collar and cuffs, and a navy skirt. Here was none of the masculine flair she had shown when she was working at Wee Care. She appeared to be sliding across the continuum of style into the feminine range.

Kelly scanned the courtroom as she proceeded, seeming completely composed. She carried a Bible and white plastic rosary beads, the crucifix dangling over her clasped hands in which she held an illuminated picture of Christ. She smiled passing her parents on her way to counsel table. Kelly sat down.

As everyone waited for the judge to appear, Jed Philwin watched Sara Sencer's interaction with the parents in the gallery: her eye contact, her mannerisms, her vocal intonations. Sara seemed to have them reined in. Then he narrowed his attention to the parents, assessing. If the defense used a mass hysteria strategy to explain away the allegations, they would have to elicit hysterical behavior from the parents on cross-examination. But these men and women appeared capable of control. Besides, in his opinion, they were from such diverse ethnic, social, religious, and occupational backgrounds that it would be difficult to demonstrate a group psychological phenomenon like mass hysteria.

When Judge Harth took the bench, Kelly didn't move, didn't flinch. Before allowing the defense to enter a plea, the judge recommended that the defendant be removed to the empty jury room to go over the indictment, and Jed and Bob escorted her there. Bob sat across from Kelly at the jury table and slowly read aloud every one of the charges. He and Jed had met with Sara Sencer several days earlier to be apprised of their nature, but Kelly was hearing them for the first time as Bob now read: knives, forks, spoons, urine, feces.

He observed her reactions closely, saw the shock, as she exclaimed, "Where would they get this from? Why would they say that?" For an hour and a half Bob and Jed discussed the indictment with their client. Kelly indicated that she understood everything.

Meanwhile, out in the courtroom, the Wee Care parents watched Harvey Meltzer closely. Well-dressed and evenly tanned, Meltzer was a svelte man in his early forties wearing large glasses resting on a narrow, hooked nose. He wore a lot of gold and carried himself with assurance, even swagger. Several parents whispered concern to one another, intimidated by his high-powered look.

When Kelly and her attorneys had returned to the courtroom, the defense waived the reading of the indictment. Kelly did not react; it was as though everybody were talking about someone else. Meltzer rose and entered an encompassing plea of not guilty to all 235 counts.

In consideration of the new indictment and the increased number of counts, Judge Harth ordered a new bail hearing to be scheduled, and Kelly Michaels was once again remanded into custody. She stood and turned toward the officers who were coming for her. As she was being led away with a dull look on her face, consciousness suddenly gripped her features, and glancing over to her father, she mouthed, "I love you."

■
■ ■

Kelly was confined in protective custody as she had been back in June. A mesh of bars surrounded and protected her, a gentle, unassuming young woman captured in a steel net. Once a day, she had a shower. Other than that, there were occasional visits from her attorneys and frequent ones by her family who were not deterred by the eight-hour drive from Pittsburgh. They demonstrated their loyalty and strength as a unit, and they faced outsiders with solidarity.

Kelly Michaels was charming to those inmates of C-tier who regularly passed by her cell, conversing with them easily and colloquially. One of them soon became convinced of Kelly's innocence and vouched for her among C-tier's other inmates. The inmates on her own tier played cards with Kelly through the bars of her cell or gathered to question her about Wee Care. Yet, Kelly's popularity was not universal: An inmate in the cell one floor below had stood on another prisoner's shoulders to bellow threats up at her through the grating.

After a couple of weeks of incarceration, Kelly petitioned for permission to get out a few hours a day to stretch her legs, but the prison staff didn't feel they would be able to protect her, and her request was denied.

When Kelly was not otherwise occupied, she sat by the bars of her cell reading Harlequin romances donated to the prison by women whom the inmates called the "Friendly People." Once, as she sat there, a fight broke out in the aisle along her cell. Kelly glanced up, smiled, then returned to her book. For a young lady in protective custody, her attitude toward proximate violence was eerily untuned. Survival in jail dictated moving away from the bars, through which a hostile inmate could reach and take hold of the throat. Necks could be broken against steel. But Kelly seemed to blank out what was happening in front of her cell.

■
■ ■

The December night had texture. It had just rained, and the black trees were in high definition against the low, black-blue sky. The Gardners were driving home from Boston, and it was too early for Joey to be sleepy, but just late enough for him to be getting punchy. He was talking to himself and giggling.

"I love you, Mommy. I love you," he said to Ellen, over and over again, laughing, fraying.

Then he wanted to tell a joke. "Why did the chicken cross the road?"

he asked his parents, already shrieking with laughter. He screamed, "To go to a dirty kind of penis party!" And he screamed hysterically, "I wish I were a penis picker!"

"What is that?" Ellen asked.

"Pick a penis, and a person pees in your mouth!"

Her husband veered off the road and jerked the gearshift. He lurched out of the car into the Connecticut night to vomit.

"How'd she get you to do that?" asked Ellen, to distract Joey.

"She threatened to whack us in the face with a wooden spoon."

There was nothing she could say. Her world was now so indelibly specific: no longer a blank canvas, no longer the three of them together going somewhere in a car. Ellen was in a private place, with these men and their feelings and their minds. She couldn't clean this out of their lives.

They drove on home, Joey sleeping, Ellen and her husband silent, listening to the sizzling sound the tires made on the wet pavement.

▪
▪ ▪

At St. George's Episcopal Church, the minister conducted a hand-holding ceremony. The minister and other staff members proceeded through each room of the church, including those formerly used by Wee Care, to say prayers and offer blessings. It was a unique occurrence in the history of the church.

▪
▪ ▪

On December 29, 1985, Kelly Michaels celebrated her twenty-fourth birthday in jail, and a month later, on January 27, 1986, Kelly, looking heavy and dumpy, dressed in a bulky winter coat, was led to the court-house building in a chain gang of prisoners. She fiddled nervously with her manacled hands. A folded piece of paper seemed to distract her as she flipped it around in her fingers. Kelly looked ill at ease, self-conscious.

Again, Judge Harth's courtroom was thick with media. The defense had filed a motion to order the sheriff's officers to remove Kelly's shackles and restraints prior to any court appearance. Judge Harth had acceded, so that Kelly was now led into the courtroom, proud, no longer chained.

In open court, Sara Sencer argued that in light of the much greater number of charges against the defendant, her incentive to flee had greatly increased, and likewise the bail bond should now be increased to the five hundred thousand dollars (fifty-thousand-dollar cash alternative) that the state had originally requested.

Harvey Meltzer countered that because Kelly's family was out of financial resources, such a bail provision would be equivalent to denying bail, which would be improper in this case as a capital offense was not involved. He reminded the judge that the defendant was "innocent until she is proven by the state to be guilty." Then he added, "This is true even in Essex County." Meltzer pointed out that prior to the December arraignment, the attorneys had all known that at least one hundred more counts were coming in later indictments, and yet, knowing that, still Miss Michaels had returned from Pittsburgh to be arraigned.

Judge Harth ruled in favor of the defense's position and continued the twenty-five-thousand-dollar cash alternative despite the increase in charges. He noted, "Bail is not preventive detention." This time the terms of her bail included that Kelly had to work full-time so that the court would always know her whereabouts. Kelly would therefore take a job doing secretarial work at her father's office. The defense team had fully expected their client's bail to be raised, so the judge's ruling was a decided defense victory.

Leaving victorious, the Michaels party descended the courthouse steps in a cancan line, Kelly, her parents, one of her sisters, and her monied girlfriend, arms linked at the elbows, fists raised in defiance to the television cameras. As they neared their cars, Kelly and her friend embraced in the street and kissed each other good-bye. The friend held Kelly's hand as she stepped into her car, and the two stretched to hold contact as Kelly pulled away. The local TV camera crew filmed the entire defiant exchange.

．
． ．

Sara couldn't help but think that if thirty-one women had said they'd been raped by the same man, they wouldn't be going to trial: The defendant would have pleaded guilty. However, as these victims were children, denial was conceivable because, in the eyes of the public, the words of children still meant little. The specter of the child's hazy mind (hazy because adults were judging it from their own fuzzy recollections of childhood) haunted many adults.

Peg Foster held that the experience of a child today in the criminal justice system paralleled that of an adult female rape victim fighting for the right to be believed and to be treated with dignity by law enforcement. Since the mid-seventies, the situation for women had infinitely improved. For children, whose suffering in sexual ways was still just beginning to come to widespread public attention, things had begun to change and crimes against children were getting recognition.

And yet, among the plenitude of reasons to grieve over child sexual abuse, the false reasons served only to trivialize the real. The fact that the child loses the status of virgin is not one of the reasons sexual assault is a tragedy.

Children and sexuality are often seen as antithetical: While few dispute that little children are very sensual (in the limited context of what feels good), adult men and women still don't always know that children masturbate and that infants have erections. Children are not supposed to feel the contractions of sexual pain or of sexual identity confusion, each of which contradicts the mirage of a child's pristine, untouched beauty.

Just because a child has been poisoned does not mean the child is poison. Cleanliness is not at all defined by purity, emptiness, nothingness. The virgin ideal exploits erotic images of something to be corrupted, waiting to be smirched, a fantasy of something ripe.

Each disappointment that life delivers to the child is doubly bitter to the parents, as it taints not only their child's childhood, but also their own symbolic one. Nothing can be lost so easily as the status of child, and nothing can corrupt a childhood so readily as a hardship or a realistic concern. The image of a child too repellent to consider is that of a child struggling with crime and pain and the paradoxes of identity—the image of a child too repellent to consider is the image of child as adult.

Female victims of sexual crimes are often considered to be more radically impaired than male victims, as if a daughter is still a commodity to be auctioned off, with the hymen a value-enhancing seal of freshness. All this emphasis on virginity does a disservice to the little boy victim, too, by imagining him so much more intact than the girl. The glorification of the girl victim's loss at the expense of the boy's robs him of the right to suffer and, more to the point, robs him of full claim to his parents' sympathy and sorrow.

Children are light, bright, beautiful things, but not in an iconic way, and any harm they might come to is tragic because it damages the child, and not because it damages the ideal. All the things that are beautiful in children—openness, growing, inexperience—are exactly the things that make them vulnerable to crime. Criminals pick on children precisely because they can, and exploit them because they are so able.

Today, even with thirty-one accusers all standing in agreement against her, the assessment of the odds was that Margaret Kelly Michaels had an excellent chance of discrediting the children and being acquitted.

7

∴

In the new year, the defense attorneys turned to developing their case. They had cartons crammed with discovery materials, including copies of the state's audiotapes, sworn statements, Grand Jury transcripts, and documents confiscated from the school, as well as papers of Kelly's that she had turned over to her lawyer.

Technically, the defense had thirty days from the date of the arraignment to file a diminished capacity plea or to inform the court that they did not intend to file, but when February 1986 rolled around, the state had yet to receive any such notification. Sara Sencer still needed to know how the defense planned to proceed so that she could design her own case.

To be successful with diminished capacity, the defense team would have to prove not simply that Kelly had experienced abuse, but that she had sustained such a prolonged pattern of abuse that it had mangled her ability to discern the wrongfulness of her acts. If the defense did use diminished capacity, then the prosecution was going to have to focus on proving the knowingness of Kelly's acts. For that, Sara would emphasize the secrecy: threats, tiptoeing, cleaning up with paper towels and mops.

In court appearances, the defense lawyers claimed to be having difficulty obtaining the psychiatric evaluations of the defendant necessary to determine whether or not they would use the diminished capacity plea. They wanted a Maryland forensic psychiatrist, Dr. Jonas Rappeport, to conduct the evaluation, but they were having trouble getting the PD Office to agree to pay for the nationally known psychiatrist. The PD Office wanted a local opinion, and while the defense struggled to make arrangements, Judge Harth continued to grant extensions.

▪
▪ ▪

When Sara leafed through Kelly Michaels's roll book, passing the purple crayon squiggles all over one notebook page (she must have let a child do that), she came upon a poem written by hand on one of the last, unused pages of the book:

truth indescriminate [sic]

Are you
going about this
the wrong way?

He says what do you want?
I say Hey, what did you say?

But I know
with the smell of your flesh, (I know)
in a flash as you dress
your body will leave me.

What was this doing in Kelly's roll book?

Sara was intrigued to know whether this poem was copied from something other than the walls of Kelly's own mind, whether this was an original poem or something favored and transcribed. The lyrics to "Both Sides Now" were also etched onto the roll book: not original. But Lewis had said, "She didn't want the other teachers to know," so obviously then they had dressed in a flash. Was Kelly transmitting signals? Jumbled, confused, did she hope to be caught?

Truth indiscriminate?

▪
▪ ▪

Joey's self-image was terrible. He constantly cut himself off in the middle of a sentence to announce that he was stupid or ugly, and if he thought he had made a mistake about something or a slip of the tongue, he'd bash himself in the head. And Joey had headaches. Sometimes he told his mother: "I don't think of the bad things that happen. I get a picture of her in my head." Ellen would hear her son whine: "I can't think!"

Ellen's imaginings of the inside of her son's mind terrified her. What was he going to see years from now when he bumped into one of the Wee Care children in a restaurant somewhere? Would his peers help Joey to feel understood, help him to know that this wasn't something that had happened only to him because he was somehow bad? Or would their existence reintroduce the humiliation? The children had suffered shared ownership of their bodies: How were they going to remember one another?

Everything in Joey's life had been touched, and there was no precise way of knowing just how warped he felt, how embarrassed, how transparent. Ellen wished she could know where her son stopped hurting, but for answers to some of her questions about the extent of the damage, she would really have to dissect Joey's brain.

He was acutely self-conscious. Walking down the street with his mother, Joey insisted that strangers could look right through him, and he cringed into himself. He was terrified that no one would like him because of the terrible things he'd done, the things that everybody knew about. When people laughed, Joey Gardner heard them laughing at him, ridiculing him, hating him. He didn't believe that people laughed just because they were happy: His mind transformed a room full of lighthearted people into a personal disaster of condemnation.

Something other than hatred tormented her son. Ellen thought back to the time when Joey had told her that Kelly had said, "Take off your clothes and I'll be your best friend."

He loved her too. Their relationship was deep, fingered, felt. Slowly, sickeningly, Ellen began to see the full, coherent picture, as when Joey later explained, "Tears still come out of my eyes sometimes because I feel so bad because Kelly was my best friend."

Kelly Michaels had touched her baby—touched him.

．
． ．

The Wee Care families tried to cope with a never-anticipated intimacy with post-trauma existence. They had never been without problems, but most had assumed they were protected from this more personal, invasive type of crime. Psychological trauma was physical, ugly. Elizabeth demanded to see her mother and her boyfriend have intercourse, saying specifically she wanted to see him put his penis in her mother's vagina.

Meg inserted a toothbrush into her little sister's vagina. Alison wanted to urinate outside.

Following denial, an overwhelming anger was the parents' most common reaction, a formless emotion that could take them in so many negative directions: toward bitterness, withdrawal, blaming their spouses, hating themselves. Some channeled their restlessness by becoming involved in child abuse organizations, trying to address in the context of an organized effort what they found so difficult to address in the context of their own lives.

A number of the fathers felt colossal guilt, particularly those who were police officers or in the protective services. These men protected all kinds of anonymous people, and yet they hadn't been able to protect their own children, and they now suffered with the sense of male responsibility that demanded of them omniscience. Then many of the fathers shut themselves in with their feelings and refused to talk about them, even with their wives.

As Sara Sencer continued to hold meetings with the families about the legal process, and as Dr. Susan Esquilin addressed groups on behavioral problems, many of the fathers dropped out of the process: They scheduled business meetings or business trips to overlap with Wee Care meetings. A woman complained that her husband had sand coming out of his ears, he was so desperate to ignore the abuse. While a number of the husbands *were* as involved in dealing with this crisis as were their wives, most of the coping was left to the women. Wives resented their husbands' inability or unwillingness to offer emotional support, and marriages suffered. For a handful of the mothers, their informal support group provided a crucial release. It was empowering for these mothers to know that women they admired could burn with the same feelings of inadequacy, resentment, and self-condemnation.

Since the time the investigation began, many of the parents had placed themselves in therapy, not only to treat problems they were having with their child, but also to treat the strains and estrangements in their marriages. The sexual problems caused by new mental associations and disabling inhibitions only exacerbated any existing estrangement, and for those parents whose child was now sleeping in their bed, sex was suspended for the time being.

Several marriages began to break apart in disputes over the child's victimization. A few of the fathers initially denied their child's involvement in the abuse, and as their wives became engrossed in assisting the child's recovery, the spouses were driven apart by the divergent vehemence of their feelings. Tragedy didn't always bring families together, but rather, like any test, raised to the surface what was already within.

.
. .

Sara Sencer's irritation mounted. When Judge Harth began to pressure her for lists and schedules of her trial witnesses, she countered by refusing to do any work on the case until she was apprised as to whether or not the defense was going to argue diminished capacity. It seemed clear to the prosecutor that the defense strategy was to stall in hopes of delaying the trial until the children had forgotten a lot of what had happened.

She wanted to get this case to trial so that the children and their parents could put it all behind them, but she wasn't concerned that a delay might hurt the case. Certainly, the children might forget certain details or even entire events, but she suspected that the increase in their vocabularies and their verbal skills as time went by would counteract that loss. Furthermore, she felt that the longer they waited, the less intimidated by Kelly the children would feel. Postponing the trial would only increase the chances for a conviction.

Meanwhile, Jed Philwin still believed his team was seriously pursuing the diminished capacity idea, but evidently he was the only one.

.
. .

The Prosecutor's Office assigned as co-counsel on the Michaels case a trial lawyer from the Special Prosecutions unit, a unit made up of excellent attorneys used on cases requiring special handling or trial expertise. Assistant Prosecutor Glenn D. Goldberg was considered by many to be the best trial lawyer in the office, a cross-examination assassin. He was the strong silent type, although when Glenn finally did come out with a comment, it was invariably a tin pun.

He shared with Sara Sencer a genuine love for children and, not so deep down, a childlike affinity with them. Glenn was a forty-four-year-old man who looked twenty-four, read science fiction books, and hung a solar-system mobile over his desk. A master of gadgets, he carried a computerized pocket phone book in his jacket and had a car steering wheel outfitted to do nearly aeronautical functions. If ever a Wee Care child happened to be in the office, Glenn entertained the child with magic tricks. His magic coloring book was a clear favorite: The illustrations disappeared at Glenn's command.

While waiting for pretrial hearings to begin, the newly assigned prosecutor began to study the statements of the teachers and aides. A teacher had alleged that Kelly had sauntered across the playground toward her and another teacher one afternoon and had asked if her zipper was undone. They'd glanced and told her no. "Good," she'd said, "'cause it'd be pretty embarrassing if it was, 'cause I don't wear underwear!" Then she had walked off, laughing.

Glenn thought about the meaning of her flip remark. In describing how Kelly took off her clothes, one child had said that Kelly started her undressing with her socks, then her pants, then her shirt, then her bra. The child had left out underpants. Maybe that omission was meaningful. Then again, maybe Kelly had been lying to her co-workers about not wearing any underwear. Glenn set that statement aside.

He saw that several teachers had commented that Kelly had played "Jingle Bells" on the piano constantly, even many months past Christmas. Glenn wondered if by playing the song in the gym with other teachers around, Kelly had communicated to the children in her own language, perhaps reminded the children with music that she could touch them sexually even out in the open. Perhaps she was flaunting her sexuality to the children in front of the other teachers. When the children heard "Jingle Bells," they heard sexual abuse, never imagining that the other adults present heard nothing.

The kindergarten teacher stated that she had frequently heard piano playing coming faintly from the choir room next door. It had never occurred to her to check the room because the school had nothing to do with the church rooms, no responsibility for them. The kindergarten teacher had assumed that someone affiliated with the church, perhaps the choirmaster, was in the choir room using the piano.

These recollections about Kelly were consistent in that they depicted her as daring, taunting, and Glenn wondered if Kelly had been saying to the other staff members, "I can do things and you're not even going to know about them." Were these power plays, a celebration of her absolute freedom to take and touch whatever she pleased? Or was she trying to get caught? Did she want people to know what was going on? Did it add an element of excitement or danger? Possible. It was clear to Glenn that Kelly harbored deep, even resentful contempt for those who were in charge of the school and whose ineffectiveness permitted her to get away with these crimes.

Glenn Goldberg couldn't wait to get Miss Michaels on the stand.

．．

Alison Steadman entered her first grade classroom sobbing, holding out a sandwich she'd removed from her lunch bag. She scrunched it, crying, "I don't wanna eat it! I don't wanna eat it!"

Karen hurried in behind her, and the teacher intercepted. Alison had started eating peanut butter again months ago and was fine with it, but something had set her off this morning. Karen explained to the teacher, "She's been hysterical all morning about Kelly. I'll be back with a new lunch," and ran out.

Alison's teacher went over to her student and said, "You don't have to eat the sandwich." Then she lifted the peanut butter and jelly sandwich out of the little girl's tensed hand and threw it into the garbage.

By the time Karen returned with a bread and butter lunch, Alison was fine.

Later that morning, her teacher approached her. "Allie, that sandwich wasn't any good, huh?"

Alison said, "No. That was Kelly. All bad Kelly."

•
•   •

Robert, who had been one of Kelly's "special helpers," told his therapist that there were two Roberts, and it was the other one who had cleaned up the pee and chased the children for Kelly. This other Robert had red hair, not brown, and when the teacher wasn't looking, he did these things to the children. Then, using a boy and a girl doll, the little boy simulated intercourse.

He drew a picture of the other Robert running after Joey Gardner yelling, "Come back here! Come back here!" Then he depicted himself (not the special helper), and this time he had tears on his face and a penis that he'd crossed out after drawing it. When he drew a portrait of Kelly, Robert described what he'd drawn: "She's happy. She's hurting the children, but I don't like it."

Through private sessions, Robert was gradually learning to accept himself as being the one and only Robert who had been Kelly Michaels's special helper.

•
•   •

Negligence suits had been filed by a number of the Wee Care families against Wee Care, Arlene Spector, and Margaret Kelly Michaels, and Harvey Meltzer was hired by Kelly's parents to represent her interests. But Meltzer's co-counsel Jed Philwin was distressed because if they went diminished capacity, they might have to attempt to establish that Kelly had been abused as a child. The parents could be the key to that argument. And Jed confronted Meltzer: "How can we attack the parents if one of us is on their payroll?"

Of course, the defense had not yet filed a diminished capacity trial plan, and it finally dawned on Jed that Harvey and Bob had no intention of pursuing that strategy, that he and the others had really been at cross-purposes ever since the defense investigation had begun.

In early June 1986, Jed Philwin entered a motion to withdraw from the case. His co-counsel suspected that Jed felt undercut by Meltzer because he himself hadn't won the position on the civil case, but as his reason for withdrawal Jed stated a potential conflict of interest created by Harvey Meltzer's civil assignment.

Saying that he could find no evidence of wrongdoing on the part of Harvey Meltzer, Judge Harth nevertheless officially released Jed Philwin from the obligation to defend Kelly Michaels, and Harvey Meltzer assumed the position of lead attorney for the defense. Bob Clark took up his position at Meltzer's side, but left most of the legal argument to the team's new leader. Civil proceedings were soon frozen by Harth pending the outcome of the criminal action.

. .

Sara Sencer became Sara Sencer McArdle in July 1986. At the end of August, the defense attorneys finally notified the court and the state that they would not, in fact, be employing a diminished capacity defense. The defense team now had reports from a local psychiatrist and from Dr. Jonas Rappeport, and the two doctors had ruled out that possibility by determining that, in their judgment, Kelly knew the difference between right and wrong.

Rappeport stated, "I did not find any serious mental illness in Kelly Michaels." In his seven hours of interviews, he detected no deception in her manner of answering questions, and he noted, "This was one of the outstanding things about Miss Michaels, is that she did not do the usual thing that I might expect from my many years of experience in examining defendants, that she did not play some of the games that they usually play, the deceptions, forgetting, leaving out material, leaving out something that might be embarrassing, etcetera." In addition, Rappeport maintained that he didn't believe this defendant possessed the psychological characteristics consistent with the profile of a sexual abuser. Meltzer and Clark stored away this last observation for use at pretrial.

When he was asked what the defense had achieved by going through all those preliminary motions for diminished capacity, Bob Clark acknowledged: "About six months."

■
■ ■

The trial date for the Michaels case was postponed to early 1987, because nobody was ready. In the delay, Sara turned her attention to the prosecution's need for an expert witness to assess all the evidence and to testify on the principles of child development: physical, cognitive, sexual. From talks with other attorneys, she came up with the name of Eileen Treacy, a New York psychologist who had done extensive work evaluating allegations of child sexual abuse.

When Treacy agreed to take on the Wee Care case, the first thing she did was give Sara the titles of books and articles to read on child psychology, child development, and child sexual abuse. And as she read, Sara started to become an expert on the nature of children and sexual abuse, on theories of suggestibility, and on the finesse involved in preparing a seamless prosecution.

In late October 1986, Sara set out to visit the children in their homes in order to see which ones were going to be able to testify. What she had to work with were several dozen children, now four to six years of age. In making her rounds, Sara discovered that the children desperately did not want to talk about the abuse over a year after the fact, some remaining entirely mute. Shortly after she'd begun, Sara suspended her visits and asked Eileen Treacy to see the children herself and determine which were capable of testifying.

A few parents refused to have their children seen by Treacy—they'd had enough. However, Sara arranged for eighteen parents to take their children to Treacy's New York office, and throughout the winter, these children and their parents traveled to the Bronx to be evaluated. While Eileen interviewed a child, the mother would fill out a checklist on behavior changes she had noticed during and after the Wee Care school year.

The consensus among most of the investigators and even most of the parents was that one of the most common things the Wee Care parents had not understood about their children was regressive behavior. Regressive behaviors (baby talk, or bed-wetting or soiling after having been toilet trained, or sleep disturbances) were not acceptable over an extended period of time or when manifested with intensity. Of course, concern was not warranted if a child came home talking baby talk after playing with his baby cousin, or if a child wet his bed once or had a not-too-demonic nightmare. But if a four-year-old who had been toilet trained for two years started soiling his pants, the parents should have questioned his behavior and not simply taken it in stride for fear of embarrassing the child.

The other most common thing the parents had lacked was an understanding of the principles of normal sexual development. Sexual acting out was a particularly strong behavioral indication because most young children had few sources of sexual knowledge, and so the possibility of abuse as the source became plausible. A child wanting to be a dog and licking his parents between the legs was not normal. A child sticking a pierced earring in the crotch of a Barbie doll was not normal. A child begging to see her parents having intercourse was not normal. When Peg Foster or another investigator explained these principles to parents, they acknowledged that they had been afraid to cut down their children with criticism.

When the Wee Care parents had erred, they had erred on the side of freedom, accepting all sorts of outrageous behavior from their children because they did not want to infringe on individuality or experimentation. The parents allowed themselves too broad an acceptance of behavioral aberration, a free rein which perhaps would have been more appropriate during adolescence, when their children would be capable of much more personal responsibility.

The mothers catalogued for Eileen Treacy the behavioral changes that had symbolized their children's trauma. When Ellen Gardner filled out Treacy's behavior questionnaire, fury unexpectedly seized her, and she surprised herself by penning a tirade on how Kelly Michaels had wrecked her son's self-image. She described how Joey used to think his body was great: He had moved well in it. When he was two or three, Ellen would be reading him a bedtime story and Joey would touch his penis. She would ask him offhandedly, "Does that feel good?" and it was no big deal.

Now Joey didn't masturbate at all. Unlike many of these children who had begun to masturbate excessively following the abuse, Joey had rejected his body. Over the course of the Wee Care school year, his drawings had changed entirely, until finally he had stopped drawing arms and legs altogether. Now he'd say, "I don't wanna draw bodies! I hate my body!"

Karen Steadman made the trip to the Bronx several times because Alison kept asking to see Eileen. When Allie met Treacy, she immediately fell in love with her, and despite all Allie's fears, somehow Eileen had reached in and soothed her. Being a therapist required clinical training, but it wasn't a clinical relationship.

Karen shared with Eileen her concerns about a mental turning off and tuning out that Allie had been using to block out her trauma. Eileen told Karen that dissociation was a particularly troublesome defense mechanism—at its extreme close to psychosis—by which someone spaced out, leaving his or her own awareness. If it wasn't treated and stopped, the lapses could become involuntary over time, and as an adult, Alison could have memory blanks. Eileen suggested to Karen an exercise to handle Alison's panic attacks when "Kelly was in her head."

So, when Allie would blank out and say, "Kelly's in my head!" Karen would tell her to close her eyes, then she'd begin to narrate: "Now we're on the beach. The sky's blue and there are flowers everywhere. Can you smell the water? The birds are flying up near the sun. See them . . . ?"

Slowly, Alison would grow calm, and the panic would release her.

. .
. .

Eileen Treacy settled on fifteen children who she believed could withstand the renewed stress of appearing in court, and Sara resumed making the rounds. Imagining that the children would be more at ease within familiar surroundings, she went to the children's houses whenever possible or had the child over to her own house. Sara traveled the area at night and on weekends when the children weren't in school.

Sara met with Nina Anderson and tried to fortify Nina for the coming confrontation. She asked, "Did you feel weak with Kelly or strong?"

"Weak."

"In court you can be strong. Can *I* go to court for you?"

"Yes," said Nina, hopeful.

"Nooooo." Sara shook her head extravagantly. "Only people who saw with their own eyes and heard with their own ears can go to court. Who saw and heard what happened?"

The girl was clever. "Kelly."

But Sara was ready for this. "Do you know what *Kelly* says?" Sara's eyes were wide, curious. "She says nothing ever happened. Is that true?"

"No."

Sara nodded. "Well, who else saw with their own eyes?"

Nina looked blank.

"Can I go to court for you?"

"Yes."

"Was I at Wee Care? Did I see with my own eyes?"

"No."

"Who did?"

"The kids."

"So who has to go to court?" Sara gave Nina a long opportunity to answer.

Nina finally said, "I do."

Sara explained the roles: "My job is to make the jury believe you. Your job is just to tell the truth." Then Sara told her that there were fifteen counts in the indictment just for her, but the little girl was disappointed. Nina retorted, "Fifteen? It shoulda been a thousand."

Sara was confident that Nina would be capable of taking the stand, but she couldn't be sure that, in the clutch, this child would come forth with what she knew about the abuse. Nor could Sara be certain what any of the other children would actually say on the stand. As a result, the prosecutor intended to use at trial all the children who could testify.

Given the lack of an adult witness to the abuse, and given the unevenness of the physical findings for lack of proper examination, the children *were* the case. And two schools of thought were popular regarding child witnesses: One held that children never lie about sexual abuse and should automatically be believed; the other school held that preschool children don't know the difference between fact and fantasy and should never be believed. Sara wanted the jury to weigh the children's credibility the same as they would any other witness's: based on how their statements fit with the rest of the evidence in light of the facts, and not in the smear of some spray-paint slogan.

8

∴

Justice rolled up its sleeves for a rapid succession of preparatory maneuvers commencing March 4, 1987, the first day of full-week pretrial
hearings. Harvey Meltzer requested a three-month continuance, claiming
that the defense hadn't had sufficient time to prepare, but Judge Harth
denied the motion. In the ensuing twelve weeks of hearings, the prosecution and the defense teams jockeyed for rulings on various evidential
and procedural issues. Kelly Michaels had the right to be present, but
after attending for several days, she waived her appearance and returned
to Pittsburgh.

Sara had George McGrath check up on Kelly's bail status and learned
that Kelly was in fact working only two days a week, as opposed to the
full-time requirement. In addition, George was unable to locate Kelly at
her parents' house, leading Sara to wonder whether Kelly was really
living there at all. The state entered a motion to revoke bail. In response,
the defense argued that the state had no right to force the defendant to
work and insisted that whenever Kelly was not working she could be

found at home. Judge Harth denied the state's motion, and Kelly remained free.

While the attorneys from each side gave the appearance of trying to be both professional and friendly, the wrangling over pretrial issues rubbed their politesse raw. As they argued motions in the informal atmosphere of juryless proceedings, the four attorneys frequently unfastened the girdle of decorum.

Judge Harth heard extensive preliminary argument pertaining to expert testimony, and he previewed several of the incoming professionals so that he could give rulings as to which subjects they would each be allowed to address. The defense attorneys planned to call numerous experts to testify on a variety of subjects, including child development, suggestibility, interviewer bias, and mass ("contagion and contamination") hysteria. An expert witness could not profess superior knowledge of anything he felt like talking about, but rather the trial judge had to approve in advance all his areas of testimony. And the witness's specialty had to involve more than common knowledge and common sense: An attorney would not be allowed to call an expert to testify as to why a gagged victim wouldn't be able to scream for help.

The pretrial hearings also addressed the procedural question of how the children were going to testify. An adult witness had to appear in the open courtroom, but a New Jersey statute provided for testimony via closed-circuit TV if a child witness (sixteen or under) could be traumatized by the open court experience.

This statute raised the issue of the defendant's Constitutional right to confront her accuser, and legal opinions varied. Some interpreted the right of confrontation to mean the right to cross-examine. By this thinking, the use of closed-circuit testimony did not deprive the defendant of confrontation because her attorney was indeed allowed to examine the witness. Others interpreted the right of confrontation to mean the right to eyeball the accuser. By this thinking, the use of closed-circuit testimony would deprive the defendant of her right by excluding her from the room. The highest state courts had yet to rule on the legal interpretation of this statute.

While Sara and Glenn had considered not even motioning for video testimony on the assumption that a live witness might be more persuasive to a jury, ultimately they had no choice but to invoke the statute because several of the children's parents threatened to withdraw their children from the trial if the prosecutors could not protect them in this manner. Therefore, Sara McArdle went forward with the argument that each child would suffer additional psychological damage if forced to testify in front of the defendant. The New Jersey statute required particularized findings regarding each child, so Sara made a separate case for each child witness and presented a therapist and/or a parent to testify on behalf of each one.

The defense countered that the closed-circuit procedure would not only conflict with the right of confrontation, but would also send an implicit message to the jury that Kelly was guilty, as demonstrated by the fact that the children needed to be shielded from her. Meltzer stated, "Using closed-circuit TV would be tantamount to having my client come in in shackles." The defense team also argued an issue of fundamental fairness, claiming that they were at a disadvantage in even addressing the closed-circuit motion because their own expert witnesses had not had the opportunity to interview the Wee Care children.

After extensive hearings, Judge Harth ruled to allow testimony via closed-circuit TV.

The defense further argued that their own experts should be permitted to see the children to determine whether, in their opinions, the children really did manifest symptoms. The judge ruled against them in this as well, saying, "We recognize the rights of the defendant, but we must not ignore the rights of the victim." He then cited potential emotional trauma, embarrassment, and intimidation, pointing out that extensive discovery had already been provided, and the benefit of further interviews was uncertain.

Meltzer and Clark had received the medical and psychiatric reports, and Sara believed that this was all they were entitled to, that the defense experts had no legal right to see the children, any more than a rape victim could be made to be examined by the gynecologist of the accused's choice. However, Sara did appreciate that in trial Eileen Treacy's opinions might carry extra weight because she had personally interviewed the Wee Care children. Therefore, to equalize the state's and defense's experts' relative positions, Sara promised that when she came before the jury, Treacy would not divulge the fact that she had met with the children; instead, she would base her conclusions solely on the evidence presented in trial.

The judge also heard argument pertaining to the admissibility of hearsay at trial. While most forms of hearsay were inadmissible under the rules of evidence, special provisions were made for witnesses who were children of "tender years." The state argued that the children's parents and therapists should be allowed to relate statements made to them by the children during the initial months of disclosure. Judge Harth granted the motion.

On April 30, 1987, precisely two years to the day from when Jonathan Moore visited his pediatrician for a rash, the defense motioned for the entire 235-count indictment to be dismissed on the grounds of insufficient evidence. Bob Clark argued that the children's taped statements had been tainted because the investigators had held repeated interviews, asked suggestive questions, and promised rewards for answers. Clark gave the examples: "I'll keep Kelly in jail," and "I'll let you play with my badge."

Sara conceded that a few of the tapes contained leading or suggestive material, but she pointed out that many suggestions of answers made by the interviewers were rejected by the children, and she added that some children had reported disclosures to their parents before they had ever been seen by an investigator.

The defense attorneys had requested that Judge Harth listen to the audio-tapes of the investigators' interviews with the children. Harth had done so, and he did not share the defense attorneys' view of the tapes, stating in his ruling: "I see no overreaching by the State . . . no evidence that individual testimony was tainted. . . . The children were not brainwashed or forced to do anything." (The defense's own expert, Dr. Ralph Underwager, had conceded in pretrial that although he felt the interview tapes raised questions of adult influence, those findings did not in themselves invalidate the children's testimony.)

Harth knocked down the motion to dismiss. He held: "There is absolutely no reason to dismiss any of the counts in this indictment on the grounds sought by the defense." The Grand Jury's permission to go to trial was thereby officially reinforced.

■
■ ■

While Eileen Treacy was testifying at pretrial and listening in on the defense experts' testimony, Sara took the opportunity to question her on the principles of child development. The two women lingered long hours in the Prosecutor's Office, drinking bad coffee, while Sara fired belligerent questions at her expert. The prosecutor was trying to anticipate every attack the defense was going to make on the credibility of the children.

Sara would start out by accusing: "They can't remember!"

Eileen Treacy drew her opinions from the entire body of professional literature. She would say, calmly, "The memory of children over four years of age is just as good as an adult's, except that preschoolers retain only the central details of a situation. They lose peripheral detail."

Okay, that was consistent with what Sara was seeing: All the children fixed on the primary mental image that captured them at the time of the abuse ("Meg was crying." "We made a birthday cake"). Secondary features (time, place, duration, frequency) usually escaped their observation.

Eileen would explain further: A child's personal perspective determines what is central to him, so he may well forget things an adult questioner would assume to be important. Because children don't have the wide-ranging, observing minds of adults, their memory tends to be skeletal, but what they remember they remember reliably.

Eileen explained the various factors that could improve a child's memory: If the perpetrator was someone the children had liked and trusted (how personal was the betrayal?); if the events had been traumatic; and if the children had not merely watched, but had participated in the abuse. The Wee Care children satisfied every criterion for improved recollection that Eileen laid out for Sara.

Sara threw down another question: "So then we taught them what to say. We trained them to accuse Kelly, to repeat it like a story."

Eileen smiled. "Sara, children don't lie to *make* trouble for themselves; they lie to get out of trouble. And cognitively, they simply wouldn't be able to memorize the lies even if they wanted to. At these ages, they're not capable of retaining a script because their thinking is static; they can't focus on several aspects of a given action at the same time. They can't *do* narration."

"Fantasy, then! They imagined this, and now they think they're telling the truth. But it never happened."

"Normal children are able to distinguish fact from fantasy," Eileen answered. And she explained, "If they believe that Superman is real, they will then explain that it's because Christopher Reeve plays Superman, and so, in a fashion, Superman does exist. They've experienced him. Conversely, children know Smurfs are make-believe. Children's imaginations are limited by their inability to think in the abstract until around the age of seven. So, little ones can only fantasize about what they've experienced."

Sara acted doubtful. "They play make-believe constantly. This is fantasy."

"Children pretend to be mommy or doctor or superheroes or wrestlers, but preschoolers have very limited sexual imagination. They can only pretend what they've physically experienced or seen in real life."

Sara then had to consider what actual knowledge a preschooler could be expected to have about sex.

Eileen gave Sara a mini-lesson in sexual development: "At three, a child is aware of genitals as being associated with the difference between boys and girls. At three, children become very curious: They want to look at naked bodies and watch people in the bathroom. They'll ask where babies come from, but if they're told explicitly, the information just sails over their heads.

"Preschoolers are curious about waste and defecation, but at four, despite his or her continued voyeurism, the child begins to develop modesty. While wanting to invade other people's privacy, he demands privacy for himself. At six, children begin experimenting, playing doctor, but rarely penetrating themselves or another child."

Eileen went into the ways children could know about sexual activity. Children could learn about sex from television, but even if they saw two soap opera actors moving, writhing about under the sheets, or even one actually on top of the other, a preschool child would not extrapolate from that a penis in a vagina.

Sara had checked with all the Wee Care families, and none of them subscribed to pornographic cable channels, and many of the children's television habits were monitored by their parents. TV didn't seem to provide a likely explanation for these children's outrageous sexual knowledge.

Sara asked Eileen about the occasional child who did in fact have some explicit sexual knowledge: Couldn't such a child have sexual fantasies?

"A normal child will not fantasize about sexual assault or abusive acts. Children use fantasy to empower themselves, to explore their capabilities and daydream about limitlessness. The only children who will fantasize to *dis*empower themselves ("She hit my penis with a fork." "We each drank some of the pee") are severely disturbed children, like those in institutions."

For all her showy skepticism, Sara McArdle was sure the Wee Care children weren't fantasizing about Kelly Michaels inserting a knife in their rectums. After all, Heather Brennan could barely utter that allegation. Hers was no titillating fantasy of a four-year-old, but rather it was a disempowering, degrading experience that the little girl wanted to forget.

It was Sara's conviction that each one of the children had told the truth.

▪
▪   ▪

Alarmed by Jonathan's suicidal behavior, Claudia Moore and her husband had consulted a psychologist. First, their son had drunk a bottle of cleaning fluid. Then he had started saying that he wished he were an angel.

Throughout the 1986 school year, Jonathan had been withdrawn, aggressive, unable to concentrate on his schoolwork, until at last the Moores had pulled him out of school. To this day, he continued to kick and spit at people, acting extremely threatened whenever a stranger came into their house. And he would hear things that nobody else heard, then demand frantically, "Did you hear that?"

He refused to be left alone in any room of the house, and given Jonathan's inability to sleep out the night in his own bed, neither his parents nor his siblings were getting sufficient or regular sleep. It had gotten to the point where he was even having night terrors during the day: screaming, crying, seeming to be awake, yet unable to be awakened. When Jonathan would finally come out of it, he'd remember nothing.

In play therapy, Jonathan and his psychologist enacted scenarios with little human figures: It was generally the same plot line over and over. Jonathan controlled a group of male figures while his therapist handled a particular dark-haired, female figure. This lady doll was a bad guy, a robber, and the male figures were always trying to catch her, trap her, bring her down. For all the repetition in his therapy sessions, the game still hadn't come to a conclusion.

As yet, Jonathan and his troops hadn't succeeded.

■
■   ■

Ellen and Joey were in the dressing room at Bloomingdale's where she was trying on slacks. Joey sat cross-legged in the corner of the cubicle. He moved in on the safe moment.

Boldly peering up at his mother, Joey stated, "You know, Mommy, I peed on my friends."

Ellen's wrists tingled as they held a pair of pants at her ankles. She looked at him and stepped cautiously back out of them.

■
■   ■

At first, Sara suspected, the children had enjoyed Kelly: Playing the pileup game might have entertained them, with its free-form exhibitionism; seeing their naked teacher play "Jingle Bells" with her breasts bobbing around had to be a scream. Sara thought that Kelly sang the other version of the song, "Jingle Bells, Santa smells. . . ." She remembered one of her investigators telling her that. In the beginning, the children must have found it exciting doing something that they knew was a little bit bad, something they couldn't tell Mommy, something that didn't really hurt yet.

Certainly, most of the children had known that sexual interaction wasn't acceptable behavior. They all knew that people don't go out in public without their clothes on, so they knew they shouldn't be disrobing in school; they knew that people use bathrooms, so obviously it was wrong to defecate in the choir room and in the presence of a gathering. The children knew they were doing "bad" things.

The children had told the investigators that Kelly had paired the boys with specific girls for various sexual acts. Apparently, she had even mocked adult romantic intrigue by making Joey and Lewis vie for the same little girl, each taking turns with her. Not knowing how to handle this alien feeling of sexual tension, the two boys had become aggressive with each other, fighting and tumbling. Robert, the little boy in awe of Lewis Dixon, had been paired repeatedly with the little girl named Lucy. Now, more than anything else in life, Robert wanted to see Lucy, terribly afraid that he might have hurt her, but Lucy refused to see him.

The interviews showed that Kelly had stimulated the boys manually and orally. At first, it had probably felt good, until the sexual activity had progressed to the more explicit and frightening acts. As a result, now the children were experiencing conflicting emotions. Most of the girls seemed to have hated the sexual abuse directly from the start, the pain of the insertions overshadowing all other impressions. Kelly didn't seem to have stimulated the little girls clitorally, so they didn't experience a physical pleasure to counteract some of their other impressions. Yet, in varying degrees, the girls, too, had enjoyed the nudity and the naughtiness. And by the time the sexual abuse became clearly painful and illicit, the children had already been compromised.

Sara thought, The perfect little perpetrators, doing things to each other. Then they really couldn't tell, because if Kelly was bad, so were they.

■
■ ■

The defense attorneys had proposed expert testimony on the profile of a child abuser, their position being that a profile did exist and that Kelly Michaels did not fit the model. Dr. Jonas Rappeport proposed a profile based largely on the opinion that women do not sexually abuse children, saying, "I cannot remember seeing a female child sex abuser." Such a profile would, of course, immediately exonerate Kelly Michaels, and in fact Rappeport avowed that the charges against Michaels were baseless. The doctor noted the violent nature of the alleged acts and stated that women do not ordinarily sexually abuse in these ways.

The state argued against the basic premise of a viable profile of an abuser, taking the position that no one can predict reliably what another human being has within him to do, including sexual damage. No category of person is doctrinally safe, and any cleanly delineated definition of "child abusers" would only delude someone into a false sense of order and safety.

Special Agent Ken Lanning of the FBI appeared at pretrial specifically to counter the claims that women who are not psychotic do not sexually abuse children. He brought with him fifteen photographs of female perpetrators to document his point. Over eight years of specific research on child sexual abuse, Lanning had developed a breakdown of the various patterns of behavior seen in sexual abusers. His distinctions were not psychiatric, but designed to aid law enforcement in investigations.

Lanning identified two major categories of abusers: preferential, or adults who prefer children as sex objects (known as pedophiles in psychiatric terminology), and situational, or adults who act out some type of anger, hostility, rage, on any available weak individual, including children. He explained that if a situational abuser were to resign her day-care job and take, for example, a position at a nursing home, she could very likely enter into the same type of abuse, but this time with the elderly as her victims. (Even Dr. Rappeport conceded that people who were not ordinarily child sexual abusers and had a normal history of sexual development could commit such acts if under severe stress: "situational molesters.")

Lanning noted as the distinguishing feature of preferential abusers the fact that their erotic imagery and sexual fantasies focus on children. By contrast, he explained, the criminal activity of a situational abuser is not clearly sexual in motivation, despite the sexual actions. Lanning speculated that the fantasies of some situational abusers could focus on rage and anger and revenge on the person or thing that inspired their need to assert control. These people could engage in sexual acts and feel sexual things, although anger, not sex, was often their primary motivation.

Lanning pointed out that he had seen sexual behavior in the service of non-sexual needs, and then, alternatively, non-sexual behavior (defecation, urination, beating) in the service of sexual needs. The allegations against Kelly Michaels contained dozens of acts in which Kelly was said to have physically interacted with the children, but throughout the investigation, the theme of voyeurism had developed: Kelly's pairing the little boys and girls and watching them perform sex acts on each other, showing them tampons and watching them urinate, and, turning it around, playing "Jingle Bells" with her clothes off and having the children watch.

When asked if Kelly got in the pileup, a little girl had answered, "She watched." Another had said that after the children came out of the pileup, Kelly had told them, "You did a beautiful job. You did just what I asked you to." The children did not depict Kelly as asexual. One imitated her teacher's heavy breathing, and one reported that Kelly "touched her own vagina and hole." Nevertheless, some of Kelly's activities seemed to have little to do with sex. A little girl alleged that Kelly "forked my hair." Another said that she had made the children look at a picture of a girl getting sick.

Sara McArdle had heard of prosecutors who refused to prosecute cases against a female because of their certainty that juries wouldn't believe that a woman would sexually abuse. Certainly, it was unusual to have a female acting alone in such an extensive circumstance. But, if all the allegations were true, Kelly Michaels was no ordinary perpetrator. She couldn't be put into a sadomasochistic model, nor a satanic model, nor a pedophilic model. The alleged activities displayed elements of each: the painful, the ritual, the sensual, but deviated from them all as well.

Judge Harth disallowed expert testimony on a profile, noting that too much of the thinking about perpetrators was based on myth. Harth said, "In child abuse, there are no usual suspects."

.
. .

Jury selection began on June 1, at which time Kelly reappeared in court to sit surreally through the proceedings reading a paperback novel. Each side was granted a number of challenges with which to knock prospective jurors off the panel. The prosecutors went into the process with twelve challenges. Due to the seriousness of the charges, the defense was accorded an extra advantage: twenty peremptory challenges with which to outmaneuver the state.

When the judge told prospective jurors that the trial could consume three or four months, most of them wanted off. Those employed jurors who were eventually chosen would continue to be paid by their employers in accordance with the policies of their firms. One juror who was selected subsequently had to be released from duty because he learned that his employer was not going to continue his salary. In a trial of such duration, the court protected the financial well-being of the jurors, in addition to remunerating them for public service. But the five-dollar daily wage paid them by the county was subtracted then from their corporate paychecks.

Jury panels were presented to the attorneys for review, and the lawyers made notes on their first impressions. Glenn Goldberg found only one juror who, on sight, he registered as an unreserved "Good," placing an asterisk next to her name. This woman, who listed her occupation as housewife, lured the prosecutor with her gracious smiles.

The bailiffs had distributed a questionnaire for all the panelists to fill out, and after they had completed it, prospectives were privately interviewed in the jury room by the four attorneys and Judge Harth. Kelly was present while these interviews were conducted and, the prosecutor noticed, positioned herself at the table so as to be the person closest to the potential juror.

A panelist in his sixties, a slender man in work clothes, had a concerned expression on his face. He sat beside Kelly, who was making up to him with flirtatious eyes. The man responded yes when Judge Harth asked whether there was any reason why he thought he would be unable to serve fairly, and the judge asked him to explain his answer. The man then gazed directly into Kelly's wide eyes and said clearly, "Anyone who could violate the bodies of little children such as she did should be drawn . . . quartered . . . hung . . . and shot."

The smile disintegrated from Kelly's face, and the potential juror was excused.

Judge Harth asked the same question of every juror who was being seriously considered. Given the fact that this was a large case involving many witnesses and a sizable indictment, would the juror feel that "where there's smoke, there's fire" and, consequently, be biased toward a foregone conclusion of guilty? No panelist who didn't swear to be undaunted by the amount of smoke surrounding this case made it onto the jury.

Following each day's session, the defense ordered transcripts. Ordinarily, daily copy of jury selection was ordered in death penalty cases, when the consequences of overlooking some flaw in a juror's attitude were dire. In most other cases, the cost (four dollars a page) was considered to be prohibitively expensive; however, Kelly Michaels's attorneys ordered copy.

By June 17, seventeen jurors were chosen. They included an electronics technician, two word processors, a clerk, a wiring mechanic, a letter carrier, two secretaries, a retired banker, a plant supervisor, an employee of an investment company, an assistant manager with New Jersey Bell, a retired postal clerk, a production assistant at NBC-TV, a hospital diet aide, a traffic administrator at ITT Aviations, and a millwright at Bell Labs.

Every juror had completed high school. Two of them had B.S. degrees in business administration, one of whom also had an associate degree in accounting; another juror had a B.A. in English; another a B.A. in communications; and still another an undergraduate math and history degree along with a paralegal degree.

The housewife who had seemed to Glenn Goldberg to be such a supportive potential juror never got called, because by the time her group came on deck, the jury was filled; however, Sara and Glenn were pleased with the jury panel: Each member seemed to love children and to be intelligent and balanced. Eleven of the jurors were parents, seven grand-parents.

By the time the full panel was selected, Sara and Glenn had used ten of their twelve challenges, Meltzer and Clark several less than their twenty. Both sides, having challenges to spare, were clearly fully satisfied with every one of the panelists. The defense team's theory had been that for an intricate medical and psychological case like this, they would require sophisticated jurors. Bob Clark wanted intelligent panelists who could enter into the proceedings with an open mind and sustain that isometric approach throughout a long trial—because trial was inevitable now.

There had never been any chance for the case to settle without going to court: The defense attorneys knew that the prosecution would never come down to where they'd even consider a plea. Eventually, Harth had inquired, "Is there any meaningful plea bargain?" and the attorneys had agreed that there was not.

The structure of trial dictated that after each attorney made his opening remarks, the state would present its complete case first, the defense witnesses following. The prosecution would therefore have the jurors' attention while they were still fresh, the slight configurational edge given to the state by a system that grants itself its own advantages. When the time came for closing arguments, after both the prosecution and the defense had rested, the state would once again have the advantage, this time in the form of the last word.

By now, Sara knew the Wee Care schedule inside out: For any given day during the 1984–85 school year she could rattle off the names of all the people who had been in that building, even pinpoint where they were supposed to be and what they were supposed to be doing. She had charts, tables, cross-referenced lists. To the best of her ability Sara McArdle had, in two years of hard work, caulked every gap in her information about the case.

Eighteen children were expected to testify, four fewer than the twenty-two who had appeared at Grand Jury. Paul, the little boy who had introduced the allegations of knives, forks, and spoons, wouldn't be testifying because his family had relocated to another state when his father had been promoted.

Sara scheduled the children to testify before her other witnesses so that they could be finished before the 1987 school year started. The prosecutors agreed to put Jonathan first: He was a starting principle. Freddie Mercer was listed as a witness, but he was unlikely to testify because he was so young, so immature, so manic with sexuality. With the reduction in the number of child witnesses, dozens of counts in the indictment had to be dismissed, so that going into trial Kelly Michaels faced 163 counts.

Preschool children were impressionable and weak and, therefore, superior victims. Their minds were only just growing, their verbal skills just developing, and they were, therefore, inferior witnesses. Sara resolved, privately, that no matter what the legal outcome of this ordeal, the Wee Care children who went to court were going to emerge from their experience with the justice system empowered by their own courage.

Part

THREE

9

.·.

The animated woman was easily the most riveting person in the courtroom. She was trim, though it looked to be an act of will to retain
control over her flesh. Her cheeks, her eyelids, her chest, her mouth,
were drawn in tiny, delicate lines just a little overfilled with flesh. And
every curve was cinched in thin summer material. A lacy white blouse
held her waist in a snug circlet, its sleeves gripping her wrists in tight,
pleated bands. Her clothes might have been simple and sweet on a little
girl, but on a twenty-five-year-old body they seemed to strain in a sexual way.

Kelly was at most five-four, but everyone always seemed to be looking
up at her. Strangers felt compelled to turn toward her and strain to hear
what she was saying, to hear the voice buried too deeply in her throat
for them really to understand her words. Kelly was no longer enshrined
with icons; her image had changed: There was no Bible, no rosary, no
illustration of Christ.

Reporters packed into the press rows, right behind their court artists who occupied the first row: No cameras were allowed. The artists began to lay out their paints and pastels and to maneuver their mini-binocular eyeglasses over their eyes. Spectators, many of them curious courthouse employees, filled the remaining benches, agonizing because their coffee breaks were wasting away and the trial had not yet commenced. No Wee Care parents were present because they were all named as prospectives on the state's witness list.

The last few jurors were led by a bailiff through the viewing gallery and across the floor of open court to the jury room. Sara McArdle and Glenn Goldberg entered the courtroom behind them, loaded down with accordion files and legal references. Their dress was loose and comfortable, and their expressions were loose and comfortable. They talked to each other in low voices, laughing occasionally, but they waited quietly in their seats for the trial to begin. Sara noted that the woman behind her was a transformed Kelly, tens of pounds shy of the awkward, lumpy girl who had vehemently denied all allegations more than two years ago in the Prosecutor's Office.

The defendant stood separated from her family by the half wall that divided the spectator area from open court. She faced her parents and sister who had seated themselves in the front row of the right-hand side of the courtroom: the ''defense side.'' She didn't look anywhere but at them.

The Michaels family formed a protective enclosure for her. Kelly's father was a tall, portly man, with a bald, glossy head rimmed by several inches of dark hair. He wore a sports jacket and toted a beige plastic cooler filled with their lunches. Kelly's mother was a slack-bodied, middle-aged woman with pink plastic glasses and a stern visage. The young woman standing next to Kelly was unmistakably a sister, a heavier version of the same person. Within their circle, Kelly spoke quietly to them, her features taut and insistent.

The doors to the courtroom opened, and Bob Clark ambled up to counsel table in his good-natured way, wearing a Cheshire grin. He gave the appearance of being a big friendly bear of a man. A minute later Harvey Meltzer followed in his nipped-and-tucked-to-within-an-inch-of-his-life suit, his face meticulously bronzed. His shoulders dipped right and left as he walked on, and his whole body smiled when he greeted the prosecutors.

The bailiff notified the judge that all parties were present.

▪
▪ ▪

Jonathan Moore waited in the wings to be, once again, the first Wee Care child to tell. According to Judge Harth's pretrial ruling, the children would be allowed to testify in his chambers. Only a limited audience would be present, among them the judge, a prosecutor, a defense attorney, the court reporter, and the video technician. Each child could be accompanied by a support person of his choice and as many stuffed animals as he could hold. A closed-circuit TV setup would transmit live testimony to the jury, the defendant, and the spectators who stayed out in the courtroom.

As in the Grand Jury procedure, each child would have to be qualified in a competency hearing prior to his or her appearing before the jury. Once the judge deemed each competent to testify, the examination could begin.

The bailiff announced, "The judge is coming out. Please rise."

Harth entered from a door behind the bench wearing a glossy black robe.

"Good morning. Please be seated," he said, his voice scratchy but strong. Sixty-one years old, William Harth had been on the bench for almost fifteen years.

Harvey Meltzer immediately initiated a motion, respective of the closed-circuit testimony, requesting that Kelly Michaels be present in judge's chambers during the competency hearings of the alleged victims.

Meltzer began, "Your Honor, as we are all aware, there exists in the state of New Jersey a statute which addresses itself and is entitled *Minors, Sexual Offenses and Child Abuse—Closed Circuit Television Testimony* —and I wish to underscore the word *testimony*. . . . Your Honor, what we have here is a situation wherein the court has seen fit, over the objection of the defense, to permit the testimony of these children on closed-circuit television in the judge's chambers. This being the case, Your Honor . . . we have a situation where a child will be testifying on closed-circuit television because the state has indicated and has been able to convince the court—"

Harth interrupted and corrected: "Has met the statutory requirements and also the requirement of *State* v. *Sheppard*. You may proceed."

Meltzer rolled onward: "Nowhere in the statute, nowhere in the commentary, does it identify that children should be protected (to coin the position of the state) from preliminary hearings."

The judge's voice was reasonable. "Now, what was the purpose of this court allowing the children to testify in the court's chambers?" He paused to give Meltzer a moment. "Was that not . . . because of problems of testifying in front of the defendant as well as in open court? That was the reason.''

"*Testifying* underlined," said Meltzer.

"That's right," Harth conceded. "Now, do you feel on the voir dire, where I must determine the competency of the children, the fear would be any less, or the reasons less, Mr. Meltzer?''

"Your Honor, what we're dealing with—''

"Just think through logically.''

"I am trying to, Your Honor.''

"Then succeed.''

"Your Honor," Meltzer protested, "we are dealing with testifying. We're not dealing with the qualifying of a prospective witness. We are dealing with testifying. That's what *Sheppard* addresses. That's what the closed-circuit television statute addresses also, Your Honor. That being the case, it is the defense's position that my client's due process rights, as protected by the Constitution of the United States, would be violated if she were not permitted to be present during this particular aspect of the trial. And therefore, Your Honor, it is our position with respect—''

"How will her rights be violated?" asked Harth.

Meltzer stood, his right arm crooked stiffly behind his back, fiddling with a gold pen. Then he said, "The accused's presence bears a relationship, reasonably substantial, to her opportunity to defend.''

The defense motion was denied.

■

■ ■

While the jury remained enclosed in the jury room, both Glenn Goldberg and Harvey Meltzer headed to Harth's chambers for Jonathan's competency hearing. Before sending him into chambers, Sara and Glenn had asked their witness which one of them he wanted to go in with him, and Jonathan had chosen Glenn. Jonathan often became inhibited around Sara—he seemed to react negatively to women as a corollary to his feelings toward Kelly—so she was relegated to the courtroom with the other spectators. Mr. Moore accompanied his son into chambers as his support person.

While in chambers, Harvey Meltzer communicated on speak-a-phones with Bob Clark, who remained in the courtroom. Kelly also wore headphones which would enable her to talk to Meltzer when he questioned the child. There were two large-screened television monitors, one facing the jury box and the other facing the gallery. Two smaller TVs were placed at other angles in the room. An additional small TV was set on counsel table exactly in front of the defendant.

Face-to-face with Jonathan Moore sat Kelly wearing a cleared brow, the oversimplified face of innocence: emptied of everything. She had a pile of papers in front of her, on top of which was a spiral notebook ready to receive her impressions of the trial.

There was a great visual silence in the courtroom as the spectators and jurors, their curiosity palpable, strained to see a figure form on the blank screen.

A small boy with white-blond hair appeared, lying back in an oversize, yellow leather armchair. Jonathan was six and a half years old.

"All right, we'll begin now," Harth said. "Good morning, Jonathan. How are you?"

"Good."

"Where do you go to school?"

Jonathan told him.

The judge asked, "Jonathan, what color crayon is that you're using?"

"Red. Bright red."

"All right," said Harth, his voice soothing. "Red. Could I hold a red crayon?"

Jonathan handed over the crayon.

"Now, if I said this was a green crayon, would I be telling the truth?"

"A lie," said Jonathan.

"A lie," agreed the judge. "If I said it was a red crayon, what would it be?"

"The truth."

The judge asked if either the prosecutors or the defense attorneys had any questions for the witness. The state had none.

Harvey Meltzer faced Jonathan. "Have you ever told a lie?"

"Yes," he answered, his frankness scoring a laugh in the courtroom.

"Do you know the difference between telling a lie and telling a white lie?"

"I don't get that."

"Do you know what a fib is?"

"Yes," said Jonathan.

"Have you ever told a fib before?"

"No," he said, "but my friend has."

Meltzer asked Jonathan a few more questions, then informed the judge that he had no further questions. Harth inquired whether any of the attorneys had an objection to the child testifying, and all present responded no. Accordingly, the court ruled that the witness was competent to testify. In the courtroom, TV screens blackened and the jurors were called back in so that the taking of testimony could commence.

. .

The television screens became animated again, showing the tall, thin judge at a long boardroom table opposite a small boy. Harth addressed Jonathan: "We have a job for you to do today. It's not a hard job, but it's an important one." His voice rolled soothingly. "Now, when you're asked a question, if you don't know the answer, don't say yes or no. It's not like a test in school. You don't have to guess. Just say, 'I don't know.' Okay?"

"Okay," Jonathan said. He wasn't looking up, but was coloring with vigor, scraping at the paper.

"Good morning, Jonathan," said Glenn.

"Morning."

"How are you today?"

"Good."

"Good." Glenn paused. "I'm going to ask you some questions. You know that, right?"

"Yes," said Jonathan, "'cause you were over my house last night."

"That's right." Glenn proceeded with caution. "Jonathan, do you like baseball?"

"Definitely."

"What is your favorite baseball team?"

"White Sox."

"And is that Daddy's favorite team too?" Glenn asked.

"No . . . Yankees."

"The Yankees." Glenn pondered. "Doesn't that make you want to like the Yankees best too?"

"Nope." Jonathan shot him down. "They're my last favorite." Slyly, he looked over at his father, ready to giggle, willing to disagree.

"Well, who is your favorite baseball player? Is there anybody you like more than the others?"

"Don Mattingly." Jonathan lay across the table on his stomach and continued to color with full arm power.

"Why do you like Don Mattingly so much?"

"He's my type," Jonathan explained. "We both throw by both hands."

"Do you remember the name of your teacher when you went to Wee Care?"

The little boy's head smashed down onto the table. Softly, he said, "Joan."

"And what kind of things did you used to learn in Joan's class?"

Jonathan murmured, "How to paint."

"I can't hear you when your face is on the table," said Glenn, and asked Jonathan which children were in his class at Wee Care.

"I have to go to the bathroom," said Jonathan. Harth called for a break.

When testimony resumed, Glenn opened a discussion of napping. "Did you like nap time?" he asked.

"Hated it."

"Did anything happen during nap time that you didn't like?"

The answer was slurred: "Yes . . . One time was the time Kelly took my temperature." Glenn asked him to tell him again a little louder.

Jonathan tilted his head back, stretched his mouth out to its most gaping limits, and shrieked suddenly, piercingly: "Kelly! took! my! temperature!"

People in the courtroom jumped.

Glenn, quietly, sounded curious: "Why did Kelly take your temperature?"

"I don't know."

"Jonathan, was Kelly a nurse?"

"No," Jonathan replied. "No way, José."

"What?"

"No way, José." Jonathan was intent on the selection of crayons, changing every few seconds which colored stick he used.

Glenn asked, "Did she do anything with the thermometer before she took your temperature?"

"Yeah," said Jonathan. "Put 'gasoline' on it."

"When Kelly took your temperature, where did she put the thermometer?"

"My bum," he said, making his voice deep and heavy. Jonathan stood up in the yellow chair and pointed where he meant.

"What?"

Jonathan brandished an opened mouth and screeched the two words again.

Glenn asked, "Did she say anything when she took your temperature?"

"No!" he snapped.

The state had no further questions at this time, so Judge Harth turned the witness over to the defense.

"Thank you, Your Honor," Meltzer said. "Are you there, Jonathan?" Jonathan was not responding.

Judge Harth stated for the record: "Jonathan is under the table."

"Come on up, big guy," called his father.

Meltzer suggested, "Jonathan, you want me to ask you questions while you're there?"

"Yes," said the voice.

"Okay." Meltzer tried to make the little boy more comfortable. "Are you afraid to talk to me?" Underneath the table, he walked over on his hands and knees to poke at Meltzer's feet.

"No."

"You're sure?" said Meltzer.

"Yes," answered Jonathan's voice.

"Then why are you hiding from me?"

Meltzer paused for the response, but the voice thrower was silent.

"Do you want me to go underneath and talk to you under the table?" Meltzer offered, willing to play by Jonathan's rules.

"I'll tickle you," Jonathan warned.

"C'mere, big guy," said his father. "Just a little bit more."

Suddenly the witness was shouting: "I don't wanna sit in the camera! I don't wanna get with the camera!"

Harth called for another break, and when testimony resumed, miraculously Jonathan was once again seated at the head of the table, facing the video equipment. But he was growling, groaning, gurgling.

Meltzer and Clark had no intention of browbeating the children. Their expert, Dr. Ralph Underwager, had advised that it was best for a defense attorney not to go after a child in an aggressive, hostile manner. One, it wasn't necessary. Two, it reinforced the stereotype of defense attorneys in sex crimes cases.

Meltzer asked Jonathan about his interviews with Sara and Glenn, seeking to establish that the child had been taught to recite a pre-arranged script. Meltzer asked, "Did Glenn talk to you about what Kelly did to you at Wee Care? What did he say happened? Do you know? Do you remember?"

"I told *him* what happened!" Jonathan shrewdly corrected.

"Okay. Okay," said Meltzer, backing off.

Jonathan paged through the coloring book, continuing, "I told him that Kelly took my temperature and that she's a nerd." His father stroked his son's back, as if to absorb the anger like a lightning rod.

Meltzer then asked, "Did you ever tell Arlene?"

Jonathan answered no.

"Did you ever tell Diane?"

Jonathan answered no.

"What about Joan, your teacher? Didn't you tell her that?" There was no response. Meltzer waited awhile, then tried to get his attention: "Earth to Jonathan."

Jonathan was wielding crayons and making whistling, fizzling explosion noises. "No, no, no. That's the ninth time I said it," the witness complained.

Then, with a big explosion sound, he lobbed a crayon bomb at Harvey Meltzer.

Meltzer asked, "Did somebody tell you that Evan's temperature was taken and Alison's temperature?"

"Uh-uh, you can't trick me!"

"Who said I was going to trick you?"

"That's what I heard. . . . Like you were going to say your mom told you to say this stuff."

When Meltzer tried another question, the child cut him off: "One more question and then I want to go home."

"Jonathan," Meltzer asked, "are you having fun?"

"No," he answered.

"No more questions." Meltzer concluded cross-examination.

The state now had the opportunity to redirect: to probe areas relating to any new information or new lines of questioning that had been introduced during cross-examination.

Glenn asked Jonathan, "Did anything happen at Wee Care that you don't want to tell us about?"

"Many things," he admitted.

"Why don't you want to tell us about those things, Jonathan?"

The witness was already packing away crayons. "So I can go home, and I forgot all of them." Jonathan finished on a note of ambiguity.

·
· ·

The TV monitors were removed to the side of the courtroom floor, and Jonathan's mother, Claudia Moore, took the witness stand.

Meltzer inquired, "Before the nurse took Jonathan's temperature, did she tell him what she was going to do?"

"No."

"You mean she just came right up and slid that thing right in?"

"Well . . . she might have said, 'I'm going to take your temperature.' "

Meltzer asked, "And wasn't it after she said that . . . Jonathan said 'That is what she does to me in school'—before the insertion took place?"

"Oh, no."

Kelly dangled her fingers over her mouth and spoke urgently from behind them to Bob Clark.

Harvey Meltzer asked Mrs. Moore a basic question: "Did you ever ask Jonathan what it was that was inserted into his rectum by my client?"

"No," said Claudia, "because at the time I assumed it was a thermometer." She paused. "I couldn't allow myself to even consider that anything besides a thermometer went up my son's rectum."

Moving on, Meltzer broached the topic of the Moores's marital difficulties, requesting the witness to correlate Jonathan's behaviors with his parents' fighting.

"Some of them caused the arguing," said Claudia, not giving Meltzer what he wanted. "The fact that Jonathan was such a wild man and that I had no control over him, that he didn't sleep nights, and that I was all the time having to stay up, and I wasn't getting any sleep. I was short-tempered. He was short-tempered. We had this crazy kid, and it put a lot of stress between my husband and I."

Meltzer suggested, "You don't think the stress between your husband and you caused the incidents with the child?"

Claudia answered, "My husband and I had arguments at about this time. I don't think those affected Jonathan. I think Jonathan's stress affected us a lot worse than that."

■ ■

Sara and Glenn met with Jonathan and his parents downstairs in the Prosecutor's Office, chatting with him to help him unwind. Then they presented their witness with a letter, a formal congratulation from the Essex County Prosecutor's Office that Sara had composed to give to all the children. Before handing it to the little boy, she read it out loud:

Dear Jonathan,

On behalf of the Prosecutor's Office, and all of the other children who have had an experience similar to yours, we would like to thank you very much for your bravery today.

We have watched you over the last two years, and have seen what a terribly difficult thing this was for you to talk about. It takes a very grown-up boy to do a job like the job you did today.

Today you took Kelly's power away and gave that power to children across America who need to be protected. You stood up and said what you had to say so that other children wouldn't have to undergo the experience that you went through.

There's no doubt in our minds that today you were and are America's most outstanding citizen.

Sara handed over the document. "Thank you, Jonathan," she said.

▪
▪ ▪

Late in the afternoon on one of the first trial days, the court's administration office received a phone call.

"Is this the Superior Court of Essex County?" the voice asked.

"Yes," answered the secretary.

"Is this where the Michaels trial is being held?"

"Yes."

The speaker was a youngish-sounding man. He said, "I just want to let you know that I'm gonna save the taxpayers of Essex County a lot of money. She's never gonna see the end of her trial."

The secretary, stunned, was silent, and the caller, too, waited. Both parties battled the lull, before the secretary made a valiant attempt at secretarial decorum. "Would you like to speak to someone who can help you?" she inquired politely.

"No," he answered. "I just want you to know that she's not gonna make it. I'm gonna put a bullet in her head."

"Oh."

The silence evaporated. He hung up, and the secretary called her superior to report the death threat.

After a series of *in camera* meetings with the attorneys, Judge Harth instituted reforms. All spectators were to be scanned with hand-held metal detectors and were to register daily on a sign-in sheet. The sheriff's officers were to make periodic checks of the hallway and bathrooms. And to protect the defendant and her family when they were the most exposed, while they were in transit to the building, the Michaelses were to travel with an armed escort of sheriff's officers. They would also be permitted to park in a restricted county parking garage.

▪
▪ ▪

Inside the courtroom, Kelly was sitting on the right end of counsel table with her back to the spectators, seemingly confused about what to do with her neatly manicured hands. She sat forward on her chair and tried clasping them behind her back, then brought her arms to her sides, her long nails flicking, then coyly clasped her hands behind her back a second time. At last, she jerked them forward onto the table so she could play with her fingers.

Meg Barnes was the scheduled witness. The state was putting the children on the stand in the mornings so they would be fresh and also to avoid making them wait around the courthouse for some other witness to finish testifying.

Before the jury was brought in, Meltzer registered an objection. In pretrial hearings, the court had handed down a sequestration ruling: Any person who was going to testify was to be absent, sequestered, during the testimony of any preceding witness. The ruling was intended to prevent the problem of parrot perjury, or the adjustment of the latter witness's testimony to match what he had already heard the former witness say. Meltzer objected to Meg's choice of her private psychologist, Dr. Susan Esquilin, as her support person in light of the fact that Dr. Esquilin would later be testifying about Meg's case.

Meltzer opened, "Most respectfully, Your Honor—"

Judge Harth interrupted: "You needn't say 'most respectfully' with every sentence."

"Yes, Your Honor," Meltzer conceded, and rephrased, "With the greatest amount of respect," and he paused for emphasis, "I am of the opinion that the state has perpetrated fraud on the court, hiding behind the rule that kids can be traumatized by testifying. . . . The court has already ruled on the Constitutionality of that issue, so we're living with that decision."

Meltzer stated his concern that the choice of Susan Esquilin as Meg's support might allow her to inherit testimony from Meg. And he went on to question the children's need for a support person.

Sara, indignant, rose to say that Mr. Meltzer obviously had no idea what, for example, Jonathan Moore had gone through when he testified.

Judge Harth recalled, "Mr. Moore was under the table at one point."

Sara took her seat.

Harth ruled that Dr. Esquilin's report on Meg's case already delineated her testimony, so she would be allowed to act as Meg's support person. The procedure was established for the future that if a parent or therapist insisted on acting as support prior to having given testimony, then he or she would not be permitted to testify to anything not already given in a prior statement.

The closed-circuit setup was prepared, but the court waited for Harvey Meltzer to finish changing into the casual outfit that he felt would put the kids more at ease.

Meg's gilt hair was pulled back in a ponytail, but the wisps around her face made her seem ethereal. Her mouth was open, usually to smile, sometimes to let her think. About four teeth were already missing from the top row, making her smile even more open.

Kelly fondled a well-worn airmail letter that she drew from the pile of papers in front of her.

Harvey entered chambers wearing jeans and a summer plaid shirt. Meg was still smiling, but her baby-blue lamb was being handled furiously, repeatedly coming up to touch and cover her face. Her bare knees, too, came up into the big yellow leather armchair to shield her face.

She swung her legs as Judge Harth asked her the first competency question. "Do you know what it means to tell the truth?"

"Yes," Meg answered, looking scared and shy and faintly bewildered.

Kelly stared at the screen set up a foot from her face. She was chewing gum. Bracketing her head was the set of speak-a-phones, her hand pressed to them. Even after the preliminary hearing was concluded, and the TV screens blacked out to allow the jury time to file in, Kelly sat rigidly, as if once she had struck her pose she had hardened into it.

Meg leaned way back and tapped the arms of the chair with her fingertips. Her mouth hung open in a listless pause while Harvey Meltzer handled the cross-examination.

The defense attorney asked Meg if during the Wee Care year she had ever told her teacher or her mother that she didn't want to go to the choir room.

"Nooooo," Meg hummed, pride and certainty elongating the word. She had protected them all.

"What about Kelly?" he asked. "Are you afraid of her?"

Meg didn't respond.

"What about now, sitting with your knees above your head. Are you afraid of her now?"

"I don't know." Meg answered through an eyehole she made between her knees.

"Do you like Kelly?" he pressed.

"No."

"Why?"

She whispered, "I don't know."

Pinned by the images on the TV screen, Kelly watched, her hand still fingering her face.

Without transition, Kelly sank into her airmail letter again.

Meltzer asked, "I'll bet you, are you still in your pink room? Do you still live in your pink room, or have you changed the color of the room yet?"

"It's still pink," Meg answered warily, the ground shifting.

"You used to have two fishes called Heckle and Jeckle, didn't you?"

"No. Birds," she corrected.

"Birds? You're kidding. I figured that was a funny name. What about, you had some, you have fish, don't you?"

"Yes."

"Do you remember telling me about the black mollies and the catfish and the zebra fish?"

"Yeah," said Meg weakly.

Then Meltzer asked, "Did you ever speak to me?"

"Uh, yeah," she answered.

"Besides today? Remember about a year ago we spoke?"

"No." Meg looked blank.

Meltzer acted amazed. "You don't remember that? Did ya ever try to put anything inside yourself, like a toothbrush?"

Meg denied that she had.

Sara wondered, Do we know that Meg *did* speak to Mr. Meltzer a year ago? She interrupted, "I don't know that Meg told him. I think that's a little confusing to the child to confuse truth and not truth."

Later, when Meltzer had finished cross, Sara framed her last question on redirect. "Meg," she asked, "what did we tell you last night was your job in court?"

"Tell the truth," answered Meg, clarifying her intentions for anyone who had doubted them.

.
. .

Sara realized now where Meltzer had gotten the details about Meg's private life: He had read them in Eileen Treacy's report of her own interview with Meg. In essence, Meltzer had distorted that client-privileged information to mislead the witness. The jurors were sent out of the courtroom, and Sara opened legal argument. She quoted the *Rules of Conduct* and asserted flatly that Mr. Meltzer had lied to Meg Barnes about having met him a year ago.

Meltzer pushed back his glasses with spread thumb and pinkie.

Sara continued, expressing her belief that the children had come to the conclusion on their own that Kelly's lawyers would try to trick them. She placed on the record her assurance that neither she nor Mr. Goldberg had ever told a child the other lawyers would trick them, but instead they had explained that Kelly was saying these things had never happened and her lawyers would try to convince the jury of that. The children must have therefore interpreted the defense lawyers' role as tricksters.

Sara then returned to the problem at hand and asserted that defense counsel's ruse was an attempt to confuse Meg and discredit her with the jury, who would naturally assume that she had forgotten the incident.

Meltzer rose to rebut: "I am ready to appear and be sanctioned if it's necessary, but the only way I can elicit information from these children whom the state has had access to for two whole years before I even got a chance to see them is to set up these children the way I've been told, and I have told them, I'm going to trick them. If the state has advised them I'm going to trick them, by golly, that's what I'm gonna try to do, Your Honor. . . . I perceive the tricking as leading them, suggesting and things." Meltzer's tone was defiant, rebellious.

Harth queried, "I gather you feel it's proper to tell an untruth to the child?"

Clark leapt, indignant. "Untruths *have* been told to the children!" Now both attorneys were on their feet.

"Don't you feel Mr. Meltzer can handle this?" asked Harth.

"At times," Clark answered.

Sara interposed. "Judge, he never informed the tribunal that in fact he had not seen the child. He left the tribunal with the false impression that he had seen the child and the child didn't remember. But for us checking, the jury would've thought that he saw the child."

"May I?" asked Meltzer.

"Yes."

"Thank you, Judge. If the court may recall, I attempted to identify in my opening statement that I hadn't seen the children, and that is why I was changing into street clothes, in order to reduce any barriers. . . ." Meltzer was becoming agitated.

Harth said, "You've lost me now, Mr. Meltzer."

"I know it's tough. I'll go slower. Maybe you can follow. It's my position—"

"I think if you go more logically, I will follow," instructed Harth.

Meltzer retorted, "Most definitely, if I went logically, I think I would definitely lose you."

"Gee whiz—" Glenn rose to his considerable height, flabbergasted. "I'm professionally offended by Mr. Meltzer's conduct as a representative of the bar. Members of the public are present; members of the press are present; and Mr. Meltzer is now maligning the dignity of this court."

The court was silent. Meltzer said nothing.

Harth was forgiving. "Did you really mean that, Mr. Meltzer?"

"Did I really mean it?" mimicked Meltzer. "Maybe it was a slip of the tongue, Your Honor."

Making a last attempt to explain himself, Meltzer tried to joke that he had only been going on a fishing expedition with the little girl, but the joke sank. Harth agreed to remedy the misrepresentation of the child's credibility by making an explanation to the jury. When the jurors were reassembled, Harth advised them only that Mr. Meltzer had never met Meg Barnes before today. He left the deception for the jurors to infer.

.
. .

Next to take the stand was Meg's father, a dark, handsome man wearing large glasses that blended easily into a strong, loving face. He proceeded slowly and chose his words with caution. As he spoke, his voice wove a cradle of understanding and sorrow.

The first few words emerged with effort, and he broke down quietly, so that it was some moments before anyone knew he was crying. He removed his glasses and leaned way back in his chair as if he was trying to tighten up a composure that had come unraveled. Then, head in hand, he caved his body onto his knees.

Kelly studied Mr. Barnes, then resumed writing in her spiral notebook, her back twitching with muscular activity.

Sara held up a photograph and asked the witness if he was familiar with the picture.

Mr. Barnes confirmed that he was, and Sara asked, "What is that a picture of?"

"It's Meg's class picture from Wee Care."

Sara approached the stand and handed him the photo.

"And what did you do with that picture?" asked Sara.

He held it delicately, taking a long look down. "When Meg told me that Kelly had done bad things to her, I asked her if Kelly had done bad things to any of the other children, and she said yes. Then I went to the bookshelf and got out her class picture, and I showed it to her and said, 'Can you tell me which children?' "

Mr. Barnes looked at the photograph full of children, holding it so gently his fingers barely touched it. The courtroom was riveted. Very tenderly, he placed the picture face down on the witness stand and lowered his head to his hands.

Judge Harth interposed and sent the jury out on a break.

Kelly scuttled over to the waist-high wall that separated her from her family. They whispered and laughed, their hands across their mouths.

When the jury returned, Mr. Barnes finished calmly. He said that when he had asked Meg which children were involved, she had told him all of them and pointed to each child in the picture, one by one. As he related this, he never once looked away from the picture, transfixed by the faces there.

Among the defense's many theories of the case was that the children's parents had taught them to lie about being abused. The defense postulated that the children had been brainwashed so that the parents could lay claims against Wee Care's purported three-million-dollar umbrella policy. The hypothetical motive was greed, and the circumstantial evidence was the fact that the parents were suing Wee Care, Arlene Spector, and Kelly Michaels for monetary damages. In his cross-examination, Harvey Meltzer asked Mr. Barnes why he was a plaintiff in a civil suit.

Meg's father was looking at him from a distance, as if Meltzer couldn't touch him. He said, "I'm told, or we now know, that into the future, and, well, starting now, there will be need to address—"

His last few words caught in his throat—"the . . . care of her."

▪
▪ ▪

Innumerable motives lured people to the courtroom. Some spectators knew one of the families involved in the case; some had experienced sexual assault and were empathetic; many more had morbid curiosity to satisfy. Among the standard spectators were those called *buffalo* by the judges, the connoisseurs who roamed from courthouse to courthouse, Federal to Superior, attending the trials they fancied. The buffalo, most of them retired or unemployed, extracted vicarious pleasure from courtroom battles well fought and special pleasure from having insider knowledge. After a while, they became known quantities at the Michaels trial.

Regardless of what drew each to the courtroom, no participant remained neutral. Opinion among the spectators wasn't formed solely on the basis of the evidence. Gut reactions to the attorneys were often decisive in determining viewer opinions, but the single largest influence in shaping opinion was the demeanor of Kelly Michaels and her family.

Many spectators were outraged by the Michaelses' apparent levity. To them, Kelly was acting as if she were in court for a motor vehicles violation and was praying the judge wouldn't suspend her license. And though her sotto voce discussions with her lawyers appeared earnest, her public display discussions were teasing and almost flip. As they rode up and down in the elevators, the entire family acted as if they were going to a cookout.

Kelly's physical appearance, too, inspired conversation. Her shimmery pink nails and her delicate, antique-looking rings, her salmon lipstick and her thigh-gripping skirts—all seemed part of making the jurors believe that such an attractive woman wouldn't need to molest babies. But there were many who suspected the defense would have been better served if she had worn simple suits in accordance with the solemnity of the occasion.

Kelly herself seemed a little afraid of being too aggressive, of losing the helplessness appeal. When she would lean in to tell Harvey her opinion of something, her expression would be intent, but then she'd back away and soften her face into a neutral expression, her arms at her sides in an exaggerated pose of relaxation.

Kelly's family hung in orbits around her, screening her from observers, and escorting her wherever she went. The Michaelses seemed to show the jurors how little they thought of the charges, treating the proceedings with disrespect. They directed their greatest animosity toward Sara McArdle: guffaws and grunts from their seats behind her back. Glenn Goldberg, who had entered the case late, seemed to escape their notice. Glenn's own personality encouraged this civility: He didn't intrude on the Michaelses' privacy, didn't glance sharply at them during the proceedings, as Sara regularly did. His courtroom presence was understated. Quiet and unassuming, Glenn was an as yet unmeasured threat.

10

∴

The eleven women and six men of the jury were of very different backgrounds, but they shared a real camaraderie. When they were cleared out of the courtroom so that a child could be qualified or legal argument could be conducted, laughter and the wet-salt smell of popcorn emanated from behind the closed door of the jury room. As the jurors came and went, they turned the courtroom aisle into a conveyor belt for home-baked foods being scrolled into the jury room, and Judge Harth had already advised them that a fifteen-pound weight gain over the course of the trial was an odds-on number.

As the prosecutors looked at it, whatever they presented to the jury could be modeled into evidence for the defense. The children's fears of going to jail could be interpreted as their consciences nagging them for lying about Kelly. The children's agitation while testifying could indicate that they were under the gun, squirming under scrutiny while trying to remember the script of accusation the prosecutors had taught them. The children could be lying. Kelly could be lying. Or all this could be a devastating mistake, an innocuous statement by one child to a nurse relayed into dozens of suburban households phrenetically searching for "the truth." As Harvey and Bob cried: "HYSTERIA."

Perhaps the overzealous prosecutors and their misguided DYFS investigator had stuffed adult-size words into the children's mouths before the children had time to utter the words they really wanted to say: "Nothing happened." The defense could offer a vast number of tangled theories to explain away the allegations.

Taking interim pulse readings of the jury, the attorneys displayed varying degrees of confidence. Meltzer and Clark talked of acquittal, but they also hedged by making frequent mention of appeal. Bob Clark felt good enough about his case to engage in a little puffery with his opponent. Running into Sara McArdle at a local hangout bar, Clark pronounced that the defense would win this case outright or, at the very worst, hang the jury. And he tried to psych Sara out by claiming to be the "King of Hung Juries."

Despite the defense team's bravado, broadcast both in court and in the press, Glenn Goldberg, a pathological optimist, was personally confident of having the jurors' support. Sara, more of a naysayer and doomsdayer, was wary of overconfidence and continued to agonize about winning them over.

The jury, as a body, exuded good nature and ease; however, when in the jury box, they were stone-faced and arid. No tears, no sweat—no moisture.

■ ■

Alison Steadman had never been given a choice about going to court. Her parents told her straight out that she was going to, no question. Karen and her husband were in agreement that Allie had to learn that when something bad happened to her she couldn't run away and leave it for someone else to clean up. They also considered testifying to be an opportunity for Alison to face her terror and take another step away from using dissociation as an escape mechanism.

Alison's black hair had a sophisticated above-the-shoulder cut, with blunt bangs. Harvey Meltzer was handling the seven-year-old witness, while Eileen Treacy, Alison's support person, held the little girl on her lap. Both Sara and Glenn were now present in chambers, having decided to examine the children together to make speaking out in court more like a natural conversation.

Once the jury had been sent out, Harth initiated the qualifying procedure, and Alison smiled and answered him with alacrity. A big teddy bear lay comforted in her embrace. Harth asked her if calling a pencil a baseball would be the truth or a lie, and he asked her if it was good or bad to lie and to tell the truth. Allie distinguished easily between truth and falsehood and willingly promised to be truthful.

However, when asked what would happen to someone who lied, Alison couldn't come up with the word *punished*. She was asked again, "Is it good to tell the truth, or bad to tell the truth?" and she answered appropriately. But when she couldn't go on to say what would happen if you lied, Harth was forced to start over. Harth, Sara, Glenn, and even Eileen Treacy all tried to phrase the question just right so as to trigger comprehension. Harth tried the approach: "Do your parents teach you about God?" but got no helpful answer.

Kelly faced her TV screen, her left hand propping her head.

Alison was asked "What happens if you lie" close to ten times. As the adults watching her from all around the table repeated the question that Alison couldn't understand, she felt their exasperation. Her expansive smile began to fall inward, and a confused and desperate look rose from its ashes.

The judge asked if she knew what "punishment" meant, and Alison started to cry. He might as well have asked for an essay on retribution. Alison huddled under Eileen's chin, withdrawing completely from the proceedings.

Meltzer objected to this child testifying.

Clearly, Alison was stuck, but Harth apparently suspected it was nerves, or even a question of phrasing. Instead of disqualifying the witness, he called a recess.

The screens blacked out while Alison took a break. When the hearing resumed, Alison's first grade teacher was in the big leather chair with her, rocking her gently on her knee. She now had two support persons in the room, her teacher and Eileen Treacy. Alison sat there in her yellow jumper and white T-shirt, her tears erased, a willing look back on her face.

In Meltzer's next objection to the witness's competency, he claimed that this child couldn't appreciate the importance of telling the truth because she didn't understand the concept of God.

Alison had said she didn't know if she went to church, but the law did not require a belief in God for her to be allowed to testify. Harth asked Alison whether a judge would be happy or sad if someone told a lie, and Alison said the judge would be sad if someone lied in court. He asked her, "If you did something bad and the teacher punished you, I may have to punish you too. Do you understand that, Allie?" And, relieving the knotted stomachs in the courtroom, she nodded.

Alison Steadman was legally qualified to testify.

.
. .

The corridor was empty except for one bailiff at the sign-in table. Karen Steadman was leaning over the water fountain when Harvey Meltzer came up to stand beside her. She looked up, rose.

Meltzer said, "Regardless of what you think, I have a job to do. I would never want to hurt your child."

Karen was dumbfounded, but she muttered, "I understand."

He was already moving away.

.
. .

The jurors returned to the jury box, unaware of the small siege on Alison's credibility that the little girl had withstood. Until the witnesses were deemed competent, the jurors could not see them or hear them. All they knew was that the court was now ready to hear testimony.

One of the first things Glenn had Alison address was why she didn't like Kelly.

Alison explained, " 'Cause she touches the kidses' private parts," carrying into the present tense a memory that as yet wasn't securely in the past.

Sara asked, "Allie, did Kelly ever do anything with another part of her body besides her hands?"

"Her mouth," said the witness, and as she confessed that Kelly had put her mouth on her vagina, Alison's admission had physical force. Tears choked her eyes. "She licked privates with her mouth."

"When she licked your privates with her mouth, where were you?" asked Sara.

"In the classroom."

"Who else was there?"

"All the kids in my class," Alison answered.

"Was that a good feeling or a bad feeling?"

"Bad feeling." Alison sat with her shoulders shifted forward over her lap, as she waited for another question.

After a brief delay, Glenn stepped into the examination. "Did Kelly make any strange noises?"

A deep humming sound issued from Alison.

"And did Kelly ever breathe funny?"

She began to pant.

"Did the children hear Kelly making these noises?"

"Yes." Her statement escaped quietly.

Alison said that she and the children had undressed because Kelly had told them to take their clothes off.

"Kelly didn't really tell you to take your clothes off, did she?" Glenn asked.

"Uh-huh." Her face was an ice sculpture, under heat.

"No!" He poked at her with skepticism.

Alison insisted, "Yes."

"She didn't really, did she?"

"Yes"—irritated—"it's true!"

"You sure?"

"I'm sure!" she snapped, unable to smile anymore.

Glenn deliberately provoked Alison to demonstrate that she would stand by her testimony, even when faced with seeming disbelief and disapproval from an adult she might want desperately to please.

Alison further shocked the viewers in the courtroom when she testified that Kelly had forced the socket end of a light bulb into her vagina.

Glenn asked, "What did Kelly do with the light bulb?"

"Stuck it up in the front."

The court reporter looked sharply over at Kelly.

Meltzer objected. "I can't see where there is any relevance to the crimes that were allegedly perpetrated on this individual child." He cited that the indictment mentioned knives, forks, and spoons, but nothing about light bulbs, or what later, in open court, Harvey Meltzer referred to as "being shtupped with a light bulb."

Glenn spoke up. "If the relevance isn't clearly apparent, nothing we could say could make it so."

Harth allowed the testimony.

In the cross-examination, Meltzer devoted substantial energy to logistical questions, such as how many lights were on, in what rooms events occurred, if the doors were closed. He also posed numerous questions about the time frame: what time of year, what time of day, how many times altogether, how many times in a day.

Throughout his questioning, Alison stole glances at Sara and Glenn, her round eyes hesitant and searching, as if each time she was surprised and relieved to find them there.

The areas of time, quantity, and sequence were beyond the cognitive abilities of a child Alison's age, as Meltzer himself had been instructed during pretrial by Eileen Treacy's extensive testimony. Yet, in the course of these questions, Meltzer did elicit some two or three temporal inconsistencies.

"May I have a moment, Your Honor," Meltzer requested. During his pause, Alison's teacher leaned forward and distracted her student by pointing out interesting things in a coloring book.

Kelly watched them together on-screen and shook her head.

Harvey produced five plastic forks and directed Alison to select the one most closely resembling that which Kelly had used on her.

Glenn watched keenly as Meltzer began the experiment.

The array of utensils included four nearly identical, small white forks and one green fork. Alison meticulously selected a specific white fork. She was certain about her choice: She charged at that fork and brandished it in front of the court. Meltzer had the fork marked as an exhibit.

Finally, Meltzer, addressing the fact that Alison slept in her mother's bed, searched for an explanation other than trauma. He asked the child whether her own room was nice, if it was pretty, and Alison told him yes.

On redirect, Glenn asked, "Do you want to sleep in your mother's room or in your own room?"

"Mine," she said.

"When do you think you'll be able to do that?" he asked.

"Today."

"Why is that?"

And Alison answered, victoriously, "'Cause then I won't think about Kelly anymore."

.
. .

Alison's mother entered the courtroom and took her place on the stand. Karen Steadman wore a navy skirt with a wide red belt and a bright yellow print blouse. Her short brown hair spiked a bit in the bangs. She had a long jaw and her cheeks were high on her face, which always seemed capable of smiling, regardless of the situation. But when Karen started telling Sara about her daughter's medical history, she had to stop. Sara held her next question and stood aside to give Karen time to get through what she was feeling.

Moments passed, and the courtroom was still, when Harvey Meltzer stepped in and called for a recess.

Meltzer strolled over to Kelly's family.

"I shouldn't have to call for a break for her. That's not my job," he stated. "That's not my job."

Shaking their heads, the Michaelses commended him on his compassion and glared, as one, at the heartless prosecutors.

When Karen retook the stand, her aspect was glum, but her voice was alert. She seemed to have confidence in the jurors' goodwill, and she turned to address them when she spoke, opening herself.

Karen told how she had tried to tease her daughter out of wearing her pajamas to school underneath her clothes. Once she had even tried to pull the pajamas off her body, but Allie was unyielding. Karen finally understood that her daughter had been trying to add one layer too many for Kelly Michaels to strip off.

Karen cried again discussing her daughter's behavior, but she talked through the tears. Alison had developed a superhero fascination that focused on Superman and He-Man. She had made her mother cut out a cartoon picture of He-Man (a Master of the Universe) and paste it up over her bed, a protective icon.

Alison exhibited sexual behaviors as well, though many of these started the summer following disclosure, as when Alison wanted to urinate outside. Whenever she was alone, and seemingly without thinking, Alison would put toys or pencils or fingers into her vagina. With her hands around her mother's face, she would go into heavy, sexual breathing and moan: "Oh, honey." Once, she'd said to her mother, "Lick my boobies."

Karen told the court, "It seemed like someone turned her on sexually. She was just in a constant state of being sexual."

Harvey Meltzer stepped to the plate for the defense and swung through various lines of questioning, again in search of an explanation for Alison's behavior other than sexual abuse. The Steadmans were involved in a number of business ventures run out of their house, and Harvey suggested that theirs was a chaotic household.

Karen responded, "Yes and no. Even though it seems to be confusing to an outsider, it's our routine."

He followed up with: "In March 1985, is it true you were experiencing a period of financial difficulty?"

Karen grinned and said, "I'm in a constant state of financial difficulty."

He then asked, "Have you ever been prescribed medication for a nervous disorder?"

Sara and Glenn objected simultaneously and loudly, and Harth called the attorneys to the sidebar of his desk for a private conference. When the lawyers had returned to counsel table, the judge turned to the witness and asked her if she had ever taken a muscle relaxant. Karen responded that she had once had an eye twitch, and a muscle relaxant had been prescribed.

The witness glanced over at the prosecutors, a bitterly sarcastic smile on her face. The disproportion of language was amusing to the spectators, and some whispering in the gallery broke into laughter.

Because Alison still insisted on sleeping in Karen's bed, Meltzer challenged: "You see no correlation between Alison sleeping in your bed and the sexual activity she expressed?"

"No," said Karen, deadpan. She later added, "I don't think I have to say what it did to my sex life."

Cross-examination had already strewn across three draining days, and Karen was worn. She was also as cold up there on the stand as she could ever remember having been. The court reporter had lent her a sweater.

Karen confirmed for Meltzer that Alison had referred to there having been two Kellys, and he inquired, "Do you know if those were imaginary playmates?"

She answered that she had no idea.

Meltzer tried to explain it to her. "Isn't it true that the good Kelly was Kelly Michaels and the 'good and bad' Kelly was the Kelly taught to her by the psychologists and prosecutors?"

Glenn jumped up to object.

Harvey turned to the Michaels family with a snide smile and whispered, "Temper, temper."

. .

That night, Alison set out to sleep in her own bedroom, proud and excited and intent. A bit later, she propelled herself off the bed and rushed next door into her parents' room, ten feet away.

"Mom, can I stay just a few more days?"

. .

The proceedings were stalled. Waiting for the TV monitors to go on was always a nerve-racking time.

The screens flickered on and there he sat, a black six-year-old wearing an elbow-length pale blue shirt, one wrist banded by a bright red Swatch. Navy-and-white suspenders bowed from the sides of his solid torso. His mother sat outside in the courtroom holding a rejected Alvin the Chipmunk stuffed animal: He had his therapist in chambers for support. Lewis Dixon's ears were tipped forward a little to receive incoming, and he had a big smile with remarkable gaps among the front teeth. His personality beamed forth from him: He was beautiful.

The jury had left the courtroom so that transmission of the competency hearing could begin. Judge Harth noticed, "You like TV, don't you?"

as Lewis waved heartily into the video camera and rotated his smiling head from side to side.

"I love it when I'm on it," Lewis answered, not even turning away to look at the judge.

While Lewis played with a pen, first fiddling with it, then doodling on a pad, Harth asked Lewis what happened to him if he didn't tell the truth.

Lewis responded with a raucous grin. "You know how you put a bar of soap in water?"

A few people laughed.

"Pretend I'm the water," he continued, "and she puts the bar of soap in the water." And then came the rousing finish: "In my mouth!"

Lewis glanced up, then down. His grin lessened in volume and became a little sly as he pretended not to notice they were all laughing.

When the jury had been reseated in the jury box and direct examination had begun, Lewis was ambushed by Glenn's first material question: "Do you remember when you went to the Wee Care school?"

Lewis looked up into the camera full face, abruptly serious and suspicious. "Yes."

Glenn's line of questioning arrived at the subject of what Kelly had looked like when naked, and he asked Lewis to describe Kelly's vagina. Lewis told him it was sometimes white and black, and sometimes red, white, and black.

"What's the red?" asked Glenn.

"Blood."

Lewis's eyes, alarmingly white and wide, snapped over to the judge. Then he dropped his head down, and shifted his attention back to his scribbling. While he drew, he explained that Kelly had told the children to eat the blood, and they did "because she wanted them to."

Glenn asked, "Did the kids want to eat the blood?"

"NO." His eyes went to Judge Harth, wide and fast, defying him to disbelieve.

Glenn moved to another area of questioning and asked if Lewis ever saw anyone pee.

"Yes. Kelly."

The six-year-old described a game in which Kelly had peed on the floor, and then the children had passed a spoon around, each taking a sip of the pee. As he spoke, Lewis swallowed knottily and contorted his lips. This had only happened once, he said. His shame clung to him. Even as he answered, he looked down, intent on his notepad.

Only ten minutes of testimony had been taken, but Lewis was extremely agitated, so they took a break.

Kelly ventured over to the court artists to offer them some Life Savers, and she leaned over their boards to examine their work. She joked with them, then returned to her seat.

When testimony resumed, Harth waved a piece of paper before the video camera and addressed the jury. He explained that Lewis had just handed him a piece of paper which he had written on in front of all the attorneys. This paper had passed through no one else's hands.

When Lewis was asked why he'd given this note to the judge, he answered, "'Cause I wanted him to see it."

The note read: "I am going to get Kelly for hurting my friends. Kelly is a bad person."

Bob Clark objected to the paper as an exhibit. He stated that the prosecutors had helped Lewis write it.

"I know what I *saw*, Mr. Clark." Harth denied the defense objection. Meanwhile, Lewis was bashing a Nerf football (Judge Harth's) against his head, as if he were punishing or rejecting himself.

Harth excused himself to check the audio-visual transmission to the courtroom. Lewis took this opportunity to beg for a break, but Harth insisted that they all needed to do some more work. He soothed Lewis with the promise that when he came back they'd play some football.

Glenn asked Lewis, "What'd Kelly do with a spoon?"

"You have any dolls?"

Sara pushed a pile of dolls across the table. The witness took one and dangled it behind his back, then dumped it on the floor. He lifted two others and rhythmically bashed their heads together. Then Lewis took a little boy doll and pulled down its pants. He named another doll Kelly and asked, "Okay. Ready?" He then meticulously wrapped its tiny fingers around a wooden spoon and used the spoon to stroke the other doll's scrotum upward, lifting. When asked how it felt, he said it "tickled a little."

Judge Harth reentered the room.

"I'm gonna play football!" Lewis informed everyone. "Excuse me."

In a moment, he had hopped off his chair, cranked back, and let the Nerf rip through chambers. From off camera came the sound of a shattering cartoon crash, but the room sustained no serious damage. The judge returned the red, white, and blue football a few times, then joined Lewis in lamenting the fact that they had to get back to work again.

Back in business, Lewis explained that on their way to the music room, which he said contained a violin, a guitar, and a "tangerine," the children had tiptoed ''because Kelly didn't want the other teachers to know where we were going.''

As the examination continued, Lewis evolved to a horizontal position in his chair, his eyelids limp. For the nth time, he asked, ''When's this gonna be over, please? Am I gonna be here till midnight?'' The attorneys and the judge tried to cajole their antsy witness.

''Is there a soda machine around here?'' asked Lewis, flipping the football around in his hands.

Harth asked him to sit up and try to be patient; with a little more persuasion, Lewis stopped angling for a break. Having made everyone laugh seemed to satisfy him.

Sara asked him how he played duck, duck, goose.

Lewis needed to know: ''When Kelly was around?'' Then he explained that the children hadn't said duck, duck, goose: ''Kelly changed the rules.'' In her version, they'd said: ''Penis, penis, penis . . . butt.'' However, he added modestly, the children were dressed, not undressed.

Lewis said that he had had to put his finger in Kelly's butt, and he made a breaststroke motion to show how while Kelly was lying down he had spread the cheeks: ''Like, opening it, and then. . . .''

He wanted to use dolls to show everyone, and he was undressing a female doll to be Kelly when he laughed and in a shrill voice demanded, ''What's this?''

Nobody answered him.

''Is this a boy or a girl?''

When he still got no response, he repeated the question.

Glenn asked him which he thought it was, and Lewis pointed to the eyelashes and lips, which were clearly a girl's, and then pointed out, laughing, that the doll also had a penis. He smartly rejected this doll and replaced it with another one. He undressed the Kelly doll and seemed just about to put his own finger into the doll's tush, when suddenly he balked and asked for a second doll.

''Where's me?''

''Well.'' Sara hesitated. ''You have to show me which one to get.''

''A black one!''

He couldn't bring himself to use his own finger, but using a doll to represent himself, Lewis showed that he had had to insert his thumb into Kelly.

After Lewis demonstrated, Sara reached across to take back the dolls. Lewis held on to the black one and said, smiling but threatening, ''Don't even touch it.'' He propped the doll, sitting beside him.

Glenn asked Lewis if Kelly had threatened him or told him not to tell anyone. Although Lewis had graphically described numerous sexual acts, when asked about fear, he laughed, embarrassed, and said softly, "I can't talk about that one."

When Glenn persisted, Lewis continued to stall until Sara suggested that he pretend to be Kelly and say what she had told him in Kelly's voice. The witness said he thought he could do that, so he put on his best husky voice and said, "Don't tell your mother, or I'll hurt your mother and grandmother and grandfather!"

"How did she sound?" asked Glenn, and Lewis said she sounded "mad, angry, and frustrated." Clark would later cross-examine Lewis as to whether he knew what the word "frustrated" meant; Lewis couldn't define it.

Finishing up his direct examination, Glenn asked, "What's the worst thing Kelly ever did, do you think?" and Lewis described the time in the choir room when Kelly had put on a black robe and belted it.

The witness leaned his head into the microphone, conscious of his audience out there somewhere, and told everyone: "She said, 'This'll be your last day,' and we got the wrong idea. We thought it was our last day to live."

He delivered Kelly's single line in a doom-filled voice, then laughed because the children had misunderstood. But Lewis's comic attitude wasn't a mask for his fear; it was a language for it.

When Bob Clark, ready to start cross-examination, made a pitch for the witness's attention, Lewis turned to the judge and said, "Can I ask you a question?" He moved to stand next to Harth and whispered in his ear, "Is he Kelly's lawyer?"

The entire courtroom heard the question as well as the affirmative answer, because the microphone happened to be right under Lewis's mouth.

Puzzled, the child whispered, "What's he doing in here? My lawyers are in here."

Harth pointed out that there were a lot of people in the room: the lawyers, the court reporter, the judge's law clerk.

"What's a law clerk?" Lewis wanted to know.

"It's someone who has a very good job." Everybody laughed.

Lewis settled back into his chair, as much as Lewis Dixon was ever settled, and Bob Clark took the helm of the examination.

"The sooner I ask the questions and you answer, the sooner we can all go home. Is that okay?"

Lewis smiled wide and clapped his hands in a million different positions, then he looked up into the camera and leaned over to clap into the microphone in case the audience had missed the excitement.

Clark asked where Lewis took his nap, and Lewis said in his classroom. "Could you describe the room for us?"

After a brief silence, Lewis said, "When the lights are off it was blue." He paused, and his poetry sank in. "But even when the lights are on, it's blue."

Lewis lifted his pen for a takeoff. Then he began to shake his head playfully, prolonging the motion, enjoying the rhythm. Through the course of the testimony, Harth had noted the deterioration of the big little boy's demeanor. "Lewis," he now offered, "do you think you could keep going today, or are you getting tired and want to come back and see me tomorrow?"

Lewis was nodding wildly, and after all his complaining, he answered, "Keep going today."

"You'd make a wonderful assignment judge," Harth complimented.

Lewis lay back in the yellow armchair, his chin supported heavily on his chest. Suddenly, he chirped, "No. Come back tomorrow."

Everyone looked around.

"I'd rather go home and go to sleep. I'm pooped." He paused. "I'm outta here," he said. Then he just got up and walked off camera.

Back in the courtroom the judge pointed out, "Members of the jury, I am learning that all authority is relative." Court was recessed until the following day.

Loud enough to be overheard, Meltzer predicted, "Well, now they'll take him home and coach him some more."

▪
▪ ▪

Judge Harth opened the next day by encouraging Lewis Dixon to sit up and pay attention: "You look so big and strong when you sit up like that."

"I might be big, but I sure am tired," lamented the six-year-old.

Bob Clark elicited from Lewis a list of the children with whom he had tiptoed to the music room. While Clark paused to check his notes, Lewis looked over at the judge and giggled. He'd picked the judge to be on his team, and subsequently he directed a lot of his humor in Harth's direction.

While Clark cross-examined, Lewis actively licked pen marks off his hands, long, lapping motions that went on for minutes. The witness was barely attentive, but Clark remained determined as he struggled to get some answers. Within minutes, Lewis complained that he wanted a break.

Harth humored him, saying he could have a break if he wanted, but he was going to get only one, so if he took it, he wouldn't have it to use again.

"Would you do that to a little guy like me?" Lewis wheedled. He leaned back, resigned to facing more questions.

Clark commanded, "Lewis, let's make a little eye contact here so we can speed this up? You *look* at me, okay?"

Lewis's eyes flitted over toward Clark.

Lewis had been the first of several boys picked to be Kelly's "very special helpers," along with Robert and Joey. Clark wanted to know if it was fun to be her helper. Lewis watched the stenographer's paper scroll out and pounded his face with the football.

"First it was. Then it turned out not to be."

Bob moved to another topic: Lewis's statement that Kelly had made the children drink her urine out of a spoon. He asked the size and color of the spoon, when the incident had happened, how many times, and where. Then he asked if there was lot of pee on the floor, thinking of the mess.

"Umm, enough so everybody could have some" was the response.

A long silence moved through the courtroom. When it had passed, Bob inquired, "Did anybody have seconds?"

"No!" said Lewis, scandalized, looking at Clark with big, wary eyes.

"Why did you drink the pee?"

"Because she was—because she—because she told us to."

Clark challenged Lewis: "Now, if Kelly told you to jump out of the window, would you have done that?"

"I object," said Sara.

"I'll allow it."

"I obj*ect*!" Lewis repeated, folding his arms across himself.

Lewis had told investigators from the Prosecutor's Office that he had put his finger in Kelly's butt, and Clark now pressed him on this point, but Lewis would no longer cooperate, and he refused to acknowledge having said that. He insisted he didn't remember.

Clark asked, "You don't recall saying that you didn't want to get doody on your fingers?"

"I *did* get doody on my finger," Lewis surprised him.

The more literal Clark's questions became, the more damaging the testimony to the defense.

Eventually, Clark persuaded Lewis to demonstrate with a wooden spoon the things Kelly had done to him. When he was finished, Clark reached down the length of the table for the spoon, but Lewis wouldn't relinquish it. Judge Harth attempted to intervene, but Lewis refused to give it back. Finally, the little witness handed it to Glenn and insisted that everyone pass it around the table to Clark—the long way.

Lewis's therapist asked, "You're getting mad, aren't you?" The little boy nodded.

And his nose was soldered to the back of the armchair, his face averted as he answered questions.

Clark curtly told Lewis to look at him.

Lewis stayed smashed against the chair, saying, "I can hear you with my eyes closed."

Clark insisted angrily.

Lewis turned around and glared at Clark, then smiled meanly and yelled, "You satisfied? You satisfied?"

Lewis was asked why he was afraid to tell anyone that Kelly was hurting him, and he said softly, "'Cause I thought they'd be mad at me."

"Why?"

"'Cause we did bad things."

"Why do you think they'd be mad at you if you told the truth?" But this last question burned out without a response.

Lewis plopped his chin down on the table.

Judge Harth asked the child if the boys and girls at Wee Care ever talked about these things.

The witness looked up at the judge and whispered, "I don't think so," then contorted his body, his face once again mashed against the back of his chair.

Clark again began badgering Lewis to face forward.

Lewis's therapist suggested to Harth, "He may do better not looking at him."

Sara objected: "I don't know that there's a requirement that a witness look at a lawyer!"

The therapist asked the little boy, "What could we do to make this easier for you? He's got a lot of questions he's gotta get through."

Lewis said, "One thing's for sure. I don't wanna come back tomorrow."

Clark asked, "Okay. When she pooped on the floor, who cleaned that up?"

"We did."

"How'd you do that?"

Lewis asked, "What's this called?" He pointed to his mouth.

Toward the end of cross, Sara thought she was going to lose a count when Lewis began to deny allegations he had already made.

"Do you remember seeing blood?" asked Clark.

"Nope. Okay? Okay?"

Harth tried: "Did you ever see blood?"

"Yes."

"Are you getting mad now?" interrupted his therapist.

"Yes," he answered, and looked around to face the defense lawyer. "Satisfied?"

His therapist continued: "I know you're mad, but can you answer the question?"

Clark interrupted. "Your Honor, I object to, on the record—"

"Objection overruled, mister!" Lewis cut in.

Clark shot back, "Are you the judge?"

The little boy faced him off. "No, but I can still say it!"

"All right now," Harth interrupted. "The question was, did you ever see blood at Wee Care?"

"I don't think so."

Clark put it another way: "Did you ever see anything red on Kelly?"

"Yes."

"Was it blood that you saw?"

Finally Lewis admitted, "Yes."

Bob Clark chose to reask the question, and this time around Lewis reinstated the accusation.

Lewis Dixon was kept on the stand for a total of five hours, almost all of that being the battle of wills of cross-examination, and he made it through. Then Lewis went home and relapsed jarringly into his behavior problems, at the core of which, Sara was convinced, was a fury at feeling that no matter what he said at court, he was not going to be believed.

▪
▪ ▪

Harvey Meltzer was moving down the corridor, talking to a reporter. The reporter had suggested that the large number of child witnesses could potentially damage the defense's case.

"Nah," said Meltzer. "With something like eighteen children scheduled to testify, that only increases the chances of conflicting testimony. And that's the way the game is played, I guess."

The reporter laughed weakly.

Meltzer rushed away, as if on wheels. As he moved, he summed up over his shoulder, "Reasonable doubt. Reasonable doubt. That's all it is."

Margaret Kelly Michaels, age twenty-five (UPI/Bettman Newsphotos)

Family of Margaret Kelly Michaels outside St. George's Episcopal Church, site of the Wee Care Day Nursery in Maplewood, New Jersey (*The Star Ledger*)

Sara Sencer McArdle and Glenn Goldberg, assistant prosecutors (*The Star Ledger*)

Harvey Meltzer and Robert B. Clark, defense attorneys (*The Star Ledger*)

Kelly, third from left, with her father, John, her sister Leslie, and her mother, Marilyn, while on a tour of the Wee Care Day Nursery facility with the judge and jury (*The Star Ledger*)

11

.·.

The right front row of the gallery was lined, aisle to wall, with massive bodies. The entire Michaels family was in attendance this fifth week of trial. They were a family of seven: Mom, Dad, three girls, and two boys. Every one of them looked like a linebacker. Kelly was the oldest of the five children, although her sister Leslie exceeded her in height, seriousness, and seemingly in age, given Kelly's playfulness and little girl outfits.

Kelly appeared to be growing younger and more helpless, partly because she had begun to cower and allow herself to be protected by her entourage, and also because of her attire. Today, she wore a pale pink dress with little blue cornflowers and a pink cardigan. Everything on her was childlike, except her shoes: She wore brown suede pumps which clashed with the image, cluing a trendier, funkier past.

With the clan of seven amassed, their banter and laughter all but physically altered the courtroom: The atmosphere was almost tricked into that of a family reunion. The Michaelses seemed to sneer at the prosecutors more brazenly than ever, taking numerical courage to laugh off Sara McArdle's and Glenn Goldberg's mandated power.

. .

Paula Danvers had contradictory features: She was thin and refined-look-ing, but had broad shoulders and thick strong wrists and hands. When she first appeared, Paula seemed calm, but she was many miles past serenity, tight with self-sustained rage.

Her daughter had testified earlier in the day. Julie was a lovely little girl, soft and slight in a thin, loose tank top from which her limbs protruded coltishly. Everything about her was dark: dark silky hair and dark eyes in a doll's face. Up till then, the jurors had seen only six- and seven-year-olds testify. Julie was gripping—only five years old—a living example of how tiny the children had been back when they had gone to Wee Care.

Paula had divorced Julie's father when her daughter was little more than a year old, and from that time on she and Julie had been alone together. The two were exceptionally bonded, and as Paula now made her way to the stand, the protectiveness she radiated was savage.

Paula told Glenn that on the last day of school before Christmas, Julie had come home from Wee Care with a black eye, and she presented a photograph to the court as evidence. Paula choked up: ''I remember feeling so disappointed that she would have a black eye for the holidays.'' Her hand shook. She had never learned exactly how the black eye had landed there.

Meltzer pounced on this admission and, rising, objected that this tes-timony was inadmissible. The witness didn't know how her daughter got the black eye, so how was it related to this case?

Paula glared.

''Let me just make sure of something I heard,'' said the judge, rotating toward the witness stand.

Paula looked as though she wanted to interrupt.

''Did you take your daughter to the school that day?''

''Yes,'' she said tersely. She was barely seated in her chair, ready.

''Did she have—''

''No.''

''—a black eye then?'' he continued, smoothly.

''No.''

''And did you pick her up . . .''

Paula bit through his words. ''When I picked her up at the end of the day, she had a black eye.''

Kelly's eyebrows pressed upward and stayed distorted.

"Objection overruled."

Glenn offered as an exhibit Paula's photograph of Julie with the eggplant bruise. Then continuing, he asked the witness why she was a named litigant in a civil suit.

"I had so much anger that summer," she said openly. "I had a lot of anger at Kelly, anger at Arlene, and a lot of fear about the long-term effects of what would happen to Julie." Crying, she said that when the case broke the members of the board wanted to keep the school open, despite the children's disclosures. "The idea of that drove me nuts."

Kelly's family members groaned softly.

Glenn talked Paula through various entries in her diary. Paula kicked her head back, and her copper hair was wild around her face as she quoted herself: "Don't worry, baby, you'll never see Kelly again."

Twisting her head, she looked at Kelly. Her anger was pointed, personal. The Michaelses snickered, but Kelly was ruffled, her eyes rolling at the frankness of emotion.

Julie's fears had persisted, Paula said, and over and over again the little girl had asked her mother if Kelly could get out of jail. Paula had explained that Kelly was locked up in a jail and nobody was going to unlock the cell and let her out, but the little girl's fears refused to buckle under the weight of logic. Julie had insisted: "She can go through the bars."

Kelly pursed her lips, shook her head in a steady rocking motion.

Up to now, the Wee Care parents had struggled to resist provocation and remain neutral. They knew that as witnesses their best tactic was to address the content of a question and not the form. If they discredited themselves with passion, the defense could prove their mass hysteria theory. And up to now their anguish had been held private: visible, but not hostile.

With Paula Danvers on the stand, that pattern broke. Composed throughout direct, Paula overclouded as her cross-examination by Harvey Meltzer began. Every day of that year, Paula said, Julie would cling to her in the car on the way to school and beg to come home before nap time. Paula's voice roughened to describe how frantic her daughter had been.

The Michaelses were shaking their heads. Leslie snorted.

Meltzer read aloud from her diary: "You indicated in your diary that Julie told you, 'Kelly hit me like this.' And you indicated on your direct examination that your daughter hit you with her hand. Is that correct?"

"With her fist, Mr. Meltzer." She looked out at the defense attorney.

"I'm sorry. With her fist. Your daughter did not tell you that she was hit with any other instruments at that time, besides a fist. Isn't that true?"

"Not on that evening."

The witness tried to explain that Julie's disclosures had dribbled out over a period of weeks. According to her daughter, one time, when Kelly was naked, Julie had laughed. Kelly had pivoted and, according to Julie, lifted her up and thrown her across the floor. Paula said that she herself had seen a very dark bruise on Julie's back sometime during that year.

The witness began to sob.

One of Kelly's brothers wasn't moved. He murmured, "*What* an act. It's just an act."

Sara swiveled, stared.

Meltzer had a trump. He pulled forth a photograph of Julie that had been taken by Kelly at Wee Care and confronted Paula with the surprise photograph. He believed the picture proved that Julie's black eye had not, in fact, occurred while she was at Wee Care, that Paula's picture showed a child considerably younger than Julie was in the Wee Care picture.

Sara's head lifted from the Underwager transcript she was scanning. Another little boy had said that Kelly took his picture, but Sara had never thought much about it. At the time of Kelly's arrest, Sara's office hadn't had probable cause for a search warrant, so they'd never searched the apartment for photographs or anything else. Here, though, was proof that the little boy had been telling the truth. Sara caught Glenn's eye and whispered her disbelief: Meltzer was handing this to them.

Meltzer retrieved Paula's black eye photo from the evidence box and held it up for comparison. "The child represented in both those pictures appears to you to be the same age?"

"Yes."

Meltzer tried insisting, but Paula insisted back. The girl with the black eye was her daughter while at Wee Care.

Meltzer not only lost his point on Julie's age in the photographs, but he also tipped his hand to the fact that the defense had withheld evidence from the state: Kelly Michaels's pictorial memorabilia of her alleged victims. Sara had found in the psychiatric literature evidence that many sexual abusers saved photographs (both clothed and naked) of their victims. Meltzer had opened himself up to the prosecutors' demanding the rest of the pictures taken by his client.

Meltzer moved on to a new area, turning to a page in Paula's diary which he sarcastically referenced as "that touching diary entry." He said, "On July second, your daughter visits the jailhouse. Your daughter sees the less-than-plush conditions of the jailhouse in Maplewood. And your daughter asks how come Kelly is not going to get a pillow, and don't you think she should get a pillow. Isn't that basically what your daughter said?''

"My daughter is a sweet and compassionate child, yes.''

"She was presumably *ravaged* by my client''—his voice ground out the word—''hurt severely by my client, and your daughter is *concerned* about my client?''

An objection for being argumentative cut him off.

Paula seethed.

Kelly wrote in her notebook, her writing motions jagged. She rubbed her face, soothing her skin, as if she had caught the spark of Paula's fury.

Meltzer directed Paula to read another entry from her diary, and she read aloud: "Hiding in the pantry. Julie calls out, 'Come on. Come on. Find me, you *dog*.' I asked her, 'Why do you call me a dog?' She said, 'Because that's your real name.' ''

Meltzer inquired, ''She had never used this terminology with you prior to this date?''

"No, she had not.''

"Did you ever ask her why she called you this?''

Glenn rose. "I object, Judge. That question has been asked many times in reference to this diary. The answer has always been the same: The witness was told not to press the child. She always says she didn't, and I object to the repetition of this question.''

"Objection sustained.''

Meltzer slid in: "Were you ever called by anybody, prior to this date, that name?''

"Judge!'' Glenn snapped.

"Objection sustained.''

Paula went on to describe Julie's constant fear that Kelly would come steal her away to punish her for telling. Paula had knocked herself out convincing her daughter that she was truly safe, until Julie had one day reminded her mother: "She sneaked out of the room with the kids.'' Then, in what appeared to be a non sequitur, Julie had asked, "Do you still love me?''

"Yes, I still love you,'' Paula had replied. "Even though when you're mad sometimes you feel like you don't love someone, you always still do afterwards.''

Julie had then told her mother, "I love you, even though someone told me not to love my mommy.''

"Who?"

"Kelly," Julie had said. "She told us not to love our mommies. But I closed my eyes real tight"—

Paula's throat now clamped down as she repeated the words—"and I still loved you, Mommy. She told all the kids in that big, big school."

The proceedings broke for lunch, and one of Kelly's brothers hailed Meltzer over to the bar and said snidely, "Sure, a three-year-old talks in full sentences." The Michaelses repeated the line among themselves, feeding off one another's indignation: "Yeah, yeah, a three-year-old, in full sentences!"

When the session resumed, Harvey Meltzer addressed the interview conducted by Lou Fonolleras in which Julie had first disclosed sexual abuse. Incredulity contorted his voice as he asked, "Julie told you nothing from November 1984 to June 1985?"

"Correct," said Paula.

"Then she talked to Lou Fonolleras and started telling you things?"

"Correct," she agreed.

Meltzer stated, "Isn't it true Julie's behavioral changes were in order to secure more time with you, to get attention?"

The witness cocked her head to evaluate the jurors. "Since I started working when she was three months of age, I have never seen behavior like this."

Moving ahead, Meltzer inquired, "Does Julie have a good imagination?"

Glenn objected. "What does that mean?"

"Does she have an imagination?"

"We all have an imagination, Mr. Meltzer." Harth commanded the momentary attention of everyone in the room.

Paula capitulated: "She plays house. She plays with dishes and imagines there's food on them." She paused to watch Meltzer's face. "She plays Rambo with the boys. That takes imagination."

Meltzer later parried, "You said . . . that your daughter could not imagine, or you don't think your daughter could imagine herself being—"

Paula interrupted, cutting off the suggestion. "I know that my daughter could not imagine that."

Meltzer suggested, "Could your daughter be taught that it happened to her?"

Paula grabbed her head in her hands, as if racked with the obscenity of the question. She twisted her head to the side, her eyes seamed shut. Finally, she squeaked out: "No. No. She could not be *taught*."

Meltzer zoomed in to his actual point. "Were you *present* during the interviews that your daughter had with the DYFS person?"

Paula stared dully but never had to answer.

Sara objected: "Asked and answered." The question was struck down.

Kelly's face was puffy-looking. She closed her eyes and rested one hand over her mouth. Raising her head, Kelly shook it a little. Her eyes appeared unfocused.

The jurors filed out. Paula's opinion of Kelly Michaels felt like granite.

Kelly stood alone, her back to her family, and faced the paneled courtroom wall, a tissue pressed up against her nose. She didn't make a sound. Harvey and Bob approached her, then stood guarding her sides as Kelly cried quietly, facing the wall, facing into herself.

Her transformation lit like sheet lightning.

Kelly left her lawyers abruptly and went back to counsel table with angry tears heating her face. She pounded her handbag onto the table, slapped her briefcase onto the chair. She began to thrust papers and spiral notebooks into the attaché. A paperback smacked in. Her movements were small, but a little pop sounded at each thrust. She smacked pens in after the books and jammed Life Saver wrappers and tissues into her purse.

Kelly's emotions were seldom shown in public. Even in this instance, she had waited until the jury was out of the room.

Mr. Michaels noticed Paula standing with her friends. He muttered to one of his sons, "I can't stand her."

"Neither can I," the young man confessed in a decompressed rush.

. .

Lurid trials inevitably attract crazies, and the case of *State* v. *Margaret Kelly Michaels* was a consortium for misfits. One of the men who for a short while attended court was recognized by Sex Crimes personnel ("I don't believe it! He's a sex offender!") as a man who had exposed himself and masturbated in front of a four-year-old girl in a local park. He carried a stolen police walkie-talkie and a six-inch knife. Another spectator who dropped by intermittently, presumably to lend support (he waved to Meltzer), had recently been accused and then acquitted of rape in a smaller Essex County case involving preschoolers at a summer day camp.

One grim-looking woman became part of the courtroom backdrop on the first day of testimony and never left again. She was nearing forty, a slight woman barely edging over the five-foot line who sat in the left-hand front row of the gallery, the earpieces of her sunglasses stuffed back into her moussed and blow-dried reddish hair. At every courtroom break, she drew back the swinging door from open court to allow the jurors to pass. With the glasses off, she stroked her lips with an earpiece, her murky eyes shuttering spasmodically.

Startled, Glenn immediately recognized this woman as having been a potential juror during jury selection, in fact the same demure housewife who had smiled at him endearingly throughout selection. Early in the trial, he approached her in the cafeteria. She looked kempt, but her obviously expensive clothes were rugged, no longer demure.

"Hi. I noticed you're coming to court."

"Yes," she said. She was tight-featured, her face thick with young wrinkles, more like folds than cracks.

Glenn asked, "How's it going? How're we doing?"

She chop-stepped away from him, nervous. "I don't think we should be talking about the case," she said. Turning abruptly, the woman hustled out of the cafeteria.

And Glenn felt a twinge of nausea as he recognized that if he'd had his way, this mercurial woman would be upstairs right now sitting on his jury panel.

She came to be known as Juror Eighteen, an honorary title given to her as the only doctrinally mute viewer of the trial other than the seventeen jurors. Soon after, a juror was released from duty because her husband had been transferred to Hong Kong, and there were only sixteen jurors left, but the name stuck anyway: This woman remained Eighteen. She showed up every single day of trial dressed in jeans or animal skin pants, a T-shirt, and some short, efficient jacket: nothing that would impede movement. Generally a day's attire would be all of a color, the single-mindedness of an extreme personality. Statistically speaking, red, black, and white were favorites.

In the morning before the trial day began, and during breaks, Juror Eighteen would position herself at the end of the hallway, leaning against the wall or gazing out the window, chafing in her leather. She carried no notepad and sat in court each day without taking down a word or speaking to anyone. The regular spectators (press, interested attorneys from the Prosecutor's Office, the PD Office) avoided her, not extending the usual chatty probes.

Somehow, through either her looks or her military bearing, she communicated menace. She met no one's eyes, ate alone (buzz-sawing her salad with a stunningly capable plastic knife), walked alone, and showed no reaction to the proceedings other than to laugh when the children testified, as if their little speeches baffled and amused her. The judge had to admonish her for her chuckling, warning that she was to desist or the court would take the appropriate action.

Technically, the first two rows of the gallery were reserved for members of the press, and so, within several weeks, Eighteen was forced to move from her accustomed seat. She relocated herself deep in the back left-hand corner of the courtroom, one jeans-gloved leg cocked up on the bench, and her scrawny but powerful arm braced against its back, issuing a silent challenge with her physical arrogance.

▪
▪ ▪

The investigation had ended more than two years ago, but information kept dribbling in, with Sara still uncovering new things about the case. A mother whose child was in the indictment but who was not scheduled to testify told Sara of having lost her daughter one spring afternoon.

The children had been playing outside on the playground at the end of the day, their coats and bags piled up along the curb, when this mother came by to collect her daughter. She found all the waiting students squirming around on the lawn, a human jungle gym, but her own child was nowhere in sight. Though she checked inside the building, her daughter was not to be found.

Hoping she had been dropped off at home by someone else, the mother left Wee Care and hurried home: She lived just around the corner. When she got there, the house was empty. Terrified, she raced back to the school and immediately spotted her daughter out on the playground with all the other children. And the mother reasoned that she had probably been in the bathroom or exploring the slope around the side of the building.

Sara learned from this that in the spring a mother could take a child home without needing to interact with a supervising teacher because the child's possessions were already at the curb. In fact, the curbside system could almost be construed as having been designed to liberate the teacher from having to worry about packaging a child for transportation. The danger, of course, would have been that a child Kelly had spirited away to the bathroom or the gym or the choir room would be called for during her absence.

Sara added this mother to the witness list.

▪
▪ ▪

A skinny little girl bloomed into focus. She looked directly into the camera, her big dark blue eyes bordered by shoulder-length brown hair and an overhang of wide bangs. She bit her lower lip to think, baring big front teeth splayed by some serious gaps. Her shirt was candy-cane-striped, and a necklace of white plastic beads hung from her neck. Seven-year-old Nina Anderson had a sweet voice and a generous face.

Glenn asked her what Kelly did with silverware.

"Put them in kids' private parts," Nina said as she leapt up in her seat.

"Did she ever put them in your private parts?" he asked.

"A little," she said, and paused. She slid down into the chair. "Sometimes." Nina was considering, playing with the tonal qualities of her words, so that she seemed to be singing her sentences.

"Which private parts did she put them in?" Glenn asked blandly. He knew that if his voice was anything stronger than blank, he might lose her to silence.

Nina said, "Almost every."

"What did she put in your front private parts?"

"Everything." Nina smoldered a dark look in his direction from under her brow.

Glenn asked her about the pileup game, but Nina wouldn't tell him how the pileup game was conducted except that they had piled up on top of silverware. Her answers remained vague, until she asked, "Can I draw it?"

Rubbing her forehead, Nina leaned over the provided paper and, taking her time, drew the scenario. Her hair fell down over her face, but her bangs were so wide that she could still see what she was doing. She drew a pileup with four figures: three children and a larger, Kelly figure on top. The children in the picture all had grimaces or straight-line mouths, but the Kelly figure was smiling.

She drew with relish and at her leisure. The adults present were patient and waited for her. The act of drawing absorbed and soothed.

When she finally finished, Judge Harth asked, "Nina, could you do me a favor and print your name on that piece of paper?"

"Uhhm. I could do it cursive or regular," she said, looking up to take in his decision. Harth selected cursive, and Nina signed the coloring paper.

Glenn resumed the examination, asking, "Did anybody tell you not to tell your mommy?"

"Uhhm. Kelly."

"What did she say?"

"She said, 'Don't tell your mom or else I'll kill you.' "

"Did she say how she was going to kill you?"

"No. No," Nina said, resistant.

He tried, "What did she say she was going to do to you?"

Nina answered, "Throw me out the window."

"Did you do anything to make her, make somebody want to throw you out the window?"

"No."

"And was the window open or closed?"

"Closed."

"Did she say whether she would open the window before she threw you out?"

"She said, 'I will leave it closed,' " Nina said, delivering an impressively complete sentence.

During cross-examination, Nina clutched two Cabbage Patch dolls to her chest, constructing a pyramid of three heads. She sat quietly waiting for Bob Clark's questions, sucking a white mint that she exposed to the camera.

Clark asked, "Did Kelly ever put peanut butter on you?"

"No."

"Do you like peanut butter?" he pursued.

"Yeah."

"What about jelly? Do you like peanut butter and jelly?"

"Umhm."

"Good."

Clark asked her about the pileup game. "When Kelly got on top, did it hurt?"

"No."

"You didn't feel squished?" he asked, ogling skeptically.

"I felt squished," she agreed. Nina's elbows leaned into the table, and she held on to a strand of hair.

"Pardon?" he asked.

"I felt *squished*."

Nina stretched back in the yellow armchair, elongating by a few feet the distance between herself and Clark.

"Now, did you ever see Kelly do any bad things in the nap room?" he asked.

"No."

"When you first came in and you were talking to Sara and Glenn, you said that Kelly did bad things to the kids, and then you named the nap room." Clark's question was complicated for a child's mind. He appended to it: "Now did someone tell you that Kelly did something bad in the nap room?"

She pondered. "I think so."

"Was it another kid?"

"I think it was Meg or Elizabeth, I think," she said, and Sara winced.

"They told you something happened in the nap room, but you believed them?"

"Yeah." Nina went a little vague.

Clark cooed, "Did your mommy ever tell you what happened at Wee Care?"

"No," Nina said, his childlike language not lulling her. She examined and adjusted her bracelets as she listened for another question. It was "Could you describe what Kelly looked like when she was your teacher?"

Her answer was initially a little unclear. "I know one thing: Her face changed. It wasn't like . . ." She wondered, then repeated, "Her face *changed*." She spoke as if she was sharing an insight, a secret.

Clark didn't quite understand. "It changed during the school year?"

"No."

The state's position was that these children were too traumatized to face Kelly in the open courtroom. Had this little girl actually seen Kelly since the case broke? Bob Clark displayed no excitement. "What do you mean, changed? Have you seen her since then?" he asked.

"Yeah," she said. "I seen her on television and the newspaper, with her sister. I didn't know which was her. That's why I don't know who she was." She was confused because Kelly's sister looked more like Kelly had at Wee Care than Kelly herself did now.

Clark went on: "Did that frighten you, seeing her on television?"

"No."

"Would you like to see her now?" he dared.

"All right," she said in a small, capitulating voice, but her accommodating smile flattened out.

Clark backed down and dropped the challenge, and her testimony was complete.

Each child remembered different amounts of information, and each had his or her own degree of freedom to move about within those memories. Nina's testimony was at the low end of that range of freedom, so much so that she almost sounded like a child who might be making up answers as she went along. Nina's testimony was undeniably weak. When all her statements were tallied, she testified that she had forgotten duck, duck, goose, peanut butter, being hit or hitting, cat and dog game, licking. And her credibility took its most devastating hit when she told Bob Clark that she thought something bad had happened in the nap room because some other children had told her so.

In her closing arguments Sara intended to tell this to the jury: If the state were rigging the children's testimony, Nina Anderson would have been better, or else she wouldn't have appeared as a witness.

. .

Kelly stood across the waist-high wall, joking with her family. She had extracted a teacher's attendance book from the evidence pile.

Sara shuffled through documents on counsel table, then turned to Kelly's back.

"Kelly, can I have that please," she asked, her voice uninflected. Sara felt stiff: This was the first time she had ever addressed Kelly casually.

A brother grunted, "Huh?" at the unexpected, but Kelly was careful not to act startled. She turned with a bemused smile, and without hesitation handed the book to her prosecutor.

"Thank you," said Sara, and turned away.

After leaning over counsel table and looking something up, Sara turned back. "Here you go," she said, holding out the document. Kelly responded instantly, spinning around and taking it back with a tight smile. Sara left the room.

Kelly turned to her family. "That's the first thing she's ever said to me, besides"—and she gestured by unfolding her hands—"hurling insults."

. .

Joey Gardner and Lewis Dixon had been best friends at Wee Care. They shared an intensity: tragic and comic masks worn over faces of equal suffering. Lewis scintillated with comic desperation to make people laugh in a blatant effort to shield others from his pain and anger. Joey brooded: mournful, tragic.

Lewis had finished testifying, but Joey still had to make the decision whether or not to participate. Ellen didn't believe he was going to do it. Months earlier, Glenn Goldberg and Sara McArdle had met with him to prepare for court, and Joey had been a little demon, refusing to talk about Kelly, swinging his legs over the edge of his chair, gripping its arms.

Glenn had alienated the little boy by reasoning that he was just going to have to talk about it. Turning bright red, Joey had told his lawyers, "I'm not going to court! Leave me alone!" and that was good enough for Ellen.

. .

As the trial developed into a slow, certain pace, media attendance dropped off until only the two major northern New Jersey papers and one New

Jersey news program offered consistent coverage. The Michaels family continued to be in court every morning, scrunched to the far right corner of the first bench, though once again it was just Kelly's parents and her sister Leslie in attendance. Only Mr. Michaels made any attempt to assimilate into the general courtroom population of bailiffs, spectators, and reporters, barking hearty greetings and little jests at those in attendance.

When Beth Anderson took the stand, Meltzer placed an objection, claiming the defense still hadn't received the witness's diary to prepare for cross-examination. More than once, the defense had not received a mother's diary much before the morning of the day she first took the stand. Many of these books contained dozens of pages of material for review, and although cross-examination had thus far averaged about two and a half days per mother, it was burdensome to review the diaries concurrently with the examination.

Harth appreciated Meltzer's position and looked inquisitively toward the prosecutors. Sara explained that often she didn't have the diaries in her possession until the day of testimony. She also added that on occasion Mr. Meltzer had received the diaries in the mounds of discovery and then didn't realize he had them.

Meltzer suggested that the court order the state to phone each mother who had not yet testified and ascertain whether or not she had written a diary. That way, on the morning the witness arrived, the prosecutors wouldn't be in the position of "learning" about a document. They could then deliver the material to the defense team with time to spare, instead of dumping it on them the day of the author's arrival.

The judge supported this suggestion, and Sara promised to seek and secure the rest of the diaries and turn them over. As Beth Anderson had indeed turned over her own diary long ago, Meltzer withdrew his specific objection to her testimony and Sara began the direct examination.

Nina's mother was spritely looking, her sprawling glasses serving to emphasize the sharpness of her features. She was very controlled, as if control came easily.

Beth Anderson described Nina's behavior during the Wee Care school year: how she had stopped eating with forks and spoons and had taken to shoveling food into her mouth by hand, then jumping up from the table and running around the room until either her mother or father made her sit down. She had begun to masturbate so often that there wasn't really a time when she didn't, and she had had nightmares: terrible, warped images of spiders and gigantic monsters, and deep water surrounding her, so deep that she couldn't get to the bottom. In the spring,

Nina had had tiny scabs all over her body from picking at herself, pinching her skin with her nails until she bled.

Beth's voice was sharp with the incisive edge of pain. "I tell myself all the time: 'Beth, you were a jerk. Here was a kid who was showing you all these behaviors. . . .' And *I didn't see* it. I was ignoring the behaviors, denying the behaviors, hoping she would outgrow the behaviors. I was *stupid* . . . ignorant. I feel like a fool sitting here and telling you these things . . . with my educational background. It was in my own house, and I didn't *see* it." She buckled beneath the gravity of her blindness.

Kelly cocked her head. A ringlet dangled as she looked down and wrote something in her notebook.

Cross-examining, Bob Clark asked Beth, "Nina disclosed to you after speaking with Lou Fonolleras?"

"Yes," she said.

"But prior to her interview with Lou, she told you nothing about abuse?"

This line of questioning was headed toward the usual "did she disclose before she disclosed" tango, when Beth surprised Clark.

"She told me twice that Kelly hit her." Silence loomed in the courtroom like a suspended slap.

Beth and her husband had both assumed their daughter meant a little girl named Kelly who had attended Wee Care, and they told Nina she would have to learn to get along.

As Sara approached the witness stand for redirect, she blatantly evaluated the jury with her hooded eyes. Then she concentrated on Beth. All the children had been educated about touching with strangers, good touch versus bad touch, but there was a blind spot in their education. Therefore, Sara inquired, "Did you ever tell Nina, if your teacher touches you, do such and such?"

"No," answered Beth. "I never thought of such a thing."

"Did you ever tell Nina what to do if someone close to her touched her?"

"No."

That was simple enough. Sara wandered back to counsel table and poured herself a mini-cup of water.

"Mrs. Anderson, why are you involved in civil litigation against Wee Care, Arlene Spector, and Kelly Michaels?"

Beth had had two long years in which to design verbal forms to fit her shapeless anger. She answered promptly: "I have three reasons for suing civilly. The first reason is accountability. The people at that school must be held accountable for what happened to my child while she was there. . . . The second reason I'm suing is because I want it to stand as a warning for other people who work in child care. They must be vigilant.''

The rhythms of the word reverberated, every strong foot of it. *Vigilant*.

''The third reason I'm suing is for compensation. . . . My daughter needs a fund set aside for her for continued psychotherapy.''

Recrossing, Bob Clark risked asking, ''As far as the compensation reasons for suing civilly, did you make a demand for what would be reasonable compensation?''

And Beth answered absolutely predictably, ''I have no idea what reasonable compensation could possibly be.''

. .

Elizabeth Kelsey's mother, Jackie, had promised to sit close, just outside the door to the judge's office. Jackie had asked if Elizabeth wanted to take her doll in with her, but her daughter said no, she didn't want Kelly to see it. So instead, Jackie drew one of her business cards out of her wallet and gave it to Elizabeth to hold on to, a talisman.

Waiting for the proceedings to start, the little girl grilled some bailiffs on what they were going to do when, seeing Elizabeth on TV, Kelly stood up to go after her.

''She won't get up,'' they told her.

And when Elizabeth insisted, the bailiffs reassured her that ''when'' Kelly stood to go after her, they would be able to stop her.

Just to be sure, Elizabeth had three friends out in the courtroom to protect her from a rampaging Kelly: her cousin, her father, and her mother's boyfriend, each of them a large-to-huge man.

Elizabeth Kelsey, normally an animated, expressive child, appeared in testifying to be the most physically composed of any child so far, but her demeanor was too smooth, her features without vitality.

She described a pileup arrangement in which the children had lain naked in the shape of a star. Calling this ''the star pileup,'' Elizabeth depicted it by cross-hatching six pens to make a Star of David.

Harth began to describe the figure for the record: ''Making a—''

''Star.'' Elizabeth pounced, helping the judge.

''I don't understand,'' he pretended. ''Did you play the game with pens?''

''With us.''

''So all the pens are kids,'' he said.

''Yes.''

Glenn asked her, "How did you get to the choir room?"

"Snuck up."

"How?"

"We tiptoed very quietly."

"Why?"

"'Cause Kelly didn't want the other teachers to know," she said, directly corroborating Lewis Dixon's testimony. For the moment, her mother's business card lay lightly on her upturned palms.

On cross, Clark asked, "Did she threaten you when you tiptoed so you wouldn't make any noise?"

"No."

"Did you make noise?"

"No."

"Why not?" he asked.

"She said she would hurt us," she answered.

Cleverly, Clark asked, "But after the first couple of times you knew she would hurt you, right? So why didn't you make noise?"

Sara objected, concerned that this question might be too confusing, too abstract. Harth asked Elizabeth if she understood the question.

"Yes."

"Can you answer?" he inquired.

"Yes. Because we didn't want to get hurt," she said, insisting. No matter how many times Kelly had hurt her, she had kept hoping for her not to.

Elizabeth had testified that Kelly had made a birthday cake out of poops and pee: "She made us eat it." Clark asked if she was certain the cake had been made from poop.

"Yes." She gripped the card in her lap.

"Kelly gave you tissues to wipe yourselves?"

"Yes . . . we threw them in the garbage."

He then asked Elizabeth for a temporal opinion. When had the bad things started. "Before Halloween?" he suggested.

Elizabeth agreed, but Sara objected. "Which Halloween?"

Clark retorted, offended. "We're only talking about one year!"

Sara looked at him. "That's what *you* think you're talking about."

Harth recommended that he clarify his question, so Clark amended it: "That year you were at Wee Care, did the bad things start before Halloween?"

"After."

On redirect, Sara asked for corroborative detail: "What did Kelly look like with her clothes off?"

"Funny," the witness answered.

"What was funny about her?"

"Her fat stomach."

When Jackie collected her daughter to leave the courthouse, Elizabeth gave her back the business card. Two gray holes were worn almost through the fabric, holes engraved by a child's thumbs as, with stiff arms, Elizabeth had pinioned the card to her lap, focusing all her agitation into the motion of squeezing and abrading the tiny piece of paper.

■
■ ■

Jackie Kelsey had prepared an answer to one question only: When Harvey asked her if she thought her daughter could be taught to say these things, her answer was going to be "Yes, I think she could be taught. If Kelly Michaels shoved forks and knives up her vagina and butt, I think she'd learn it very well." As it happened, Meltzer never posed that question.

Jackie's nose was red, standing out from an otherwise light complexion. She wore her boyfriend's suit jacket over her dress: By some perverse law of inversion, the courtroom was too hot in the winter and too cold in the summer.

Glenn unearthed some papers from his brown accordion file and showed one of them to Jackie, a drawing made by her daughter. He asked her to describe it. It was a picture of Nina Anderson, Elizabeth's best friend from Wee Care. Jackie began to cry as she read aloud what Elizabeth had written on the drawing: "Nina, before Kelly made her take her clothes off."

Harth, noticing her distress, announced a five-minute break.

But Jackie interjected, "I'm fine."

Court remained in session, and Glenn moved on to the subject of her journal about Elizabeth. Jackie insisted it had been her own idea to start it.

Her voice was shaky, and her fingertips pressed numbly into her cheeks as she said, "I started the day after Lou Fonolleras talked to Elizabeth."

Glenn asked, "Did you want it to be used in court?"

"No."

"Why did you turn it over last week?"

Jackie sounded rueful. "I needed to use it to refresh my memory."

"And why did you let it be used in court?"

She smiled. "Because you insisted."

"Why didn't you want to?"

The transition to anger was instantaneous. "This was written for me. This was written for my *kids*. It has personal thoughts. *Feelings*." She ended abruptly.

Kelly's face was red. She dropped her pen.

Jackie explained that she had finally stopped filling in the journal: The whole process was just too painful and morbid. "I thought, I don't want to hear any more. My mind cannot absorb any more." Jackie paused, collected herself. "This is my baby we're talking about."

She was crying, furious.

Kelly massaged her eyes, fingers splayed.

Harvey Meltzer handled Jackie's cross-examination. He was taut.

Jackie had testified that Elizabeth had sung "Jingle Bells" well past Christmas and into the spring, all the time, and at inappropriate times. He asked, "Is it your opinion that your daughter associated 'Jingle Bells' with Kelly?"

Harth interrupted. "Now you're asking for an opinion." Only experts were entitled to give their opinions in court. The judge warned Meltzer that this witness was not an expert, reminded him that it was within his rights to prevent her from launching into a personal opinion.

Clark called out, "Mr. Meltzer! Could we have a moment, Your Honor?"

Bob and Harvey huddled, then Meltzer addressed the court: "I'll move right along, Your Honor."

"All right." Harth settled back into his throne.

"You indicated at some point in time your daughter started sleeping in the hallway?"

"Yes. Outside my door at the top of the stairs."

Trying to clarify this layout, Meltzer directed, "Could you draw it on the chart on the piece of paper behind you, please?" He pointed to the small bulletin board on the wall.

Jackie remained seated. "Well, it's two doors that are next to each other, and she would lie there." She described with her flattened hands.

"In between the two doors . . . ? Could I impose on you?" Meltzer asked.

"Is it really necessary?" asked Harth. "She's indicated."

"Your Honor, but the record doesn't show left-hand side, right-hand side, and in between which hands, sir."

"If you insist on it, I'll allow it, but I'd like to move this trial on. I don't know how it's going to assist the jury. But do you insist?" Harth stretched his eyes at Meltzer.

Meltzer swallowed. "Yes, sir."

"All right."

Jackie rose disdainfully and faltered over the pens.

Harth inquired, "Any special color you'd like, Mr. Meltzer?"

Meltzer played along. "What're my choices, Judge?"

"I think we have orange and black and red."

"Red sounds nice."

"All right."

Kelly tapped on her pad.

Jackie sketched in scant red lines. "This is Elizabeth's door, my door, stairs. Elizabeth would be along here."

Harth said, "You may sit down now. Thank you very much. That helps me a great deal."

"You're welcome, Your Honor," Meltzer replied.

Kelly didn't trade looks with Bob or gaze up at Harvey. The connection between Kelly and her attorneys seemed to have dissolved.

"I never would've suspected it," finished Harth.

Meltzer inquired about Elizabeth Kelsey's Grand Jury appearance, bringing up an incident that seemed to reflect the prosecutor's overzealousness: when Sara Sencer McArdle had grabbed Jackie's wailing daughter out of her arms and carried her off into the Grand Jury room.

Jackie said that Sara had later apologized for the misunderstanding, but she also offered, "She thought that it was something I wanted."

"Did you give her any indication that that's what you might want?"

Harth interrupted. "Objection. Sustained. Too peripheral."

"I hear no objection," Meltzer pointed out.

"I have no objection, Your Honor," said Sara.

Harth didn't let the moment pass but instead addressed himself, finally, to the defense's persistent objections to his own involvement in the proceedings. The judge explained to the jury, "We have long since receded from the arbitrary and artificial methods of the pure evidentiary system of litigation which regards the opposing lawyers as players and the judge as a mere umpire whose only duty is to determine where infractions of the rules of the game have been committed. It's not something that's rare. . . . The judge may, on his own initiative, within his sound discretion, interrogate a witness. . . . The court is responsible for the conduct of the trial. All parties have rights, and the fact that the defendant has rights does not mean that the alleged victims' mothers have not. Questioning should be pertinent, should be relevant, should be reasonably worthwhile in the consumption of time. Thus, the court does object from time to time."

Meltzer returned to the witness and asked circuitously, "So everything your daughter told you happened at Wee Care happened after disclosure, after she spoke to Lou Fonolleras?"

Harth struck down the question: asked and answered.

Meltzer moved in to attack the diary entry of Elizabeth's disclosure that Kelly had put a knife in her vagina. He challenged Jackie: "Elizabeth didn't cry because Kelly told her not to?"

"That's right." A field of derision undulated between lawyer and witness.

Kelly was at present the most animated that she had been yet during the trial: fidgeting, shaking her head, making an intense note.

Meltzer queried, "What is her threshhold of pain? Is it slight?"

"Objection, Your Honor!" said Sara.

"Sustained."

Meltzer pounded on. "Does she cry a lot, your daughter?"

Jackie was distant. "In regard to what?"

"When she gets hurt. When she hurts herself," he began, but soon dropped this line of questioning.

Court broke a little early for the day, at defense counsel's suggestion, and with the jury in the jury room preparing to leave Meltzer took the opportunity to place an objection to the judge's sarcasm during the drawing of the diagram. His discourse was lengthy, but he concluded with the simple complaint: "I don't believe it's appropriate for the court to respond in the manner which it did."

Glenn rose to defend the judge. "As far as sarcasm goes, for the record, I think most of the sarcasm in this trial has been directed by defense counsel to the court, and frankly I think that's overdone quite a bit."

Harth, in turn, addressed the underlying issue of contention: the dragging pace of Meltzer's cross-examination of the state's witnesses. Harth said, "I don't think witnesses must go through a trial by ordeal. There was absolutely nothing to be gained by the diagram at all. Nonetheless, counsel insisted on taking the time to draw a diagram that has added absolutely nothing to the case.

"Sometimes, at the length of questioning, I do ask myself, is the purpose to get information or to be able to use daily copy the next day: that's the thought I have had, Mr. Meltzer, very frankly. And in fifteen years almost on the bench, I have never had those thoughts before." Harth instructed lightly, "I trust you will guide yourself accordingly hereafter."

Meltzer's nose was pinched as he responded. "I am personally offended by what the court has concluded its observations are."

"Those are my thoughts."

"Well, I'm advising this court and any other court I come before: Nobody, including a judge, will tell me how to run the defense of my client's case. My client is exposed to a whole pile of stuff that I think is absolutely garbage, and I have the right to cross-examine any witness, be she child, adult, whatever, and I don't like it every time we, Mr. Clark and I, are cross-examining a witness that we are, for lack of a better expression, getting the rush from the court.''

"All right. Anything further to add to the record?" asked Harth.

Sara spoke up. "I would have an objection to any adjournment until this witness is finished." Jackie was adamant that she didn't want to return to court, and Sara had promised to do everything she could. At the very least, she felt it wasn't necessary to wind up early today simply because Mr. Meltzer thought he was at a good stopping point.

Sara continued: "I think these witnesses have been dragged back day after day after day at this time. It is also my perception the purpose of this is daily copy, whether you like it or not, Mr. Meltzer." She pierced Meltzer with her eyes.

The judge, however, accommodated the defense and dismissed the witness for the afternoon.

The following day, Meltzer explored Jackie's diary entries at great length. Elizabeth had told her that she hated their house, and she wanted to move far away where Kelly could never find her and punish her. Meltzer then asked about her daughter's sleep disturbances: "Have you ever experienced any other children having night terrors?"

Jackie answered, "I've heard people describe them. They're nowhere near the terror I see my daughter going through when she's roaming the house, screaming."

"She was asleep when she was walking through the rooms, right? You couldn't—"

Jackie interrupted. "I cannot awaken her from these things. She's asleep. She's roaming in the house and she's screaming. How many times do I have to say it?"

Meltzer was impervious. "And this happens more than once an evening?"

"Sometimes it happens many times an evening."

"Did she ever explain to you what was going on at these times when she was roaming the house?"

Tears were rolling down Jackie's face. She tried to affect a safe, uninvolved monotone, but her voice accelerated and became strident. "She wakes up fine, tired the next day, doesn't remember what was happening. I can only tell you what she says when she's roaming. She wants me. When I hold her, she pushes me away. She screams for me.

When I hold her, she pushes me away. She screams to me, 'Let me go home! Please let me go home!' ''

Meltzer exclaimed, ''To the house she hates?''

''Objection!'' said Glenn, outraged.

Harth responded with neutrality. ''Objection sustained, and that remark will be stricken from the minds of the jury. Any more questions, Mr. Meltzer?''

''Yes, sir. We're moving along.'' He turned to Jackie, fingering his gold pen nervously. ''When did the sleepwalking start?''

''Part of the night terrors is sleepwalking. She's roaming the house. I have to put the gates up on the second floor. She roams the house.''

''To the best of your recollection, did anything happen when the sleepwalking or the night terrors commenced? Did anything precipitate the sleepwalking and the night terrors?''

''Which episode?'' Jackie asked.

''The very first episode of sleepwalking.''

Jackie looked him in the eye. ''Yes. She disclosed that Kelly Michaels raped her.''

Meltzer recoiled. ''Your Honor, I'd request that that comment be stricken, because I don't believe the child used those terms.''

''Why should that be stricken?'' asked Glenn. ''He asked the question. She answered.''

Kelly leaned her right shoulder into the endeavor of writing, holding the pen so tightly her knuckles veed.

Harth judged: ''I will define for the jury at the conclusion of the trial the definitions of the various terms. You asked the question. Answer was responsive.''

''Thank you, Judge,'' said Meltzer.

12

.˙.

The prosecutors imagined that the hardest thing for the jurors to accept could well be not the fact that someone had perpetrated these crimes, but that no one had detected them. Sara and Glenn planned to request that the jurors make a trip to St. George's Episcopal Church.

The judge had long ago heard legal argument over entering into evidence a scale model of the church and school that had been provided by the state. Meltzer and Clark had contended that the precise scale of the model was misleading. The student architect who had built the model had used a scale of one half inch per foot, and the model was constructed accordingly within those proportions. However, the defense attorneys had argued that the entire scale should have been altogether smaller because the overall largeness of the model made it appear as if the building was sprawling enough to make non-detection of the abuse plausible.

Harth had missed the logic of the complaint. ''It depends what you're using the model for,'' he had said. Harth had drawn on his nautical background and suggested, "Let's take naval architecture. You feel you'd have the same scale for the *QEII* as you would for a tugboat?"

Glenn's reproach to the defense argument had been blunt: "Novel argument. 'It's too big, too clear. Let's have it on the head of a pin.' I'd put the whole *building* in evidence if I could!"

And, in a manner of speaking, this is what he and Sara now did. In a leftover swatch of courtroom time, the prosecutors proposed a visit to the building itself. Having made their motion, the prosecutors then waited, expectantly.

"Objections?" asked Harth.

Unexpectedly, the defense attorneys received the suggestion with smiles. "None whatsoever!" said Meltzer, and he informed the court that if the state hadn't requested the visit, the defense would have asked for it themselves.

The surprising concurrence exemplified the collision of attitudes: Every piece of evidence appeared to engender directly opposite interpretations. In this instance, the defense intended to prove how small St. George's really was and that it was inconceivable that such conduct could have been hidden when the three basement classrooms were extremely close together. The state stressed the vast and sprawling layout of the entire church building.

On a midweek morning in August, the jurors, the judge, the attorneys, the court reporter, the bailiffs, the Michaels family, and members of the press all journeyed to Maplewood to visit the remains of the Wee Care Day Nursery. St. George's no longer housed a school, although recently DYFS had received an application to license a new day-care center on the premises. Apparently, that application had been squashed. St. George's remained a church only, the school's back rooms now used for Sunday school sessions.

The neighborhood was serene. The physical deceived, unmarked by what had transpired within.

Kelly showed no reaction at having returned to the scene of the crime or, alternatively, to the bitter scene of the frame-up. The press corps was in full display. The field trip had conferred new interest on a trial that was becoming media-rote. The defendant and her family chatted with reporters while they waited to enter the building.

Before entering, the judge cautioned the jurors that what they were now seeing was not to be considered as evidence. This viewing had been designed solely to give them a reference point by which to visualize and understand the testimony they heard in court. With that, the trial party passed through the doorway and entered what had once been Wee Care.

The group toured the downstairs schoolrooms, Judge Harth going first as chaperone to the jurors, then the defendant and her family, and next the attorneys. Members of the press intermingled with the trial party.

Wee Care had been closed for over two years, but the placement of the classrooms and the geography of the entire complex remained the same. The art room and block room, the lower floor's pair of classrooms, were dusted with cloudy light. When Wee Care had used the building, the curtains (the same yellow gingham) had always been drawn shut, and the rooms had been gray and shadowy. As the jurors twisted from the corridor into the connected rooms, Kelly stood and watched intently as they filed past, a hopeful look on her face.

The art and block rooms were connected to each other by an accordion door. Kelly's father hung back when the jurors passed through from one room to the next. Then, with the accordion door pulled almost to the shut position, he suddenly succumbed to a coughing fit. The implicit message seemed to be that if Kelly had touched a child during nap and the child had cried out, the teacher across the divider would have heard something.

Up on the third floor, the jurors made a quick foray into what had been used as the kindergarten room. The window set into the door was high enough up so that a preschooler could have walked past on the way to the choir room and never appeared in view. At the moment, the question of visibility was moot because the window was opaque, covered with a cardboard decoration.

When the trial group reached the choir room, they found the doors girded with push-bar locks, a new feature on what had once been an easy-access door. Formerly, the room's walls had been dingy, paint peeling; now they were glossy and clean. The members of the church board had had the choir room whitewashed several weeks before this visit, and it sparkled. The jurors explored the room. It was larger than it had sounded from testimony, with an elevated ceiling and several layers of pews, clear light washing in through the remote windows.

As everyone filed out of the room, a few jurors, in passing, mindlessly tapped on the piano keys. Judge Harth heard the notes and quickly told them to refrain. The jurors had all passed from the room back into the hallway, when, fresh from the judge's admonition, Harvey Meltzer (bringing up the rear) confronted the piano and banged loudly on the keys. The noise was a commotion rather than a tune, communicating to the jurors that Kelly's playing "Jingle Bells" nude would have roused the communal dead. Harth, apparently furious, stopped the jurors in the corridor and instructed them that there were many ways to play a piano, with variations in volume, pitch, tone, etcetera. He took Meltzer aside for a private admonishment.

The group began to unwind back through the building. Curving, ducking, twisting their way through the passageways, the reporters whispered comments among themselves: "God, you could get lost in here! Look, another hiding place."

The cameramen, who hadn't been permitted to join the tour, waited outside, and when the trial party finally emerged into the contrast of a well-lighted day, representatives of the press swarmed the attorneys. Harvey Meltzer told them in a subdued voice that returning to Wee Care had been a difficult and uncomfortable challenge for his client: "It hurt to come back." Meanwhile, the Michaels family lounged on the lawn, posing for a photograph that became known as the "Lawn Party" picture: Kelly looked prepubescent, baby fat hugged by the thin material of her sundress; Mr. Michaels clenched a fat cigar between his teeth; and Kelly's mother and sister smiled, enjoying the sun.

▪
▪ ▪

Sara McArdle took Joey Gardner and another little boy who had already testified out for ice cream. Sara studied Joey as he held his cone. She thought him the most beautiful child. The two boys conferred over sweets. The other little boy didn't tell Joey anything about his courthouse experience other than to say, "They asked a lot of stupid questions." Later, Sara dropped the boys home.

Joey knew that a little kid could testify against Kelly and live through it.

▪
▪ ▪

The behavior of Juror Eighteen became progressively more overt. At lunch and recess she tailed the jurors and (fist on hip, staring them down) staked out their coffee breaks. State's witnesses were also her targets: She trailed them into bathrooms, stairwells, phone booths, elevators. She even followed them to their cars. Eighteen was willing to lunge between closing elevator doors to share the ride with the prosecutors or their witnesses. And when the elevator didn't hold human lure, she used the stairwell, racing up and down the eight flights of stairs to intercept targets on another level. Small wonder she carried no dead weight.

▪
▪ ▪

A major choke point of the defense's suggestibility theory was a five-year-old named David Kirschner. So far, the defense's examination of each parent stressed the fact that the children's disclosures followed the state's interviews, thereby implying that the allegations had been tainted. But David Kirschner had disclosed to his mother without ever having been seen by any of the investigators.

Janet Kirschner had been informed by another mother that her son had been named as a victim, so she had said to David, "The other kids are telling their mothers about the bad things that happened at school."

His eyes had dilated like saucers. Janet had held herself in and asked him, "David, what'd ya think would happen if you told me?" and he'd answered, "I thought Kelly would come in at night and take off my pants and come into my room and put sticks in my tushy." Janet had left the room and collapsed.

Over the next few days, David had disclosed the insertion of forks, knives, spoons, toys.

Janet and her husband had made the decision not to allow David to participate in the state's investigation. They agreed that maybe down the line, depending on how David was doing, they would let the prosecutor use him as a witness at trial. Until the first trial date approached, David hadn't even spoken with the prosecutor.

At first, Sara had been put off by Janet Kirschner's refusal to participate in the investigation, but at this point in time David was like a witness preserved in amber, intact and devastatingly accurate. This child was the tactical star witness of the state's case, a miniature demolition machine aimed at the defense's suggestibility theory.

His mother testified first. Janet hunched over the microphone, her broad shoulders and tall, thin frame relaxed into an armed but easy slouch. She constituted a separate and equal threat to the defense, being herself a sharp, experienced attorney. Janet's reputation preceded her, and the courtroom shivered already in anticipation of the cross-examination face-off.

Sara led with a few basic questions, then stepped back to counsel table and let the witness continue, leaving her to steer her own course. And Janet fulfilled expectations. From the moment she opened her mouth, the defense began to take a beating.

Janet first shrugged off her jacket one shoulder at a time, not rushing to talk. She leaned in and bracketed the microphone with her elbows, then began to enumerate David's pre- and post-disclosure behavior changes. Earthy and unstressed, she described David's fear of windows, his fear of being alone, his regression to baby talk and toileting accidents. She described his complaints of rectal pain which, like other mothers, she had assumed were the result of careless wiping. In all her answers, Janet was articulate, comfortable with language.

The most disturbing behavior was David's night terrors, which she described: "He only had 'em twice, but they were awful. The first time was after Christmas. We had rented a movie, and thirty seconds into it, David fell asleep. Then he woke, his eyes glazed, like from another planet, horror-movie terror, shaking uncontrollably, awake and not awake, asleep and not asleep."

At the time, she had sought some explanation of this that she would be able to accept, and she had found it in a popular child psychology text. "I looked it up and found it in Dr. Spock: 'Terrors.' I figured, 'It's in Spock, so it's something kids have.' "

She had told herself: "Kids have nightmares. You hear them crying, and you go in and say, 'Was it a nightmare?' And you hug them, and you generally live happily ever after." But Janet learned otherwise, as her peace of mind slowly decayed.

Talking it out had not been a purifying experience for her son. David's sense of danger had only heightened with his betrayal of Kelly: He awaited her promised revenge.

Janet informed the court: "After disclosure it seemed like it was one big nightmare."

Sara asked, "Did you want him to be involved?"

"No way in hell."

But David had been involved, and as his disclosures fumbled out, her first priority became to take care of her son. David told her things like Kelly had put a knife on his penis, and told him she could do magic, and said Jesus Christ was the most powerful man that ever lived and could change you into a dog if you didn't listen. Janet put him into therapy. "Taking care of myself was part of it too, and I had to get therapy." She wasn't ashamed either for thinking of herself or for seeking help.

Janet reclined with her hands behind her head. Kelly stiffened next to Clark.

Sara asked, "Why are you a named litigant in a civil suit?"

"I'm suing because I feel I have an obligation to my son to sue. The way our society is structured, the people who do injury to other people have to pay for it. And just because it's painful to me and my son doesn't mean we shouldn't do it."

Harvey Meltzer rose and walked very slowly to the witness stand. He seemed to hoist himself as a massive, cumbersome weight. Janet Kirschner was a very dangerous witness, and their interaction was paced and taut as they faced each other, lawyer to lawyer.

Meltzer asked whether, pre-disclosure, David had told her that he had been sexually violated.

"No. Not verbally," she said gently.

Did he tell his brother?

"No. Not verbally."

Did he tell his sister?

"No. Not verbally."

Meltzer's voice had lost its bombast: He sounded tired today.

Janet offered, "We had a hard time explaining that we didn't know. . . . He felt that he had told us, and yet we had let him go."

Meltzer indicated that he too had trouble understanding how, in all that time, no one had discovered the alleged abuse. He asked if, during that year, she and David had ever talked about whether children were sad at the school.

Janet attacked the innuendo: "Believe me, Mr. Meltzer, if I had any clue that anything was going on in that school, he would've been out of there that minute." Before Meltzer could rebut, she continued: "I even got through that period from May to David's disclosure in June believing my kid had walked through the raindrops—and not gotten wet.

"You have to understand," she said, as if willing him to understand, "these were individual behaviors." She gestured toward the chart of her son's behavior changes from the start of the Wee Care school year through the present. "If you had shown me this chart in January 1985, Mr. Meltzer, and said, 'Janet, do you realize all these things are going on with your kid?' I would've said, 'Holy—' something I couldn't say in court."

A shoulder dipped so that her fist could support her head. Angled, she watched Harvey, all readiness.

Kelly watched vacantly.

Janet willingly discussed her son's behaviors. Sure, David was doing weird things. For instance, he wasn't eating his lunch. "But I didn't know to make the connection that he had doody all over his lunch table instead of his lunch."

She tapped her paper cup on the judge's desk to get his attention, then stood and poured herself some water from his pitcher.

The witness described one night when David had been particularly scared. She talked holding her cup of water.

Meltzer asked, "Did he wake crying that night?"

"Right, right," she replied, then added, "and he did it before that too, Mr. Meltzer. Every night."

Meltzer jerked toward the judge. "May we have that stricken, Your Honor. That last remark is not responsive."

"No," said Harth. "I feel it is responsive. It gives a complete picture."

"If I wanted a complete picture, I would have asked if it occurred," Meltzer responded into iced silence.

Harth retorted, aghast, "Well, *I* want a complete picture, Mr. Meltzer, and it will remain."

"Absolutely, Judge," said Meltzer.

Harth scowled, "And I'm sure the jury wants a complete picture."

Meltzer turned back. "They will *get* a complete picture, Your Honor," he promised curtly. He spun and walked back to Kelly's family while jiggling his big gold watch until, loosened, it spiraled down his wrist.

.
. .

Most mornings, the jurors waited nearly an hour for the beginning of the taking of testimony. They were exceedingly patient, even on days when they spent more time on breaks than in listening to witnesses. But they themselves were scrupulous about being prompt, appreciating the fact that if one member of the jury was late, over twenty other people would be unable to accomplish anything.

A juror was late.

David Kirschner waited for the parties to assemble. During the delay, the judge played football with him in chambers to distract and relax him. Half an hour later, the missing juror arrived.

David planted his elbows on the table, angling his hands forward to frame his eyes, like blinders. His curly brown hair was slicked down and parted on the side, the dark of it offset by the pale blue of his rugby shirt. His mouth was tiny and unhappy, even smaller in contrast to his big ears and large, intelligent eyes. Janet Kirschner sat beside her son as his support, but he kept within himself and didn't exchange glances with her, sulking politely.

David crisscrossed his forefingers inside his mouth and nervously poked out the opposite cheeks while Sara began the slow process of drawing out fragmentary testimony. She asked him if he had ever liked Kelly. He removed his fingers and responded, "Yeah," then qualified, before "she did bad stuff."

"What did Kelly do the bad stuff with," Sara asked, and he answered lingeringly: "Uh, forksh, knives, shpoons . . . uh, Legos." He sounded as though he were talking around something, as though he had marbles in his mouth.

The prosecutor handed him a doll so he could demonstrate.

"Can I take the pants off?" asked David.

"Yes," Sara said, and mindful of the listening jurors, she added, "if that's what you need to do to show us."

Taking off only the doll's pants, the boy meticulously inserted an assortment of objects into its rectum.

Sitting there, dwarfed by the boardroom table and his own knowledgeable eyes, David told Sara that the children had played a game of pretending to be animals. With their clothes off, they had crawled around licking one another.

Meltzer objected, claiming that the charges listed in the indictment didn't make any mention of David Kirschner and licking.

Sara agreed that this particular testimony did not address a specific count, but it was not intended to do so. This testimony was offered to characterize the overall criminal nature of the transaction at Wee Care.

Janet interrupted because her son was confused about the meaning of "objection." "Judge, David just asked me what that meant. Could you explain it to him?"

"Certainly," answered Harth. He addressed the boy, who sat practically inert: "You see, David, when the attorneys have a question or disagree about whether a question is a good question or not a good question, then I sort of act like an umpire at a baseball game."

Harth overruled the objection, agreeing that although Miss Michaels wasn't charged with a specific count of licking involving David, the testimony would address the overall tenor of events at the school.

Glenn picked up the thread and prompted David to go on with his explanation of the licking game. Selecting a male doll and struggling to get the pants off, David took the eventually naked doll and lifted it to his mouth. A pulse of time was filled with dread of what he surely was about to do. Holding the doll with the penis in front of his mouth, David lapped up the inch of air that separated the penis and his mouth. Then he flopped the doll over and, grasping a leg in each hand, parted them and ran his tongue a swipe above the buttocks. Finally, his eyes downcast, he mock-licked the doll's navel.

Delicately placing the doll back on the table, David spread his right thumb and forefinger inside his own mouth and, staring emptily, distended his lips.

Glenn asked, "Did Kelly ever take your picture at Wee Care?"

Sara glanced sharply at Harvey Meltzer.

"Yes."

Glenn asked, "Did Kelly ever touch your penis with anything?"

"Yes," he confessed.

"With what?"

"With peanut butter." David elaborated dully: "She took a knife, and she put it in the peanut butter. Then she spread it on your penish."

"How'd the peanut butter come off afterwards?"

"She licked it off."

Without warning David was traded into another pair of hands.

Carrying over the subject of peanut butter, Meltzer asked the witness where Kelly had put the peanut butter on the girls.

David rubbed his arms along the lengths of the chair arms. "Vaginas," he said thoughtfully. "They didn't have penises." Everyone smiled, appreciative of his gravity.

"Did you tell your mommy that you got hit? . . . Why not?" Meltzer asked.

"I was scared."

"Why were you scared?"

David didn't answer.

Judge Harth helped. "Were you scared of somebody, David?"

"Yeah," he said, and when asked who, the answer surprised: David pointed at his mother. Shame collared him more tightly even than fear.

David's left fingers toyed with his eye, stroking all around it, flickering. He gazed through them out into space.

"Why were you frightened to tell your mother?" Meltzer asked, inviting confidence.

"'Cause I was younger, and I thought she might've spanked me," he said. Now both sets of fingers feathered around the eyes, and his timid voice sounded a little angry.

"And did she spank you?"

David stalled for a second, then he squeaked out, "After I told her, she didn't spank me."

He was drained. David reached listlessly for a cup of water on the table. Stiffly lifting the little paper cup, he dropped it slidingly into his lap. He looked down, unreacting, then smacked the side of his head hard and, erasing it, shrugged, and hunched limply with his forehead on his fists.

Harth, without remark, broke court for a ten-minute recess.

After the break, Meltzer resumed his cross-examination. David's hands were again pulling out the sides of his mouth. The judge asked David to please hold the football for him so the judge's own hands could be free to write, and in this way Harth successfully lured David's fingers away from his face. David took the hand-off and started rolling the football under his palm against the table.

Viewing the little witness who was stolidly ignoring him, Meltzer noticed a variety of scratches across David's fingers and elbows. Pointing out each one in turn, he asked, "Did that hurt?" then, "Did you tell Mommy?" David answered each time that he had told his mother about the cut.

Meltzer seemed satisfied and paused to review his notes, but cross-examination alone had been going on for over an hour and a quarter. Harth prodded Meltzer: "Why don't we get to it."

"We're trying real hard, Your Honor."

"Let's try harder."

David started to gnaw at a piece of chocolate his mother had just handed him. For a few seconds, he was bemused by the rhythm of eating.

Meltzer asked, "Did Kelly ever tell you no matter where you were she could see you?"

"Yes." David discarded the food.

"And you believed her?"

"Yes."

"Do you believe her now?"

He looked gravely at the lawyer. "No."

"But you believed her because you were just three years old?"

"Yeah," David said, rolling the football across his forehead like a rolling pin.

"You said Kelly put Legos by your tushy."

David corrected: "*In* your tushy," then stretched out a large, squint-eyed yawn.

In phrasing her questions on direct, Sara had used the word *unusual* several times, as in "Did Kelly do anything unusual with peanut butter?" Meltzer asked David if he knew what the word *unusual* meant.

"I forget."

Meltzer asked him where he had first heard the word.

"I don't know," David said. His hand was stuffed down the neck opening of his shirt.

Judge Harth intercepted. "If a pitcher pitched a football at a baseball game, would that be usual or unusual?"

"Unusual," said David.

Meltzer flapped through his legal pad, then framed his last question. "How'd it make you feel when Kelly took the peanut butter off?"

David, in hiding behind the football, answered, "Weird . . . and bad."

As the session concluded, David mechanically spun the football on the table.

. .

Sara had promised Joey Gardner that she'd give him two weeks' notice before he would be needed to appear. When she did, he surprised his mother by saying he was thinking about it.

Ellen asked, "I thought you weren't gonna talk about it?"

"Well, it's true. But it's two whole weeks away," Joey said, then he changed the subject.

A few days later he came up to her and asked, "What am I gonna wear?" And that was how Ellen found out that her son was going to court.

Joey slept fitfully, digging his nails into his arms and pounding his pillow violently. And he questioned his mother about protection.

"Will Kelly be in handcuffs? In a circle of cops?"

Ellen promised she would be. Then Joey decided that he didn't want his father to come into the judge's office, just his mother. He thought it would be a good idea if his father stayed out in the courtroom to keep an eye on Kelly. Ellen silently thanked God that Joey had new figures of power in his life.

Before Joey gave the final word that he would testify, he extracted one more promise from his parents: After he came back from court, they were never to talk about any of it again.

Sara visited Joey at his home to prepare him for court. Joey was torn because he knew that his answers could get Kelly, his "best friend," in big trouble and maybe send her to jail forever. Little of him remained uncorrupted by Kelly's touch. The two had shared both the intimacy of love and the intimacy of hatred.

Sara McArdle let Joey know that he had the power to keep Kelly from hurting other little children. He wanted to do it, but Joey was mortified, furious that he had to talk about the abuse. As Sara questioned him about what had happened to him at Wee Care, Joey kicked, bit, clawed, spit at her—intermittently kissing and hugging her—screamed, punched, and pulled her hair. Joey Gardner was unparalleled in how hard he was fighting, in how fast he held on to both hate and love.

▪
▪ ▪

Kevin Brennan presented a slight figure suited up in black tie and a baby blue suit laced with white pinstripes. His tight blond crew cut didn't go with his timidity.

Sara asked her first question: "Kevin, who spiked your hair this morning?"

"Mom." He didn't smile. His arms were folded politely on the table, his eyes intent on Sara.

Sara proceeded tenderly. "Did Kelly do something unusual with peanut butter?" she asked, her voice friendly.

He sat still and thought. "She put it on my penis . . . and on my heinie." He gazed at Sara, all the color frightened out of his eyes, eyes that were blinking with long motions.

"Did she put it on herself any place? . . . Where?" she asked.

"On her 'gina . . . and her heinie."

The judge asked, "Do you really remember that?"

"Yes," said Kevin, breaking the cord connecting his eyes to Sara.

Sara, her voice still cheery, cut in. "What did Kelly do with knives?"

Kevin didn't answer.

"What about forks? What'd she do with forks?"

"Uh, I don't wanna talk about it," he said. He shifted uncomfortably, as if he was sweating inside the suit.

"Do you remember?"

No answer.

"You wanna show us?" she suggested, patiently upbeat.

The pause extended. Kevin stared.

Harth eased himself into the breach. "Kevin, supposing you pretend this is a fork." He handed Kevin his pen. "And we have a doll here." Harth's voice left no room for fear. "Take the doll and show me what happened," he said.

Sara prompted gently, "Kevin, it's okay as long as it's the truth."

He said, "I forgot," so Sara asked him, "How do you know she did bad stuff?"

" 'Cause she did it to me," he said softly. Everything he said slipped out softly.

Harth asked, "What kind of bad stuff?"

Kelly doodled.

"Everything. I don't remember."

Sara asked, "Did you ever see Kelly do mean things to Heather?"

"Yes."

"Are you able to talk about that?"

"No." He shook his head. Kevin curled his lips in a defensive gesture. He had tiny features.

"Did you ever see Kelly do anything to Heather's private spots?" Sara asked.

"I don't wanna talk about it."

That was the end of direct-examination.

Bob Clark asked Kevin for the name of his nap teacher, but Kevin couldn't remember. Clark asked the prosecutors to stipulate for the record that Diane Costa had been Kevin's nap teacher.

"Absolutely not," Sara said. "I'll stipulate that that's where she was supposed to be."

In front of her monitor, Kelly laughed at Sara. Meltzer's own laugh was disruptive.

Kevin stared fearfully into the video camera, his father patting him gently on the back. Kevin smiled up at his dad. Then he leaned his chest up against the table and propped himself there, very still and kind of dazed.

Clark asked him: "Do you remember where you were when she put the peanut butter on your penis?"

The judge clarified: "Mr. Clark means what room."

"Bathroom," said Kevin.

"Were your clothes on or off," asked Harth. Silence gaped. "Do you remember where your pants were?" asked Harth, then waited, his face certain that a response was coming.

"Off."

Harth was making headway, however tuggingly, so he continued framing questions. "When you put your pants back on, was peanut butter still on your penis?"

"It was off," said Kevin, quietly but without hesitation.

"How did you get it off?" Harth had worded the question carefully. Kevin stared, unmoving. Judge Harth didn't give in to the clamp of Kevin's fear. He asked, "Will you whisper to me?"

Bob Clark reinserted himself into the examination. "Objection, Your Honor."

"*All* right," Harth sang. "Objection. Overruled."

"Your Honor, may I have some control over my cross-examination?"

Harth had already returned his attention to Kevin, who had stood up and now whispered in the judge's ear: "She took it off with a, uh, um, tissue."

"I object," said Clark.

"Your objection has been noted."

Kevin leaned back into the armchair, his fingers touching his forehead hesitantly.

"Can I have control over my cross-examination. Please?" Clark repeated, and asked the little boy, "Where did the peanut butter come from?"

In the absence of an answer, Harth asked, "Do you remember where Kelly got the peanut butter, Kevin?"

"No."

"Did she have it in a jar?" provided Clark.

"Yeah."

Clark questioned, "Did she use something to get it out of the jar?"

"Yeah."

"What?"

"A knife."

"How did she put the peanut butter on you?"

Another silence stretched. Harth started to phrase a question and registered the disapproving expression on Bob's face. He said chillingly, "Yes. Go ahead, Mr. Clark. I'm sorry I tried to clear it up."

His voice surly, Clark fed Kevin a final question that would turn out to make his version identical to and corroborative of David Kirschner's: "Did she use the knife to put the peanut butter on your penis?"

"Yes," said Kevin, sheepish.

"Where else did she put peanut butter?"

"On my heinie."

"And did she use her hand to put peanut butter on your heinie," Clark suggested.

"Objection," Glenn interrupted. "A hand with a knife or the hand itself?"

Clark amended: "Was it a hand or a knife or nothing?"

"A knife."

Clark paused over his notes.

"Next question," said Harth.

The pause lingered.

The tireder Kevin got, the more he looked over at his parents, his look pleading, "Take me home."

"Anything further, Mr. Clark?"

"Did you ever fall on your back at Wee Care?" Clark asked, fishing for something to explain away the bruises Kevin had come home with that year.

"No."

Clark returned to knives. "Did Kelly ever cut you with a knife?"

"Mm, no." He lightly stroked his nose with his pinkie.

"Did Kelly ever tell you she would cut you with a knife?"

"Yeah." Kevin tilted his face down onto the table, giving Sara a little smile when he found her there in his sights.

"What'd she tell you?"

"I don't remember."

Clark asked, "Did you ever see Kelly do anything to your sister?"

"Yeah," said Kevin, stunned, caught in the headlights.

The lawyer pressed: "What'd she do."

"Uh, I don't wanna talk about it."

Harth tried to phrase the question in an easier way. "Did Heather ever see Kelly do bad things to you, Kevin?"

"I don't know," he whispered.

"*All* right," said the judge. Good boy, the voice said.

▪
▪ ▪

Kevin Brennan's sister, Heather, was the most unequivocating of all the Wee Care children in her hatred of Kelly Michaels. From the beginning of that school year, Heather had been very clear that she didn't like Kelly. Her mother could never understand why.

Ann Brennan remembered going to Wee Care for a parent/teacher conference with Kelly. Kelly had seemed nervous. She'd told Ann, "Heather's really liking me." Without a word about her student's class-work, and without looking Ann in the eye, Kelly had spent the following quarter of an hour discussing her own relationship with Heather. Ann remembered Kelly's saying: "At first she was uncomfortable, but now she's really trusting me."

Following disclosure, Heather Brennan had fixated on Kelly's super-human powers. She had been convinced that Kelly could come in through walls, lift beds, pick up entire houses whole, and float through walls. Her father had tried everything to prove to Heather the existence of physical limitations—trying to pick up beds, throwing himself into walls—but his daughter's fears were unyielding.

Her mother knew Heather needed a champion. Ann Brennan told her daughter that there are good people in this world and bad people and that Sara McArdle was one of the good people. Sara was going to protect her.

The little girl, now six, sat on her mother's lap, dainty in a china-blue print dress. She was gloriously beautiful, with serious, dark blue eyes. Her dark hair was drawn back in two stubby propeller pigtails with glossy white ribbons circling them. Her face was wide open, bangs snipped high to provide maximum visibility, and a band of teeth was missing from her mouth. Heather stroked a fluffy white baby seal. Her stuffed animal was new for coming to court: new symbols, new associations.

Heather pulled at the seal's nose and said its name was Sara. Every once in a while she patted it, making sure it was still in place.

Meltzer's first questions concerned logistics: how Heather had gotten from the classroom to the "attic"; what colors the walls were; whether she'd eaten lunch before or after playing duck, duck, goose. Her first series of answers contained many "I don't knows," but Meltzer persisted, attempting to discredit her recollection with her inability to make these bridges.

Then he asked, "Who took all your teeth?" He looked at her.

Finally Heather answered, "The tooth fairy."

Meltzer asked, "Did you ever get peanut butter inside your vagina?" He drew on Ann's diary for his questions.

Heather looked wily and afraid. "No," she said.

Sara, watching, could see the tears: The child's eyes were full.

"How did you get the peanut butter off?" he asked.

"She licked it," said Heather. Heather turned and nestled into her mother.

Harth got Heather's attention. "Are you ready for a glass of water and a bit of recess?"

"Mmhm," she thrummed, touching her hair.

"I thought you might be."

Meltzer continued after the break. "What do you remember about the orange monsters?"

"I remembuh that she said, if you tell your mother, she and her friend can turn into an orange monster and they'll come and get your mommy and daddy."

"Did she tell you who her friend was?"

"No . . ."

"Were you scared of the orange monsters?"

"Yes." She looked quickly at her stuffed animal.

"Did you tell Kevin about the orange monsters?"

"Yes . . ."

"You said Kelly crossed her eyes and that made you scared."

"Yes."

"Did you ever cross your eyes to make your brother scared?"

"No . . ."

"What did Kelly put inside of you?" he interjected.

Tears pooled in her deep blue eyes. "A knife, a fork, and a spoon."

"Did she ever stick blocks inside of you?"

"No."

"Any sticks?"

"No."

"Any Legos?"

"No." Her chin lowered defensively.

On redirect, Glenn asked, "Heather, what's the worst thing Kelly did?"

"She made us eat the poo poo, and the peanut butter."

"Are you sure it was Kelly and not some other teacher?"

"Yes."

He then asked, "How do you know who did this?"

" 'Cause I saw."

Meltzer tried turnabout on recross. He asked, "What's the best thing Kelly did at school? You just told us the worst thing. What's the best?"

Heather answered, "Told me about the orange monster."

"Told you about the orange monster? That was a good thing?"

"It wasn't, but it's the best thing," she said, biting her lower lip.

"Anything further?" asked Harth.

Sara was laughing. "No, Your Honor."

Kelly, writing in her notebook and ignoring the screen, finished a thought and hoisted herself with her punctuation.

■
■ ■

In Bloomfield, a search related to child pornography turned up hundreds of seized photographs. Among the photos of children, police found a snapshot of an adult woman, naked except for stockings, lying on her stomach. On the backs of her thighs were laid a knife and a fork. The sexual imagery publicized by the Michaels trial was beginning to appear in other incidents. In Montclair, a woman was accused of using silverware to penetrate children of preschool age.

These crimes did not appear to be copycat crimes: One of the suspects told police he had picked up the sexual use of silverware from pornographic movies.

■
■ ■

The Michaelses wore all the trappings of a normal family, the large family next door where someone was sure to be home to baby-sit if you called, and where the mother would keep a key to your house just in case your children ever locked themselves out. The Michaelses were articulate, educated people, versed in national affairs and possessing, in their current crisis, a special knowledge of child sexual abuse and some of the latest books and articles regarding legal and professional procedures. They had made themselves knowledgeable in the field so as to be able to help Kelly, as well as to make some sense out of what they had been living with for over two years. Mr. Michaels made a point of recommending *The Politics of Child Abuse* to some reporters.

The sympathetic best seller *When Bad Things Happen to Good People* accompanied the family to court for several weeks and was followed by other popular books. When Kelly wasn't busy with the religious pamphlets that were frequently scattered in front of her on counsel table, she read erudite works. For a time she read an anthology of major American plays of the 1960s. Then, for several days, she carried C. S. Lewis's examination of how education develops man's sense of morality, *The Abolition of Man*.

Kelly's father, John Michaels, wore a boutonniere of unwilting cheer, bantering and teasing and joking (particularly with the female reporters) as if refusing to be the outcast. His only interest was in saving the life of his little girl, but as he was helpless in this supremely frustrating situation, he busied himself in his function as goodwill ambassador. He left the courtroom when he could no longer stand it and loitered in the hallway, conducting business out of a pay phone, smoking, or drinking coffee.

Mr. Michaels appeared to be in his own, distinct experience, separated from the women in his family by his joviality, and often sitting apart from them, behind or to the side, softly lulling himself over and over again with the head-shaking refrain: "Fantasy. Fantasy." Mr. Michaels danced around his family, providing food and drinks, and lugging the lunch cooler, but the core of the group was his wife, Marilyn.

Mrs. Michaels was the pump of self-righteous anger. She shook her head, superior, and tsk-tsked her way through the testimony. Kelly and her sister Leslie replicated their mother's behavior, although Kelly was radically less animated. Frequently, Kelly would flutter over to the spectator rows and sit on the bench with her mother and her sister, the daughters two wings bracketing their mother's body, folded in close for confidences.

．
．　．

Ann Brennan, Kevin and Heather's mother, testified to wrenchingly intimate details of her daughter's pre-disclosure life, details she obviously had difficulty verbalizing. Ann testified that after disclosing the abuse, Heather had started to masturbate showily and to excess. Whichever room she happened to be in, Heather would lie on her back, spread her legs, and spread her genitals.

Ann's voice sank. Her husband rose and left the courtroom.

"Here, it's all right," said Harth, stretching over the bench to offer a cup of water.

Collecting herself, she finished: "And she'd say, 'Smell my vagina.' "

Heather, while a year younger than Kevin, had always been much more independent, more vivacious, and she had been eager and excited to join him at school. So it was strange when, early in that year, Heather had started complaining about school and telling her mother that she didn't like Kelly.

Ann started to repeat what she had said to Heather at the time.

The witness interrupted herself: "I can't believe I said this." Ann laughed, a little frantic, then she quoted her own words: " 'Kelly's your teacher. Sometimes she's gonna do things to you you're not gonna like. But in the classroom, she's the boss.' "

When Ann Brennan was released from the witness stand, she threw a party for her children. The party had been Heather's idea: It was a Kelly-goes-to-jail party. Sara and Kevin McArdle joined the Brennan family, and they all had pizza and ice-cream cake out in the backyard. On this day, although the trial was not far along, Sara for once felt very solid about winning a conviction. For Heather, at any rate, it was over, and Kelly was going to stay in jail forever. Here was the party to prove it.

13

⠂⠂

Local TV news programs periodically covered the Michaels trial. And it seemed that Harvey Meltzer was on the air as often as the media would have him. One reporter affirmed that the defense lawyer's most endearing quality was his consistent availability for comment. Meltzer's public statements to the effect that the state had presented absolutely no physical evidence were abundant. And his comments reinforced the doubts of adults who feared that a child's mistake could ruin their lives in a moment's frayed synapse.

At first, the prosecutors had refused to appear on camera and would make no comment to reporters outside the courtroom. When Sara McArdle did grant interviews, her comments always addressed the misguided fears about the credibility of children. She told one reporter: "It would appear that in the absence of a videotape rolling in the midst of a crime, the state should shrug its shoulders and say, 'Case closed.' The defense wants you to believe that children are little immoral animals who will tell adults whatever they want to hear."

Bob Clark and Glenn Goldberg made their television appearances as well, but their statements were less frequently used than those of their colleagues. Sara McArdle and Harvey Meltzer were considered the two lead attorneys, and it was their interpretations of the testimony that were most ardently solicited. Within the courthouse, though, Glenn had his own fan club: Several women employed by the courts regarded him as the hero of the trial, and one swore she was going to send him a dozen roses when he "delivered her" a conviction.

If a station was covering the trial on a given day, there would be cameramen lurking in the corridors to spring the cameras on Kelly Michaels, her family, and her attorneys as they made their way to and from court. Kelly was shown on-screen with every broadcast, but always simply entering or leaving the courthouse: The defendant never granted an interview. Nevertheless, the permanence of publicity condemned her as accused.

Coverage in the newspapers was limited mostly to the local papers. The editors of family newspapers, morning newspapers, had to exercise discretion in the wording of articles, and they had to ask themselves the question: "Would you want to read this over coffee and a muffin?" As a result, many editors neutered all the explicit testimony. In one such article, the initial draft described testimony about "anal penetration and oral penetration." The same phrase was adjusted to read: "one type of abuse and another type of abuse."

• •
•

Six-year-old Angie McMahon bit down on a tremendous potato chip, as if to prop open her mouth. She was plump and confident, and her ash-blond hair seemed to dawdle by her face. She was lying back in the chair, tipsily verging on the horizontal, her right leg bobbing. Angie chewed with great interest, her eyes taking in the legal preparations in chambers, sliding side to side under the high crescent cut of her bangs.

Angie concentrated harder on the snacks than on the prosecutor's questions, and Judge Harth cautioned the attorneys: "We may have to be more patient with this child than we have with others." Angie's responses were shot all over the place.

Glenn asked, "What did you see Kelly do with peanut butter?"

"She, uh, put it on herself," said Angie, in long, wide words. Then, swirling her finger in her mouth, playing with potato chip mulch, she provided the next bit of information: Kelly had used both peanut butter and jelly.

Glenn asked: "Where did the jelly come from?"

Angie was breathless, little gasps between her words. "Mm, um, from her vagina."

Out in the courtroom, her grandfather groaned.

"Did you have to lick that off her?"

"Yes," she slurred.

Feet braced on the conference table, Angie reached forward for the bag of chips.

Meltzer, in cross-examination, asked Angie whether, after hurting the children at lunchtime, Kelly had followed them outside. Angie sucked salt off her finger. The attorney inquired, "Did Kelly come outside with you or stay in the back?"

"She-stayed-in-the-*back*," Angie snapped, examining the bag's insides.

"Did another teacher come in there?"

"*No*," she said sarcastically, looking deep into the chip bag, then she glanced up at him to see if he'd heard it.

Meltzer asked, "Where did she hit the children?"

"Everyplace."

"The head?"

"Yes."

"The back?"

"Yes."

"The arms?"

"Everyplace," she repeated.

"Toes?" asked Meltzer.

"No."

"No toes?" he said, incredulous.

"No toes."

"Why did Kelly hit you?"

Angie answered, "'Cause she wanted to," humming a little.

"What parts—" he began, then said, "Strike that."

Angie's head jogged forward, and she halted a potato chip midair. "What?" She pursed her mouth flipply, sassily.

Meltzer requested, "Tell me what Kelly did with the fork."

"She hit people—and their body," Angie said, keenly.

"Where?"

"Everywhere."

Angie began to toy with a box of Chiclets, and soon she was chewing raucously. By the time Meltzer had asked his final questions for the defense, Angie McMahon was saying no to everything.

"Did Kelly ever do anything to you that you didn't like?"

"Ummmm, *no*."

"Did anyone ever touch you at Wee Care?"

"Nobody touched me."

"Did Kelly ever do bad things and hurt you with a spoon . . . knife . . . fork?"

She answered no to each instrument.

Redirecting, Glenn fit in one last question. He asked, "Did you tell Mr. Meltzer today what happened at Wee Care?"

"*No*," Angie stated, winning relieved laughter from Sara and Glenn and a helpless little laugh from Harvey Meltzer.

■

■ ■

Throughout the presentation of the state's case, the appearances of child witnesses were interspersed with other witnesses, including grandparents and other relatives of the children who testified about the children's behavior during the 1984–85 school year, as well as therapists and psychologists. In their own testimony, Arlene Spector and the former teachers and aides came to theoretical blows over how the Wee Care Day Nursery had really functioned.

Arlene insisted that attendance had been taken first thing in the morning, and that the rosters specifying where each student napped had been adhered to strictly. The teachers said that the children had floated; one said during nap Kelly had occasionally opened the accordion door and offered to take the children who were misbehaving into her adjacent nap class.

While Arlene did admit that she herself had rarely intruded on a nap session, she testified that parents could and did enter the school unannounced but were discouraged from being disruptive. And she conceded that if, during the course of the day, she were to have walked into Kelly's classroom and found it empty, she wouldn't have been alarmed.

Contrary to what the prosecutors anticipated, Arlene did not admit ever having said that Kelly Michaels could have gained solitary access to the children. The prosecutors were therefore forced to question all the teachers, aides, and parents who subsequently appeared as to the lack of order at Wee Care and as to Arlene Spector's poor supervision. Mothers came forward and swore that Arlene was never around. An aide said, "Things were neglected." In the press, it appeared as if the state was vilifying Arlene Spector, but the prosecutors responded that the nature of Arlene's own testimony had made necessary this attack on her credibility.

Peg Foster, who hadn't seen Arlene since the end of the investigation, felt sorry for her, despite the fact that resentment against the school's former director generally ran high on the state's side of the case. With the public attacks made against Arlene and the personal feelings she must have, Peg believed Arlene had paid enough for having let Kelly Michaels into her school. You couldn't take the fingerprint of someone's heart.

Kelly's former co-workers didn't only talk about their former employer. They also attested to the strange behavior of the children. Children had masturbated constantly and made grabs for the teachers' breasts; several had wet their pants daily; they had stopped asking for peanut butter; almost every single one of the children had refused to nap; and Lewis Dixon, her special helper, had hung on Kelly, wrapped around her like a familiar.

Because the teachers had noticed behavioral changes in the children, the defense attorneys, for their coercion theory to work, would have to convince the jury that all the parents and all the teachers were lying. Otherwise, they would have to grant that the behaviors had not been fabricated and then rely on other stresses in the children's lives to explain away those behaviors.

Late after trial one night, Sara and Glenn were conferring with a former Wee Care teacher about her coming court appearance. Glenn was leaning in the doorway of Sara's office, bored out of his mind. For hours they had been going over and over the same things: how poorly the school had been run, how much opportunity Kelly had had. Suddenly, the teacher remembered a bizarre statement Kelly had made. In the gym one day, Kelly Michaels and she had been griping about the school when Kelly had exclaimed, "This school is run so terribly. Arlene just sits in her office upstairs. I could be molesting the kids, and nobody would ever know!"

Glenn started to laugh. This was too good to believe! He even hesitated to present it to the jury for fear of appearing to have contrived it. Who had made this statement? Joan? Brenda? Christine? No. Kelly Michaels, the only one accused of child sexual abuse.

Glenn got in touch with some other former employees to inquire whether they remembered any such dialogue. He discovered that at a later date Kelly, while talking to another co-worker, had asked, "How do they know I'm not some kind of child molester?"

The state presented this testimony to the jury, and as the prosecutors expected, the defense dubbed it an embellishment, conspicuously recalled years after the fact and on the eve of trial.

In their cross-examinations, the defense stressed all the things the aides and teachers had never noticed. No teacher had seen any abuse, nor smelled any urine, feces, or peanut butter in an unexpected context.

Well, Glenn thought, and no teacher had ever seen Kelly taking pictures of the children either, although some of them had known for a fact that she had carried a camera. So, where had she been when she took those photographs?

▪
▪ ▪

The Michaelses in one car and Meltzer in another were leaving the courthouse when they spotted a third car following them. Their pursuer drove a Datsun 300ZX, T-roof, black with red trim, and made no attempt to camouflage herself by dissolving into the porous lanes of traffic.

The three-car convoy reached the rectory at which the defense party planned to have dinner, and Mr. Michaels stepped protectively out of his car. He reached the driver's side of the Datsun, and the driver accommodated him by lowering the window.

He demanded, "Why are you following me?"

Eighteen glared at him out of her squinty, blinking eyes and assembled a retort. "Don't question what I do!"

Mr. Michaels watched, dumbfounded, as the electronic control silently seamed the window of communication shut. She had said all she wanted to say, her entire grand purpose, her statement of self.

The following morning, testimony was preempted by matters of security. The death threat phoned in at the trial's outset made the implications of Eighteen's conduct somewhat more serious. The four attorneys convened with the judge in chambers to evaluate the possible threat this woman represented.

Judge Harth sent a bailiff to escort her into chambers. She had just arrived in court, as usual a latecomer. Seeing the bailiff advance down the hallway, Eighteen moved brazenly to intercept him, eager for the confrontation.

Harth relaxed behind his desk. Eighteen sat directly opposite, clenched muscularly on the edge of her chair, leather jacket and rigid spine forming a perfect, upended hull. She refused to sheath her blood-brown sunglasses, seeming to draw strength from their plastic impenetrability, the dark talisman of her nerve.

The judge tried to establish who this woman was following and why. She freely admitted that she was following all members of the defense party. She denied following Sara McArdle.

Sara frowned at Glenn in contradiction: The woman certainly had been following her.

Harth tried to discern if she had an employer, if she had a partner, if she had an intention, if she had a mission.

Finally, he asked directly, "Do you intend any harm?"

"No," she answered. Then graciously, she added, "You don't have to worry about that."

When the woman had been dismissed, the attorneys and the judge entertained the possibility of barring her from the courthouse. Sara felt that her own physical integrity was at stake and thought that Eighteen's "mission" was to create a mistrial, in the belief that this trial was a miscarriage of justice. Glenn agreed completely. He felt Eighteen was deliberately adopting a paramilitary stance and costume, and he was adamant that the jury had the right not to have her staring at them and harassing them throughout their service on this trial. Sara and Glenn wanted the woman barred from coming to court.

Meltzer and Clark were dead set against taking such action. They wanted her here, where sheriff's officers might keep an eye on her, and not on some rooftop at the other end of a rifle sighting. Harth just wanted her to allow the trial to progress unimpeded, and his retort to speculation on her mental state was always: "Don't try to apply logic to illogic."

The status quo remained intact. It was too early.

. .
. .

Joey called Sara "Vomit," but Glenn was the one he really hated, and so the two prosecutors agreed it would be best if Glenn stayed out of judge's chambers during Joey's testimony. Bob Clark was back in chambers for the defense, so that left Glenn and Harvey to watch the version transmitted into the courtroom. Consoled by the knowledge that this was the last time he would ever have to talk about Wee Care, Joey was behaving as his mother had told him was proper in court: without physical combat.

The seven-year-old stared down at the table, his nose centimeters from its surface, and refused to make eye contact with anyone. He held his head in a deadlock, clamping the curly brown hair as if he were holding down the pin of a live grenade.

Sara questioned the little boy, her voice sweet and loving. "Did you like Wee Care?" she asked.

He peeked out from under his hands. He grimaced. "Yes and no." Joey's voice had a drag in it.

"Why wasn't Kelly nice?" she asked.

Joey breathed heavily, now mushing his hair into his face. "Because she . . . aw, shh. . . ." He jerked his head side to side, then hung it as if he'd been decapitated. "She touched me on my private parts."

Harth stepped in. "With a football like this?" he asked, holding up the Nerf.

"No. With her hands!" said Joey, impatient. He pulled out his face to mock a strained smile.

Kelly, in her private industriousness, wrote and wrote.

Sara asked, "Where did Kelly have hair?"

Joey put the heels of his hands to his eyes. "In her vagina," he said, voice dull.

"Did you ever see Kelly bleed?"

"Yeah."

"Where?"

His answer, "In her vagina," came out all slurred together.

"Did the blood get on anything?"

"Yes."

"What?"

"Me."

Sara paused, readied herself. "What part of you?" she asked, as Joey squirmed his head around and started flailing at the air with it.

He answered, "My penis," then smeared his eyes with his hands.

"Where was your penis that it got blood on it?"

Joey's face was completely covered by hair and his frantic hands. "Inside her vagina."

Sara elicited the testimony that Kelly had urinated on Joey, and she asked him, "Did she ever do anything with doody?"

Quietly, he confessed, "She pooped on me," and lifting his head, he repeated the statement, breathing wetly, as if a sodden sock had been shoved down his throat.

"Did Kelly ever have you go to the bathroom on *her*?"

Joey looked up, wounded. He seemed surprised and hurt that she was asking him these things. "Yeah. . . ."

"Did you see Kelly touch the other kids?"

"Yeah."

"What'd she do to them?"

Joey tried to speak. His mouth moved, then he looked down and considered. "I can't remember."

"Did Kelly ever hurt you?"

Joey glanced up at his lawyer. "Yeah!"

"What'd she do to hurt you?"

He lay his head sideways on the table. Then, chanting his answer metronomically, his voice swinging backward then forward, he intoned,

"She *stuck* a *knife* in me. She *stuck* a *fork* in me. She *stuck* a *spoon* in me." He kept hitting the table solidly with the edge of his hand.

Sara inquired, "Did Kelly tell you, 'Go home and tell Mom everything that happened?' "

"No . . . She said, 'If you tell, I'll turn you into a mouse.' " Joey yawned.

When Bob Clark initiated cross-examination, Joey was hanging himself off the rim of the table by his chin.

The defense lawyer said, "My first question is, would you like a break?"

"Yeah," Joey huffed, and letting go with his chin, slid down the slick, worn leather armchair to beneath the table.

Following the break, Clark asked, "What type of knife did Kelly use?"

"Metal." The witness stood up on his knees to take off his navy oxford vest with its royal blue pattern.

"What end of the knife did she put in your butt?"

Sara picked up the vest and put it right side out.

"The sharp part." Joey turned his back on Clark and coiled over the arm of the chair.

Clark asked if they had gone to the piano room after lunch. Joey twisted forward to face him. "Yeah."

"Could you show us how far the fork went in?"

Joey approximated the distance with his hands, holding the pose to let the judge estimate for the record: six inches. While Clark made notes, Joey reverberated from side to side in the chair.

Clark resumed, "What part of the fork did she stick into your butt?"

"The part, oh my gosh—" He ran out of breath.

"The part you eat with?"

"Yes . . ."

"Did she ever make you bleed?"

"Yes."

"A lot?" asked Clark.

"No."

"How did you know you were bleeding?"

Joey grimaced.

"Did you see the blood?"

"Yeah."

"Did you tell anyone?"

"No." Joey squirmed.

Clark continued: "Are you frightened of Kelly?"

Joey hunched on his knees facing up against the back of the chair. "Now? No." His body shot up out of the chair.

Referring back, Clark asked, "Kelly said she'd turn you into a mouse? Did you believe her?"

"Yeah."

He asked, "Did she show you how?"

"No."

"Why did you believe her? Had you ever seen anyone turn into a mouse before?"

"No."

"Not even in cartoons?" asked the lawyer, his voice stretching.

Joey capitulated: "In cartoons, but cartoons aren't real."

Clark asked Joey if he had ever had any fights with his buddy Lewis Dixon.

"Yeah," answered Joey, nodding with a smile.

"What'd you fight about?"

Joey was vague. "We didn't really fight about anything."

"Did you yell?"

"Yeah." Joey paused, then became sly. "We ripped apart each other."

Clark inquired, "With words?"

"With bare hands," Joey answered, with a wry smile.

A belly laugh escaped from Clark, as the tension in chambers broke momentarily.

But when Joey said that he'd seen Kelly poop on Lewis, he gyrated as if he were built on the principle of agitation. He was telling on his best friend.

Clark asked, "Are you a big boy now?"

He estimated: "Sort of."

Clark, to conclude, brought up Joey's appearance at Grand Jury in the summer of the investigation. Two years later, Clark asked his witness, "Do you remember when you were asked if you were telling the truth, you said you were telling 'lies, lies, lies'?"

"Yes. I remember that," Joey answered, with a small, private smile.

Thus, Clark ended dramatically: "No further questions."

Sara asked, "Why did you say that you would tell a lie, Joey?"

Joey fingered the football. "Because I wished they were."

. .

With the completion of Joey Gardner's testimony, the state had only two more child witnesses to go, and the jury was excused for an extra long weekend because the defendant was at home with the flu. At this time, the defense moved for a retraction of Judge Harth's order that the press conceal the identities of the children and their parents.

The attorneys convened in the empty courtroom. The dependable rhythm of the jurors' cheerful movements through the courthouse always offered some relief from the choking atmosphere of trial. With the jury box vacant, the courtroom seemed dim.

Harvey Meltzer stated that he had been remiss in playing along with the court's directive, and that to bar the press violated his client's right to a fair and public trial. He now demanded that the gag order be rescinded. Then, pointedly, he reminded the judge that the presumption of innocence was guaranteed by the Constitution.

Harth tried to understand. He said, "So you want infants to be named in media."

"I want [the press] to have the option. I can't force them."

Sara interjected, "I have a 'standing' question, Your Honor, whether Mr. Meltzer has the right to assert the rights of the press."

Glenn added his observation: "They want to use the media to investigate their case for them!"

The Wee Care parents had participated in the trial believing that the court would protect their identities, and today mothers came out in force to be present at this after-the-fact negotiation of the rules. Even Ellen Gardner (much as she hated the atmosphere of the trial) made an appearance, tense and anxious.

The prosecutors remained present for argument, but most of the motion consisted of the defense attorney and the judge arguing law with each other. Sara sat in the jury box with Karen Steadman, who had boldly moved out into the open court to get a better vantage point.

Meltzer explained his position: In the course of the trial, he had received phone calls from three individuals, all claiming to have knowledge that certain state witnesses (all of them parents of alleged victims) had lied. Apparently, the informants had read newspaper accounts of the testimony and, although the gag order prevented witnesses from being identified in the articles, had guessed the identities of the witnesses and called Meltzer to share their information. But all three informants insisted on sharing this knowledge anonymously. None of them was willing to come forward.

Meltzer speculated that if the identities of the child victims and their parents were published, other people would come forward with information exculpatory to his client.

Judge Harth now asked the defense attorney to cite those cases that related to the legal issues at hand.

"How does *Globe Paper* sound?" Meltzer suggested, naming a case in which *The Boston Globe* had been denied admission to a trial because the rape victim was under eighteen years of age. On appeal, the paper had won the right to cover the case.

Harth responded, "This court has not impeded attendance, we can agree. The front rows in the gallery have been marked off for the press without any request from the press. Court artists have been allowed to sit within the bar to sketch and to come sketch chambers and the closed-circuit TV setup."

Harth pulled a stack of sign-in sheets toward him and proceeded to read all the entries from a single trial date. On July 2, 1987, WCBS, WNYW, Fox-5, WABC-TV, WCBS radio, Channel 7, TV3, WNJR, NBC, *The Star Ledger*, CNN, TV-employed court artists, and dozens of spectators had attended the trial, and, Harth added, "Even someone from 'Solid Waste.' "

"Can we all agree this trial has been extremely open?" he asked, looking around the room for acknowledgment. "There is no such exclusion here as in *Globe*."

"Allow me to interject my thought to this process," said Meltzer. "*Globe* only disallowed press when the child testified, not the parents."

Harth responded, "Can we agree that to identify the parent is to identify the child?" He was met with silence, then a reluctant "yes," followed by more silence.

Harth released the pressure by coming to the point. He inquired, "Tell me how the interests of our public, the respect for our government, is enhanced by allowing the names of three-, four-, and five-year-olds to be released and known to their school friends? Let me ask you, how does that enhance it?"

Harth continued, "This is reality, and this is life. Now tell me how the court's reasoning, and the First Amendment, would be enhanced? . . . Tell me, Mr. Meltzer."

Meltzer countered, "Let me ask you, is it your view of your role to make rulings that will find favor with the public?"

"Mr. Meltzer, if one seeks public popularity, don't become a judge. Because there's always a loser before me. . . . Now, what specific language do you want me to refer to that says this court has no authority to direct the press not to reveal infants' identities. Direct me to the language. I have my casebook, I have my bifocals, and I'm ready to go."

Meltzer stared at his notes for some minutes.

Harvey and Bob were alone at counsel table. Sara was still in the box with Karen, and Glenn stood off in a corner of the courtroom, having stepped away from the table. Bob Clark was only a shadow there, an all-but-silent partner, shuffling papers and occasionally muttering low-frequency instructions to his colleague. He flipped to useful pages and slid papers to Harvey across the desk.

Harth, waiting for the attorney to refer him to the language, interrupted the silence: "Take as much time as you like, Mr. Meltzer."

Finally, Meltzer began to read from *Globe Paper*, leaving off, however, just as he reached legal language that contradicted his own motion. Meltzer twiddled his Cross pen behind his back while Harth corrected Meltzer's account. The judge read from where the attorney had left off. The case provided for situations in which there existed "compelling government interest" that justified restricting the press's right of access to a trial.

Harth went on to list from the same opinion those factors that a judge was to consider: "Ages, the nature of the act, therapy and the problem of possible relapses, the difficulty of childhood, the right to privacy."

Harth paused, gravely, and stared. Without glancing back down at the book, he finished, "The right to mental health."

Meltzer shouted, "What do we do then, Your Honor? Bind our hands behind our back?" Harvey stood and held his wrists joined together before him, and adjusted his neck with a twitch.

Harth pulled out the New Jersey statute that provided for the protection of the identities of juveniles, both alleged victims and defendants. Having read aloud the statute, the judge asked, "Are you maintaining that the condition of our state is that a juvenile defendant's identity is to be unwaveringly protected, but the juvenile defendant's juvenile victim's name should be published?" He drove a long look into Meltzer.

"We'd be turning things upside down," said Harth, finally releasing Meltzer by curving a comic glance across the parents in the gallery.

Harth pressed further: "Or is it your position that when an adult is accused, the protection of the alleged child victim becomes *less* than when a juvenile is accused?"

"No, sir . . ." said Meltzer. "But," he pointed out, "we're not talking about logic, reason, or legitimacy. We're talking to Constitutionality, whether [the statute] is proper or improper."

"Run that by me again?" said Harth, a curl in his voice. He directed the court reporter to read back the last remark. Harvey stood, on his feet for the full-force battle. He listened to his own words, twirling his glasses as if indifferent.

In the courtroom quiet that followed, Meltzer leveled a flat accusation: "You're impeding the range of freedom of the press!"

"That was exactly my purpose." Harth laughed, and swirled his chair.

"That's why we're here, Your Honor. *You don't have that power.* Most respectfully!"

Eventually, finally, Meltzer said lamely, "I feel a little embarrassed to be up here by myself because I would think some press would've come forward."

Harth responded, "Maybe it's because they think there's no issue."

But Meltzer claimed that some reporters had in fact called him and vowed their support, although . . . they wouldn't come forward.

Harvey Meltzer at last acknowledged that he knew of no ruling to show that the court had no authority to protect individuals' privacy in sex cases. At this impasse, Meltzer called for the creation of innovative new rulings to reflect societal developments, saying, "We must see how things change and make new rulings."

Harth hesitated. "Well, I don't know that the right of privacy is a diminishing right in our society."

"I'm very distraught that we're taking these things lightly," said Meltzer.

"No. I'm not taking them lightly. I'm taking them accurately."

Harth denied the defense motion.

▪ ▪

From the back of the courtroom behind the closed door came a scrabbling sound. Several jurors turned around to see, then faced front again. Lester, the bailiff, peered through the window in the door: to the left, then right, then vanished.

The scuttling resumed, and some squeegee sounds suctioned, like rubber on linoleum. Suddenly, a little grinning black face flew past the window. Fred Mercer's slim fingers flailed for the window rim, and as the bailiff started to lower the child, a baby voice pleaded, "I wanna! I wanna!"

After more than two years of near catatonic terror, Fred had to get a glimpse of Kelly.

Fred's actual court appearance as the last child witness opened with a shot of the tiny gymnast doing a pull-up on the back of the yellow armchair. Fred Mercer (he wasn't Freddie anymore, now that he was all of six) was a very difficult child to examine, given his pronounced immaturity. Sara and Eileen Treacy had both doubted that Fred would be able to corroborate the counts in his name. Sara predicted that Fred was either going to testify that he never went to Wee Care, or he was going to look right at Harth and order, "Take off your robe, Judge!"

Fred had only just turned three at the beginning of the Wee Care school year, and he was still a wisp: narrow hips and shoulders and thin, elongated arms and legs.

He wouldn't concentrate. He asked, "What's in there?" inclining toward the mike.

"That's a microphone," Harth answered, and touched the device. "That's a wire that goes to the VCR camera."

Fred stuffed four of his fingers into his mouth and angled his body through the axioms of armchair geometry.

Glenn wanted Fred to show him with dolls what Kelly had done, just as he'd shown him yesterday when they'd prepared for court. He asked Fred to demonstrate. The cameraman panned artfully to the corner, revealing Fred bending over to sort through a pile of dolls. Fred selected a white female doll and a black male doll and returned to the conference table. He named the first one Kelly, but he balked at calling the second one Fred. He named the little black doll after Joey and handed the two of them to the prosecutor.

Glenn held them apart at arm's length, and Fred proceeded to give direction. "Closer," he said.

Glenn inched the dolls closer, cautious not to overinterpret.

"Closer," Fred repeated.

The dolls moved in on each other.

"Closer."

They almost touched.

Fred evaluated his work. "Hold them higher, please." He waited. "Him. Down lower."

Fred stretched his skinny arm forward and, lifting the Kelly doll's arm, awkwardly patted the doll's hand on Joey's crotch.

"Now can I put 'em back?" he asked, and restacked the dolls into the corner. "Now is it time to leave?"

"Anything happen there you don't wanna talk about?" Judge Harth asked soothingly.

"Yeah."

Glenn offered, "Do you want to tell the judge what you don't want to talk about?"

"I know 'em. I just don't wanna tell 'em." Fred's eyes were lowered to the table.

Bending over the microphone, Harth said, "Even to me?"

"Yep," Fred stonewalled, and executed a headfirst vault over the side of his chair and disappeared under the table.

"Could you come up? We can't hear you," said the judge.

Glenn reminded, "This is your last chance to tell the judge what happened!"

Fred emerged and approached Harth with the intention of whispering some secret. He sat himself down on Harth's lap and nervously stroked the microphone, effecting excruciating communications with the courtroom. He angled to get closer to Harth's ear. Finally, secure in his confidence, he whispered to Harth (and directly into the nearby microphone), "She touched people in our private parts."

The witness's fatigue was cause for a break. Returning, Fred tore the veil of spontaneity off the aspect of the prosecution by asking, "Glenn, what do I have to say again?" But Meltzer didn't follow up on this statement on cross-examination.

When Meltzer initiated cross, Fred asked the judge if he could stay on his lap. He could, and he did.

Meltzer opened: "Do you know why you're here?"

Fred smiled and looked up from the table. "Testify."

He clicked a plastic box of crayons against the microphone, and a bailiff hurried into chambers with shell-shocked ears. Harth handed Fred the Nerf football to draw him away from the mike, and Fred hugged it to himself with a big smile. It rolled down his legs under the table, and Fred darted under after it.

Meltzer, sensing the end of Fred's serious participation in the examination, strung together a list of Fred's previous allegations and fired away: "Did Kelly?" "No." "Did you?" "No." "Did anyone ever?" "No." Meltzer set them up and Fred knocked them down, a complete recantation.

The defense had no further questions.

Glenn redirected one question to Fred. "Do you like talking about Kelly?"

"No," he said.

"I have no further questions."

But Harth carried on. "I don't understand. Why don't you like to talk about Kelly?"

Fred answered, "She did bad things."

"What kind of bad things?"

Fred looked over at Harth and, exasperated, pointed down the length of the table toward Harvey Meltzer. Fred retorted, "He said 'em all already."

Harth clarified, "He asked questions, and you said no to them."

"I said I don't *think* so to some of 'em," corrected Fred. He put a piece of legal paper on top of his head, standing it up vertically. It hovered for a moment, then wafted off.

.
■
■ ■

An investigator from the Prosecutor's Office was clearing the televisions to the side of the courtroom. He approached counsel table and began to remove the small TV set that sat in front of the defendant. Kelly, looking up at him, smiled.

"Well, it's the handsomest man in this whole courthouse!" she said.

Harvey Meltzer, waiting for his client, said wryly, "Thanks a lot."

■
■ ■

That night, following his appearance in court, Fred's bedtime prayers were as follows: "Thank you, Jesus, for my mommy, my daddy, and my friends. And thank you, Jesus, I had the courage to testify."

14

∴

Lou Fonolleras was the target of the defense, the alleged maestro of
dozens of children's cries of rape. Bob Clark suggested that perhaps
at one time Lou *had* been an objective evaluator, but in his opinion Lou
had been beaten down by the sheer magnitude of this case, given sixty
children to interview. Clark speculated that Lou had become predisposed
to find abuse and had validated sexual abuse wholesale.

The jury had heard extensive cross-examination of witnesses as to
when, how many times, on and before what date, and behind what closed
doors, etcetera, the children had talked to Lou Fonolleras. Although
George McGrath, Rich Mastrangelo, and, to a lesser extent, a handful
of others had conducted interviews, the defense innuendo danced around
Lou Fonolleras time after time, as the tactical linchpin of the suggestibility
argument.

When Sara McArdle announced that the state's next witness was Louis
Fonolleras, Jr., the jurors hitched themselves up and craned around to
observe his entrance, their faces averted and stiff in suspended judgment.

Lou stood well over six feet tall and walked with the studiously soft tread of a big man. He wore a deep navy suit and a pale yellow tie. By his leaden eyes, downcast as he crossed the floor, and by his rhythmic, lulling gait, everyone could see that he was concentrating. Lou knew he had a lot to answer to.

Sara McArdle set Lou up with a series of knockdown questions: "Have you ever before heard a child disclose about peanut butter?" "No." " 'Jingle Bells?' " "No." "The use of excrement?" "No." Swift, streamlined, she cranked out the answers regarding the ways in which Kelly had hurt the children. And she elicited that the Wee Care case was the first time that Lou had ever heard anybody accuse the insertion of utensils, pileups, nudity games, the use of urine, peanut butter and jelly, menstrual blood.

Meltzer listened intently: Lou Fonolleras was going to be his witness. Though he was losing his tan (autumn was fully in control), Harvey still looked dapper in a sleek, tailored suit and the ever-present pink paisley tie.

Sara ran Lou through a brief synopsis of the chronology of his involvement, then she announced, "The state has no further questions."

Lou had held the witness stand for just over ten minutes. Sara's examination hadn't even peeled back the first page of Lou's own, half-inch thick report detailing the dozens of interviews he had personally conducted. Closure was stunningly abrupt.

Meltzer rose to address the court. He asked, incredulous, "Am I to believe the state is finished with this witness?"

"You got it," Sara said, staring, as Meltzer bent down to adjust his socks.

Meltzer requested, "May we come to sidebar, Judge?"

But Sara had anticipated the problem. Arguably, cross-examination was not supposed to take up any issues that hadn't been covered on direct, and this direct had been skimpy, minimal. She understood Meltzer was concerned that his cross-examination would be cut short, so Sara stipulated, "I don't intend to object to beyond the scope." Now the jurors would know that she wasn't afraid of anything Meltzer could ask: Lou had nothing to hide.

When cross-examination started, Harvey Meltzer faltered with general questions about the witness's background, uncharacteristically gentle and patient. Lou was expecting "Isn't it true?!" types of questions, and he found this politeness from Meltzer disconcerting.

The examination was aimless, filled with frequent repetition, and a great deal of pen activity between questions. The lawyer had Lou describe the children's drawings in detail, rather than submitting them to the jurors.

Lou's voice, naturally soft and low, rasped a little: He was still uptight. The tension seemed to live in his neck, which he turned gently to ease. His fingers tapped on the stand.

Meltzer retraced some of Sara's small steps, and he elicited that Lou had seen only fifteen of the twenty children named in the consolidated indictment; he established that Lou had never even spoken with Jonathan, whose statements had led to all other statements, nor had he ever spoken with Sean.

For the first half hour of cross, Lou was petrified, but then he started to pick up Meltzer's rhythm. Lou sensed that Harvey didn't know how to handle him, other than to get him angry to show the jury how intimidating the DYFS worker might have been to a child. As the day went by, Lou eased into the rhythm of attack/absorb, and soon he had lost his initial defensiveness.

While Meltzer meandered, the jurors studied the witness as if to gauge whether this was the monster of malice and ineptitude that Meltzer and Clark had portrayed.

Lou was so soft-spoken.

Kelly stared at him, her hands in a prayerful pile, her shoulder pad askew.

Lou explained to the defense attorney that, even if a child initially denied the allegations, he couldn't simply terminate an interview: "The interview process is essentially the beginning of the healing process for them. It's a very hard decision to make."

Meltzer asked, "You perceive yourself as a healer?" with an insinuation of fanaticism.

"I didn't say that, sir." When Lou looked in Kelly's direction, he noticed her watching him, and he didn't like it.

As everyone waited for more questions from Meltzer, who seemed occupied in deep personal deliberation, Glenn Goldberg rose to point out that the record did not reflect these long stalls between questions and the extensive page turning and milling about.

Meltzer was obviously not prepared to cross-examine. It was his pattern to buy the transcripts of direct testimony and then reframe the questions that had been asked on direct. This morning, the defense had been thrown onto the stage without having had a chance to memorize its lines.

Toward the day's end, Meltzer unexpectedly provided a surprising climax. He asked the witness how many children had attended Wee Care.

Sara listened carefully, ready to object, her chair straining on its two back legs.

"Sixty," Lou answered.

Meltzer inquired how many were interviewed during the state's investigation.

"Fifty-one."

Meltzer sounded defiant when he asked, "And it was your evaluation that all fifty-one of these children had sustained sexual abuse from Kelly Michaels?" Meltzer peeled off his glasses and grinned unnervingly.

Lou held his gaze and said calmly, "Yes, sir."

Sixteen jurors imprinted one another with devastated looks.

The defense had introduced into this trial evidence that would never otherwise have come to the jury's attention. Only twenty children were named in the current indictment, therefore the state's case was restricted to evidence pertaining to those twenty. The prosecution would not have been allowed even to refer to the existence of the thirty-one other known victims, until this moment when the defense clearly opened the door to Sara and Glenn.

The defense attorneys topped off the effect by announcing that it was their intention to play for the jury the audiotapes of Lou's interviews with the children. If Sara had tried to enter the tapes into the record, the judge would certainly have prevented her because the statements were self-serving hearsay, not covered by the tender-years exception. However, the defense attorneys were certainly permitted to interpret the tapes differently if they so chose. From their perspective, the very same tapes could be used to impeach the children's credibility and prove that Lou had tainted the children's testimony with suggestive questions.

Sara believed the playing of the tapes would benefit the prosecution, but she did, however, request that the judge instruct the jury that the state could not have introduced these tapes as evidence. She didn't want the jurors to speculate that the state had tried to cover them up. Meltzer "strenuously objected," pointing out that this legal issue would be confusing to a jury of laymen.

"Judge Harth is fairly articulate. Any other reasons?" asked the judge.

"I guess I have no reasons."

All parties settled into agreement to play the tapes.

．
■ ■

Glenn was talking with Bob Clark in the hallway when Kelly came up to offer her lawyer a piece of hard candy. The Michaels family was well provided with sweets, the floor beneath their front row bench always littered with crinkly-clear wrappers.

Kelly turned to the prosecutor. "Would you care for a piece, Mr. Goldberg?" Her face was open and charming. A bumblebee was embossed on the chunk of candy.

"No thank you," Glenn said, mindful of what he knew Sara would do to him if he accepted.

Kelly coaxed, "There's honey in it."

"No. Thank you anyway." He was more than a head taller than Kelly. Amazing how helpless she tries to seem, he thought, and how off she must be to offer her prosecutor candy.

As Kelly moved away, Glenn muttered to Clark, "Sara'd kill me if she heard I took candy from Kelly."

Clark slipped him a drop from his own handful, and Glenn put it into his case file.

▪
▪ ▪

With the testimony of parents and children completed, the ruling barring future witnesses from the courtroom no longer applied, so that a handful of mothers now attended the trial daily, among them Karen Steadman, Jackie Kelsey, and Paula Danvers, while several others attended sporadically: All the regulars were the mothers of girl victims. They took over the left-hand front row of the gallery, taking notes and making suggestions to Sara and Glenn in an attempt to use some of their otherwise crippling anger. The presence of these women in the courtroom bolstered Sara, giving her a group of friends with whom to joke, gossip, make trial critiques. But whenever the jury was assembled, Sara limited her contacts to craning her head around and checking for reactions, stifling outbursts with her eyes.

Karen would watch Sara as she sat there, her elbows surrounded by papers, chewing on her pen and rocking the chair. She would grab Jackie's arm as Sara gained speed. They'd hold on to each other, waiting, dreading, trying not to laugh or call out: That chair was in such tantalizing danger of falling over.

For her part, Karen had a violent need to know every last detail of what had happened to her daughter, to be there, every day, listening to what everyone else remembered. In one of her fantasies, Kelly decided to tell all, and Karen sat her down and learned, from Kelly's own mouth, everything she had ever done to Alison. Karen's need had nothing to do with her daughter's virginity. She craved control over the situation, and something in her sensed that if she could know every detail, every article of clothing, every day, every place, how many times and with which children and how and in what room, and what Alison had been thinking—then what?

Karen didn't really know.

■
■   ■

The entrance of Juror Eighteen was emphasized by her tardiness and enlivened by her appearance: the clanking chains on her boots, the Day-Glo glare of her red bodysuit. Before she had even cracked the courtroom door on Lou's continuing testimony, the metal detector was shrieking a warning out in the hallway. Eighteen settled in to observe the witness, hollowly sucking the rim of her glasses like a fish.

As the first audiotape rolled and the timid sounds of a child's voice infiltrated the proceedings, members of the press stopped taking notes. They had all witnessed the closed-circuit testimony, but these taped conversations were stunningly different. They touched the heart of a child while the pain was new, constant, the largest thing in his or her life. The children's voices, voices that had already been enriched by two years' maturity, were naïve once more, voices that hadn't breathed a word of this to anyone, voices sometimes giddy, sometimes terror-stricken, sometimes so filled with paralytic reluctance that they were barely audible.

The defense played its first three tapes: Robert and Evan's joint "Buffalo Bill" interview, Kevin and Heather's joint interview, and a late interview with Freddie Mercer.

Lou noticed Kelly looking at him again. This time he peered into her eyes. Instantaneously, she looked away to write furiously in her notebook.

The jury heard Lou's tenderness with the wounded children. When Lou said to Kevin, "You feel better now that you've started talking about it, it's not a big secret anymore? I've talked to other little kids feeling the same way," it didn't sound like an attempt to exploit peer pressure. And when he joked with the children on tape, it didn't seem that he was tricking or suckering them.

Days into the cross-examination, Harvey Meltzer held a transcript of one of the audiotapes and proceeded to ask the witness, "Did you ask the child . . . ?" and Lou responded yes. Meltzer asked, "Did he answer . . . ?" and Lou responded yes. Finally, Glenn pointed out that the jury had already heard the tape and that defense counsel was eliciting no new information with this method of questioning.

"What's the point, Mr. Meltzer?" inquired the judge.

Meltzer answered, "There is no point. I'll move on."

As Meltzer continued working through the content of Lou's interviews, Glenn objected repeatedly to the length of time between questions, the equal devotion of time to silence as to talk. Glenn insisted, "It's not fair to have a witness return a second day because we only did half a day's work."

Cross-examination was slow, circuitous, and repetitive, and when Meltzer asked Lou, yet again, where in the interview room he had placed the pig puppet when he was with a child, the judge preempted Lou's answer: The Court had already heard this testimony. Harth recounted, "It was on the shelf."

"Were you there too, sir?" sniped Meltzer.

"No. I heard the testimony. Behave yourself, please."

"I am, Your Honor," Meltzer said, inserting the last word.

The pig puppet in question sat up on the witness stand, an obscene, flesh-colored protrusion, its red-painted tongue lolling out of its grin. The witness seemed to have been forgotten.

Bob Clark patted Meltzer on the back, urging him to ease up.

■
■ ■

The letters started arriving, typed letters sent to Judge Harth accusing him of participating in a prosecutorial conspiracy and of having taken away the presumption of innocence by revealing a bias against Kelly Michaels. Eighteen warned that he would be dealt with accordingly. Occasionally, the judge read portions of one of her letters in open court, establishing a record of her "involvement" and sometimes taking the opportunity to inquire of the woman about her intentions.

Sometimes an entire hour would be robbed from the day as the attorneys met in judge's chambers to confer over the morning's letter and then consult with its author: "What do you want? Why are you doing this? What are your intentions?"

Harth would apologize to the jurors for the delay: "One of life's minor contretemps," he lamented.

At the same time as the correspondence multiplied, Eighteen's behavior grew more reckless, as she continued to tail the jurors. State's witnesses, past and present, were also targets: She followed them into bathrooms, stairwells, phone booths, elevators. She couldn't get enough attention.

All four attorneys respected the danger presented: the danger of a disheveled mind. As soon as Eighteen's conduct was brought to his attention, Judge Harth made an announcement in court: "There will be no following." He elaborated briefly, and then instructed that, as the courthouse provided two cafeterias to choose from, all spectators were to dine in the one not used by the trial's jurors. And he placated everyone, saying, "The duck à l'orange is just as delicious in both cafeterias, I assure you."

▪
▪ ▪

Sara apprised the judge that the state's copy of Joey Gardner's interview tape was much clearer than the one she had turned over to the defense. Harvey Meltzer, however, insisted that his own copy be played, and the tape rolled.

Shortly into the replay, Sara cut in. "Your Honor, I'm gonna have to object to this. This is not how our tape sounds."

Meltzer said, "Your Honor, this is the tape that was provided to the defense by the state. If the state's alluding to the fact that we tampered with it, I object strenuously."

"That's not what the state is alluding. Mr. Meltzer is soooo quick to take umbrage," said Sara.

"Usually with good reason during the course of this trial," piped Clark.

Harth interceded. "We will not go back and forth. Where is the other tape?"

Sara answered, "Downstairs. There is some gap for several lines. I don't know how that happened."

"Your Honor, this smacks of Richard Nixon!"

"I don't know that Mr. Nixon had to put up with you." Harth smiled.

"He has never been honored that much."

Sara pointed out, "Transcripts were provided well in advance of that gap being created in the tape." Then she hurried out of the courtroom, the swinging doors banging shut behind her, and ran down to her office. George wasn't around, so she rooted around in the file cabinet, tossing aside transcripts and tape cassettes and dehydrated uncapped pens.

Glenn spoke up in court: "I'm sure we can play this tape during that portion."

When Sara returned ten minutes later, Meltzer had prepared a comment: "Your Honor, I'd like the record to reflect that I object to the entire process that we've been forced to go through. We've been listening to inferior-quality tapes all along, like, apparently, this tape." He lifted and rattled his cassette of Joey's interview.

"Mr. Meltzer," said Sara, "if you had problems with the tapes, you should have come to me and asked for other copies."

"I did not do that because I thought they were the same as what you had. . . . And also, Your Honor, if we're arguing about doing things right and doing things wrong, why in God's name weren't these children videotaped? Why were they audio-taped? Why are we missing the body language that I'm asking this witness to attest to and you're precluding me from getting it from him? Why did that happen?''

The judge's voice dragged into a drawl. "Oh, Mr. Meltzer, I'm picking on you so poorly. I'm sorry.''

"Thank you very much. I would like the record to reflect, in spite of the fact that there is no jury, there was a demeaning descriptor and tone to the judge's comment.''

"It was accurate.''

Glenn intruded on the pas de deux. "The self-deprecating comments that Mr. Meltzer makes, even in front of the jury, invite that type of response. He seems to glory in taking the part, the role of the underdog, the martyr. He's not a martyr, and I object to that type of attempt to bait the court.''

Harth surrendered to bewilderment and said, "I think I should put on the record: This November thirtieth will be my fifteenth year on the bench and nineteen years of practice before that and one year law clerk. I've *never* seen the conduct I've seen in this court . . . !''

"As long as we're putting things on the record, let's be frank about the whole thing,'' Meltzer responded. "I am attempting, in as professional and as gentlemanly a fashion as possible, to advise this court that I am distraught with the way this court is performing.''

Harth sighed. "We might put on the record that all this has come about because the state has a clearly more audible, plainer tape, and because of the court's ruling allowing the clearer tape to be played—''

"Absolutely not, sir.''

"—Mr. Meltzer has caused all this, including interrupting the court.''

When Joey's tape finally started to roll, the jurors were stricken. The flitting schisms of tone in Joey's voice were like a mania, otherworldly.

Meltzer addressed Lou, the long-forgotten witness: "There seems to be a lot of laughing by the child during the taping.''

"A lot of it was nervous laughter too, if you can hear it.''

"What is nervous laughter?''

"I think it was demonstrated on the tape, sir, during certain portions.'' Lou paused to listen as Joey droned pathetically, as if every word weighed a ton, and then, seized by mania, shrieked in a thin, stretched laughter.

Lou went on: "He'd try to exit the interview mentally, emotionally, by laughing.'' But Lou's clinical explanation couldn't kill the feeling: The taped laughter sounded sinister, like that of an ancient.

The defense attorney touched on the atmosphere at Wee Care during the joint investigation. "Did any teachers say they saw Kelly sticking knives, forks, or spoons into the children?"

Harth said, "I don't believe the state ever claimed that."

"Judge, believe me," Sara interjected, "that would've been the first witness on the witness stand."

When the playing of the tapes was finally concluded, Meltzer's next tactic was to try to enter questions about children who were not named in the indictment. He had derived these questions from the existing audios of their interviews. Of course, the jury couldn't hear those tapes because they didn't pertain to the indictment.

Harth said, with some irritation, "We're not interested in children who are not part of this case."

Clark argued the defense's position: "Your Honor, it's not a difficult logical leap to see the connection, Your Honor, with regard to . . . we have children who *are* in the case who have been interviewed by this particular witness that we do not have transcripts of. We do not have any indication of what was said or transpired other than this witness's recollection, and his notes that even he has indicated are less than perfect. What we're suggesting, Your Honor, through this line of questioning, is an attempt to demonstrate through the transcripts that we *do* have his state of mind during the course of his investigation at Wee Care."

But Harth remained firm in his ruling: "The state of mind might be relevant as to the children that are in this case. As to those who aren't, it has nothing to do with this case. It's a collateral issue. Your next question, Mr. Meltzer, please."

"Did you have an occasion to interview—" and Meltzer named a child not listed in the indictment.

"I did," said Lou.

"Did you have occasion to ask him how—"

Harth sustained his own objection. "We're not concerned with—"

"We *are*." Bob Clark jumped up.

"I have ruled, Mr. Clark."

When Meltzer still continued to frame questions about children not named in the indictment, he attempted to justify himself to the judge by saying, "We don't know what transpired, we don't have transcripts, and what I'm trying to do is to find out if he did the same thing with Julie Danvers, for example."

Harth had a different solution. He advised: "Then you ask the question directly as to Julie Danvers. We've had a lot of words, but the reasoning remains the same. It's a collateral issue."

Meltzer rested cross, and Sara stepped back in. Her redirect examination was extensive. She worked through all those areas Meltzer had explored on cross, affording Lou an opportunity to clarify or elaborate on key ideas and emphasize important distinctions that Meltzer might have short-changed. In effect, by abbreviating direct, Sara had simply reversed the order of who went first.

Because she had perceived boredom, even irritation, on the jurors' faces, Sara introduced a concise system of questioning so that Lou could synopsize his Wee Care involvement. He testified that he had been the first of any investigator to hear of ''Jingle Bells'' and the use of utensils in the pileup, but that most of the other types of allegations had first been disclosed to a different investigator, including the very first allegations of naked duck, duck, goose, insertion of utensils, peanut butter and jelly, the ingestion of feces, and the presence of urine and vaginal blood. Lou also calculated that the total time he had spent with each child averaged about two hours apiece. The implication Sara left was that, compared to Kelly Michaels, Lou had not been given a lot of time for brainwashing.

Lastly, Sara returned to the volatile topic of fifty-one substantiated cases of abuse. She asked her witness, ''You've substantiated abuse in fifty-one children. Are you able to discuss why in each case?''

''Yes,'' he answered.

Going no further with the subject, Sara left this carrot/stick dangling within the defense's reach and rested her examination. On recross, Meltzer declined to explore why Lou Fonolleras had concluded that all fifty-one children had been abused.

The defense had opened the trial with statements lambasting the state's investigators: Meltzer had indicated that those authorized by the state were unskilled social workers. However, once the tapes had been played, it became obvious that Lou was not a liar, a zealot, a conspirator, or even a poor interviewer.

The destruction of Lou Fonolleras had not gone according to plan, although Meltzer had established one important point: Certain allegations had been made to Lou and yet to no one else during the entire course of the investigation. If the jurors did not trust the purity of Lou's conclusions, then his widespread influence in the case might be considered cause for reasonable doubt during their deliberations. To achieve such an outcome, the defense needed Lou to be unprofessional on the witness stand, but Lou's great size housed a penetrating calm.

▪
▪ ▪

Her most overt letter yet introduced a twist: It was addressed to Kelly and handed to her in person out in the hallway by Number Eighteen herself, empowered by her blood-brown sunglasses. The letter railed at Kelly's persecutors, then stated: "Kelly, I could go on and on. . . . However, my objective was never to cause you concern, but I cannot allow this to continue. . . . It's happening sooner than I thought. As I see the need, I shall perform. . . . You shall be acquitted, no thanks to your attorneys. Know that I am with you. And I shall contend with those that are against you."

The highly formal, archaic language seemed an attempt at order.

When the woman continued to follow the jurors contrary to the judge's order, a plainclothes sheriff's officer was assigned to follow her as she staked out the panelists over lunch. In a formal hearing (always out of the presence of the jury), the judge heard testimony from the officer, and then asked Eighteen whether or not she had understood his directive as to the cafeterias.

"The court's directions do not apply to me, sir." Eighteen insisted that she was a peaceable person and that no harm would come to the judge. She inquired, "Does that concern you, sir? . . . Contend, sir, does not mean physical harm, sir, as you have thought. That's very narrow-minded, sir."

Further conversation was fruitless, so finally, after months of the game, Harth ruled: "In view of your conduct, you may well be in contempt of court, although I do not want to refer to that remedy. . . . You are not to enter this court complex."

Eighteen claimed not to believe Harth was within his rights to so order. Consequently, she reappeared in his courtroom the very next day. Harth called her up to counsel table and demanded an explanation of her conduct.

She sounded wounded, outraged. "You fail to see my position here, sir! You are disrespectful!"

He inquired, "What have I done that is disrespectful?"

"I don't wish to tell you."

"How can I understand if you won't tell me?" he asked.

"You are supposed to use wisdom and discernment."

Harth stared at her blankly, then deemed her to be in contempt of court and sentenced her to ten days in the county jail annex at Caldwell. He peered down at her, commanding her with his eyes to understand what he was about to say. "Now if at any time, it could be a half hour from now, you feel you could obey the court's order, all you have to do is obey."

■
■ ■

Investigator George McGrath had been in and out of the courtroom since the trial began, scheduling and then chaperoning the witnesses, holding them in abeyance until the attorneys were ready, running documents up to the prosecutors. Whenever he appeared in the courtroom or passed them in the hallways, George scrupulously avoided waving hello to or even smiling at the jurors. Nevertheless, when the investigator finally came in to testify, the jurors were not weighing the credibility of a total stranger. His was a familiar face, a controlled, capable, laughing face that they had observed in hundreds of configurations of friendliness.

As George entered the courtroom, his confident strut was muted to an intent stride. Still, as he took the stand, George pulsed with authority.

"Please state your name."

"George! McGrath!"

At an early morning break, Glenn rendezvoused somewhere to confer with his witness, and by the time they made their way back to the courtroom, George had changed. Sara first saw the results when Glenn demanded offhandedly, "Where's my witness?"

George, standing next to him, beamed serenely.

"Here he is!" answered Glenn. "The *New* George McGrath!"

When George retook the stand, the adjustment was subtle but distinct, calibrated to Glenn's refined taste. The witness was calm, patient. George's testimony offered details of the unit's investigation that defied the witch-hunt theory. He described the state's initial reluctance to interview girls, as well as the long delay between the first investigation and the eventual, more thorough joint investigation.

Throughout George McGrath's first day of cross, Meltzer attacked him on lack of personal knowledge of certain statements in his own report, asking again and again, "Where did that come from, sir?" And it seemed that George's testimony might be shaken. However, by the next day when he returned, George had sorted out the sources of each and every remark in his report. And he informed the jury that this report, written after the investigation and specifically at the request of defense counsel, "was composed of all information of all investigators who may have dealt with that particular child."

·
· ·

The area was experiencing a stretch of warm November weather, but Alison Steadman insisted on wearing long-sleeved pajamas to bed each night. At one time, Karen might not have questioned this, but by now she knew to question.

Allie was reluctant to acknowledge that she was dressing this way for any special reason, but Karen kept at her. Finally she explained to her mother that out on the playground at school she had overheard her friends talking about a news story about a man who had picked up a hitchhiker, raped her, and then chopped off her arms with an ax. Alison was expecting this man to come during the night and chop off her own arms. She was trying to cover them with the pajama sleeves.

Karen could see the terror in her daughter's face, but she didn't know how to console her. How could she tell Alison: "It won't happen here. You're safe here"?

15

.·.

Generally, both Sara and Glenn were open with spectators about their
case strategy: what witnesses they were going to put on, what testimony was coming. Sara in particular was eager to chat about prosecution
plans with anyone who was willing to give her an opinion. She'd walk
up to a stranger and ask, "How we doin'?" or indulge her twinges of
anxiety by soliciting reviews from court reporters and bailiffs.

But now something was definitely different, because for the first time
in five months, no one in court knew who was scheduled to testify.
Harth's courtroom was packed, a full house. George McGrath sat at
counsel table with Sara and Glenn, and in the audience were Lou Fonolleras, Peg Foster, and Rich Mastrangelo, along with a contingent of
parents and a dozen newspeople, half of them with camera crews.

The next two state witnesses were the closest thing to surprise witnesses
this trial had yet heard. As Officers Wanda Dean and Betty Sheffield of
the county jail annex at Caldwell appeared, tremors reverberated through
the courtroom. The two officers had been assigned to the tier housing

Kelly Michaels during her incarceration, and the guards' combined testimony reconstructed an account of Kelly's life there.

During her two stays in the jail annex, Kelly Michaels had been held in protective custody because, as Wanda Dean explained, prisoners facing these types of charges "don't do well in prison." For her own protection, the guards had intended that Kelly have no interaction at all with the inmates; however, on one occasion, a number of inmates had gathered in front of Kelly's cell. Officer Dean described how, curious, she had edged behind the electrical break box, the control box by which the officers gained access to the locked tier.

"I was eavesdropping," she said frankly.

Everyone except Miss Michaels could see her there, but nevertheless, the inmates continued their conversation. The rest of the tier population was out of sight, some at their prison jobs and others in the television room at the opposite end of the tier.

Dean overheard the inmates asking Kelly about her function at the school. They wanted information, and, Dean explained, "They weren't going to use the harassment approach. They were going to be her friend."

She heard Kelly say that she told stories and nursery rhymes, and then, as the other women encouraged her, Kelly shared with them one of the stories. Illustrating with her hands, Kelly recited: "These are my eyes and they're to see with. This is my nose and it's to smell with. This is my mouth and it's to talk with."

The guard paused and broke out of her baby-voiced imitation. She finished by saying, "Then Kelly mentioned her breasts."

At this point, Officer Dean had signaled with her hand to another guard, and as Dean left the scene, Betty Sheffield took up the post listening in on the exchange. Sheffield heard Kelly tell of having taken her clothes off in front of the children. Sheffield added, though, that Kelly had explained, "What the one little boy said actually didn't happen. He just didn't understand what she was trying to show him."

Officer Sheffield had listened for only a minute when she decided to break it up. She wasn't about to wait for Kelly to say something to upset the other women and start a fight; she didn't want to deal with that, so she moved in and dispersed the group, warning the gathered inmates to stay away from the door to Kelly's cell.

When they were alone, Sheffield said, "Miss Michaels, these ladies have no business being around your door, and you shouldn't be telling them about what you're in here for."

Kelly retorted that she didn't feel she was doing anything wrong.

"Why do you feel that way?" Sheffield asked.

"Because I don't feel what I did was wrong," she said, belligerent.

"Why not?"

As Sheffield now told it, Kelly then braced her fist against her hip and said defiantly, "Well, I just feel that whatever a person's sexual preference is is their own business." On saying that, she turned her back on the officer and went and sat down on her cot.

Sara McArdle checked the jurors' faces and saw shock.

Neither guard had submitted an incident report about that day's events, because, they explained, such reports were generally reserved for something like a physical confrontation, the setting of a fire, verbal abuse, a suicide attempt. But in his examinations, Bob Clark stressed the fact that no report of the alleged gathering had been turned in, insinuating that these tales were after-the-fact embellishments.

When the two guards left the courtroom at the end of the day's testimony, press spokespersons wheeled around them, and the evening news was full of their unexpected corroboration of the children's allegations. Sara believed that this could very well be the turning point in public sentiment. For all those people who couldn't find it in themselves to accept the victims' words, here were the words of the one person they might believe, the words of an adult: Kelly Michaels.

The Michaels family stormed out of the courtroom, Kelly crying and escorted by her two attorneys. On his way to the elevators, Harvey Meltzer confronted one of the mothers and challenged, "Wait till it's over, sweetheart! Then we'll see!" On the news that same evening, Harvey appeared, his eyes sparking and his hair flyaway as he called the day's testimony "just another shoveling that they're piling on top of a pile and they're hoping something's gonna stick." On a different TV channel, he pointed out that the two officers had discussed their testimony prior to appearing in court and added, "I think there's something foul in that situation."

The next morning, Harth offered some gentle media advice: "Sometimes, it is wise to think before we speak." Then, after fielding complaints about the defense party's interaction with the state's ex-witnesses, Harth assigned to the Wee Care parents an empty room in which to congregate, drink deadly coffee, and sit out boring segments of testimony without having to come into contact with members of the defense.

．
．　．

The next witness was being escorted up to the eighth-floor courtroom. Kelly ventured out into the hallway where her mother stood in the corner drinking coffee. Kelly arched her arms over her head and pirouetted on tiptoe toward her, then slowly, gracefully, widened her arms, still on pointe. She said nothing, a mirage from *Fantasia*.

■
■ ■

A twenty-three-year-old inmate, serving a sentence for aggravated manslaughter, appeared to testify against Kelly Michaels. Officer Dean had testified that while Kelly was in jail, no one had been closer to her than Charlene, and Charlene herself said now, "She'd confide in me—like I was a friend."

Charlene testified that at first she hadn't wanted to get involved with the Michaels trial because she believed that all that was at issue was Kelly "pattin' babies on the back. Whatever she's here for, I had other things on my mind." In addition, she hadn't been sure how the other inmates would react if she testified. Then, after thinking it over by herself, she had decided to cooperate. Her decision, she maintained, had nothing to do with any favors from the Prosecutor's Office. Presently, Charlene was already serving the maximum sentence for her crime and had been denied an application for a sentencing review. And Sara had told her she would make no special appeal on Charlene's behalf, although if her case ever did come up for review, Sara would notify the judge of Charlene's cooperation with the state.

Charlene spoke with great composure, even nonchalance, as if easy in a system which had already judged her. Throughout her stay in Caldwell, she said, Kelly had repeatedly told her that she hadn't meant to hurt the children. Kelly had also insisted that the four-year-old was lying when he said she'd stuck instruments up him, insisting that she hadn't hurt him in the way he said she did.

After seeing a clip about Kelly on the news, Charlene had confronted her fellow prisoner: "You were on TV, and they said you had the kids pile up butt-naked."

"Oh yeah?" asked Kelly.

"Yeah," Charlene retorted, then asked, "Did you really harm those kids the way they're accusing you of?"

And Kelly had answered, "Not all of them."

Usually, Charlene said, when Kelly realized that she was discussing her own case, "she'd shut up and go on to the mumbling stage." If Charlene then asked her what she was saying, she would answer, "Oh nothing. I'm just talkin' to myself."

Bob Clark attacked Charlene's credibility on cross, setting out to show that she had cut a deal with the Prosecutor's Office for reduced jail time.

As Bob interrogated Charlene about her criminal record, he lingered on such points of insinuation.

After repeated and overlapping questioning, Harth interjected, "Now Mr. Clark, I've got to ask, what is the point of this?"

"Thank you," said Charlene, her eyes narrowed to their densest state.

But Clark ambled on and asked Charlene if she could correlate her December 1985 statement to Investigator George McGrath with her January 1986 sentence.

The witness angled her head back to the judge and asked whether she was on trial.

"No," said Harth, smiling.

"Just curious."

Clark continued to attack her motivation for testifying, pounding on the vulnerable nerve the state had bared by daring to place a convicted killer on the stand.

Finally, Charlene interrupted him: "All right, it's like this. When Goldberg talks, he makes sense. I mean—" Laughter drowned her out. She waited.

"So, I don't make sense?"

Charlene was calm, almost humorous, even as she complained. "No, because you be trying to pile everything up. I mean, you ask me about my case, and you ask me about something else. I mean, how can I answer three and four questions?"

Clark answered, "Easy. You listen to the question, then you respond. If you have a question, then you can ask it."

"I listen, but sometimes you make things difficult."

"Great! I'm doing my job." He chuckled.

Finally, a sense of the preposterous struck her. In her own trial, Charlene had pleaded guilty to aggravated manslaughter, so she queried, "If I'm not gonna lie for myself, I'm not gonna lie for Kelly. That's why I'm sittin' in jail, now."

"Because you wouldn't lie?" Bob asked, snide.

"Yes."

"It has nothing to do with shooting someone?"

"Yes, it does. With shooting someone and pleading guilty. Because I knew I was guilty."

Bob Clark unfurled a piece of evidence to prove that Charlene had always believed Kelly to be innocent. He presented the witness with a letter she had written to Kelly just after Kelly had been released on bail. In the letter, Charlene called Kelly her "friend for life."

The witness explained, "I used to write a lot of letters," ten or sixteen a day.

Bob quoted from the end of the letter: " 'I'll always believe in your every innocence, no matter who may disown you.' "

"That was out of the goodness of my heart."

Glenn interrupted, indicating that Clark had omitted the fact that on Charlene's letter the word *innocence* was in quotation marks, and down by the signature, the sign-off word *Sincerely* was followed by a question mark.

Clark laughed and countered with the observation that there were marks all *over* the letter. Bob now informed the court that Mr. Goldberg hadn't mentioned that the *i*'s in *innocence* and in every other word were dotted not with dots but with stars.

Charlene interjected from the witness stand: "She had a thing about stars. I don't know what it was."

When Glenn retook control of the examination, he asked Charlene about those stars, and Charlene elaborated: "Her whole room was flooded with them, silver stars that you give little kids. Red, blue, green: on her face and all over the walls."

Meltzer listened, literally biting his fist.

Charlene knew where the stars had come from: They were from a box of teacher's reward stars. And she knew this because when Kelly had eventually made bail and left Caldwell, she had given Charlene a collection of items, including a writing tablet, a picture of some famous painter, some glitter, and the box of stars. Thinking of Kelly and wanting to please her, Charlene had placed stars over the *i*'s in her letter: She knew Kelly liked stars and would be dazzled by them.

Bob Clark contended that Charlene had found her jaunt to court to be a pleasant outing, but in fact she had risked alienation from her fellow inmates for cozying up to the criminal justice system. Charlene believed that in testifying she had done something she felt was right and at the same time useful to society. George McGrath, who had shepherded her through the system, received a letter from Charlene after she returned to prison, thanking him for giving her an opportunity to feel worthwhile again.

▪ ▪
▪ ▪

In the elevator one afternoon, a stranger addressed three of the Wee Care mothers: "Let me tell you something. We had a guy messing with kids in our neighborhood, but we didn't call the police. We just took him up to a rooftop and threw him off."

The three women peered at the speaker, skeptical.

She finished, "And that was the end of that problem."

With gallows humor, dozens of onlookers, cocky vigilantes, threatened Kelly Michaels's life if she were acquitted. The retribution fantasies of these presumably upstanding citizens somehow balanced their internal scales of justice.

One wanted to slip her a note that said, "If you win, you lose. If you lose, you lose. Enjoy the rest of your trial!"

•
• •

New York child psychologist Eileen Treacy had testified in seven mass-abuse cases. At the age of thirty-five she had already seen 1,000 sexually abused children (150 of them between the ages of three and five) and 2,500 non-abused children. Treacy also had four years' experience teaching day care.

A judge in another case had described Eileen Treacy as a walking encyclopedia of professional literature, and she demonstrated why: She footnoted with corroborating sources just about every statement on which Harvey Meltzer challenged her. She even went one step further to list contradictory articles and then explain why the detracting opinions were faulty. Sara's spirits lifted dramatically during the week that Eileen testified.

On direct, Sara just pointed Eileen in a direction and let the witness hold forth fluently. In her evaluation, a child was never reduced to a number: Eileen researched and took into account the child's statements and bearing, prior sexual knowledge, developmental history, and behavior *changes*. As Sara had promised, Treacy did not include in her opinion any materials from her own interviews with the children, but based her conclusions solely on the evidence presented at trial. In this way, she availed herself only of the same evidence to which the defense experts had access.

Treacy had coined the term *confounding variables* to denote any clinical explanation other than sexual abuse that might account for some or all of a child's behavioral symptoms. Out of all the children in this case, she had found three with a new baby in the house, three whose parents were having problems in the marriage, one whose parents were separated, one who had never known his father, one who lived in a hectic household, one who had witnessed family violence at the age of one year old, another whose mother had a live-in lover, and, finally, one boy whose little brother had allegedly been sexually abused by a male baby-sitter (the case had not yet gone to trial). This last child, Pete, had himself been discovered to have a bruised penis prior to the Wee Care school year, causing his parents to wonder if perhaps a baby-sitter had abused him as well. For all the remaining children, Treacy could find no confounding variables whatsoever.

Treacy explained the difficulty of evaluating which behaviors were caused by which stresses: "Human beings are not like math problems in that there's a lot of overlap in how we deal with stress." Taking into account all the alternative explanations, Treacy was able to confirm that nineteen out of the twenty children in the indictment did have symptoms consistent with sexual abuse: In these children, only sexual abuse could sufficiently explain the full range of behaviors. For example, a new sibling in the house could not explain a child's acting out sexually or refusing to eat with silverware.

The only child's evaluation in question for Treacy was that of Pete, whose brother had alleged sexual abuse. This particular confounding variable made the evaluation too complicated for Treacy to say with certainty that Pete's current behaviors were related to sexual abuse at Wee Care.

Treacy stated that the evidence on the nineteen others was "consistent with sexual abuse," but refused to testify that they had been abused, believing that the ultimate question of guilt was for the jury to decide. The closest Treacy came to attesting to the veracity of these allegations was to say, "There is no question in my mind that it was not the interviews which prompted symptomatology. Interviewers are just not that powerful, and they can't produce pre-disclosure behaviors as well as post."

When Harvey Meltzer confronted the witness with the suggestibility theory, the core of the defense, Treacy laid out some ground rules about children's cognitive abilities and inabilities: "It is possible to suggest particular answers to children. Whether they'll accept is another matter." She explained that children do sometimes say things to please parents, but when it comes to sexual abuse, not saying anything is how they try to please, by trying to protect their parents from the abuse.

Treacy said, "Children lie, adults lie, people tell lies. It should be noted, though, children lie to get out of trouble, not to get into it."

The witness's delivery was rapid, precise, and devastatingly comprehensive. Kelly listened, heavy lids pushing down on her eyes.

Treacy testified that children also know the difference between fantasy and fact. Otherwise, she pointed out, "We'd never let them watch cartoons, with their decapitations and edible bombs." And the witness stated as she had to Sara that normal children do not fantasize about degradation and abuse, that only severely disturbed children will fantasize to disempower rather than aggrandize themselves.

Meltzer then confronted the witness with the suggestive build of the "so-called anatomically correct dolls," contending that the genitals were oversized in proportion to the rest of the doll.

Treacy responded, "Children don't have the kind of sexual turn-ons we have." She explained that even sexually abused children don't touch breasts unless that kind of touching was involved in the abuse. Eileen Treacy stated repeatedly that abused children do not need these dolls to act out sexually: They'll use anything. They'll act out on themselves, on other toys, on a Barbie doll, or, yes, on an anatomically correct doll.

Meltzer wanted to know if it wasn't true that normal children are inquisitive about adult anatomy and will try to touch, purely out of curiosity. Treacy informed him: "A child may look, but it's quite uncommon to explore, to go and touch, especially private-part touching. A child of this age is very frequently voyeuristic. They like to look. . . . Note, this is also true of kids who were breast-fed: They still don't fondle breasts in a *sexual* manner."

Leslie Michaels was smiling smugly. Her sister sat poised and pretty, a paper cup in front of her stuffed with the cellophane wrappers of the hard candy she had consumed.

Meltzer inquired, "Why would a child confide in a complete stranger that she was sexually abused, and not advise a parent?"

"Confide is an inappropriate use of language. Children don't just walk up to people and say, 'Hi! I'm sexually abused. . . .' The interviewers make it clear that their job is to take care of children, they're strong people, that they're good at protecting children. This breaks down the power of the perpetrator. Also, these strangers don't punish the children. David Kirschner feared being spanked by his mother."

"Does a child of David's age have the cognitive ability to have a conflict within himself?"

"Yes."

Meltzer asked, "If it didn't happen, and someone told a child for two years that he was brutalized, and the child was made to talk to strangers about what had happened, will a child of five or six have the cognitive ability to have conflict about what he knows to be true within himself?"

"The probability of a child being able to maintain a complicated lie, particularly with a story line—it's remarkably improbable."

He tried again. "Cognitively, isn't whatever an adult believes is true, true to kids?"

"No. Children in this age group are too egocentric," she answered, then pointed out, "If that was true, you'd have kids making immediate disclosures."

Finally, Meltzer asked whether three-, four-, and five-year-olds have "the inherent or incipient sexual drive that exists in adults." Referring to the drives toward orgasm and sexual intercourse, he demanded, "It doesn't exist somewhere in their subconscious or in their physiological uncontrollable being that they're unaware of?"

The jurors laughed and fidgeted as Meltzer spiraled down the drain of Freudian excess. But Treacy's answer was no, normal children do not.

In putting together her witness list, Sara had learned that many lawyers disputed whether or not expert witnesses accomplished anything in a day-care abuse trial, or whether the understanding of the psychological issues was simply a matter of common sense. Experts were time-consuming, expensive, and one step removed from the primary witnesses.

Sara was convinced that Eileen Treacy's testimony was crucial to her case, that Treacy, who spoke brilliantly, had managed to unknot the complex psychological and behavioral issues that the defense attorneys were trying to confuse.

When the witness stepped down, Sara rested her case.

■
■ ■

Joey said to his mother, as if it was some sort of revelation, "I told God I was innocent. And innocent means good."

"Well, I'm glad, because you are good," Ellen said.

"I am?" Joey was amazed. Kelly had known him in a reprehensible way, but still she had a home in his mind.

Ellen herself had gained some distance from the time when everything was raw, but on an invigorating, clear winter day she paused, waiting for a light to change, trying to place a feeling she had forgotten. There was something in her day that she couldn't quite remember, and she was fitfully certain that the thing she couldn't remember was the thing that mattered most.

■
■ ■

Christmas of 1987 was two weeks away (as was Kelly Michaels's twenty-sixth birthday) when, after 105 witnesses, 254 exhibits, and over 20 weeks of testimony, the prosecution concluded. Ultimately, nineteen children had appeared, and a twentieth remained in the indictment on the basis of his parents' testimony. Rich Mastrangelo and Peg Foster had not testified: Sara had decided that their testimony would simply repeat Lou's and George's, and she didn't want to provoke the jurors. For a while, there was some talk by Kelly's lawyers that the defense might call Rich Mastrangelo as a hostile witness so that they could introduce into evidence Rich's interview tapes, but they dropped the idea. In Sara's estimation, Rich's interviews were very good, with no leading or suggestive questions, and she wasn't at all surprised when Meltzer and Clark declined to call Rich to the stand.

As all the inculpatory evidence that would be put forth had now been presented, Judge Harth dismissed the jury for several days while he reviewed the evidence and determined which counts in the indictment should be dismissed for insufficient evidence. The attorneys convened in the empty courtroom, and Judge Harth listened to argument.

Of the 163 start-of-trial counts, Harth ultimately dismissed over 30 of them because the state had not proved its case. Some charges had been substantiated only by what the children had said on the audiotapes, and Harth would not allow such hearsay material to be considered as proving the truth of a charge. (In the end, thought Sara, the tapes primarily helped the defense case by providing them an opportunity to attack her unit's investigative techniques.)

Harth ruled that the state had not established a sufficient factual basis for a number of the terroristic threats. Several of the children had testified that Kelly had threatened their parents, but back in 1985, Sara had worded those counts of the indictment as threats made against the children themselves, because that was what the children had been focusing on at the time. Consequently, Judge Harth dismissed those counts. About a dozen more counts were dismissed in response to an appellate ruling against the inclusion of certain types of hearsay. A total of 131 counts would be going to the jury.

As the defense attorneys readied their own witnesses to testify, Meltzer and Clark ran into a problem: Dr. Underwager, Dr. Rappeport, and, most particularly, Dr. Elissa Benedek had yet to review the testimony of the children. Harth was warned: "What we're talking about . . . is a world-class expert, and she may not have time to get here." So, the defense entered a motion to copy all the videotapes and mail them out, round robin, to its experts.

The prosecutors opposed the motion, given that in another large trial the identities of the child victims had been compromised in exactly this way when the tapes had somehow fallen into wider circulation. Instead, Sara offered to keep a VCR available in the Prosecutor's Office so that at any time of day or night the defense experts could have a private viewing.

Judge Harth stated, "I am taking judicial notice of the geography of the United States, and also taking judicial notice that we are in the jet age," and then he ruled against the defense.

In this intermission, the state also requested materials to prepare for the coming defense witnesses: a completed witness list, experts' reports. The main question Sara and Glenn wanted answered was whether Kelly Michaels was going to take the stand, but on that issue Kelly's attorneys were teasing both the media and the prosecutors, with a Meltzer collection of "you never know" comebacks.

Kelly Michaels had no obligation to prove herself innocent: The state shouldered the entire burden of proof. In fact, Kelly had no obligation even to submit a defense.

■
■ ■

A Wee Care mother attended a meeting at her daughter's public grade school: A new child abuse prevention program was being previewed for the parents. The recommendation the program made to the children was that they tell their assailant no, and then run to an adult for help.

The mother of the victim objected: "If you think this is gonna help, you're out of your mind. It's gonna hurt. These kids aren't running down a street looking for a policeman!"

The program also emphasized that children be wary of strangers, and the mother tried to point out that preschoolers were never alone with strangers: The people who had access to them were known figures, trusted friends and caretakers.

Still disturbed by the lack of understanding, following the meeting the woman made an appointment with the school nurse. She tried to make the nurse see that her own child would never say no to an adult: According to the way we raise our children, every adult is an authority figure. And children are taught, in no uncertain terms, to do what they are told, to obey their elders, to respect unquestioningly. If an already abused child such as her own was told to say no to an abuser, that child's guilt and sense of being at fault, being bad, would only be reinforced.

She suggested that perhaps children should not be expected to decide when a situation calls for "no." And perhaps children should not be expected to have the strength of will necessary to say no to an adult.

Kelly Michaels was known to teachers and parents as being able to discipline a misbehaving child with simply a look. She was able to silence a child who was crying hysterically merely by lifting that child onto her lap. Kelly was the teacher, a grown-up, the boss, in charge, and the children knew to do what she said.

And even if a child uttered no, what abuser could be counted on to obey?

The mother told the nurse that to put the onus of prevention on the children is less helpful than teaching them that they can tell their parents if they have been hurt or made to feel uncomfortable in any situation, made to do something they didn't like. Just maybe they will tell, she said. It was impossible to prevent an unforeseeable crime, but she felt strongly that parents had to be responsible for protection.

To this mother, the most important thing was to listen to her child. When a child insisted he didn't want to nap in school, the parent should weigh that preference as a legitimate desire, with seriousness. If it seemed whimsical, it might well be. But if parents were going to set out to educate children to wield their perceptual tools, then they needed also to educate themselves to have regard for their children's forthcoming insights.

Part

FOUR

16

.˙.

The defense case was oriented toward expert testimony and leaned particularly heavily upon the testimony of Dr. Ralph Underwager, a Minnesota psychologist who had gained prominence by testifying in one of the early day-care cases in Jordan, Minnesota. Now the doctor spent 60 to 70 percent of his professional time traveling and testifying in child sexual abuse matters.

Dr. Underwager had no formal training or certification in either child development or child psychology. Child sexual abuse was not his field of knowledge; however, it was his field of courtroom practice. He proliferated his opinion, "No one knows how to tell accurately whether a child's been abused," throughout the nation's courts. And he maintained that no known interviewing techniques could be relied upon to yield credible statements. Consequently, as Underwager had stated at the Jordan trial, he felt it to be "more desirable that a thousand children in abuse situations are not discovered than for one innocent person to be convicted wrongly."

Underwager had testified in thirty-five states, via satellite in two or three foreign countries, and, he noted, in the military. His scorecard tallied about thirty day-care cases and, when family court matters such as incest and custody were added in, involvement in more than two hundred trials overall. Yet, Underwager was not a diplomate of the American Board of Psychologists ("I made the judgment that it really was meaningless"), and he had never had work published in a professional journal. He was, however, working on a manuscript for publication.

The first thing Harvey Meltzer asked the doctor was why he testified all over the country and all over the world. The expert braced his long arms against the edge of the witness box and inclined his weight heavily onto his palms, as he answered mellifluously, "There are very few mental health experts who are willing to speak upon the kinds of issues that bear upon the child sexual abuse issue, because of the kinds of pressures." And he acknowledged having received death threats.

Kelly watched him. Her entire back could have fit into just one of Dr. Underwager's colossal shoulder blades. He was much larger than Lou Fonolleras, and less fit. He hulked, carrying his portly six feet five and three quarter inches bent forward.

Meltzer asked, "What about the interview process itself as a teaching aid?"

The doctor catalogued the improper techniques used by interviewers that, in his estimation, had led to false allegations of sexual abuse. He drew vaguely from the materials of the Wee Care case:

"The interrogator wants the response, 'The clothes are off.' The interviewer doesn't stop, repeats the question over and over again. . . .

"The dolls are almost invariably introduced as 'these funny little dolls.' What's funny about them? What's funny about them is they possess genitalia. And that's a very powerful message to the kids. It says, 'This is what I'm gonna focus on. . . .'

"When Miss Kelly is referred to as being in jail or being bad, this is also a very powerful message to the children. 'This is what we want to talk about. This is the attitude we want you to have.' "

If a child said, spontaneously, "Kelly hit me," and the interviewer then repeated, "Kelly hit you?" Underwager would consider that repetition to invalidate the child's statement because the interviewer had reinforced the allegation.

The doctor generalized his complaint about investigative techniques: "When a child is kept in the process of mixing about in a whole series of events . . . emotions . . . the child is taught."

Sara and Glenn sat at counsel table watching and listening to the testimony. Glenn had warned Bob Clark that when he was finished with Ralph Underwager, direct and cross-examination would become known as B.C. and A.D.: Before Collapse and After Decimation.

Meltzer's direct was lengthy, but Underwager's most fundamental point seemed to be: "We have two very basic, well-established facts. Adults are very powerful influences on children . . . that influence is much more powerful than most of us tend to be aware of. And the second basic fact is that children are vulnerable to adult influence. Their very survival depends on one way or another producing enough of what the adult wants from the child so that the adult takes care of the child. That's a very basic fact of a child."

When direct was over, Glenn stood before his opponent to begin. Underwager had a powerful, Assyrian-shaped head stretched with gleaming pink skin, a rectilinear chin carved into shape by a stiff, white beard. Glenn queried, "Doctor, would you say that there is no conclusive proof that allows us to say anything with certainty?"

Kelly looked up from her journal with a quizzical scowl.

Underwager replied, "For human beings, there is no certainty."

Glenn asked, "Doctor, do you use the scientific method?"

"Yes."

"Is *that* a way of proving anything?"

The doctor answered with a stale smile: "Only as a probability. Nothing more."

Glenn attacked the suggestibility theory head on. "Have you yourself, Doctor, done any experimentation to determine whether children are, in fact, more suggestible to influence?"

The answer was no.

"Would you say that children have amazingly accurate detail recall?"

"Yes." Underwager smiled at the jurors.

"Doctor, you yourself have used leading questions in dealing with young children with sexual abuse."

"I'm sure I have."

As an example of the witness's own use of suggestive statements, Glenn then read aloud the line of introduction Underwager had once used to begin an interview with a particular little girl: "I'm here to talk to you about things that happened to you sexually."

Kelly's father had his right hand up his pant leg, nervously rubbing his calf.

Glenn moved on to ask, "The problem with interviews is that the question elicits the answer?"

Underwager nodded emphatically. "Yes."

"Isn't that always the way of it, that a question elicits an answer?"

"Yes."

Glenn introduced the subject of an evaluation the witness had once conducted of another little girl alleging abuse. The child had been accompanied to Dr. Underwager's office by her father.

Quickly, Bob Clark angled his body into a half-erect posture and requested a proffer of where the prosecutor was going with this line of questioning.

Glenn turned to Harth. "I don't want Dr. Underwager to know where I'm going just yet."

"Well, can we have it at sidebar?" suggested Clark.

Harth refused and allowed Glenn to continue.

Glenn resumed, and asked an innocuous question: "So, the father was the suspect in the allegations of sexual abuse against his daughter?"

"Yes."

When Glenn then went on, "And you didn't ask that she be brought to your office by an impartial person?" Underwager retorted that those arrangements had been left to the court and the local Prosecutor's Office.

But Glenn pursued him. "Isn't it true that if anyone else in the world were to bring her, it would have been a much less coercive situation?"

"At the time there was no more than an accusation. The child was still in the custody of the father."

"But wouldn't anyone else have been better to accompany her to your offices?"

Underwager's eyes flickered to the jury; he looked down as if taken aback. "You're assuming he was guilty."

Glenn disagreed. "No. I'm not assuming anything. Say if, *if* she had actually been abused. When she came to your office, you didn't know whether or not she had, in fact, been abused. Is that correct?"

"Yes. Although, in this case, the fact that she had gonorrhea made it more likely that she had been abused."

Glenn had a special reason for stressing this child's case. In a previous court appearance, Underwager had declared that his own interview with this little girl from Connecticut was a model for how to interview a child. Intent on forcing Underwager to divulge exactly what this model process had been, Glenn instructed the witness to describe his procedure with the girl following preliminaries.

Underwager responded, "In the course of the afternoon, I spent more time with the child."

"Doing what?"

Underwager flinched. The answer unstuck slowly. "What I described before."

"Letting her play with toys?"

"Doing what I do."

"What's that?" soothed Glenn.

"We interacted."

Glenn asked patiently, "What'd you do after letting her play with toys?"

"I let her go." Then Underwager stipulated, "I behaved like an adult. I did not get down on the floor with the child." He spoke with pride.

"But you never asked about sexual abuse. In fact, you were very careful not to," Glenn checked.

"Yes."

Underwager explained that he had read a book to the little girl, so Glenn nudged, "You're reading a book on whales, and what happened then?"

Underwager reconstructed the scene: "The baby whale is born, grows up, goes off on its own. I'm reading the book, she begins to ask me questions about the baby whale being born. . . . Then she began to ask me about how babies are born. Then I responded frankly, as accurately as I could, not talking down to the child. . . . She then asked me some questions about how babies start. I responded with a fairly brief discussion of how human beings make love."

Glenn stopped the doctor. "Let me interrupt for a second. By reading this book on the whale giving birth, you introduced the subject of sex to her?"

Underwager demurred: "I gave her a free recall opportunity. I don't think I introduced the subject of sex to her."

"Well, who picked the book out? You or her?"

"I did."

"So you introduced the subject of sex."

"I introduced the subject of whales and whales giving birth. Yes."

"What did you leave to free recall to her?" Glenn paced silently, one hand in his pocket, his jaw thrust forward a little on the attack.

Underwager sidestepped the question, never answered.

The little girl had eventually told Dr. Underwager that her uncle had abused her, though her father had been the initial suspect. Eventually, she had said, "That's what Uncle Jack did to me." Glenn now reminded the witness, "You went to a court in Connecticut and said, 'This is the maximum reliable statement that a little girl four and a half years old can make.' But Doctor, isn't that exactly what happened with Jonathan Moore?''

"No," said Underwager.

"You're right! It's not! Isn't what happened with Jonathan Moore even *more* reliable?''

Underwager didn't cave in. "No. He said, 'That's what my teacher does to me at school. Her takes my temperature.' I think that's much more ambiguous, much less clear.''

But Glenn had shown that the only difference between the allegation of the girl from Connecticut and that of Jonathan Moore was that the girl had had the subject of sex introduced to her, while Jonathan had not.

Glenn asked, "Dr. Underwager, when the judge asked you what the little girl said Uncle Jack did to her, what did you tell him?''

"Gee, I don't recall.''

"Wasn't that the most significant thing the girl said to you?''

Meltzer objected. "Could my client, I mean the witness"—Meltzer didn't seem embarrassed by the laughter over the slip—"possibly be given the luxury of the transcript I happen to know Mr. Goldberg has before him. We all have trouble remembering things. I don't remember what I said yesterday.''

Harth refused. "Memory may be tested as well as credibility. I will allow it.''

Mr. Michaels smacked his signet ring against the wood of the bench.

Glenn probed, "What was your description of how human beings make love?''

"Oh, I don't recall.''

Glenn asked the witness, "You expect little four- and five-year-old children should be able to give details of incidents by virtue of free recall?''

"I've said that.''

"And haven't you testified that the interviewers should have questioned the children using free recall rather than the way they did?''

Underwager answered that the research showed that the most reliable statement of a child was one given through free recall, but he added, "The interviewers would be best advised to do whatever they could to get the child to tell their story.''

"Is it your testimony that if free recall doesn't produce statements of sexual abuse, investigation closed, that's it, end of case?''

Underwager concurred that if free recall produced no statement, "It should not be prosecuted, case closed. I think the risk of false positives is too high.''

Glenn, hooking a line, asked, ''Do you think if I were to ask you some leading questions, do you think that would bring to mind some of the specific materials you reviewed for this case?''

The doctor smiled, self-amused. ''Mr. Goldberg, I believe your manner of leading questions would introduce a lot of error in the testimony.''

''Well, let's see,'' Glenn challenged, constructing a game. ''Did you review police reports?''

''Yes, I did.''

''Did I introduce any error yet into your testimony?''

''No. You've just repeated what I already said on direct.''

''Did you review the report of George McGrath?''

''I don't recall.''

''My asking didn't cause you to say yes?''

''No, it didn't.''

Glenn shifted. ''Let's try this. Isn't it true that you reviewed the gun involved in this case?''

''No, I didn't,'' said the doctor, laughing as if to make light of the conversation.

Bob Clark objected. ''There's been testimony regarding the suggestibility of children three to five. Doctor Underwager has testified that he's about fifty-eight. I fail to see the relevance.''

Judge Harth reasoned: ''There have been certain theories advanced by the doctor regarding free recall, and the prosecutor is exploring certain stimuli. The doctor has testified he believes error will be produced, and Mr. Goldberg is testing the theory. Overruled.''

Glenn continued, relentless: ''You did review transcripts, didn't you?''

''Yes.''

''Very suggestible question. No error introduced.''

''Yes.''

Glenn said, ''You didn't review the gold bars Kelly used in this case.''

''No, I didn't.'' Underwager's voice lost its swagger.

''Very suggestive. No error yet.''

''No.''

''Am I interviewing you or interrogating you?''

''Interrogating,'' said Underwager, not sensing the trap.

''So! Even as an *interrogator*, I'm asking you leading questions, but I haven't yet caused you to tell the jury something that isn't true!''

''To the best of my knowledge, no,'' the witness answered.

Glenn turned to the nineteen audiocassette tapes made during the joint investigation, of which the doctor had listened to fifteen. Glenn stated, "Four out of nineteen tapes were garbled, so you didn't hear them, so that's twenty-five percent?"

"Yes."

Harth interrupted. "Twenty-five percent of nineteen? Twenty percent."

Underwager was jubilant. "You're right, Your Honor! The mathematician strikes again!"

Meltzer chimed in, "Error has been introduced by the prosecutor!"

"You're right. It works! It works!" said the doctor, laughing thinly.

Glenn picked up, asking, "Did you interview the investigators involved in this case?"

"No."

"Did you ever talk to George McGrath?"

"No. I think that would get me into jail in Newark if I did that," Underwager said, giggling.

"Did you ever attempt to talk to the parents—"

Clark jumped to his feet and, one notch below a scream, declared, "Your Honor, I have a serious objection to this line of questioning. He knows the defense investigator, and defense team in general, hasn't had the opportunity to talk to the parents because they exercised their right not to."

Harth answered calmly, "No. He's asking if he *attempted* to talk to them." The judge was standing up behind his tall chair, leaning against its back edge. Occasionally, he got restless.

Glenn seconded Harth: "Yes, I'm asking if he tried to contact them."

Underwager settled it. "No."

Clark took his seat.

The prosecutor asked, "Did you ever interview Kelly Michaels's co-teachers at Wee Care?"

"No."

"Did you read transcripts?"

"Some of Lou's testimony, cross-examination of Eileen Treacy, George McGrath's testimony."

"Would it be correct to say then that you did not read the testimony of any of the parents?"

"That is correct."

"You did not read the testimony of any of the children?"

"That is correct."

"You did not view the videotapes of the children as they testified in judge's chambers?"

"That's correct. I believe, though, that they have another expert coming in to do that," answered Underwager.

Glenn pushed forward. "So, as you sit there now, you do not know what the children said before this jury."

"That's correct."

"Do you still feel you have all relevant data for your testimony?"

"For my testimony? Yes."

Glenn questioned, "You consider yourself an expert on suggestibility?"

"I don't know if I would say that."

"So, you're not an expert."

"I wouldn't say that."

"Then you are?"

"The American Psychological Association says—"

Glenn cut him off. "No. I want to know what you think, not someone else. Are you an expert in suggestibility?"

"I have some special knowledge of suggestibility," the defense expert conceded.

Glenn sounded confused. "But you're in court, testifying as an expert witness."

"For the purposes of this court, I'd say I was."

"Oh! So for the purposes of this court you're an expert, but outside this court, you're not?"

"The difficulty is—" Underwager stalled, then finished, "that our profession discourages calling yourself an expert."

Glenn retrieved from the court clerk the plastic forks that defense counsel had used to question the children. He knew the witness hadn't seen the testimony to know yet what the children had done. Glenn gave Dr. Underwager the five forks and an open question: "If those were to be presented to a little boy or girl with a request to pick one out, do you have an opinion? Which one do you think the child would be most likely to choose?"

"I don't know."

"Well, what are the differences among the various forks?"

"One is broken, differences in color, discoloration, one is bright green and the rest are white." He moved the forks around on the stand.

"Doctor, would you say from your knowledge of suggestibility, if you had to figure out or imagine which fork a child would pick out, the principles of suggestibility would dictate they'd pick the green one that stood out?''

"No. It would depend on the mode of presentation."

Glenn provided: "If the forks were dropped on the table in front of the child."

"Pick-Up-Stix? The child would do what I did, pick the nearest one."

"So, you think it would be a pure chance selection? Whichever fork happened to fall closest to the child, he'd pick up?''

"No. That's not at all what I'm saying."

Glenn appeared not to hear, continuing, "So, all things being equal, the child will randomly pick what's nearest to him?''

Underwager grinned, hanging his head demurely. "Oh! But all things are *not* equal.''

Glenn pounced: "And the thing that made it not equal was that the child was asked what instrument was used in the abuse, and the child *knew* he was abused, so he picked the ordinary white instead of the standout green! That was the variable that makes it not equal.''

The doctor paused. "It might be a variable."

The following day, Glenn was still investigating this question. He asked the doctor, "You don't think the child would pick up the farthest? Just as likely?''

"No.''

"Or pick up one in the middle? Just as likely?''

"No.''

Glenn had arranged for the televisions to be brought back into the courtroom, and now he played back a portion of Alison Steadman's testimony. Still in her yellow summer jumper, Alison watched Harvey Meltzer drop five forks onto the tabletop in front of her. Passing over the bright green fork resting nearest to her, she reached across and carefully selected the white fork that was farthest away.

Glenn paused the tape. "Doctor Underwager, which fork did the little girl pick up? The closest one?''

"Yes," he said.

Glenn, isosceles eyebrows raised, repeated the question: "The closest one?''

"Yes. Closest to her right hand." The doctor's eyes taunted.

Glenn was confounded. He repeated yet again, "Didn't she pick up the farthest fork?''

"No. It's the closest—closest to her right hand.''

Glenn shook his head: The man could think on the run. He fast-forwarded the tape to Meltzer's identical experiment with the plastic spoons. This time Alison chose a white spoon from the middle of the pile.

"What happened, Doctor Underwager?"

"She apparently picked one from the middle."

"She didn't do what you said she'd do, did she, Doctor Underwager?"

The expert witness stated, "The behavior speaks for itself."

Abruptly, Glenn was scathing: "Isn't it true that, whatever you see, you are going to find some excuse to explain away whatever the child did other than showing what Kelly did to her?"

Bob Clark objected.

"Objection overruled."

"No," answered Underwager. Underwager's small, round lips curled back in the bud of a smile.

Glenn next played a sequence from Julie Danvers's testimony, and Julie picked the utensil in the center of the batch. Underwager attributed Julie's failure to choose the fork closest to her to the fact that there were too many people in the room.

Harth inquired, "In what way does the number of people present . . . influence the child holding a clump of utensils, lead to selecting one as opposed to another?"

Dr. Underwager spoke with a wink in his voice. "The parent is holding the child, and as the child was performing the task, who knows but whether or not the hand on the leg pushed a little bit harder."

At day's end, Harth dismissed the jury and asked the prosecutor how much longer he intended to go. Glenn estimated two to three days. Meltzer objected to Glenn's thoroughness and stated, "I think we're cutting the baloney roll a little too thin."

"I agree," said Glenn. "It *is* a baloney roll."

Kelly, sitting beside Underwager on the bench, brushed some lint off the doctor's shoulder.

The courtroom had just about emptied out, but Glenn was still packing up his papers. While closing up her equipment, the court reporter mimicked, "Is your name Underwager?" and then answered herself, "Not necessarily so."

Glenn entered in: "Is it the opposite of Underwager?" then answered, "*No.*"

▪
▪ ▪

"Bring her up," Harth ordered.

The judge wanted to confer with Eighteen before her scheduled release from jail, hopeful that reiteration would effect a cure and she would stay away from the courthouse.

The bailiffs brought her in. She looked slightly drawn sitting at counsel table adjusting her handcuffs and pushing them farther up her wrists. The Michaels family exchanged bemused looks.

Kelly sat near the windows at the far end of the table but didn't look at her would-be protector. Kelly wore a large silver bracelet over the cuff of her blouse, a detail that seemed to connect her to Eighteen.

Meltzer and Clark were both standing off to the side of counsel table. Neither prosecutor would get close to counsel table: Sara sat in the viewing gallery, and Glenn was at his post in the jury box. All the lawyers had deserted.

Eighteen loosened her jaw, pointedly patient.

From feelers Harth extended, it sounded as though Eighteen had every intention of defying his order and returning to court the moment she was released from Caldwell. Harth suggested to her that she might wish to consult with the attorney whom he had waiting here on her behalf.

Eighteen declined.

He then suggested that she consult with her family members.

"That will not be necessary."

Eighteen was returned to Caldwell to serve out the tail end of her sentence, and immediately upon her release, Eighteen revisited Harth's courtroom.

With disgust, Harth stated, "You are just plain interfering with this trial." The judge stared at her, anxious for any sign of comprehension he could glean.

The woman's voice was gruff. "Your rulings do not apply to me, sir. I have told you I am here for a purpose, and you refuse to adhere to that."

"You won't describe that purpose."

She intoned like a preacher: "Are you so blind that you cannot see, sir?"

"Anything else?"

"No. That is it, sir."

As Harth opened his mouth to resentence her for contempt of court, she interjected, "I see you have not obtained any wisdom or discernment. Sir."

"I must hold you in contempt of court" was his response.

She barked, "You are very foolish, sir." For the first time, she was revealing anger, vehemence.

"Why?" asked Harth.

"That is it, sir."

As the woman rose to meet the sheriff's officers who were closing in, she grinned and lifted her fists, slowly, carefully, connecting them at the wrist.

They cuffed her.

"You see the color in her face?" a bailiff remarked.

The laughter began as she turned her back to the judge to be led, a leather stalk, from the courtroom. She cackled diabolically. She could still be heard as the guards led her down the corridor, this time to be held for psychiatric observation.

She obviously needed structure in her life.

.
.   .

Kelly looked demure in an all-white dress with a stretched bodice. She continued to write in her notebook, now working in two narrow columns, like a theological text.

Dr. Underwager had offered his opinion on the limited ability of pre-schoolers to feel emotion in an interview. He had claimed: "Children do not yet have the cognitive ability at this age to do the abstract thinking necessary to have emotions, like embarrassment or shame. What they can do is feel anxiety at not being able to answer."

Glenn asked "whether he had testified that children can't remember threats."

"Out of the presence of the perpetrator, threats will lose their hold, they won't control the child."

Glenn struggled to get it straight. "Children can't feel shame, embarrassment, or remember threats, but you're saying that they can remember phony stories told them by an interviewer for years to come?"

"What I think I said was when children are repeatedly reinforced and given by adults the social influence that leads them to construct the image of being a victim, that that has long-lasting effects."

"What other emotions besides embarrassment, shame, threats, can't children feel?"

"Now, children show physiological responses, but they have not yet learned to think abstractly, to learn what label to give. That's part of growing up, and that's what makes it a mistake for an adult to look at a child and to project on to that child the full adult construct: embarrassment, shame, anxiety, whatever that label might be." He limited children's emotional range "to avoiding something negative and seeking something positive. . . . There are even some psychiatrists, though I don't agree, who question whether children experience love, or are children just responding to the warmest fuzzy they can find?"

Harth asked, ''Would a caveman fear the water before he learned either the word for fear or drowning? Adults learned emotion before they even had language, didn't they?''

There was a long wait for the answer, which was no.

Kelly wrinkled her brow suddenly, without any apparent impetus for her consternation. She seemed to watch an altogether different channel of daily life.

Moving to a new area, Glenn asked the doctor to address the effect of sexual abuse on preschool children.

Underwager answered, ''The effect on most children of repeated abuse by an adult would be very damaging. . . . For a given child, the specific signs of damage would depend on the child, and would range all the way from developing ulcers to becoming angry and hostile.''

Glenn was aglow. To his knowledge, no other prosecutor in the country had ever gotten Dr. Ralph Underwager to acknowledge under oath that sexual abuse could provoke behavioral disorders in child victims or even cause harm.

Glenn got specific: ''Doctor, what would be the effect on a young child of being forced to drink urine?''

''There could be some gastrointestinal distress,'' said Underwager.

''What about *psychologically*?''

''Some children, as I've said, could find it attractive, enjoy it, reinforce their fascination.'' Underwager eventually embellished this thought: ''I think the kind of fantasy a child has about waste frequently does include consuming, in one form or another, urine or feces.''

Glenn challenged him: ''Have you ever come across any child finding the drinking of urine attractive or fascinating?''

''I haven't.''

Glenn pushed, and the doctor could not cite a single professional study that corroborated his own opinion that children fantasize about ingesting waste.

The next area Glenn invaded was Underwager's ''Time and Motion Study,'' an assessment of the children's allegations in terms of feasibility constraints. Dr. Underwager and his research staff had considered several specific acts Kelly Michaels stood accused of to determine the time that she would have required to accomplish those acts. The results of the study specified a low- and high-time estimate for each given act.

First off, Glenn asked Underwager, ''Have you taken the time or effort to visit the place where the Wee Care Day Nursery was located?''

The doctor answered no.

''How far were the children's classrooms from the choir room?''

"I don't know."

Glenn probed Underwager for the specifics of his scientific method, and to help him focus, Glenn directed Underwager's response to one specific example involving seven children in a nude pileup, lying on top of utensils. He asked how he and his co-workers had determined the length of time it would have taken for the children to move from one part of the school to another.

Underwager was exceedingly serious: "Based on our own experience and judgment of how long it would take."

"Doctor Underwager, what experience do you have lying naked on the floor and having children pile on top of you?"

"Objection," said Clark, "as to the form of the question."

"Objection sustained," muttered Harth, barely able to speak.

Glenn read back a statement from direct examination: " 'Of course, we hadn't seen the building itself. But we're relatively familiar with buildings and rooms and how to move from one to the other.' " Now he inquired, "How could you do this without knowing a specific measure of feet?"

"Oh, rather easily. You visualize . . . imagine how long it takes."

"The jurors have been to the building. You haven't. And they have the same ability to judge buildings and rooms. Who better to estimate how long it would have taken? The jury or you?"

Underwager hurrahed: "The jury!"

The study had defined a low-end estimate of eight minutes and a high-end estimate of twenty minutes for Kelly to have gotten seven children to the choir room. Glenn needled, "Is there any reason to believe it couldn't take only *seven* minutes?"

"No."

"It could take only seven minutes?"

"Conceivably."

Glenn shifted up. "Why is the maximum twenty minutes? Couldn't it've been twenty-five minutes?"

"It could've been. Certainly."

Glenn worked in this way through the examples of Underwager's time and motion study, widening the values for the high and low estimates, and greatly damaging the study's claim of precision.

Glenn concluded, "Doctor, are you saying you used subjective experience to make your estimates?"

Underwager answered, "Yes."

"Isn't the scientist who"—Glenn quickly found his copy of the doctor's manuscript and quoted Underwager back at himself—" 'who bases his findings on unchecked subjective experience regressed to the level of an untrained witch doctor?' ''

''No.''

Glenn read the quote again: '' '. . . the scientist who bases his findings on unchecked subjective experience . . .' ''

Poking his finger through the loophole, Underwager howled, joyously: ''Unchecked! This is not unchecked!''

''Good, Doctor. Tell us how these findings are checked,'' Glenn requested.

''Intersubjective Confrontability.''

Harth exclaimed, ''Wow! That's a tough one. Tell us what that means.''

Underwager explained that two researchers each developed their own time estimates, then they compared their results, and if they each had similar estimates of elapsed time, the results were deemed to be more or less accurate.

Harth extrapolated: ''Then if a *few* witch doctors got together, they could get the same finding you got?''

''Yes,'' was the shocking response.

.
. .

At the end of the day, Harth once again inquired how much longer the prosecutor anticipated being with this witness. Glenn explained that this was the defense's most important witness—Kelly mouthed, ''He's not!''—and gave his usual refrain: ''Not much longer, Judge. One more day?''

Kelly, waiting in the gallery for her family to gather their belongings, shook her head. She protested, ''It doesn't matter! It's so stupid! Even if Dr. Underwager didn't testify, we still have a case. We still have a case.''

.
. .

Karen Steadman drove slowly through Newark. She wasn't in any rush to get to the courthouse.

Newark was a sprawling urban area, scarred by abandoned housing projects and empty, littered lots. Karen passed an elementary school, a tar-top basketball court (no net) enmeshed with fifteen-foot fences. She glimpsed a few little children lining up on the blacktop. Their obliviousness shattered her.

.
. .

Underwager must have sensed that he was in trouble because early into cross-examination he appealed to Judge Harth (in the presence of the jury), saying that Mr. Goldberg was trying to destroy him professionally. He had already said that he felt persecuted by an association of district attorneys who allegedly perceived him as the number-one enemy expert witness.

In response, Glenn Goldberg assured him, "Certainly not anymore, not after testifying in this court."

Mr. Michaels hung his head, shaking it lightly, and laughed to himself.

The doctor went so far as to distance himself from his own writings, qualifying statements that he had made in his own book manuscript, so that finally Glenn asked him, "Doctor Underwager, aren't you willing to rely on the material in your own book, knowing the author as well as you do?"

"Yes, certainly," he answered, with the little smile.

In his testimony, Dr. Underwager partitioned the set of the ways children can communicate and left no area undiscredited, emotional or verbal: Courts were not to believe either children's feelings or their words.

Sara told Glenn in her precious, whispered kiddie voice: "If I were God, there'd be a very special place in Hell for people who go around the country doing this to little children . . . a very special place in Hell."

For his part, Glenn was outraged at how grossly unprepared to testify Dr. Underwager had been, outraged at the doctor's almost total ignorance of the facts and evidence in the case.

Yet Underwager vigorously attacked the prosecuting parties: "The behavior of the parents, investigators, and prosecutors in this case can be likened to the behavior of the adults in the Salem witch trials."

"Who specifically?"

"Mr. Fonolleras and Mr. McGrath."

"Did you ever hear any tapes of their interviews?" asked Glenn.

"No."

17

.·.

January had nearly elapsed, the trial had just filled seven months on the Superior Court docket, and Sara and Glenn were still demanding notification of if and when the defendant would testify. If so, there was much physical preparation to be done: a line-by-line review of Kelly's police statements, the teachers' testimony, the school roll books, the time cards. Dozens of hours of work still had to be scheduled.

Sara and Glenn tried to extract a promise that they would be given one week's notice by the defense if Kelly was to testify, but Meltzer and Clark arranged with the judge that the prosecutors would be told two days in advance. The mechanism was put into place, but the prosecutors weren't expecting any such notification for quite a while: Two experts and five, possibly six character witnesses were still slated to testify.

In the past several weeks, the defense had put various employees of St. George's on the stand. The warden of the church testified that he had never paid any special attention to what the children or adults were doing at Wee Care. The two secretaries for the church, however, both insisted that the abuse could not have happened: They had been in the habit of wandering into the choir room bathrooms (they were cleaner than the bathroom closest to their office) and they had never seen or smelled any peanut butter, urine, or feces, nor seen any stray items of clothing or scenes of abuse. They did, however, acknowledge that there was no way the children should ever have been in the choir room to learn what it looked like.

The secretaries' claims to having been in the choir room at unpredictable times of the day was damaging to the state, but on cross-examination Glenn Goldberg got them to admit how little knowledge "all those people in the building" really had about what was going on at Wee Care. Both women admitted to knowing absolutely nothing about how Wee Care had run or its schedule, even of where the children had eaten lunch. As one of them finally protested, "I'm not responsible for the children!"

The other secretary acknowledged that she had never checked, when she saw children coming up the stairs, if they were following a Wee Care schedule or not. Kelly could have been headed toward the choir room, this secretary said, and she would not have questioned it. This same woman stressed that she had heard no piano playing from the choir room and insisted that she would indeed have heard if anything had been wrong. To back up this claim, she testified that one time she had heard a child crying and had been so alarmed by the sound of his voice that she had mentioned the incident to Arlene Spector a week later. Glenn turned her testimony against her, inquiring, "If you were that concerned about unusual crying and noises, why didn't you go down to the classroom?" The woman retorted, "Mr. Goldberg, that's not my job. I assumed there were plenty of teachers there."

Dr. Jonas Rappeport took the stand for the defense, but because his proposed testimony on the profile of an abuser had been struck down in pretrial, his testimony in large part overlapped that of Dr. Underwager. Rappeport believed that the children in the case had been abused by law enforcement by the repeated interviews during the state's investigation. He said, "These children have been so traumatized since this whole thing started, anything they say now is invalid." In addition, he pointed out the possibility that the children had alleged abuse simply to please their interviewers: "Kids don't like being scolded. They want to please adults."

When Glenn asked him whether that also applied to pleasing teachers, the witness answered, "Sure."

In many areas on which the prosecutor asked him to comment, the doctor had not reviewed the appropriate materials. Attempting to pinpoint the doctor's basis for claiming that these children's allegations were the result of suggestion, Sara rose and asked, "Did you in any way attempt to figure out who was the first child to say, for example, the insertion of a spoon, and where that allegation came from?"

Dr. Rappeport responded vaguely, "I recall it came from suggestion."

Interestingly, despite the fact that Dr. Underwager had testified that he had not viewed the videotapes of the children's testimony because another expert was coming in to comment on them, Dr. Rappeport claimed that it was Underwager's field to review children's testimony. Rappeport himself had seen no children or victims in a professional capacity—he maintained that he was qualified to testify as an expert in this trial because he had raised three of his own—but had interviewed hundreds of perpetrators. One of his sessions with Kelly Michaels in 1986 had been videotaped "for educational purposes," although in criticizing the children's statements, Rappeport claimed that interviews were never as good when a tape recorder or camera was on.

Surprisingly, Dr. Rappeport contradicted Ralph Underwager on a number of important points. Rappeport acknowledged freely that abused children might display behavioral changes, and he confirmed that abused children often become more modest, demanding more privacy in the bathroom and concealing their sexual features: for example, overdressing, or adding another protective layer of clothing. (Karen Steadman sat up, startled, on the bench.) Rappeport also admitted that children feel embarrassment and guilt, emotions that can lead to a child not immediately disclosing abuse.

In other areas of his testimony, the doctor claimed to rely not upon a review of the evidence but upon the representations of defense counsel. A case in point was Rappeport's understanding that when Jonathan Moore told his nurse, "That's what my teacher does to me at school," the thermometer was not yet in his rectum. Rappeport claimed that to his knowledge the nurse's hand was on the child's back, and so that was the kind of touching to which Jonathan's "disclosure" had referred. Of course, when Glenn inquired why, if that context were accurate, Jonathan would then have gone on to say that she used Vaseline, the witness had no explanation.

Just before releasing the doctor from duty, Glenn asked the doctor if he recalled having at pretrial recommended to Assistant Prosecutor Sara McArdle the book, *The Politics of Child Abuse*.

"Oh yes!" said Rappeport.

Glenn dug in a little further, establishing that the doctor selected the publications upon which he relied on the basis of their authors. Then Glenn drew a sheaf of papers from his accordion file and presented the packet to Judge Harth to review. Harth glanced through the materials, then had a bailiff carry them over to defense counsel. Bob and Harvey began to laugh.

Meltzer spoke up: "Can I have this copied when we're done with it?"

Glenn retrieved his copies of *Finger* magazine and waved them before the witness, in the process giving the jurors to his left an eyeful of a naked man and woman sprawling, legs splayed, amidst several inflated dolls. On the inside pages were photographs of children being raped, a child standing over an adult and urinating into the adult's mouth, written pieces detailing sexual experiences with young children, both incestuous and extrafamilial, and the exhilarating feelings experienced by the sexual abusers writing in.

The coauthors of the doctor's source book were also the publishers of *Finger* magazine. Glenn asked the witness: "Are you aware that [the authors] of *The Politics of Child Abuse* publish child pornography?"

Dr. Rappeport had had no idea.

Glenn next asked if, knowing this, the doctor would withdraw his recommendation of their treatise on sexual abuse. Glenn was still holding up the magazines. On the cover of one, the title, *Finger*, was drawn as little pieces of fingers all pieced together to form phallically curved letters.

Rappeport responded, "No. I'd say they present another side of the picture." From a personal perspective, he qualified, "They obviously are bad people whom I wouldn't associate with."

After the jury had been dismissed, the defense motioned for a mistrial.

Glenn defended the admissibility of this evidence: "This prejudices only his own credibility. . . . That he'd still consider the opinions of this book demonstrates the total lack of validity of his opinion, if pornographers are believed."

Harvey Meltzer countered, "Your Honor, it's my understanding that pornography is in the eyes of the beholder."

Clark added a comment as well, on "the prejudicial and inflammatory tactics of Mr. Goldberg."

The judge ruled: "All witnesses can be questioned on their credibility. Experts can be questioned on their qualifications as well, including education and their reading of treatises."

.
. .

Bob Clark had watched over Kelly, aware of the tension created by her having to sit at counsel table day after day, unable to respond to the attacks being made against her. Whenever he had sensed that Kelly was nervous, he had attempted to disarm her, most often with dark humor, which she liked. The energy of her frustration was obviously being directed into her writing: She had written voluminously since the trial had begun.

The defendant, her family, and her attorneys had grown close over the course of this trial: They had been together every day during breaks and lunch and the stressful course of proceedings. Harvey Meltzer had even named his new Doberman puppy Kelly.

All of them shared a great deal of anger about what was going on, and as a result, they found solidarity as one extended family. The families of the two lawyers had also become involved in the dynamics: Meltzer's wife and son frequently attended proceedings to support Harvey's client, and Clark's mother made infrequent appearances. The Michaelses had adopted her as one of their own. The group even socialized on occasions after court: "Do you want Chinese or Italian?"

Spirits on the defense side of the courtroom appeared to be elevated now that control of the trial had turned over to their team. Kelly had a steady influx of experts to rally around her and articulate her interpretation of the evidence. Along with presenting the best defense possible, her legal team continued to load the record with their comments as to the perceived prejudice of the judge against their client and their objections to statements of his which they considered sarcastic. Meltzer was quite vigorous in his comments, so much so that at times Judge Harth had to defuse him: "Mr. Meltzer, Mr. Clark is pulling on your sleeve. You've already won. You can't win twice."

.
. .

Dr. Elissa Benedek, possibly the most qualified of all the defense experts, wielded a mighty triad of specialties: She was a board-certified psychiatrist in adult, child, and forensic psychiatry. She had been in practice in Michigan for over twenty-three years, and her particular areas of expertise were child psychology and sexual abuse.

Benedek's massive (twenty-seven-page) curriculum vitae boasted assorted credentials: guest lecturer at Harvard, consultant to the Secret Service, speaker to the army troops stationed in Germany, and, most impressively, one-time trustee on the board of the American Psychiatric Association. Currently, she held the office of secretary of the APA. The doctor already had six day-care cases to her credit, as a consultant in five and as a witness in one, but she had never yet testified in such a large day-care case.

Her manner betrayed that this was a debut: Instead of advancing toward the witness stand, she stood awkwardly in the middle of the courtroom floor to be sworn in. She was dressed in a beige blazer and skirt, her blouse buttoned to the base of her throat. Benedek was shorter even than Kelly.

Meltzer conducted direct examination, but on her own initiative Dr. Benedek spun away from his questions.

She described her preparation for trial: "I reviewed all materials provided to me. In summary, I reviewed all the videos of interviews by various police officers and DYFS people, all the Grand Jury testimony, Dr. Rappeport's reports, a videotape of the defendant, Kelly Michaels. I reviewed portions of experts in this case, including Doc—*Miss* Esquilin and *Miss* Treacy, medical reports, videotapes of two children: Joey Gardner and David Kirschner."

The timbre of her words was defensive: "*I asked* to see all of the children; *I asked* to see all of the parents; *I asked* to see all of the videotapes of the children. I was not afforded the opportunity to do so."

Sara objected—loudly. "She certainly was!"

Benedek shook her head pityingly.

The doctor defended herself: "I work a fifty to sixty hour week. I was more than willing to review the material in my home, with my family. I was not going to fly all the way to New Jersey." The tremors of an uptight witness thrummed through her answer.

Meltzer asked her to comment on the demeanor of David Kirschner during his court appearance, and Benedek responded, "David Kirschner showed very little affect. He was basically flat and disinterested, except for the time when David asked what an objection was and the judge explained in a very nice way . . . and David smiled. But for the rest of the time, he really was a child repeating material which had, for the most part, been carefully rehearsed."

Glenn objected to Benedek's conclusion: "She can testify that's her opinion, but there's been no evidence."

She elaborated: "David showed very little emotion like he was reliving the experience—no anger, fear, nothing spontaneous."

Benedek shifted her attention to Joey's testimony, the only other videotape she had reviewed. She stated, "Joey looked annoyed that he had to be doing this again. He was a typical seven- or eight-year-old. . . . The only flashes of spontaneity he showed were when he was given a break. Neither child showed evidence of traumatic reliving."

Meltzer derided, "Didn't you see David turn his face and Joey turn his face from the questioner when a painful question was asked?"

"They turned their *face*," she conceded stiffly.

Harth cautioned, "Objection. That's leading, Mr. Meltzer."

Meltzer directed his witness to David Kirschner's testimony about peanut butter. She described the scene: "David didn't remember about peanut butter when the question first arose. If a child did not remember the first time, he was asked a second time and a third time. What happens with children is that if they are asked repeatedly by authorities to endorse particular things, they eventually give up—and endorse those things. A kid can only hold out so long."

Kelly nodded in increments, as if she were ticking each word off a checklist.

Meltzer asked Benedek to confirm from the transcript what David had said in his testimony, but Harth interrupted. "Mr. Meltzer, it's not the function of an expert to tell the jury what was said in an interview." He turned to Benedek. "Do you have any *opinion* as to what David was saying?"

"Do you have any opinion as to what David was saying," Meltzer mimicked.

"My opinion is the questions were leading, that they introduced new information to the child, that they were coercive to the child, that the child was not allowed to narrate freely the events of the allegation. He was asked no corroborating details, like what was he thinking, what'd the peanut butter look like, etcetera. . . . He was asked how'd it feel, and he said, 'It felt bad,' but that's certainly not the kind of elaborate answer that would corroborate an allegation."

Harth pursued the point: "You said to ask what peanut butter looked like. What sense would there be to asking, unless he'd never seen it before?"

"The sense of that is to see how the child answers those questions spontaneously. Peanut butter on the penis and butt looks different from peanut butter in a jar. It looks more crunchy. It looks less crunchy. It looks more fluid. It looks less fluid."

"You'd expect a child to say it looks more fluid?"

"No." Benedek gazed off and mused. The answer came to her. "More wet," she said.

She returned to David's demeanor while testifying, her delivery smug: "If an event is really that traumatic to a child, it's not that easy to reenact it. You don't get answers that easily. It's not that spontaneous."

Just moments ago she had said that the testimony seemed false because it was rehearsed, not spontaneous; however, now she declared that it was too spontaneous to be authentic.

Meltzer asked, "The jury has heard children asked how various things tasted, and the word *yucky* came up. Does that word mean anything to you?"

Dr. Benedek laughed. "Yes. It has a very special meaning to me. . . . When I hear the word *yucky*, a red flag goes up. . . . Too many children say sexual abuse is 'yucky' when interviewed by inexperienced people. The word's a *red flag*. When a child says sperm tasted yucky, instead of salty, sweet, bitter, like a Mars bar, like some terrible chicken soup my mommy made—" She broke off, then elaborated, "Many other words can be used," then she added, in meter:

> Gushy, gucky
> Smushy, smucky
> Icky, ucky."

Discreetly, Sara wondered, A Mars bar?

Dr. Benedek stated, "I think both the adults and the children experienced contamination and contagion. First, the interviewers came in and spoke to the children. And the children were not isolated, so they went back into their classroom and said, 'Guess what happened to me?' "

"Objection, Your Honor!" Sara shouted.

Benedek's hand quivered on its pedestal.

Harth asked the witness, "Are you basing that on evidence?"

Holding the microphone and raising her voice belligerently, she said, "I'm basing that on experience with children. Also, some of the children said, 'So-and-so told me what happened.' "

"All right," allowed Harth.

Meltzer asked, "Dr. Benedek, we've heard testimony that there were group meetings. . . . We heard letters went out from the school."

Benedek's fingers clutched the microphone. She spoke directly into the grid, her voice thick and shaken: "Yes. Parents were sent a letter and told their kids had been abused."

Glenn flipped through his papers and checked the letter. Nope.

Oblivious, Benedek embellished her thesis. "They were encouraged to look for signs of sexual abuse; they were told to identify them as signs of sexual abuse; they talked about them with each other; they had parent meetings; they talked about them with the children. So now all of the information is contaminated."

Harth asked the unthinkable: "Have you seen the letter?"

Benedek answered, "No," not nearly so appalled at herself as everyone else appeared to be.

The judge ventured, "Well, so you're not answering from the actual content of the letter?"

"There is *an article*—"

Harth told her to stop the response.

"—in the literature—"

"Objection!" shouted Sara.

"—that talks about the inflammatory nature of letters!"

. .
.

DYFS's Institutional Abuse Unit had fielded many allegations of abuse since the Wee Care investigation. Lou Fonolleras had since seen a number of girls whose mothers were frightened because their daughters had vaginitis. He had questioned the mothers closely and had established that the women had read about the Kelly Michaels trial and were concerned that this inflammation could be symptomatic of abuse. Lou reported these cases as unsubstantiated (the girls weren't alleging any kind of improper contact) and cautioned the parents against paranoia. Not every symptom was a proof.

. .
.

The direct testimony of Dr. Elissa Benedek was a two-day soliloquy: Like a roller coaster, its tracks were deceptively smooth. Finally, Meltzer turned her over to the prosecutors, who accepted the challenge with the knowledge that they were facing a dangerous witness.

Glenn took the first shift with Benedek. He asked, "Would you say that you are not an authority in child sexual abuse?"

"No. I would not say that I am not an authority."

He tried the converse: "So, you would consider yourself an expert."

"My colleagues consider—"

"I didn't ask what your colleagues think. I asked what do you think."

Harth interjected: "No. That can be part of her answer. What's your next question?"

Benedek blinked behind her plastic-framed glasses.

Glenn explored her clinical experience with children of preschool age, asking, "Doctor Benedek, how many boys under the age of six have you treated for child sexual abuse?"

"I told you, I don't keep statistics on that kind of thing. I've been in practice since 1963. I've seen many children."

"I asked how many in child sexual abuse?"

"Yes, sir. That is correct. And I *cannot answer*," she said. "It's so difficult to remember all of one's involvements."

Glenn explored the doctor's preparation for court. She had not viewed the seventeen other videotapes of children's testimony, nor read Eileen Treacy's official report, despite the fact that her special purpose in coming to court was to neutralize Treacy's testimony on confounding variables. Pointedly, Glenn reminded Benedek that daily copy of the trial transcripts had been available: She had had every opportunity to see them.

Irritated, Benedek told him, "I have what I have. This is unusual to me. . . . I certainly would not say I'm unprepared. I'm confident of my opinion, but I certainly would have liked to have had other material."

Glenn considered his notes, then looked up and asked Benedek to interpret David Kirschner's excruciating discomfort during his appearance in court.

She responded, "Avoidance mechanism having to do with the uncomfortable situation. Having to go through this, what I would consider a test: question/answer, question/answer, question/answer. *Certainly* not to do with retelling a traumatic event. If a child were retelling a traumatic event, there would be some natural emotion: sadness, anger, shame. Something spontaneous."

Glenn contended, "Dr. Benedek, wasn't David Kirschner one of the saddest little boys you've ever seen?"

"Nooooo." She laughed. "He wasn't *close* to the saddest little boy *I've* ever seen." Her tone mocked.

"How long was the tape of David Kirschner approximately?" he inquired, testing her familiarity with the video.

"Oh, I really don't know. I have no idea."

"Was it less than an hour?"

"I really don't know. I didn't *time* it."

Glenn asked her to confirm her opinion that an abused child would spontaneously reenact the trauma when talking about it.

She said, "Certainly every time a child describes 'the trauma' you don't see a change in affect."

"Is your answer, then, that you would agree that there would *not* be a spontaneous reenactment of the trauma?"

"Not completely, but there certainly would be some occasional affect consistent with the trauma."

Glenn fired, "Which child's head fell upon the table at the first mention of Wee Care?"

"That's not reenactment of a trauma. That's, 'Oh no, not again. I don't wanna tell again about this stuff.' "

"Which child?" he insisted.

Benedek guessed: "Joey?"

"No. Jonathan Moore." Glenn let that error sink in. He asked, "Did you watch the tape of Jonathan?"

"No. I watched one minute, saw Jonathan dressed up, and *that* was *it*." Benedek's voice sneered.

Glenn offered as an example of spontaneity Lewis Dixon's testifying to drinking pee and motioning with his mouth to replicate his distaste. Glenn asked Benedek to comment, despite, of course, her not having watched the video.

She answered, "I'd say that is overpsychologizing. I couldn't comment on that."

"Isn't that exactly what you're doing in all of your testimony? Taking little bits and pieces out of all the material and testifying to them out of context?"

"I don't think that's what I'm doing. I have a lot of information."

Glenn had more examples. "What about the meowing behavior. Would that be consistent with the notion of spontaneous reenactment of the trauma?"

"Yes," Benedek responded, adding, "and it's also behavior consistent with childhood. They meow. They make bird noises."

Harth interrupted. "Now I want you to listen to the question, Doctor." He directed the court reporter to read back the prosecutor's question.

When the question had been repeated, Harth cautioned Benedek: "You're here as a witness, not an advocate."

Clark jumped, irate. "Objection!"

"No. In view of her role as expert and her answers," said Harth in attorney code.

Clark remained on his feet. "You're constantly telling our experts they're advocates. She answered the question." As the trial aged, the gray in Clark's hair seemed to be encroaching, as if his head were slowly freezing over.

"Let's hear the question and answer. If I'm wrong, I apologize."

Dr. Benedek looked up at the judge, said curtly, "Thank you. I *appreciate* the apology."

The reporter read through the complete transaction.

Harth readdressed Benedek. "Doctor, just answer the question."

Glenn resumed. "Doctor, do you know what meowing I'm referring to?"

"No. I have no idea. I was going to ask you," she said.

Glenn explained to her the evidence on which she had just given her opinion: "In an interview, when asked about the abuse, Joey Gardner began to meow—spontaneously."

"Those interviews were situations where kids were trapped!"

"Doctor, I'm talking about meowing."

She acknowledged the possibility that he meowed because he was uncomfortable in the situation. "I would not say spontaneous reenactment."

"Doctor, are you aware of any allegations in this case where children act like something other than themselves?"

"Yes."

Glenn's voice lilted disarmingly. "What are they?"

"Games. Duck, duck, goose. Maybe cat and dog games."

Glenn asked her if she was familiar with an incident involving Fred Mercer and his interviewer, Anne.

"I have no recollection at all."

Glenn paged through his notes for his next area of questioning.

Benedek spoke: "First of all, I'd like to comment that all these kids were sexually overstimulated: by the interviewers, by interaction with each other, by all that was going on."

Part of Glenn's job was to control the witness, to prevent these interjections when no question was on the floor, but he was actually a little pleased that the doctor was so obviously violating the rules that the judge repeatedly had to admonish her not to go beyond the question.

Glenn described the little boy Robert who had hidden himself in a closet with naked dolls and silverware. He inquired, "Wasn't that spontaneous reenactment of the trauma, Doctor?"

"No, it was not. Are you alleging that he was placed by Kelly in a closet with Barbie dolls and utensils?"

Glenn retorted, "You don't know anything about this, do you?"

Benedek sputtered.

The judge suggested Glenn move on.

Glenn described Joey Gardner's self-portrait with blood colored in between his legs. He asked her to comment.

"These kids were asked about blood from Kelly's vagina *repeatedly*," she said.

"Doctor, what would you say if I told you that self-portrait was drawn three months before any interviewer ever saw Joey?"

Benedek paused, lingered, then asked helplessly, "That self-portrait was drawn three months before any interviewer spoke with the child?"

"Yes."

She recovered. "Tell me where, when, how—and why it was saved."

Harth interrupted: "How it was saved? How does that matter?"

"Because retrospective history, particularly when people have been told what to look for, is highly unreliable."

"Doctor, would you agree, before it could be saved, it had to be *done*?" asked the judge.

"Yes. It was done."

Harth inquired, "*Why* was it done?"

"I don't know. I don't know why Joey drew that."

"You may continue, Mr. Goldberg."

Finally, Glenn asked head on: "What *would* be a spontaneous reenactment of trauma?"

In offering her own definition, Benedek adopted an urgent rasp: "If you see a youngster alone in a playroom—there's nobody around—playing with dolls, talking with the dolls, saying different things, saying, *'Don't hurt me, don't, don't do it, don't touch me there.' 'Yes I will. Yes I will.'* "

Karen Steadman rushed out of the courtroom.

The doctor stopped herself suddenly to add: "With lots of movement, lots of affect, lots of feeling. The whole gestalt thing."

Glenn proposed, "What about a simulated sexual intercourse? Is that sufficient?"

"One episode of simulated sexual intercourse in isolation, in itself, is not spontaneous reenactment of a trauma, no. First of all, it's subject to the eye of the beholder."

Harth stipulated, "Allowing that, allowing that."

"If you know young children, you know that there's a lot of sexual curiosity, playing doctor, etcetera. So one episode of playing at intercourse—" She stalled. "I'd like to know what the child has seen, etcetera."

"Do I take it, then, for anything to be spontaneous, it has to occur more than one time?" asked the judge.

"No."

The witness expanded on her answer: "Spontaneous reenactment of trauma is repeated play, often alone, sometimes observed, with a lot of affect, emotion, etcetera."

Harth suggested, "So, if a child is observed in a closet playing repeatedly with dolls and utensils, saying, 'No, no, no,' and things like that—? You gave it as an example."

"I don't remember. When?"

"Oh, several minutes ago. You don't remember?"

"No. Describe the incident."

"You gave the example. You were here. You mean you don't remember?"

Clark objected vociferously. "Your Honor, you're badgering my witness."

"Oh! I'm so far from badgering her. If you think I'm badgering, you haven't lived."

Clark laid it out for him. "Number one, you're cross-examining. Number two, you're not giving her an opportunity to answer. Number three, your tone is badgering."

Glenn interposed himself between the two, and returning to basics, he started with the simplest premise. "Doctor, do you agree there *can* be spontaneous reenactment of trauma?"

"Yes," she answered, subdued.

"Would inserting a toothbrush into her sister's vagina have a relationship to sexual abuse?" he asked, referring to Meg Barnes.

"I can see that that would have a relationship with sexual curiosity. I can see that that would have a relationship with experimentation. Not about traumatization."

"Doctor, what literature can you cite on that point?"

"Well, you're being extremely specific. They don't talk about inserting toothbrushes, but they talk about sexual curiosity and inserting objects into themselves."

"Doctor, isn't it true that children of that age don't even realize there's such a thing as a vagina, or the extent of it?"

Benedek disagreed. "Kids are more sophisticated sexually. They know the names of body parts. Four-year-olds do know their body orifices. Girls know that they have an opening in front and an opening in back. Boys know they have a penis, a peenee, a hot dog, whatever."

Mr. Michaels grinned.

Glenn handed off the baton to Sara, who had prepared the portion of the examination dealing directly with Eileen Treacy. Sara confronted Benedek with her report critiquing Eileen Treacy's findings, and asked, "Do you feel that this is an unbiased, fair report?"

"Oh yes indeed," said Benedek.

Sara asked, "Why did Miss Treacy examine the behavioral changes in this case?" Her tone was cold and crisp.

"I don't know," Benedek answered.

Sara asked, "Isn't it right in the transcript why she examined the behavioral changes?"

"Which transcript?"

"The transcript of the trial that *you reviewed*."

No comment.

"Didn't Miss Treacy herself recognize that these behaviors might not be as a result of sexual abuse, right in the transcript, over and over and over?"

"Yes, that's right. Miss Treacy admitted that."

Sara flapped Dr. Benedek's expert report. "Yet nowhere in this report does it mention that Miss Treacy recognized that the behaviors might not be a result of sexual abuse."

"I was asked to write a report on confounding variables," stated Benedek.

Sara, holding her throat, inquired, "With regard to David Kirschner, you said Miss Treacy made no comment about the confounding variables. Wasn't it correct that it wasn't that she didn't comment? It's that she *found* no confounding variables!"

"Yes. But I did find hitting in the family."

Sara read from the transcript of Treacy's testimony: "Question, 'Did you find any confounding variables as to David Kirschner?' 'No, I didn't.' "

Sara looked up. "Yet *you* say she makes no comment?"

Benedek registered confusion, so Harth asked the court reporter to read back what the prosecutor had just said. "Plain?" he then asked.

"Plain," Benedek answered.

Sara continued, "And you even go on in your report to say perhaps she didn't even inquire into confounding variables."

Benedek rested her chin on her fist. "Yes, I did."

"You see she took a full history from the family?"

"Mmm*hmm*."

"With regard to Kevin Brennan, you said no confounding variables were mentioned. Does that mean none were looked into, or none were found?"

". . . I meant no confounding variables were mentioned in the transcripts available to me."

"You said there was no comment when actually none were found."

"Yes." Benedik didn't flinch.

Judge Harth questioned, "Why didn't you simply say that?"

"I don't claim to be an expert in English or an English professor. If my report is confusing, I'd be happy to explain it, and I'd welcome the opportunity to explain it."

From out in the corridor came the sound of a baby crying. The defendant slowly swung her head around to look over her shoulder toward the door.

Sara read further from the doctor's report: "You said, 'Although Miss Treacy took into account the confounding variables, she denigrated them and didn't feel they had any importance in the symptomatology the children were displaying.' "

"Yes."

"What are Miss Treacy's qualifications?"

Meltzer objected.

Sara's voice strained, said, "Judge, she called her an unskilled clinician this morning."

Meltzer objected again. "Your Honor, that's not true. That was a generality."

Sara inverted the spearpoint of ethical pressure back toward Benedek. "But you wouldn't be calling Miss Treacy an unskilled clinician, would you?" she asked.

"I can't make a comment about her clinical skills. I don't know her." Benedek's hand shook a bit at the base of the microphone stand, but her voice was emphatic, partly because her lips were up against the mike.

"With regard to Meg Barnes, did Eileen Treacy take into account the symptomatology and the baby brother?"

"Yes. She took it into account and dismissed it."

Sara inquired: "What symptoms?"

"Well, she didn't take into account bathroom language." In her report, Benedek termed bathroom language "a common ailment" of young children, a normal developmental thing.

Harth said, "Well, there's bathroom language and bathroom language. There's quantity, extent, type of language."

"If you show me a transcript—"

Sara snapped, "I'm not showing you any transcript."

Clark tossed in an objection.

"Shouldn't that have been included in your report on confounding variables, Doctor?"

Benedek answered, "No. I don't think I should've included the answer to every question you asked me in court in the report. That's what cross-examination is for."

Impervious to the witness's tone, Sara continued: "Didn't Miss Treacy say that the confounding variable of a new baby did not explain some behaviors?"

"If so, I disagree. Certainly when there is a birth of a baby, there is a great deal of regressive behavior, separation behavior, problems with nap time."

"What problems with nap time did Meg have?" asked Sara, calling Benedek's bluff of having evaluated the situation.

Momentarily, the doctor conceded, "That information was not available to me."

Sara addressed the judge. "I'd like the court to take judicial notice of the fact that Mr. Meltzer had access to all the information, all the transcripts, all the evidence in this case."

"I think we can all agree." Harth glanced at defense counsel.

Sara went on. "Would one expect the child to have vaginal and rectal soreness?"

"No," she admitted.

"Would one expect a stretched vaginal opening?"

"Objection," said Meltzer, remaining seated. "The pediatrician said it could be congenital."

"Also, in the testimony of the doctor, he said it could be due to sexual abuse," Sara reminded.

Facing the judge, Harvey Meltzer snapped with the utmost derision: "Oh absolutely! It's consistent with everything, sir!"

18

. .

The trial resumed on a Monday morning in February following a long weekend recess. The sagging poster-board model of St. George's, with its floors slipping out of kilter and the corners of rooms dipping under their cardboard support beams, had been renovated. The state's model of the church building was now completely reset into cantilevered precision.

The winter sun glared into the courtroom, lulling away the realities of the season as Judge Harth opened the morning's proceedings. "You may call your next witness," he said.

Meltzer announced, "The defense calls Margaret Kelly Michaels."

Kelly rose and fairly skipped toward the witness stand: sweet, uncertain, like a little girl onstage, wearing a beige skirt with a silk blouse of pink and white swirls. All the members of her family were present, brothers and sisters and parents seated in a row. The Michaelses were six smiling stones.

Glenn stood. "Your Honor, can we come to sidebar?" He was furious.

Harvey Meltzer had guaranteed two days' notice before Kelly took the stand. So, Glenn Goldberg was going to ask for a two-day recess so that he and Sara could prepare as promised.

Sara glanced behind her at several astonished mothers and then joined the other attorneys clustered up at the judge's bench.

The jurors showed no reaction to the murmurs and the courtroom anticipation, sixteen professional inscrutables. They seemed to be waiting to be convinced that they would really finally hear from Kelly Michaels.

Kelly hovered awkwardly at the center of open court.

"You can sit down, now," the court clerk apprised her, and she returned to her seat.

Judge Harth relocated the discussion to his chambers to hear a lengthier argument. During the delay, the two reporters who by luck were present rushed out to the pay phones to call their colleagues and their camera crews.

The mothers in attendance went to make their own phone calls. Two and a half years ago, Sara McArdle had promised every Wee Care parent that if and when Kelly Michaels took the stand, each would have a seat in the courtroom. Now with the surprise, the handful of mothers who were present weren't going to be able to get the group together. Maybe something would happen; maybe Glenn would win his argument for adjournment.

Kelly waited quietly and concentrated.

In reality, any damage to the state's ability to cross-examine would be minor because Meltzer's direct would take a few days, during which time the prosecutors could catch up to the revised timetable. Yet, by springing Kelly's appearance on the court, her attorneys had purchased an opportunity for her to become acclimated to the stand before being subjected to the electrified environment of a packed courtroom and an onslaught of victims' parents and media. The mobs wouldn't be able to accumulate today until at least lunchtime.

Glenn was frustrated with the sudden upheaval of his own preparation plans, but though Sara wanted more time as well, she was adamant: If Kelly was ready, then Kelly had the right to go on.

Harth denied the state's request for more time because, technically, the defense had no legal obligation to afford notice. The promise to apprise the state of Kelly's date of appearance had been nothing more than a gentleman's agreement, and fulfilling it purely a matter of professional courtesy.

Before it was time for the midmorning break, the judge once again requested the next defense witness.

Meltzer said, "Your Honor, at this time once again I'd like to call Margaret Kelly Michaels."

Kelly glided across the open floor, then stood awkwardly about four feet away from the clerk while he read the oath. She nervously flopped her hand onto the Bible and swore truthfulness in undertones. Then she mounted the witness stand.

Meltzer's eyes magnetically connected with Kelly's every glance, keeping her eyes steady. "Miss Michaels, where do you reside?"

"At the moment, I'm living in Pittsburgh with my family."

Her voice was thick but clear, a sultry purr rippled through with an open, girlish inflection. She broke out of her concentration on Meltzer to embrace her parents with her eyes.

He continued, "And what type of formal education did you have?"

"I had four years of college . . . two classes short of my degree. A general degree in theater, liberal arts."

Meltzer probed, "What types of courses did you take?"

Kelly once again focused exclusively on him. This witness compelled in the great slowness with which she moved her eyes. "Gosh, a little bit of everything." She elaborated: "As far as theater: acting, movement, dance, ballet, voice. And in liberal arts you also have religion and English and math and science and that stuff."

Seated behind the desk, she looked breathtaking, almost angelic. Today, her beauty had clarity.

From his front-row seat, Mr. Michaels beamed, entranced.

"What prompted you to come to New Jersey?" All eyes were on her.

"Well, not so much New Jersey. But it's always been my dream, ever since I was a kid, to be able to work as an artist in New York City. That was always my dream. And when I finished school, it just—That was a place that I knew I wanted to end up being, near New York. I wanted to eventually go to school and I wanted to try to maybe study theater or writing or acting in New York City."

"You said you came to New York to be an artist. What type of artist were you referring to?"

"When I think of artist, I think it's a particular way of looking at things, and I wasn't really sure. I had been involved in the theater, and I had written a lot of poetry, and I really enjoyed photography, and I had a lot of interests. I just wanted to become an artist."

She paused, thoughtfully, as though trying to remember the texture of her motivation. "I know I wanted to *give that way*." Dark curls clustered around her face which was so white, slashed dramatically with dark brows, dark, embedded eyes.

She went on: "I don't know how else to explain it. And I knew New York to me—Pittsburgh is like a little pea compared to New York City—to me, it's the cultural capital of the country, and I knew I could find a place. I felt I could find a place here."

"When did you arrive in New Jersey?" Meltzer inquired, and then Kelly began to tell her story.

She opened, "I believe in the beginning of September of 1984. . . . I lived in an apartment in East Orange off of Central Avenue. . . . I lived with this girl who taught high school. She said I could live there and, until I found a job, and we could share expenses, and if it didn't work out for me, that I couldn't find employment or things didn't work out for me, then I could come back home."

"How did you come to be employed at Wee Care?"

"There was an ad in *The Star Ledger* that was very brief, and it said, 'Assistant Teacher Needed Immediately, Part-time, Full-time Positions Available, Call.' And I thought of student teacher, I'm sorry, assistant teacher. To me that was someone who corrected papers and assisted a teacher. I felt: 'I had four years of college, I'm sure I could correct papers or help a teacher.' That's something I felt would be better work than minimum-wage stuff which I was, you know, faced with. So that—You want me to go forward with . . . ?" Kelly now looked appealingly at her lawyer.

Meltzer jumped in. "How did you, was there a number with the ad in the newspaper?"

"Oh yes . . . and I just gave it a shot, and I called and spoke with Diane Costa." She had a lot of breath in her voice. "Well, I called her, and I heard all these noises, little kids, lots of noise, and I was like, 'Oh my gosh! This is a day care. . . .' And I said I had no experience at all. . . . I said, 'Well, I have experience in acting and singing, a little bit of dance, and that kind of stuff.' And she said, 'That's perfect for us because a lot of our own people—it's not necessary to have an educational degree, but we like people who have creative arts backgrounds. You sound like you also come from a big family and you sound like someone who would be good here. . . .' I told her where I was from, my family, and I had baby-sat my brothers and sisters since I was thirteen."

Meltzer intruded on the monologue. "Do you remember approximately when that phone conversation took place?"

Kelly ventured a survey of the faces around her, glanced briefly over to the jurors. There was gloss to the black in her eyes. "I know it came around the time that I was running out of money and having to make a decision whether I was going to go home and make another stab at coming to New York, maybe later with my sister when I had some more money.''

Meltzer walked away from the gallery, pulling her eyes back around to neutrality.

Following a one-day training tryout spent with Diane Costa, Kelly was hired with probationary standing as she learned the responsibilities of an aide. Kelly described: ''I started the following day. . . . Diane was the one who supervised me, watched out for me . . . the one who really, real closely observed what I was doing.'' She stressed the minutia of supervision.

Two weeks later, Kelly was made a full aide.

Meltzer asked, ''Under what circumstances did you become a teacher?'' He handled her with softness and a subtle, underplayed tone of respect.

''I'm not sure of the exact amount of weeks I had been an aide. . . . They had a temporary teacher for the threes . . . and she said she would be leaving, and they had an opening. . . . They felt that, at least temporarily, I could fill in, with, of course, an aide, fill in that three years' position as a teacher. Arlene and Diane said it was temporary, to see if I could do it. . . . They felt I was qualified, or at least able to handle the job.''

''Did you accept that position?''

''Reluctantly, yes. But I did.''

''Why?''

Kelly held out her hands importunately. ''It seemed like—it was obviously a whole lot of responsibility. As an aide, you're assisting a teacher. As a teacher, you have the responsibility of those children directly under you, and you have to work on lesson plans, and it's a lot more work. So—and I wasn't obviously—I obviously didn't have educational training. So, I felt—''

Kelly needed direction. Meltzer asked her about her personal aide. She responded, ''I know positively that Brenda at some point became my aide in particular. . . . She might go out for a couple of minutes, for a break or to take kids to the bathroom. She was primarily to assist *me*.''

''Do you recall any time period throughout the 1984–85 school year that you were not assigned an aide to work with you?''

Pointing out that her children were the youngest, Kelly protested, ''No. It would be impossible. It would just be a madhouse not to have assistance.'' She insisted further, ''For the most part, I felt that I had an aide most of the time, and I needed it.''

"Was that structure adhered to vigorously?"

She speculated, "It had to have been. It would've been a complete madhouse, if there wasn't any structure. I mean, imagine if you just had kids going—it had to have been. . . . It would've been impossible if there hadn't been some kind of structure."

"On a daily basis, Diane would pop into your room?"

"Umhm . . . Arlene sort of at random would come in whenever."

The jurors' hands were on the move, squirming in their laps. But nothing demonstrative disturbed the still life of some ten parents who had managed to break free and come to court. They were attentive and somewhat dumbstruck by Kelly's composure.

"I just wouldn't have felt secure not having an aide," she said with a voice innocently husky.

Kelly maintained that her responsibility during first lunch was to lay out the mats for the children's nap session. She didn't have to be in the lunchroom until the second lunch period when she was a monitor.

"Was there anybody helping you during the first lunch to put the mats out?"

"*Suuure!*" She sang the word. Kelly tasted her own tongue, embarrassed. "Uh, sure," she corrected.

"Did you ever have any control of the children during the first lunch period?"

"To the best of my recollection, I did not."

Sara, on the sidelines at counsel table, shook her head and made a note. She was certain Kelly had taken a few children who were supposed to be in that first lunch group up to the choir room, or even to a corner of the gym. As the year progressed, the other teachers had told her, the mats hadn't been laid out until right before Kelly's nap class started, so where had Kelly been during first lunch?

Meltzer now tried to undo the damage done by his introducing the photograph of Julie Danvers so long ago. He asked, "Were you encouraged by the administration to take pictures of the children?"

"Yes." Kelly looked at him unveeringly.

"Under what circumstances was that request made?"

"That was Arlene Spector's request. Bring the camera in because, I know, I'm pretty sure I put it down on my application, resumé. I know I discussed it with her at the time. She said it would be a wonderful idea, bring the camera in, have it with you, if the kids are in the playground, just take some fun shots."

The character Kelly was depicting for the jury was impulseless, nerveless: She took no initiative. She had answered the Wee Care advertisement, thinking the teacher's aide job was grading papers at a high school. When she had called Arlene and heard baby voices in the background, she had immediately tried to back out, realizing she had answered an ad for day care, a field exceeding her modest skills. Once she had become an aide, she had desperately not wanted to be a teacher, and when Arlene had begged her to fill the vacated position, she wouldn't even consider it without the assurance of having a full-time aide. And she *never* would have thought to bring her camera to the school had it not been for Arlene's suggesting that perhaps she could take some candids of the children, create a collage.

"Did kids ask you to rub their backs?" Meltzer asked.

She still didn't know what to do with her hands, the same problem she'd combated at counsel table through the eight months of the trial. "Oh, yes. When I came into that nap class, it had already been done. . . . Before I had been hired at the school, back rubbing had been instituted, had been used at the school. . . . It was helpful to the children. There was always going to be children who'd request it." She pasted the phrases together impressionistically.

"Were there ever occasions that you rubbed the child's back below the clothes?"

Kelly waffled. "I don't specifically recall, but I can't say that that couldn't have happened at some time."

▪
▪ ▪

Sara feared Kelly Michaels as a witness, and she was irritable all through this first day of direct. She spun through corridors, ignoring people, nervously drinking cups of water. The entire courthouse thrilled with critiques of the witness: her facial beauty, her sexual voice, her ease on the stand. That first night after Kelly took the stand, Sara heard the echoes of facile lying and was distraught, terrified that they were going to lose the case.

Kelly was unexpectedly nondefensive, surprisingly calm, disappointingly stable, and noticeably not confessing.

▪
▪ ▪

In the ensuing days, around fifty Wee Care parents, family members, and friends flexed their sorrow on the left side of the courtroom, more in a show of strength than a show of support: intimidation systems. The attendance was greater than ever before, even greater than at the arraignment back in 1985. Before they all entered the courtroom, Sara warned them all: "No outbursts! Be good!"

On the second day of direct, Meltzer moved his inquiry to the day Kelly had been brought in for questioning, and Kelly described what it was like: "I remember having just, my whole world was blown at that moment. I remember deciding, 'What am I going to do?' At that time, they had released me. I was—I thought it was over, and I decided I had to call . . . the director of the school I was at and let them know what had happened to me and what had happened that day and what they had accused me of. . . . I thought that was the only fair thing to do. . . . We talked about what I told them. I told them everything. I was honest with them, that I'm innocent."

Without warning, Kelly became vehement as she thought back: "And she said, 'They did not say they would press any further?' I said no. She said, 'You're welcome back to work here. . . . So I had gone and discussed that with her, and that day she—I resumed working at the school." And then, a few days later, the new school had released her, placing Kelly on an indefinite leave of absence.

Meltzer asked, "Where were you taken? What were you told when the knock came on the door?"

"Uh, they asked to speak with me outside of my apartment, and I had to get, of course, put on shoes and get dressed. They said it was a matter about a possibility of some isolated child abuse at the, at Wee Care. I was astounded."

"Where'd you go?"

Kelly inhaled and held it. Everyone waited a long time for the answer. "Right here. . . . I spoke to a number of people. . . . They brought me to an office. They might've said it was Mr. McGrath's office. I was spoken to by them. . . . Miss Sencer was there. She just popped in and out throughout the day, but never said a word to me at all."

"Never?" Meltzer sounded astounded.

"Never said a word, not to this day, except out in the hall, telling me to come into the courtroom." Kelly's heavy eyes thickened.

"What did they tell you? What were they after?"

Glenn objected. "The form of the question."

"Sustained."

Meltzer continued: "Kelly, ah, do you remember what Mastrangelo said?"

"Yes I *do*," she sang out, then recalled, " 'You've got to prove to us that you didn't do this. . . .' Well, he said I was going to have to prove it to him, and then he was going to have to prove it to Mr. McGrath, who was his boss." Kelly imitated a hustling cop: " 'You can confess anytime. You can confess anytime. We'll go easy on you. We'll get you help.' " She slid liquidly into the officer's persona.

Meltzer inquired softly, "Did you ever confess?"

"Never." The answer was two strong syllables.

"Why?"

"Because I am innocent. And that's why I never confessed." She elaborated, "I told them that when they came to my door. Every chance I got, but they didn't seem to be interested. . . . They wanted one of two things: They wanted *me*, or me to point the finger at anybody. Any information that didn't relate to that, they didn't want to hear."

"What was being charged at the time?"

Her hand danced attendance around her face. "At the time, it was taking a temperature improperly, it was hitting a child with a wooden spoon, and it was possibly locking the closet. That was it. That was the charges." She sniffled, and the microphone gurgled in sympathy.

Bob Clark interposed: "Excuse me, Your Honor. May I have a tissue?"

"I'm just sniffling, and the thing's so close. I'm sorry," said Kelly, indicating the microphone. "It's an odd noise. I'm sorry," she apologized, painfully not wanting to offend.

Harth handed down a tissue.

Meltzer asked, "To the best of your recollection, is there stuff, answers that you gave . . . that don't appear in either of the two reports?"

"Yes. Plenty. Plenty. Plenty."

She did finger calisthenics: Pray, curl, tap the table. Pray, curl, tap the table.

"Do you remember what time that was that you were dropped off?"

"All I know, it was the end of the evening, end of the afternoon. And I remember the sun, seeing a glimpse of the sun because I believe I was in his front seat and the sun was coming through and I hadn't seen the sun all day. So I do remember that. I remember, I know it was evening, early evening." Kelly went round and round about the sun. "I remember being so grateful to see the sun and seeing it coming. It was low enough that I could see it through the window. . . . From the sun, how low it was, I know it was late, late in the afternoon."

Meltzer let her revolve, then he addressed the judge: "Judge, I would like the court to take judicial notice that, on May sixth of 1985, the sun set at Newark Eastern Time at six fifty-eight P.M."

"All right. Any problem of my taking judicial notice of that?" Harth asked.

Glenn answered, "No, I don't think so, Judge."

Neither Sara nor Glenn could divulge to the jury that a lot of the time Kelly had spent at the Prosecutor's Office she had been taking the polygraph test, because the test wasn't admissible as evidence. Cleverly, Meltzer now encouraged Kelly to discuss the length of the day, leaving the implication that the day had been filled with incessant browbeating.

Meltzer clicked forward to the day of her arrest and her subsequent incarceration in Caldwell. He asked, "Did you speak to anyone about your case?"

"No, I did not. No." Her breathing was heavy, but she was matter-of-fact.

Her lawyer led Kelly point for point through every statement Charlene had testified Kelly had made, and Kelly denied, with great conviction, each and every one.

Meltzer then asked, "Were you the recipient of any threats?"

"Yes."

"What types of threats?"

Glenn interjected: "Judge, is this relevant?"

"I don't understand the relevance, Mr. Meltzer," said Harth.

Clark spoke up: "Well, Your Honor, I think based on—there has been certain testimony with regards to what was disclosed, or allegedly disclosed by my client while she was incarcerated, and essentially these questions are in fact relevant as far as my client's state of mind at the time of her incarceration. Common sense, and under the presence of threats would reduce the occasion to—"

Harth understood and intervened. "I'll allow it. Did you receive any threats up there?" he asked.

Kelly turned her face up to the judge, her body language innocent. "Yes, Your Honor."

Kelly described the threats: "Usually, it would be, it was like a common, harassment. It was a common—just the daily thing is what goes on. . . . The problem would be, 'I didn't hear anything, but I'll keep an eye on it or an ear out for it. . . .' I also phoned my family as well because I didn't think I could trust anybody in the jail. . . . I didn't trust any of the guards in there to do *anything*. It was *ridiculous*." Her words were soaked in sadness.

Meltzer questioned, "Did you ever tell Betty Sheffield that one's sexual preference is one's own business?"

"No. I never told Betty Sheffield anything. . . . The extent of the conversation with the guard would be, 'Can I use the phone, please. I've asked sixteen times,' 'Can I get a shower, please. . . .' That was the extent of the conversation with a jail guard."

Sara, engrossed in transcripts, glanced up and thought: If this doesn't convince them she's a liar . . .

"Did you ever have any conversations with Wanda Dean?"

"Yes. I asked her for a shower. I asked her for a phone."

"Were there ever a large number of inmates outside your cell talking with you?"

"Mm. If there were any people outside my cell, I don't believe they were talking to me, no." Kelly inhaled deeply, steadyingly. "I was *harassed* outside my cell." At Meltzer's request, she then rose and drew a diagram of the tier. Pointing, she added, "There's the phone right there past my cell."

As Harvey Meltzer began to wind up his three days of direct testimony with his client, spectators and reporters yawned from the lack of significant testimony.

In reference to events at the school, Kelly spent a lot of time describing her empathy with the children and her generosity toward them: giving them cooking lessons to make granola clusters so they could "feel like they were helping to bake"; making little puppets out of sweat socks for them to play with; taking them on walks to look at streams or visit the town library. She also made it clear that they were rambunctious and noisy, implying that the secrecy of abuse would have been impossible to maintain.

Kelly offered an innocuous context in which some of what the children had said could be true: She explained to her lawyer that she had perhaps played "Jingle Bells" in the gym at the children's request. She had never visited the choir room with the children, she stated, nor had she used the gym's back stairway up to that room until the day the jury had visited Wee Care. About the poem found in the back of her roll book, she explained to Meltzer, "It's just—kinda silly."

The hardest-hitting testimony was her representation of how Wee Care operated. Kelly stressed supervision, insisting that she had rarely been alone in her classroom, and that Arlene Spector and Diane Costa had randomly spot-checked the room or brought people in to see the school. Parents, she claimed, picked their children up at unexpected times, interrupting her nap class at times. Kelly listed what days of the week and for what hours each child had attended the school, then delineated whose morning classroom, lunch, and nap each was in. And she came up with three children who were never under her care: Elizabeth, Robert, and Joey. However, Kelly's chart didn't account for the after-nap period when she had supervised late-staying children in the gym. Both Robert and Joey fell into that group.

After reporting on the Michaels case for over two years, Trish de Gasperis of the *New Jersey Nightly News* had gone into the first day of Kelly's testimony thinking it would be one of the greatest stories of her life. And Trish was absolutely riveted when Kelly took the stand . . . for about five minutes. She soon realized that she wasn't going to know anything more about Kelly than she did before. Toward the end of her direct testimony, Kelly Michaels was even more of an enigma than ever.

Meltzer asked his client, "Kelly, are you acting?"

And she answered, "No, I'm not acting."

Meltzer was subdued as he entered his final portion of direct for the day. Quietly, he said, "You've been accused of doing some rather terrible things to these children. Did you, at any time during your tenure at Wee Care, do anything improper, or touch David Kirschner in an improper manner?"

"No."

"Did you do anything improper or touch Lewis Dixon in an improper manner?"

"No."

"Did you do anything improper with Angie McMahon?"

"No."

He inquired of Meg Barnes.

Her widespread eyes looked dark and humid, her lips collected, dense. "No."

Harvey Meltzer asked again and again, each time naming yet another child, and Kelly said no.

George McGrath sat at counsel table and massaged his eyes.

By about the fifteenth name on the list, Kelly's voice had thinned, and she nodded emphatically along with each denial.

The parents listened, unmoving, to twenty simple no's. Every single one of them was being denied: their pain denied, their child's victimization denied. And Kelly almost seduced them into fantasies that maybe all this was really just a horrendous mistake. . . .

Denial was such a seductive thing, all the way around.

■
■ ■

Kelly had a weekend through which to collect herself for the onslaught of Glenn Goldberg, thanks to Harvey's timing of the completion of direct.

Sara and Kevin McArdle decided to drive home from work past Joey Gardner's house so they could stop in and say hello. Enough time had gone by since his testimony that Sara felt a visit wouldn't upset his emotional balance. When Sara ran into his mother and asked, "How's your kid?" Ellen simply told her, "We haven't talked about it."

Sara wouldn't bring up Kelly again. She had promised Joey she wouldn't. She just wanted to remind him she was alive. As they approached the house, Joey caught sight of them: He was pumping around the street on his bicycle, working off energy. Joey waved.

He looked terrific. He seemed happy, and he had already grown a lot. His lawyer gave him a huge hug, and they talked for a while about how things were going in school. He was athletic, doing well. And he was extremely musical: He had taken up the recorder and the piano.

Sara shook her head as they drove off. She turned to her husband and wondered aloud, "Why are people afraid to show children normal affection? It makes me so sad that people think hugging a child is going to make him accuse them of sexual abuse."

Sara loved Joey because he was eccentric. Glancing behind them, Sara saw Joey racing back down his block, screaming uninhibitedly at the top of his lungs.

■
■ ■

When Kelly came in on Monday morning, she was wearing a scarlet blouse with shoulder pads and puffed sleeves.

The jurors entered the courtroom and made their way to the jury box. The men waited in the aisle so that the ladies could file in first and take their seats. After months of testimony, the jurors had formulated precise patterns of how most efficiently to file into their rows of seats.

Cross-examination could not enter into the area of the defendant's character: her trustworthiness, her sexuality, her sense of responsibility. The defense had chosen not to bring Kelly's character into question; therefore, the state would not be permitted to probe that area.

Glenn opened the examination on a humorous note: "I'm going to ask you to show how you played the piano for the children at Wee Care. Are you willing to do that?"

The defendant scrunched her eyes, concentrating.

Glenn lifted a long flat cardboard box up onto counsel table and slid out a Casio keyboard. Kelly alternated amused, suspicious looks between Glenn and the judge.

Meltzer, having only just seated himself, jumped up. "I object! He's making a grandstand type of a play!"

Harth disagreed. "According to the testimony, her piano playing was one of her substitute abilities that the school took instead of formal preparation to teach."

Glenn nodded. Exactly his point: Kelly had been hired predominantly on the personal skills listed on her resumé, skills that he intended to demonstrate she'd exaggerated.

Harth ruled, "Since there has been evidence on the state's case as well as the defense's, I will allow it."

"What he says is not true!" Kelly interrupted. "That it's a substitute. It's inaccurate."

Glenn laid the electric keyboard in front of the witness, provoking an imp face when he told her to play "Jingle Bells" as she had played it for the children.

Kelly lowered her right hand to the keys. "Uh, Mr. Goldberg?" Winning his attention, Kelly angled her face downward and played the quivery notes from the beginning of the tune up to "jingle all the way."

"That's 'Jingle Bells,' " she said, and, smiling, deferred to the prosecutor with a flourish of the hand.

Glenn observed, "So basically, Miss Michaels, is it your testimony now that when you played 'Jingle Bells' for the children it was essentially with one finger?"

"This is a teeny little keyboard—" she began, cheeks stiffening, the smile suddenly an anachronism.

Meltzer rose to object. Seeing him, Kelly mouthed, "Please," pleading with prayer-folded hands. Meltzer reseated himself.

Kelly said, "That's how I would play 'Jingle Bells.' "

Glenn went on. "My question to you now, Miss Michaels, is, when you played 'Jingle Bells' for the children, you played with one finger?"

"I don't recall."

He then asked her if she could play any other songs, and when she acknowledged "Twinkle, Twinkle Little Star" and "Mary Had a Little Lamb," he proposed: "The fact is, Ms. Michaels, that there was really no reason to be so limited to 'Jingle Bells,' was there? Because there're so many simple songs that you can play on a keyboard with one finger?"

She cocked her head, her curls sloshing into themselves. "I suppose," she agreed. Glenn left unspoken that the children who alleged nude piano playing consistently specified "Jingle Bells."

"You testified last week, Miss Michaels, that when you proclaimed your innocence, the detectives weren't interested?"

"Yes."

He cast his eyes over the police report. "And yet you were asked, 'Are you sexually attracted to any of these pupils that we just talked about,' and the detective typed down the answer, 'No.' Is that right?"

Disinterestedly: "If it's there, that's what he typed, yes."

"The detective didn't leave that out of your statement, did he?"

"If it's there, no, he didn't. No." She seemed impenetrable in her self-righteousness.

". . . You testified that they weren't at all interested in hearing about your claims of innocence, isn't that so?"

"Yes."

Glenn read from the signed statement: "And yet, it says you were asked, 'Do you have anything else to add,' and the answer was 'After nap time, I was never'— and you crossed out *never* and made it *rarely* —'I was rarely responsible for bathroom. I am absolutely innocent.'"

"Umhm." The iamb sounded like a control mechanism, a calibration.

"So the police did write down, did type into the statement what you say they really weren't interested in?"

"They typed it. They typed. Yes, they did." Her grand emptiness was difficult to interpret because, in any other circumstances, she would in fact be considered the best judge of her own mind and memories.

Glenn attacked unexpectedly to ask whether her frequent delays in responding to these questions were unnatural, speculating, "Is it because this is part of your training in terms of how to make it appear that you're giving spontaneous answers to things that in actuality you have spent a lot of time thinking about?"

"What training, Mr. Goldberg?" She was indignant.

"Training in acting."

"Training in acting? There's no training in acting that has *anything* to do with going through *anything* like this, Mr. Goldberg. I don't understand."

"Well, I'll try to explain." He sounded fresh.

The judge cut in: "No. The jury will judge."

Glenn, undaunted, flaunted her resumé, asking as he dangled it: "Do you remember that you talked about your responsibility for caring for a nine-year-old child? And you say you were responsible for the daily care, eight to ten hours a day, of a nine-year-old child. In addition to feeding and dressing this child, worked with the child to plan activities for each day, and you've mentioned some of the activities. Could you tell the jury, Miss Michaels, how you went about feeding and dressing a nine-year-old boy?"

Meltzer objected. "Relevance, Your Honor. We don't have any nine-year-old children, and this is something that took place before she appeared at Wee Care. So where is it relevant?"

"I think the relevance is obvious, Judge."

"I will allow it."

But Kelly was already poised with her answer, and when Meltzer had finished, she replied willingly: "Feeding would be preparing meals. Dressing would probably be tying shoes, things like that." She deepened into her seat, vindicated.

With skepticism, Glenn asked, "You had to tie the shoes of a nine-year-old boy, Miss Michaels?"

Kelly backed away. "I really don't remember. I know feeding would be preparation, I believe . . . making meals. As far as dressing: I don't know. I don't know."

"Aside from eating peanut butter, did the children ever do anything else with it?"

"With what, Mr. Goldberg?" she countered.

"Peanut butter."

"No. Besides eating it?"

"Yes."

"No."

"Then why did you once tell someone, Miss Michaels, that the children threw peanut butter at each other?"

"Throwing peanut butter?" Kelly widened her eyes and nearly laughed at her prosecutor.

"Objection, Your Honor," blocked Clark.

Meltzer asked Glenn, "Who was this somebody and under what circumstances? Let's have specifics, please."

Glenn addressed the judge: "The somebody was Dr. Rappeport, Jonas Rappeport, who testified on behalf of the defendant in this trial."

Harth nodded the question through, overruling the objection.

"I don't remember," Kelly answered. "I don't remember saying that about throwing peanut butter. I think that was in response, well, did he ever, could they ever have thrown it at each other. I really don't recall. If I could see the reference to the question, please."

Instead of handing her the psychiatrist's report, Glenn read aloud her entire convoluted exchange with Rappeport's associate:

Q: There is this issue of peanut butter and jelly. Do you remember that?

A: Yes, I do.

Q: How do you explain that?

A: There's no, there's no, I don't know. There's no jelly at the school, and I don't think, just peanut butter. Still, I don't, peanut butter was, ah, I told Dr. Rappeport in the last visit that we're really limited as far as the kind of food they had for snacks. They had

Cheerios, umm, Shredded Wheat, and peanut butter. They had
peanut butter every single day for snack or, ah, you know, so you
know, a lot had peanut butter sandwiches, and, I don't know, I, I
don't know if they ate peanut butter a lot.
Q: Did they play with it?
A: Sure. Um, I, I, you know, just as far as games, like I, you know,
throwing peanut butter at each other during snack time.

The answer splattered.

Glenn asked, "Is that what the children did at Wee Care, Miss Michaels? Threw peanut butter at each other during snack time? Because
you just told us that all they did was eat it."

"They *ate* it, yes." Defiance wafted through the chain mail of her
poise.

Glenn said knowingly, "They didn't throw it at each other, *did* they?"
as if he were looking right through her.

"Throw it at each other? Did they throw peanut butter? No. I don't
remember, I don't remember saying, I don't remember. No."

". . . And you went on to say," he continued: "Throwing peanut
butter at each other during snack time or dropping, you know, maybe,
you know, the things, little things the kids do, smearing each other. The
kind of things like, you know, you go over and say, 'Please don't make
a mess of each other. Clean it up.' " Once again, Glenn insisted, "You
know the children didn't smear peanut butter on each other."

"I think you're taking something completely out of context. I think
you're coming up with reasons—"

"Miss Michaels, that's why I read the whole long area." Glenn pulled
his eyes from Kelly's entreating face to look at her own words in the
report.

She tried to dig out. "I'm sure a kid could've stuck his finger in the
peanut butter jar. I was not talking about smearing across bodies or any
of that."

"What you were trying to do is convince your interviewer the way the
children got peanut butter on themselves is because they smeared it on
themselves, instead of you doing it."

"There was no smearing of peanut butter, and I was not making a
rationale. There was no smearing of peanut butter on children's bodies
at that school!"

Mr. Michaels, his arm stretched across the bench back behind his wife,
thumped Mrs. Michaels's shoulder with his thumb, a convulsive motion.
She didn't react.

Glenn dropped the sheaf of papers onto the table. "Smearing each other, Ms. Michaels, are your words."

"Smearing each other," she repeated, dull.

Glenn stood staring. "That's it?"

Listening, Meltzer clenched a Hi-Liter.

"That's the best I can do." Kelly seemed disoriented, shouldered back and forth by her testimony under oath and her own statements recorded in the psychiatrist's report.

Glenn made his voice ingenuous: "There were wooden spoons at Wee Care, weren't there?"

"*Yes*, Mr. Goldberg. Umhm!"

"Did you ever have trouble finding a wooden spoon when you needed one?"

Kelly protested, "I don't remember three years ago if I had trouble finding a *wooden spoon*."

Out of nowhere, the prosecutor directed, "What kind of child was David Kirschner? Would you describe him for us?"

"Very sensitive. Cried easily, but pleasant. Pleasant kid."

"Lewis Dixon. Would you tell us about your recollections of Lewis Dixon?"

"Lewis was, uh, gosh, a lot of energy, hyper, a hyper kind of kid, real hyper at times." Glenn had given no reason for why he asked this, and Kelly sounded rattled.

"He was pretty friendly with you, isn't that so?"

"No."

"Didn't he hang around you a lot, want to be with you a lot?"

"No. No. That's not true."

"Fred."

"Basically a happy kid. One of the younger children. Talked a lot of gibberish. . . ."

"Please describe Julie Danvers." Paula stiffened.

"Julie was kind of sweet, kind of a little spacey, sweet. She came late to, a little later than the other children, so I know that, um, that might've been difficult for her."

"But you got along all right with Julie, didn't you?"

"Yes."

"Joey. What can you tell us about his personality?"

Kelly was staggered, the delay noticeable. "I don't really—"

"Nothing comes to mind at all?"

"I don't know exactly what. I'm really having trouble understanding what you want. I just—"

Glenn started to interject.

Kelly asked him, "You want me to describe what I remember of him?" She waited, then did that. "He used to get in trouble with Lewis. They used to fight. They were good friends."

Glenn continued through the list of children, then asked Kelly to comment similarly on the teachers at the school. Kelly had had no problems getting along with any of them.

By the time Glenn had finished with her, Kelly Michaels, not realizing that she was doing it, had vouched for the credibility of every single one of the children and teachers who had testified against her.

▪
▪ ▪

For the second day of her cross-examination, the witness wore a silk blouse colored in oil spills of blue, purple, gold, and magenta, the deep colors accentuating her luminous face. The courtroom was filled: fear, resentment, hatred, enmity. People were packed into the gallery benches (Harth had had to restrict attendance to families and members of the press), the atmosphere choked with hostility.

Glenn started in on his witness: "What games did you play with the children at Wee Care?"

Kelly fidgeted, adjusting the vertical and horizontal dials on her pose. "Uh, I believe I testified, I've probably forgotten some of 'em. So, to the best of my recollection, uh, tag. We played games, at least in my class, with a bag of—a typical thing to do with kids this age—to put in a piece of felt, put in something soft, something smooth. You have them close their eyes and have them guess what it is. That type of thing. I believe I testified that duck, duck, goose at times was played. I'm sure there are some that I have forgotten at the moment."

"Did you make up any games?"

"No."

To disconcert her, Glenn bounded out of the topic and asked, "Why did you bring a camera to Wee Care?"

"I believe it was under Arlene's request . . . possibly work on pictures to put up for a bulletin board sometime, but it never materialized."

"It didn't occur to you on your own to bring in a camera to take pictures of the children? It was only as a result of a request from the director of the school?"

"To the best of my recollection. I'm not positive, but to the best of my recollection at this time."

"And what kind of pictures did Arlene tell you to take? What'd she tell you about picture taking?"

Kelly recounted, "To have the camera available, take candid shots, kids playing, that kind of thing."

Glenn got specific, asking, "What does a candid shot mean?"

"People being natural, doing their own thing. That's candid. You try to get candid. But a lot of times, when people see a camera, they're not candid anymore," she noted perceptively.

"So candid means the opposite of a posed shot?"

"Yes."

Sara listened closely. Kelly's photos were largely of distorted faces: grotesque monster faces, contorted faces, vamped faces—most appeared to be posed.

"David Kirschner testified to this jury that you took his photograph. Where is it?" asked Glenn, in a voice he would use if he were talking to a baby.

Kelly objected. "I don't have a photograph of David Kirschner. . . . I have no photograph to my knowledge. . . . Did I take one? I don't believe I did."

Glenn altered the emphasis. "Did you ever show the photographs to the children?" He sounded idly curious.

"I don't remember."

"Did you ever show the photographs to Arlene?"

"I don't remember. I don't believe I did."

"Did you ever show the photographs to anyone?" Glenn hammered to make the argument that these photographs had been taken purely for her own pleasure.

Kelly answered, "To anyone? Yes. Gosh. My folks. Of course, Mr. Meltzer and Mr. Clark."

"Why didn't you show them to the children?"

"Mr. Goldberg, three years later! I don't remember. I can't answer your question."

Glenn paged through the roll book until he reached what he called the "sex poem." He had waited months to ask: "The poem that you wrote in your roll call book: Why did you write that?"

"As I testified, I have no recollection that that is my poetry. It's my writing, definitely. I know it's my writing, but I have no memory of if I copied it from something else, if it was mine."

"You're actually testifying that you don't know if these are original words or phrases?"

"Yes. I don't know."

The prosecutor closed in, asked, "Do you understand how people could relate this poem to the charges against you?"

Meltzer and Clark objected in one voice, and the judge sustained.

Glenn recited the poem: "truth indescriminate [sic]/Are you/going about this/the wrong way?/He says what do you want?/I say Hey, what did you say?/But I know/with the smell of your flesh, (I know)/in a flash as you dress/your body will leave me."

He set the roll book aside and asked, "Was there anything going on in your life at the time you worked at Wee Care that would cause you to think and perhaps write about the smell of someone's flesh?"

Kelly, vacuous, said, "I don't remember."

Glenn interjected, "What was the reason you went from Wee Care to the Community Day Nursery?"

"Better job for me. Less responsibility."

He tried, "Your leaving Wee Care, did that have anything to do with the working conditions at Wee Care?"

". . . I don't remember, but if you look at Wee Care and you looked at Community Day, Wee Care was a little, teeny place in a basement of a church, three little rooms. Community Day was a big, spacious place, beautiful facilities."

"Was lack of supervision, was that one of your complaints?"

"It could have been occasions, umhm," she concurred.

"What do you mean, could have been occasions? I don't understand."

"I'm sure there were occasions. We would have to share two aides instead of three, or [one] would have been absent and we would have had to share an aide. That could've happened."

Glenn insisted, "*Did* you ever share one aide instead of two?"

"Yes."

"Did you ever have *no* aide?"

"I don't remember that. I don't remember that." The abrasiveness of cross-examination was scrubbing away Kelly's smoky seductiveness.

Glenn lunged. "What was your reason for telling Christine, 'I could be molesting the kids and nobody would really know'?"

Kelly answered, "I don't believe I said that. I believe it was in the context I could have been discussing with Christine a number of things."

"What do you mean, you could have been?"

"That's—we discussed many things."

"So in other words, you don't really mean, 'I could have been' discussing child molesting. You really mean to say, 'I was' discussing it, right?"

"No, I don't mean that."

"What *do* you mean?"

Kelly looked like a helpless, all-dressed-up little girl. "I'm really unsure what you're talking about."

Glenn patted the transcript lying on the table. "I'm talking about the same subject that Mr. Meltzer asked you about on direct."

"Mmhm, mmhm," she hummed, rocking her head. "Mmhm, mmhm, *okay*." Her eyes seemed a little glazed, as if she was having trouble staying in focus.

"What was the reason?" Glenn asked again.

"I said in reference to the McMartin case, we were talking about our fears as day-care teachers. . . . It's a topic of conversation among day-care teachers. It was then, and I'm sure it is now."

"Any other reason?" he pried.

"No other reason, Mr. Goldberg."

"Then why did you give Mr. Meltzer the reason that it had something to do with Christine majoring in psychology?"

"That's an incomplete answer, Mr. Goldberg, because I remember saying the same thing, because that's the truth." Kelly paused. "She did major in psychology, yes."

"Well, what did that have to do with talking to her about child molesting?"

"I have no idea."

Meltzer tried to get the floor. "Time for, excuse me, is it time for a page reference now?" he asked, gesturing toward the transcript in Glenn's hand.

Glenn ignored him as he read from the transcript: "Mr. Meltzer asked, 'Do you remember ever having a conversation of that nature?' And the first three words of your answer were, 'If that happened. . . .' "

"Umhm."

"*Did* it happen?"

"We had many conversations, and yes, we discussed the dangers of being a day-care center worker . . . but I don't remember saying those words."

Glenn read further: " 'I'm sure I could've said something along those lines, or she could have, but that has been taken out of context.' "

Kelly jumped in. "That's exactly what I've said today!"

"Who took it out of context?"

"*You*, Mr. Goldberg." Kelly gripped his name as if it were the handlebar on what they were talking about. "What I'm interested to know is when Christine remembered those conversations for *you*." She tipped her head to smirk.

"Why do you think it matters, Miss Michaels, when she discussed it with the Prosecutor's Office?"

"It matters, Mr. Goldberg," Kelly answered, superior.

"Is there any doubt in your mind you talked about child molesting with Christine?"

"No. Not the specific topic. See, it's out of context."

"Did you say to [another teacher] these exact words, 'How do they know I'm not some kind of child molester?' "

"Do I remember saying that?" Kelly squinted. "No. No, I don't. I can't remember everything she said in October of 1984, so I don't know how she remembers anything *I* said in October of 1984."

She'd sounded at first as if she carried all the answers, and that conviction had been part of her charisma, but now Kelly was evaporating with every hard-hitting challenge.

▪
▪ ▪

Sara's hair was pulled back from her face in two white barrettes. Her delivery was streamlined, not a question wasted: cutting in, cutting out. The very first question late in Kelly's second day on cross cut home: "Would it be correct to state that it was your testimony that Wee Care was a very adequately supervised facility?"

Kelly was perfectly poised facing her prosecutor: head high, unjustly accused, persecuted.

"Are you asking did I say that?" she replied.

"I'm asking if that is your impression of Wee Care." Sara kept her arms folded across her chest. She was circling around on the floor, always facing Kelly, yet looking down at her notes: foraying forward, shuffling back.

Kelly answered, "I felt for me that for the most part I was adequately supervised."

"And that was because you had an aide all the time, isn't that correct?"

"Oh. I didn't say constantly, but for the most part, yes."

"And Diane supervised you, and Arlene supervised you?"

"Yes, umhm."

In a neutral voice, Sara asked, "You've also stated, isn't it correct, that except for short periods, you were never alone with the children."

"Short periods. Except for that, yes. Umhm."

Sara knew every mention Kelly had ever made of the coverage in her classroom: She had tracked the evolution of the alibi from always an aide, to an exclusive aide assigned to Kelly who sometimes roamed, to at most times, to generally. Almost three years of living and breathing *NJ* v. *MKM* had its payoffs.

Sara stated, "You've also testified that there was no time during the 1984–85 school year that you didn't have an aide assigned to your class." Sara sounded that much more skeptical in the absence of all inflection.

Kelly confirmed, "For the most part, umhm."

"What does 'for the most part' mean?" Sara's voice steeled.

"Usually . . . Umhm. To the best of my . . . yes! Yes, usually." Kelly frayed, desperately clinging to her pleasing persona.

"When did you not have an aide assigned to your class?"

"I don't recall specific."

"Well, did you have one in the morning?" asked Sara.

"Yes, I did."

"From nine-thirty?"

"Yes."

"From nine-thirty to ten?"

"You're being very general. Are you talking about always, constantly, every minute? I'm not sure."

Sara was relentless. "It was your testimony on Monday, was it not, that it would've been impossible for you to do your work without an aide."

"Oh, yes. Umhm."

"That it would've been a madhouse in the classroom without an aide." Sara turned to glance at the gallery full of parents, her face hard.

"Yes," said Kelly.

"Therefore, is it your testimony, Miss Michaels, that you always had an aide?"

"I said for the most part, yes, umhm."

"When did you *not* have an aide?"

"I believe I testified the teacher took children to the bathroom. There would be a time when there wouldn't be an aide there, that kind of thing."

"Except for those bathroom periods, you had an aide in your class?"

"For the most part. Yes, umhm."

Sara looked over her shoulder at Glenn and George, just checking in: no looks of alarm. Sara rolled onward. "Were you having any problems controlling the children when *you* were an aide?"

"I don't think so."

"So there was no reason for you to believe, prior to taking over the three-year-old class, that you would need an aide, was there?"

Clark objected. "As to the form of the question, Your Honor."

Kelly answered, oblivious to her attorney. "Oh, yes."

Harth instructed, "Reframe the question, please."

Sara stated, "You didn't have any problems disciplining them. There was no reason for you to believe that you would require an aide all the time, was there?" Sara was asking leading questions, loaded questions, molding the witness's answers.

"Oh, yes. I certainly felt I needed assistance with the three-year-olds. Yes, I did."

"If you felt you needed assistance, did you feel that you needed assistance in the late afternoon?"

"There was assistance. I wasn't the head teacher in the afternoon."

"Isn't it a fact that you would send other teachers home who were supposed to stay in the late afternoon?"

Clark shouted, "Objection! Where does that come from in the testimony?"

"Your Honor, it doesn't have to come from the testimony," said Sara

"I'm going to allow it," Harth ruled.

Sara started to repeat the question, but Kelly cut her off. "No, I never sent any teachers home."

"And you knew which parents picked up which children at what time, did you not?"

"You had to know, yes."

"So you were very aware of that?"

"As aware as anyone was, yes. We had to be."

The prosecutor looked with frankness over at the jurors. Kelly had clasped and planted her hands, which, at the moment, were stiller than they'd ever been throughout the trial.

Sara turned her attention to the myth of "the Administration" and its supervisory diligence. She reminded Kelly that from early March onward, Diane Costa, the head teacher, had spent only half days at Wee Care. Sara added, "And Arlene was never there on Fridays."

Kelly agreed. "I believe that could be the day, umhm."

Sara maneuvered: "So there were times, weren't there, Miss Michaels, that both Arlene and Diane were not present at the Wee Care facility while you were there."

"I'm sure that happened, yes."

"And you've stated that except for very short periods of time like when there were bathroom times, Brenda would be with you?"

"I said *usually*, yes, umhm." The two women looked at each other.

Sara inquired, "What would she do for the rest of that morning period?"

"Oh gosh. Assist, take children to the bathroom, go get juice, help clean up. Umhm. That kind of thing."

"And when she went to get the juice, the juice wasn't in the classroom, was it?"

"No."

Sara was hurrying Kelly, not giving her a chance to embroider, engage, dazzle. She pushed through to the verifiable realities of the Wee Care timetable. Sara was eager to be finished, to get this all on paper.

Sara ejected another question: "Snacks. That was Brenda's responsibility, isn't that correct?"

"If it had to be done outside of the classroom, yes," the witness answered.

Kelly insisted that, once she had her own classroom, Brenda was assigned exclusively to her, and Sara attacked that premise, reading off Brenda's duties from a large poster-board chart: "She had to distribute full yellow pitchers of milk to each of the three nursery classes; she had to cut up fruits or vegetables for each snack if on hand; monthly, she had to restock the closets; she had to prep lunch and P.M. snack; she had to take children to the bathroom; she had to help other teachers if they needed help during snack; and she had to help Arlene if she needed help. So there were many times in the morning during that first period that Brenda had many other duties besides being an aide in your classroom, isn't that correct?"

Kelly sounded angry: "She was in and *out*, Mrs. McArdle, yes. But she was there for me usually when I needed her."

■
■ ■

Karen Steadman didn't believe that the sexual things had ruined Allie. It was the fear. Her daughter would have innocence sexually: Of that Karen felt sure, truly believing that the physical memories would be muted. But Allie lived her seven-year-old's life today like a forty-year-old who had seen a lot but who hadn't mellowed at all. Alison locked doors, looked over her shoulder in case someone back there was about to jump her. Alison had lost all sense of invulnerability.

Karen's child worried about how things could hurt her: about the date on the milk, and about whether or not flies could, invasive, fly up her rectum.

She's under the rock now, Karen thought to herself.

■
■ ■

Ellen Gardner was able to come to court for a day to hear Kelly testify. She couldn't believe how good the woman looked, a true transformation from her Wee Care days. Kelly was as good-looking now as she had ever been (trimmed down, and dyed and curled), and she had what looked to be a new wardrobe fitted out for her new persona (matching bags, shoes, silk blouses, accessories). The physical and material improvements made it appear almost as if Kelly had been rewarded.

Ellen shivered to think that Joey could become like this woman. The fear, at least according to the stereotype, was that a child victim could become promiscuous or frigid in later years, a backlash from the failure to adjust sexually in a normal, natural fashion. And any one of these children could conceivably grow up to be like Kelly. Robert, Joey Gardner's friend, had told his mother that Kelly had said to him: "This is what you're gonna do to children when you grow up."

Ellen wondered whether Kelly had been echoing words she herself had heard as a child. And Joey's mother hoped violently that her son wouldn't feel the need to turn his anger on a smaller, weaker creature just to be reassured of his own humanity.

．
． ．

The prosecutor rocked from foot to foot, impatient to start the third day of cross-examination. Her thick black dress, cinched tightly by wide black leather, dwarfed her, yet her voice was powerful when she finally began: "You stated, Miss Michaels, that it was necessary to stick to a schedule, and if you didn't stick to a schedule the school would be in chaos, isn't that correct?"

Kelly sounded strong this morning, and righteous. "It was—I don't believe either of you have children, and if you've ever been to a day care . . . always a few steps near chaos all the time. Just having that many children running around playing. It's just always near that. So the schedule helps, yes." Her indignation was lit.

Sara reinterpreted the answer to her advantage. She charged, "And therefore it was easy to predict when changes were going to occur?"

Kelly had a hard line to argue. If she said the school was well structured, then she supported her claim that her classroom was well monitored by her supervisors and aides. Alternatively, if she said the school was chaotic, then she supported her claim that her nap room was frequently interrupted by random intruders. Logically, she needed it to be both ways.

Kelly wavered. "I don't understand the question."

"*You knew* what was going to happen in school every day?"

"Oh, sure," said Kelly, then changed her mind. "I don't understand."

"You knew when the classes were going to change?"

"Oh, yes. Umhm."

"You knew when the snack was going to be brought in?"

"We knew approximately, yes."

"Wasn't snack, Miss Michaels, from ten to ten-fifteen, and then Brenda would go to the kindergarten?"

"I really, I don't remember. That may be true."

Sara practically ignored her. "And you were alone with those children in that room at least a half an hour, two to three mornings a week, because Brenda, who you say was your aide some of the time *or* most of the time, went to the kindergarten room?" Sara circled forward and back.

Kelly answered, "I don't remember that long of a stretch. Yes, I was alone with the children. Yes, there were times."

"Longer than what you told this jury last week? Longer than just going to the bathroom?"

Kelly tried to glue things back together. "Or other sorts of duties, I believe. But I don't remember that long of a stretch. That would have been very difficult to have handled, but I *did* state I was alone with the children at times. Yes, umhm."

Sara continued to shave down the bulk of vague testimony, working inward toward the precise shape of how time was used at Wee Care, how during first lunch Kelly had supposedly laid out mats for nap period, after which she and another teacher would supervise second lunch.

Sara tested Kelly's memory: "Who were the children in your lunch?"

"That I'm really—I have to think about that."

"You don't remember that, do you, Miss Michaels?" Sara was invasive, threatening.

"Right offhand—"

"Yes."

"If I look at the list . . ."

"Without looking at the list. Do you remember that?"

"Not really."

(Sara thought to herself: Because you never had the same group two days in a row!) She asked, "Yet you had these children every single day at lunch. . . . You had these children every day in your lunch room, didn't you?"

"Yes, ma'am."

Sara wanted to demonstrate that Kelly could have absconded with a few children from first lunch, and then, after monitoring the second lunch, hustled to get the mats laid out. This theory was important because lunch was one of the only times Kelly would have had the opportunity to abuse Elizabeth Kelsey: Elizabeth had not been in Kelly's classroom, official lunch, or nap, and she had left school early in the afternoon, missing the late-afternoon time period which Kelly had often supervised.

Sara peered right into Kelly. "You did not set the mats up until after second lunch."

"That was not the usual routine. No, ma'am. I set the mats up during first lunch."

Single-mindedly, Sara pursued this possibility. "If those mats were not getting set up during first lunch, you were not assigned any other specific activity during that time, were you?"

Kelly was vague: "Oh, there would always be a place for me to go. You didn't wander. That was absolutely—it was absolutely impossible, no time for that to happen. . . . It would've been ridiculous."

"Well, if Elizabeth says you took her up to the choir room during first lunch, and you didn't set the mats out, that would've been a time that you would have had the opportunity to take Elizabeth to the choir room, isn't that correct?"

Kelly expressed shock: "First of all, I never took Elizabeth or any child to the choir room, and second of all, I put the mats down first, during the first time period."

"And you're certain of that?"

"Yes, ma'am. I was assigned by Diane Costa to put the mats down. Yes."

Sara wryly inquired, "And you're as certain of that as you are of everything else?"

"As certain as my memory can be, as anyone's memory can be of three years ago, Mrs. McArdle."

Then Kelly testified, "I remember Arlene popping in on occasions in the nap room, randomly."

"Well, Arlene testified she didn't do that—"

"Objection." Meltzer remained subdued, but softly he added, "Comparison of testimony, Your Honor."

"Objection sustained."

Sara checked with the transcripts of the past few days. "You stated that parents were always coming and going. Which parents?"

". . . Specific people?"

"Yes."

"I remember seeing faces often coming down to get kids' coats and lunches, but that was a daily occurrence."

Sara repeated, ''Which parents would come in the classroom, Miss Michaels?'' The day was getting old.

''Gosh, I remember seeing faces, occasionally.''

Sara hit Kelly's claim of general traffic during nap time. ''Well, did Julie's mother?''

''I remember her right after nap,'' Kelly answered, her hands cupped, ladylike, on the wooden shelf.

''Paul's mother?''

''I remember seeing her. Yes, I do remember seeing her.''

Sara delved: ''Did she come in your classroom when the kids were in nap?'' leading Kelly on.

''I seem to remember.''

One more time, for clarification, Sara reiterated, ''Paul's mother came in?''

Kelly balked. ''We're talking about the beginning of nap time?''

Sara gave Kelly a clue to the flaw in her testimony: ''Paul was a nine-to-four child, wasn't he?''

''I don't remember,'' said Kelly quickly.

''If he was a nine-to-four child, he wouldn't have been picked up at the beginning of nap, would he?'' said Sara, the implication echoing: So why would his mother have been at the school . . . ?

''She was a member of the school board, so there was . . . sometimes earlier in the day . . .'' Kelly flailed for another explanation.

Sara's voice was stiff with loathing as she said, ''She wouldn't walk in through your nap class, would she?''

''I remember her face. I don't remember if she walked in my nap,'' Kelly conceded.

Sara stood with her back turned to Kelly, scanning her notes. ''Once you got the kids comfortable, you were alone with those children in that nap room, isn't that correct?''

''Yes, ma'am,'' said Kelly. At this moment, Sara was a foot and a half from Kelly's face.

Sara declared, ''And that was a time when people wouldn't come into the classroom because they didn't want to disturb the children, isn't that also correct?''

''You try your best, but there were random occasions. It was never an announced thing. . . .''

''You told Rich Mastrangelo, 'Usually, I have the first nap. Parents are always coming and going.' That wasn't correct, was it?''

''I believe that's what I testified to just now.''

Sara accused openly: ''Once you closed the door of that room, you were alone with those children!''

"I was alone with the children during my nap. Yes, I was."

Having achieved this complete admission of access and opportunity, Sara relinquished control of the witness.

Redirect and recross examination followed, but were brief, repetitious, uneventful: The denouement had already begun. Kelly's testimony hadn't introduced anything exculpatory except the exhibit of her personality.

Kelly's fists were at her mouth, and she stared with a numb, filmy look. The attorneys finished with her in less than twenty minutes.

Judge Harth spoke to the defendant: "Thank you, you may step down." He looked up. "You may call your next witness."

Kelly looked empty: paralyzed by anticlimax.

Bob Clark rose to address the court. "Subject to moving exhibits into evidence, the defense now rests."

Kelly walked back to counsel table, ladylike, self-possessed, staring out the window to her left. She was out of reach, seemingly untouched by the charges, innocent or guilty.

. .

No one knew at this point how Kelly's mind operated any more than they had years ago when the case broke. Kelly Michaels had been looked at, talked about, thought of, yet never defined. People around the courthouse tried to explain Kelly to themselves and to one another. Names of mental disorders were batted around: multiple personality, psychotic, sociopathic.

The children themselves had talked of two Kellys: a good Kelly and a bad Kelly. Those people who inclined toward the multiple-personality theory cited the children's statements as proof. Leslie Michaels told the press that when her sister had been accused of these crimes, Kelly herself had been worried: "I have no memory of abusing the kids. Do I have a split personality?" But many who believed in Kelly's guilt gave up on trying to figure her out and simply insisted that she was evil.

Even if Kelly Michaels's thoughts could be turned out like a globe of her mental geography, she might disappoint those hoping to find an intact, orderly motivation for committing sexual crimes against children. The self-conscious, knowing criminal was at least graspable, opposable, but Kelly could be just as confused about what she did and why as were those people desperate for some explanation.

Part

FIVE

19

∴

Closing arguments were each attorney's final opportunity to speak directly to the jury. Bob Clark, then Harvey Meltzer, then Sara McArdle, then Glenn Goldberg would each argue the inferences to be drawn from the evidence and provide the jurors with the words of persuasion they wanted them to take with them into the jury room. The prosecutors always had the first and last words in a trial as compensation for the disadvantage of carrying the burden of proof. Sara and Glenn had devised a plan to deliver their summations in relay style, switching back and forth, but Clark and Meltzer would speak in the traditional fashion: in sequence. ·

With a fresh haircut and looking dignified and trim, Bob Clark began summation faced with the reality that he was competing for sympathy with nineteen children. He addressed the jury: "Currently, there exists a catchword: 'Believe the Children.' It is not a question of which side did you believe. That would be an oversimplification. It is possible to believe *both*. But in that case, reasonable doubt exists.''

However, after carefully establishing that he and the children were not in complete opposition, Clark betrayed an underlying scorn for them. Meg Barnes's hefty contribution of eleven counts to the indictment seemed to amaze him, and he listed for the jurors the eight first-degree counts of aggravated sexual assault: four vaginal penetrations and four anal penetrations, each with fork, knife, spoon, and finger.

Clark summed up: "Some of everything."

He spent much of his time massaging the jurors' imaginations, trying to impress upon them the impossibility of the alleged crimes and sharing with them his own incredulity over the charges. He described the task of having to organize and undress eight, ten, fourteen children, and challenged, "Imagine what it takes. . . . I submit—incredible! But, apply your common sense."

In the same vein, he continued, "Where are the signs, the physical evidence? Did someone smell feces? No one in the course of this trial smelled anything unusual or anything out of place."

(Yeah, thought Sara, and seven of the kids were having accidents in their pants every day. The smells were all over the school, so no one would have thought anything of it if they did smell something.)

Clark added, "Kelly must have been a marvelous cleaner, a great housekeeper, and do it all within the time constraints." Reminding the jurors about the negative findings when the FBI analyzed the wooden spoon and the piano benches, he said, "Once again, incredible."

He then marveled that Kevin Brennan never once told his mother about what his sister, Heather, was doing in school. His attitude was one of sheer disbelief: "The tattletale syndrome—the brother who you almost have to beat up personally to keep from telling all your business to everybody. Kevin didn't tell? Defies logic."

Attacking the level of detail in the prosecution's case, Bob noted that just because the state had introduced testimony on minute details (a pharmacist to confirm that Evan Connors had indeed had an anal rash during 1984–85) didn't mean its cause was right. Completeness and thoroughness did not equal rightness.

Later, Clark articulated further disbelief that the children had the cognitive ability to have remembered and articulated the things they did. He reminded the jurors of the testimony: "Joey said he remembered saying 'lies! lies! lies!' at the Grand Jury." He paused for drama, then stretched his voice wide around the upshot: "He *wished* that they were lies. *Fantastic!*"

The defecation and urination allegations he just couldn't fathom. He confessed, "Quite frankly, I've had trouble getting my kids to eat broccoli, let alone feces and urine."

Then Bob Clark astounded his audience: "Some of the children I saw seemed to be . . . brats, quite frankly." He added, "I find it unbelievable that anyone would've been able to give instructions to that group of children that passed through the judge's chambers, getting them to do whatever she wanted them to do!"

He wanted to disprove the control Kelly reputedly had had over the preschoolers, but his words seemed to attest to the impossibility of the defense's entire suggestibility strategy. If no one could tell these children what to say, how could Lou Fonolleras?

Soon after making this comment, Clark apologized for the "brats" remark, and then revamped his argument to single out Lewis Dixon as the one legitimate recipient of the label. He said, "The problem I have with Lewis Dixon is that I found it hard to believe that this child, who didn't listen to the judge, his support person, who barely listened to me and was a problem child in school . . . this same Lewis Dixon who may only listen to his grandfather—"

Sara interrupted. "I object, Your Honor! *Today* he listens. The testimony is, he didn't listen *then*."

"The jury will use their recollection," said Harth.

Clark continued: "Is this the same child who Kelly Michaels was able to tell what to do, when to do it? I doubt it."

Then he delivered his opinion on why the other Wee Care teachers had given statements on behalf of the prosecution. Clark attributed their attitude to fear of being implicated, explaining, "The way it was presented and the nature of the offenses. It may rub off. People may think, 'How could you be there for seven months and not see anything?' " Clark went so far as to say, "They're all putting distance between themselves and the accused. They all believe she's guilty."

Glenn gulped.

Never in a million motions would he or Sara have been allowed to say such a thing before the jury. But now the jurors had heard that all the teachers who had been there daily, in the school with Kelly, the very people who could evaluate whether or not the sexual interaction was believable, feasible—they all believed that Kelly was guilty.

Harvey Meltzer hit hard on the quality of the investigative interviews. "The majority of [the children] didn't say anything until after they saw the magic people: Lou, George, and Rich." Meltzer overlooked David

Kirschner and Angie McMahon, who had each first disclosed to their mothers, as well as Jonathan (Harvey called him "the her-takes-my-temperature kid") Moore.

The children in this case had not been sexually abused, Meltzer maintained, because if they had, they could never have gone up to six months without disclosing. Meltzer said, "They couldn't say, 'Hey, Ma! Kelly is doing bad things to me in school . . . and you should see how she cooks a poopie cake, like no one's ever cooked one before!' " He eyeballed the sixteen jurors. "Can you *believe* that?"

The defense attorney had an explanation for why the Wee Care parents were so willing to go along with these abuse allegations: They had neglected their own children and were therefore grateful to use Kelly Michaels, the mythical child abuser, as a scapegoat. In one breath, Harvey believed that the behaviors had never existed, were just a post-indictment fabrication contrived to support the false allegations of abuse; yet, in a second breath, he held the parents responsible for those very same behaviors.

Meltzer imitated a mother frantic to find an explanation for her child's behavior: " 'It's not because of what *I* did. My housekeeper's a pretty good lady. And if not, my next-door neighbor's housekeeper is a pretty good lady. It wasn't because of what *I* did. It's because of what *Kelly* did.' " Seeking exoneration for their own crimes in parenting, he hypothesized, the parents had settled on the most denied anathema.

Moving on fluidly, easily, to another major defense point, Harvey Meltzer stated, "There is no medical evidence that any of these things took place."

Given the allegations, "Winter months in the choir room . . . disrobing in the cold temperature," he said that the kinds of things he would have expected to find by way of physical evidence were simply never found. "Kids would've gotten sick," he said.

Echoing Bob Clark, Meltzer glared at the jurors and said, "Does the word *unpossible* mean anything to you?"

Then, shifting emphasis away from the evidence, Meltzer attacked Glenn Goldberg, criticizing his concentration on Kelly's "sex poem" at the back of her roll book. He stated, "I would submit, ladies and gentlemen, that this is, indeed, a sex poem." Meltzer stared the jurors down, then hit them with it: "You'll find the same in James Joyce's *Ulysses* and in the Bible. So . . . if so, she's in good company."

Meltzer found his true voice in impeaching the prosecution: "Hasty conclusions. . . . They discounted everything that was positive and focused on everything that was negative." His summation was riddled with one-liners ("The state's case is like a silk handkerchief—all show and no blow"), flip remarks poking holes in what he considered to be a shoddy case. He slurred, "We have two miracle workers. We have Kelly Michaels being able to perform miracles on the children so they wouldn't talk, and we have an equal and opposite miracle: Lou, George, and Rich getting them to talk."

He mocked, "It would've taken twenty-five people to do what she's supposed to have done." Then, apparently at his most serious and dignified, Harvey Meltzer took the jurors back a short time in American culture and implored them: "In the immortal words of Clara Peller, 'Where's the beef?' We've heard a description of the lettuce, a description of the bun, a description of the sauce, but the state has failed to describe that beef patty, that incontrovertible piece of evidence."

▪
▪ ▪

Sara challenged the jurors: "Which expert told you about a study that says children can be taught they've been sexually abused? What study? There is no study, because children cannot be taught this. Children believe in Santa Claus, of course they do. They experience him every year. . . . The state agrees with the defense that, yes, children can be taught about sexual abuse." Sara paused, then concluded, "But it's not the interviewers that teach abuse. *Abuse* is the learning process."

Sara walked, out of her way, over to where Kelly sat. She drew extremely close and pointed a rigid finger at the defendant. Kelly raised her eyebrows and grinned, nodding invitingly. Sara repeated, "*Abuse* is the learning process."

Over her shoulder, Sara said to the jury, "When Kelly Michaels placed a knife in Alison Steadman's rectum, Alison learned what that felt like. These are the acts that taught the children about abuse. That is how they came to personalize it."

Sara turned abruptly and returned to the podium.

Glenn discussed the nature of the crimes: "Everything is invisible. Nothing shows on the child, and it's so hard to understand. The defendant, you think to yourself . . . looks good to me. Attractive young lady. Why would she do it? You may never know why she did it. . . . She may not herself know. Maybe she didn't think she did anything wrong . . . something the children are going to experience anyway, sex."

Clark objected, but Harth silenced him. "I gave you an opportunity to sum up. Now it's Mr. Goldberg's turn."

Glenn paused, tilted back his head, and sang, "Moons and junes and ferris wheels, the dizzy dancing way I feel. . . ."

Sara looked embarrassed.

He strolled over to the blackboard and turned it around to reveal a poster that said "The Dizzy Dancing Way I Feel" in red letters six inches tall. The lyrics from "Both Sides Now" had been inscribed by Kelly into her Wee Care roll book, and in Glenn's mind this line from the song epitomized Kelly Michaels. To draw the connection for the jurors, he recapped all the evidence about Kelly's strangeness: spacing out or dancing away from other teachers during a conversation; lapsing into a trance for thirty seconds in the midst of being addressed. . . .

When he had concluded this catalogue, Glenn once again sang out the first few lines of "Both Sides Now."

Meltzer objected: "Repetition. And worse the second time than the first."

The courtroom responded with sincere laughter. Harth just smiled and said, "Well, it's going no further."

Glenn quoted Kelly: " 'How do they know I'm not some kind of child molester?' "

He stared at the jurors, mouth open, then informed them: "When we heard that, we thought—"

Mocking dismay, the prosecutor propelled a handful of papers into the air, and the sheaf avalanched to the floor. "We were afraid to present this to you because we thought it might sound contrived, like we were witch-hunting. However, in the interest of completeness and thoroughness . . . and that leads to, what? Rightness?"

Sara glanced up from her papers: "Rightness."

"Rightness . . . we presented it to you."

Kelly smoothed her hair off her face, picked up her daily missive, and began to read.

Glenn asked rhetorically, "Was it sort of exciting to play 'Catch me if you can'? . . . Was it 'truth indiscriminate,' a confused kind of truth? . . . Was it that Kelly Michaels was bold and brazen? Probably so."

When Clark made another objection, Harth overruled, then admonished him on the frequency of his intrusions into the state's closing arguments. The judge implied that the objections were becoming frivolous.

Clark yelled, "Point out one improper thing I've done!"

"Just stopping him right now with what he said."

Set up in front of the jury box was a chart that catalogued the number of times Kelly Michaels had testified to various evasions: "I don't remember" or "I don't remember but I'm sure it happened" or "I don't remember but it may have happened." Glenn inquired, "And this is the person who says forget about the other nineteen eyewitnesses who said she did it . . . believe her and disbelieve them because her memory and her credibility are better?"

Bob Clark raised his voice to object: "The Dizzy Dancing Way I Feel" was still taunting from the blackboard. He wanted the poster removed. Harth ruled that it could stay.

Sara pointed at Kelly, who rolled her eyes, glittering black glass. One of the proofs of Kelly's innocence that Meltzer had presented to the jury was "She didn't run away." Sara was impatient, derisive: "That doesn't mean she was innocent. Where was she going to go? Was she in a position to go to Bolivia? She really believed she could talk her way out of the trouble she had gotten herself into."

Facing the jury box, Sara said, "The defendant says impossible, improbable, *un*possible, couldn't happen!" She lashed into Kelly's testimony, saying, "She doesn't want you to realize how really easy it was to grab children because children were always floating around. Miss Michaels would like you to believe that during nap that school was run like Grand Central Station. She has to create that illusion for you because Miss Michaels knows she was alone during nap." Sara was stressing, repeatedly, that Kelly, cold-blooded, knew what she had done.

Kelly nodded, eyes wide and mock-impressed behind Sara's back.

A Wee Care teacher had stated that the knife she kept in her classroom for making snacks had disappeared so often that she had taken to hiding an extra knife, and now Sara was incredulous: "Of all things to keep disappearing, what was missing? The silverware! And we know what happened with the silverware." She slapped the podium.

Meltzer was next to object. Harth reminded, "It's Mrs. McArdle who's summing up, Mr. Meltzer."

Glenn used Harvey Meltzer as a weapon against Harvey Meltzer. He said, "In reality, what are the effects of early childhood experience? I think Mr. Meltzer said it best. . . . Mr. Meltzer explained, 'Your Honor, with all due respect, we all have our idioms and idiosyncracies. Sometimes statements and phrases that I use go all the way back to my *infancy*, and sometimes they come out.' "

The state's summation was soon interrupted by yet another defense objection. After the judge overruled, Glenn checked his tally and mentioned that there had now been over one hundred objections, most of them not sustained.

Harth, diplomatic, deflected, "I'm sure they're doing what they feel is proper."

Clark agreed, explaining, "If appeal is necessary, they'll say we waived if we don't object."

Glenn moved on to address the eleven-day court appearance of Dr. Ralph Underwager. His words were not kind. "Dr. Underwager expressed his opinions in this case based on an ignorance of the facts. . . . And the facts were available. I submit to you, when Dr. Underwager pulls his figures out of the air, he knows what he's doing is wrong, and he even gets whole columns of figures wrong. . . . I submit to you he is a disgrace to the science of psychology."

Glenn abruptly gave up trying to explain the meaning of Underwager, and instead he ripped up the copies he held of the doctor's report and showered the pieces onto the courtroom floor.

"Yes, it was," said Harth, acknowledging Harvey Meltzer's objection that the prosecuting attorney's file had just been ripped up and thrown onto the floor.

Glenn wanted to offer the jurors an explanation for why the state had held Underwager on the stand for eight long days of cross-examination, so he offered an analogy: "We tried this case somewhat as a fireman puts out a fire. They pour all kinds of water. They don't use a squirt gun—'just enough water'—because there's always a danger that if some little ember stays among the rubble, some strong wind might come along, and it could inflame and ignite."

Now cracking a gigantic book, Glenn proposed to read to the court something that, in its entirety, epitomized Ralph Underwager's testimony. He began: " 'Twas brillig, and the slithy toves/Did gyre and gimble in the wabe;/All mimsy were the borogoves,/And the mome raths outgrabe./ Beware the Jabberwock, my son!/The jaws that bite, the claws that catch!/ Beware the Jubjub bird, and shun/The frumious Bandersnatch!' "

Glenn proceeded to chant Lewis Carroll's complete "Jabberwocky," modulating his tone with the vanity of an orator. Spectators laughed without noise so as not to interrupt the uproarious performance. When he had finished, Glenn offered a postscript: "Stands for the proposition that gobbledy gook, words that mean nothing, can sound like they mean something. He didn't want you to understand. He didn't want you to know what he was saying."

The last note of Sara's summation rang out for the children: "I'm very proud of them."

Meltzer objected. "Personal feelings!"

Kelly swung her head about slowly, as if sedated, to see the judge overrule.

Sara went on. "Victims often walk away because they're afraid to come to court. These children could have walked away. . . . These kids are truly superheroes. They've used their weapons—their courage and strength and their sense of right—to overcome their weakness and terror. . . . Neither you nor I have the power to rewrite history so the suffering of these little children hadn't happened.

"I'm turning this case over to you. The children have told you; the parents have told you. All I ask is that you do what any prosecutor would ask. I ask you to do justice. I trust that you will. Thank you."

.
. .

Neither Harvey Meltzer nor Bob Clark had made any material reference to some of the things that, in their initial remarks to the jury nine months ago, they had stressed as their strongest arguments. The name of Lou Fonolleras was mentioned only in passing. The testimony of the children's parents was not addressed. Nor was the oft-repeated defense allegation that the state was on a witch-hunt to palliate the area judge whose grandson was involved.

And they did not make use of the testimony of their own expert witnesses. Except for the $54,518 paid Dr. Ralph Underwager by the Public Defender's office, his appearance in New Jersey was left forgotten, but Bob Clark defended his team's selection of Underwager by querying, "Who else does suggestibility?"

Dr. Underwager left New Jersey, his credibility as a witness wretchedly disabled. At a future time, when prosecutions became immune to Ralph Underwager, some other expert would certainly take his place: The niche would be filled. And that next national defense expert might be someone more trained and qualified in the areas of child development and sexual abuse, perhaps someone more difficult to neutralize, a new and stronger defense expert.

Dr. Elissa Benedek, also unmentioned in closing, carried home $11,593. The prosecution had paid Eileen Treacy $25,000 for her work, although in addition she had donated four hundred hours to the case. In all, the defense had cost $421,000, the prosecution $283,101. Adding in courtroom expenses, including personnel such as the judge, the bailiffs, the clerks and secretaries, the total expense to New Jersey taxpayers of *State* v. *Margaret Kelly Michaels* came to $1.2 million.

20

.˙.

Throughout the trial, Judge Harth had aligned himself, as the impartial arbiter of procedure, with the sixteen nonpartisan members of the jury. Harth opened his charge to the jury by thanking them, in slow, considered tones, for their cooperation and attention during a trial which, contrary to all expectations, had already lasted for nine months. Back in June 1987, during jury selection, the judge had warned them that the trial was expected to last for twelve weeks.

The doors to the courtroom were sealed. Traditionally, no one was allowed to enter or exit the courtroom so as not to distract the jury and out of respect for the law. Judge Harth laid out the basic premise of the American justice system: "The defendant is presumed innocent till proven guilty beyond a reasonable doubt. The burden of proof is entirely on the state, and there is no burden on the defendant to prove herself innocent." Harth explained that if any one of the counts was not proven beyond a reasonable doubt, then on that count, "the defendant is entitled to acquittal."

The area of reasonable doubt was completely uncharted: The legal system left the difficult demarcation between the known and the insufficiently proven to the discretion of juries. However, Judge Harth offered this guidance: "Everything relating to human affairs is open to some imaginary doubt."

Reasonable doubt adjoined the tender area of unknowability, and the judge's words could be applied to the testimony of the experts as well as to the jury's verdict.

After making his preliminary remarks, Harth began the obligatory reading of the indictment by the court. One by one, he read each of the 131 remaining counts, fully describing each act charged and stating the name of the child allegedly victimized. The jurors listened quietly. As the judge inventoried the counts, a few stole looks at Kelly's parents.

The Michaels family was still here, front and center, everyone except the two brothers. By now, they were fixtures in the courthouse, and many of the bailiffs and office personnel admired their grit.

Harth took forty-five minutes to read through all the counts. When he was done, he proceeded to explain, in a businesslike manner (his voice almost monotonic), the required proofs of each crime. On the charges of sexual penetration the state did not need to prove that the instrument had penetrated a specific distance: The slightest penetration, either orally or manually, constituted an aggravated sexual assault. Harth also explained that on each of the counts charging anal or vaginal penetration, the jury might determine that the evidence did not sufficiently prove that a penetration had taken place, but that it did prove that a touching had occurred. The jury could therefore choose to downgrade a first-degree offense to a second-degree. This, Harth told them, was a "lesser included offense," and in their deliberations on the penetration counts they were free to consider that alternative.

Harth continued with the requirements of proof. The state had no responsibility to prove that terroristic threats did, in fact, actually terrorize the child. Likewise, the counts of endangering the welfare and morals of a child did not require proof that the conduct did, in fact, corrupt the child. As to all counts of sexual interaction, the law considered it to be immaterial whether or not the child victim had consented to the act. Harth explained, "The law cloaks the child with an inability to consent at a tender age," to prevent someone from taking advantage of the child's immaturity.

He apprised the jurors that the evidence for each count "need not determine specific dates and times of acts." The courts and the psychiatric community recognized that children are not able to provide these details.

The state was required to prove that the defendant had acted "purposefully" in the commission of these acts. For example, an accidental brush of the hand would not constitute sexual assault by sexual contact. However, the state had no obligation to prove the defendant's motive in crime. The prosecutors didn't have to understand Kelly, only convict her.

Finally, Harth charged the jurors as to the testimony of Kelly Michaels, saying, "The jury should not disregard the defendant's testimony merely because she is the defendant and has an interest in the outcome of this case."

The jurors slumped into their yellow bucket seats as the judge offered words of consolation for the responsibility they were about to assume: "Use your common sense. No one can ask more of you, and what's more important, you can ask no more of yourselves."

The judge's charge completed, a bailiff withdrew four slips of paper from a wide wooden box. The names of the four alternate jurors were read off, four people who, having listened to the testimony for all this time, were to be excluded from deliberations. Two of the alternates looked relieved, two disgruntled. The alternates would have to continue to attend court, but would be excluded from jury room deliberations except if and when testimony was reviewed. The court clerk gave to the twelve deliberating jurors blank verdict sheets that listed the counts along with their possible verdicts. They were forty-five pages long.

The five sheriff's officers, who during deliberations were to shepherd and safeguard the jurors as they came and went or took meals, were called forward at this time to be sworn. Judge Harth asked them all to place their hands on the Bible, together. The formality was unexpected. Harth guided them to swear to keep these jurors separate from all others and to maintain the sanctity of deliberations.

"Now go to work and be as leisurely as you choose," said Harth.

The twelve deliberating jurors filed into the jury room, and the alternates were shipped out to their own holding room.

Harth said, "All right, let's catch our breath also."

Meltzer laughed. "Does this mean it's all over?"

·
■ ■

The first thing the jurors wanted to know was whether they could plan to sit only until five o'clock each day: They wanted to arrive fresh daily so as not to impair their judgment. They also requested not to sit on Saturdays. These requests hinted at a long deliberation, although Glenn Goldberg insisted jokingly that they would be back any minute with all counts guilty.

Whereas during the trial everyone had been more or less polite to one another, managing to coexist in the small space of the courtroom, now they were too on edge to sustain the formalities. Those on either side of the case kept to themselves. The Michaels family and Kelly's attorneys vacated the courtroom, relocating to a room on a higher floor of the courthouse. The prosecutors, the press, and several mothers set up camp in Judge Harth's courtroom, finding it difficult, if not impossible, to draw much farther away from the scene of ultimate transition. Sara's and Glenn's professional responsibilities still centered on this case, and they still spent most of their time waiting for the verdict and away from their long abandoned desks.

At the end of the first day of deliberations, the red light came on outside the door of the jury room, and a note was passed out to a bailiff. Inside the jury room, jurors were laughing, stamping their feet. Glenn, lounging with a newspaper directly outside the door, commented, "The typical sound of a jury in a sex abuse trial."

The judge called down the defense party, and the jurors and alternates were reassembled in the jury box so that Harth could read aloud the note he'd just received: "We'd like to review . . . audiotaped interviews, VCR interviews, closed-circuit testimony of the children as they are listed in the indictment. We would like to see all available materials on each child one at a time, and we would like to deliberate as to each child after reviewing the materials."

Harth wasn't certain what they wanted, and he asked them if he understood correctly: "If Dr. Underwager testified as to David Kirschner, will you want to hear his testimony read back when you get to that child?"

Half the jurors were shaking their heads. One called out: "Strike that, just strike that."

"Do you want the testimony of Dr. Underwager, Benedek?"

"No. No." Several jurors were speaking at once, chuckling, moaning. Mark, the foreman, clarified that they wanted to review only the statements made by the children themselves.

The next morning, television monitors were erected on carts and the jurors reviewed the videotape of Jonathan Moore's testimony.

The jurors' faces were vacant as they watched the tape. Most leaned back, as if only faintly interested, but a few were intent, sitting forward. When the tape concluded, they returned to the jury room, and the waiting resumed.

Meltzer told the press that the request to view the videotapes was a pro-defense indication, because it meant that the jurors were focusing on suggestibility in their deliberations, but the prosecutors had a different take on it. Glenn and Sara both agreed that if they could have selected any testimony for the jurors to review, they would have chosen the children's: Theirs was the most clearly responsive to the charges.

. .

Waiting for the verdict, the parents and the Michaelses shared the same strain, both groups riding in and out on their own speculative tide. Kelly didn't look as captivating as she had when she had testified. Her features and expressions seemed to have faded, and her now-lengthened bangs gave her face an overshadowed, overcast look.

Those holding out inside the courtroom found it impossible to pass the time reading because their eyes constantly worked around to stare anxiously at the unlit red light bulb on the wall outside the jury room.

Time passed, but the jury's pace was erratic. Sometimes they found whatever they were looking for within twenty minutes of the completion of a child's video, but other times not until after a full day's deliberations.

The tapes would require forty-three hours of viewing time alone, and given the time needed between tapes, the verdict could be several weeks away. Yet, Glenn Goldberg remained certain that at any moment now the verdict would be in. He knew, just knew, that the jury members were going to view the tapes of a few children, and then admit to themselves that they believed everything.

On the third day, the jury momentarily stopped viewing tapes. The next day, however, their pace picked back up, and by the fifth day they were viewing an average of two tapes a day. Moods in the courthouse undulated, but Kelly appeared to feel good. She received a lot of support from her family, hugs and smiles, which seemed to help them in their distress as much as they helped Kelly.

The aura was like that of election night: Every local report was avidly overinterpreted. If the jurors took ten minutes to deliberate after a tape, then asked for the next one, that meant one thing. If they asked to take a walk outside after lunch, that meant something else.

Sara, desperately anxious, was too uptight to sit in the courtroom and wait. She passed time joking with reporters about the case. ''Gucci bags and alligator shoes, that's how we bribed the kids,'' she said. Then she sobered and said, ''If she's acquitted, then there is no justice for children.'' She turned and hurried back into the courtroom. If the verdict came in not guilty, it would become next to impossible for Sara's Child Abuse Unit to move forward with institutional abuse cases, because their credibility would be shot. More even than the lives of these particular victims could be at stake in this trial.

On the eleventh day of deliberations, Glenn couldn't stand it any longer. He wanted some indication of when the verdict was going to arrive. After morning roll was taken and the jurors were sent to their room, Glenn stood up and addressed the court: "Since the jury seems to be moving more rapidly than before, perhaps it would not be out of order to make some mild suggestion if perhaps the jury could give us some idea, if they want to, a day ahead."

Meltzer rose. "May I be heard, sir? How does the word *jury tampering* sound? I think we're supposed to keep the hell out, pardon my French, out of the jury room. I don't want to seem we're pushing them." Meltzer took his seat.

Harth concurred. "I don't think we should get into it."

"Judge, there is no word *jury tampering*. That's two words." Glenn, testy with the great uncertainty, was provoked. "The sound of it, though, is perfectly ridiculous. I think . . . in fact, I *know*, there will be nothing at all inappropriate with simply sending out a mild request."

"I don't think there'd be anything wrong. It's a judgment call on my part. I prefer to be conservative," Harth replied.

Harvey's knees were bent as he thought of standing up to speak, when Clark whispered, "Don't respond. Don't respond."

Harvey reseated himself.

. .
.

Juror Eighteen was back again. The county doctor had reported that she wasn't insane. But, following her release from Caldwell for the second time, Eighteen fulfilled all expectations and reappeared in court. The jury, in their deliberations, were unaware of her devotion.

Sara and Glenn had vacated counsel table. While Harth conversed with Eighteen, Kelly, at the other end of counsel table, chatted with the defense investigator, impervious to the confrontation going on at her side.

Harth initiated the encounter: "I'd thought I'd made it clear you were not to come."

Eighteen's features were clenched, but her body hung loose: casual, primed. "And I thought I made it clear to you that that does not apply to me. We've been all through this, Your Honor."

The judge recalled. "I asked you why, and you refused to answer."

What next came out of her mouth was both poetic and arch-prophetic: "I see your heart is still lifted up, sir, and you are full of pride. And your mind is still hardened. And I perceive, sir, that you will have a downfall.''

Harth asked tentatively, "Can you tell me what kind of downfall?''

"No," she said, licking her lips.

He phrased the next very carefully. "But you know what it is?''

Eighteen was in power, control. "Yes," she said, nodding.

"You leave me no choice. I find you in contempt of court.''

"Sir, I can only say that you are being very foolish.''

"Why foolish?''

"Because you should perceive my position here without having to require me to reveal it . . . *sir!*''

Eighteen refused to stay away from the courthouse, and Harth wasn't playing the game anymore. He had a jury deliberating on a nearly ten-month-old trial, and hundreds of thousands of taxpayers' dollars invested in an unobstructed verdict. He ruled, "You are in contempt of court.''

"You are misusing your power, sir.''

For all his disgust with this predicament, Harth seemed reluctant to return her to jail. He said, "I hesitate to do this. Are you sure you cannot obey?''

She responded unwaveringly: "Absolutely not, sir.''

Harth sentenced Juror Eighteen to thirty more days in the Caldwell facility, but relented just long enough to apprise her: "If at any time you feel you can abide—''

"No, sir," she said. "You have a lot to learn.'' Then she rose to accommodate the officers who were carting her away.

Kelly remarked nothing.

.
. .

Kelly and Leslie entered the courtroom conversing playfully in French. The jury called for the videotape of the last child, Fred Mercer. As the nineteenth tape rolled, Kelly seemed strong, contemptuous.

The deliberations were obviously nearing their end. Sara, at counsel table, leaned over to Glenn: "I've gotta call my travel agent.''

Bob Clark believed differently. He was confident that the jury intended to request much more testimony after they were through with the children, hoping, presumably, for the next selection to draw from the defense case's presentation. However, belying this prediction, he carried *Cruise Magazine* pressed against his side, researching the coming catharsis.

.
. .

It was April 15, 1988, the thirteenth day of deliberations: Sara was in the courthouse cafeteria when the call came. In the middle of the lunch break, the one time of day she had thought she could safely leave the eighth floor, the jurors turned over a note informing Judge Harth that they were ready with a verdict. Sara dropped her hard-boiled egg and raced back to court. The reporters and parents in the cafeteria noticed her peel out and rushed after her.

The Michaels family was already assembled in the gallery's front row, the two brothers absent. The attorneys gathered in Harth's chambers to discuss procedure.

The entire floor of the building was teeming with would-be spectators. For the first time since the trial had begun, Wee Care fathers were here in force beside their wives. Fifty friends, parents, and relatives were present on behalf of the children, along with dozens of courthouse employees who had learned via the courthouse network that the verdict was in. The members of the press numbered two dozen.

To add to the uproar, the reporters and even Prosecutor's Office investigators were being harassed at the door by guards who didn't recognize them: The Sheriff's Office had assigned an almost entirely new crew of officers to Harth's courtroom. The guards were abusive and the atmosphere charged, as if there had already been a riot.

It took close to an hour from the time Sara left the cafeteria for order to be restored in the courtroom. Every uncomfortable wooden bench was shoulder to shoulder with spectators. And twice as many people as were crammed into the courtroom were roiling about in the hallway, trying to be close to the source of commotion.

The alternate jurors were led from their holding room through the hordes, and they took their seats with cautious looks, as if apprehensive about what was to happen. Then the twelve principal jurors emerged from the jury room.

Sara watched them enter but could read nothing from their expressions. As they settled into their swivel chairs, they avoided looking at anyone in the gallery, but a few glanced over at Kelly. In consideration of the large number of counts, she had been given permission to sit throughout the reading of the verdicts.

The first verdict, though only 1 among 131, could provide an advance indication of how the jury had gone with the entire indictment. The fathers and mothers of the children waited, and stared at nothing.

Kelly was at counsel table, mute. The jurors waited silently for the judge to enter. One or two were biting their fists, gently.

Sara McArdle, Glenn Goldberg, Harvey Meltzer, and Bob Clark took their seats at counsel table.

Harth entered suddenly, moving quickly. Without preamble, he asked, "Have you reached your verdicts?"

"We have," answered Mark, the young man who was the jury foreman. He was the youngest member of the panel, but when he began to speak, it was clear that he was serious, competent.

The judge instructed the court clerk to read the first count, a count charging the most severe type of crime of which the defendant stood accused. The man read, "Count one. First-degree aggravated sexual assault upon Jonathan Moore by anal penetration."

Harth was watching Mark. The clerk asked, "Your verdict?"

"Not guilty."

Nobody moved.

The clerk continued. "Count two. Third-deg—"

Judge Harth interrupted. "You forgot the lesser included."

He directed the clerk to the place on the verdict sheet, and the clerk read, "Count one. Second-degree sexual assault by sexual contact. Your verdict?"

Mark betrayed no inflection, no partiality. "Guilty."

Kelly swallowed, dropped her head.

"Count two. Third-degree endangering the welfare of a child, Jonathan Moore, by engaging in sexual conduct which would impair or debauch the morals of the said Jonathan Moore. Your verdict?"

"Guilty."

Mrs. Michaels blanched, and her eyes widened.

"Count three. Second-degree sexual assault by sexual contact upon Sean Hurley by touching genital area. Your verdict?"

Leslie scowled, as if she wasn't clear what was happening.

"Guilty," answered Mark. The jurors watched their foreman; many then dipped their heads to study their fingers.

Count four. Count five. Count six. Guilty. Guilty. Guilty.

Sara felt no jubilation. After the first moment of glacial release, she was too busy taking down the verdicts on her notepad.

Glenn watched Mark steadily.

"Count seven. Third-degree endangering the welfare of a child, Robert Stern, by displaying blood-soaked tampon. Your verdict?"

"Not guilty," said Mark, delivering the first count acquitted completely as opposed to being reduced to a lesser offense.

Count eight. Count nine. Count ten. Count eleven. Count twelve.

Guilty. Guilty. Guilty. Guilty. Guilty. As the guardian of the jury's judgment, Mark delivered the verdicts with conviction.

The defense attorneys averted their eyes, their faces pushed down into the table by the pounding of guilty verdicts.

Mr. Michaels sat unflinching and unsmiling.

Thirteen. Guilty. Fifteen. Guilty. Sixteen. Guilty. Seventeen. Guilty.

Kelly's mother was breathing heavily. She seemed to have sunk into the bench, and with each "guilty" she emitted a high gasp.

Kelly didn't look around.

Count eighteen. Count nineteen. The alternates seemed to register new resolution as each judgment was announced. Count twenty-one, twenty-two, twenty-three (jurors studying their knees; they had nothing to do with themselves; this was what they had done), twenty-five, twenty-eight, thirty-six, fifty-four . . .

Kelly leaned over to Clark. He sighed and explained something.

A cluster of six armed guards stood behind Kelly. Three more were arranged around Judge Harth's bench, two were at the doors to the courtroom, and one stood posted in the gallery over by the windows.

A few of the parents wept, a soft sound, private, clean.

Count fifty-six, fifty-seven. Guilty. Guilty. Mrs. Michaels's face had turned red. Mr. Michaels slipped his arm around her.

Kelly rocked her head. Clark, without moving his body at all, was whispering to her.

Count sixty-six through count seventy-three: being nude in front of a child, exposing her vagina while having her menstrual cycle, hitting child on penis with a spoon, hitting child upon rear, defecating and/or urinating in front of child, anal penetration with a spoon, forcing child to put knife in her rectum, trying to force child to put his finger in her anal cavity. Eight guilty verdicts.

The jury believed every single one of Lewis Dixon's allegations.

Kelly had disconnected from Clark. She sat unmoving, a rock. Then Sara noticed Kelly wipe her eyes, shake her head. Eleven more guilty counts in the name of Joey Gardner. "No," Kelly mouthed, her face like a prayerbook held in her hands.

Sara suddenly, convulsively, realized what Joey had meant by "She pooped on me." Hunched over her papers, Sara glanced again at Kelly out of the corner of her eye: Joey had been talking about anal sex. That twelfth count had just come back not guilty.

Ninety-three, ninety-four, one hundred and five.

Leslie Michaels's face was flushed as she shook her head. Kelly's second sister, Eileen, looked dragged down, exhausted. The room was filled with sniffling sounds.

"Count one hundred and nine. Third-degree endangering the welfare of a child, Kevin Brennan, by committing sexual acts upon his sister in the presence of this child. Your verdict?"

Kelly had a little smile.

"Guilty," Mark answered.

Guilty. Guilty. Guilty. Not Guilty. Guilty.

Only one count now remained. The clerk read it off, the one hundred and thirty-first: "Third-degree endangering the welfare of a child, Fred Mercer, by being nude in front of child. Your verdict?"

Mark's voice was deep, final: "Guilty."

The reading of the verdict had racked through forty-five raw minutes.

Meltzer now said, "For the defense, I request a polling of the jury."

Kelly stared over at the jury box, shaking her head. But it did not seem to be a strong reaction, just a resettling of her hair. She sucked on her lower lip.

Before polling the jury, Harth read back his understanding of the 131 verdicts, and Mark checked the judge's hand notes against his own verdict sheet. They read together rapidly, causing but a brief delay. The rest of the jurors sat still, extremely private, not invading one another's thoughts.

Kelly talked to herself, nodding her head.

Mrs. Michaels and Eileen hung their heads just over their knees.

A man in the front row of the jury box let out his breath, settled back into his chair, and swiped his hair away from his forehead. The jurors seemed hesitant to look at either the Michaelses or the Wee Care parents.

Judge Harth was ready to initiate the polling of the jury. First, he read back the first group of verdicts in the indictment. Then he instructed, "Members of the jury, if these are your verdicts, will you please answer yes. If these are not your verdicts, will you please answer no."

The court clerk took over. He asked, "Juror number one, are these your verdicts?"

Mark answered yes.

"Juror number two, are these your verdicts?"

"Yes," said Edith.

"Juror number three, are these your verdicts?"

"Yes," said Mary.

"Juror number four, are these your verdicts?"

"No," she said.

The clerk's mouth snapped shut.

"Excuse me," Harth interrupted, polite. "You said. . . ?"

"No," Essie repeated. She said the syllable as if it was the simplest thing in the world.

Mrs. Michaels, almost completely dissolved in grief, gasped back into composure, her dead eyes suddenly startled and alert.

Mistrial? Not a mistrial? What happened now to the verdict?

The attorneys were still, silent, but spectators were glancing around the room, gauging reactions. The rest of the jurors sat complacent, unsurprised. One or two wore fatalistic looks.

The judge's voice rang out: "*All* right. Members of the jury, you must continue until you have reached a unanimous verdict. You may now return to the jury room and continue your deliberations." Harth left the bench.

The twelve jurors moved lingeringly down the aisles and back into the jury room while the alternates were escorted out of the courtroom.

Kelly walked over to the waist-high wall, bracketed by her attorneys. Her family huddled against the other side of the wall, embracing her despite the impediment. Kelly began to cry in the arms of her family. Her sisters murmured to her, patted her on the arms, the shoulders, talked to her across the barrier. Abruptly, Kelly tried to disengage herself and pointed over their shoulders into the gallery.

"He's the guy who did this to me!" she said. Kelly looked down at Lou Fonolleras who had fought his way into the courtroom to hear the verdict. Her parents and sisters all pivoted to look.

The Michaelses snatched up their belongings and left the courtroom to wait out the renewed deliberations. Halfway down the aisle, Mrs. Michaels, revitalized, shouted, "It ain't over, *folks*!"

■
■ ■

Twenty minutes later another note came out from the jury: "We are ready to resume reading our verdict."

The court reassembled, and Bob Clark rose to speak. "We would now move for a mistrial. That juror is now singled out to come in line with the other eleven jurors. . . . We believe our client, under these circumstances, is not able to get a fair trial, and we believe we are entitled to a mistrial."

In response, Harth cited a Federal Court case supporting his action in returning the jury to their deliberations. He stated, "I'm satisfied that what the court did is entirely appropriate under our state and federal law. Bring the jury in." The court clerk polled the twelve jurors again, and this time, they were all in complete agreement.

As the question was handed down the rows of jurors, their expressions varied, some soft and shy, one drawling out his yes, another loud and clear. Another's voice was scratchy, so rough it was almost a whisper, the uneven sound of sorrow. He sounded hurt to have to judge. They had sat in this courtroom profoundly involved but not interactive. Now they were speaking, and their voices were personal, poignant.

Kelly smiled, nodded, then her face fell and she shook her head. She looked at Clark, who shook his head too, with a small smile.

The jurors answered, over and over again.

With all these yeses, it felt as if the court was in the grip of the group, in the clamp of their judgment.

Kelly's back began to quiver, but she was otherwise completely still, crying but unmoving. She touched her hands to her face, held her features in.

The very last verdicts were polled, and all the jurors concurred. The man with the hurt in his voice wiped his brow after his last yes.

"That concludes the polling of the jury," said Harth.

Kelly folded her hands.

The assumption of most in the courtroom was that Essie, the fourth juror, hadn't concurred with the premise of Kelly's guilt and that she had balked in the ultimate moment of condemning. In fact, as she later revealed, Essie had a different problem with the 115-count conviction. She told a newspaper reporter that if she had "any regrets, it was because of the not guiltys we lost." Essie had judged Kelly Michaels to be guilty on every single one of the 131 charges.

Before releasing the jurors, Judge Harth charged them on their conduct outside of the courtroom, discouraging them from divulging the details of deliberations. He said, "You are not required, except on order of this court, to discuss this case. . . . But the heart, the heart of this system, is free and open discussion in that jury room. . . . Thank you, and I extend my best wishes." Then Harth added, "Members of the jury, there are rewards to being a judge. . . . Your attitude has been one of my rewards." He leaned back in his gigantic black chair. "After you go to the jury room, I would be privileged if I could shake your hands in chambers."

The jurors rose and began to leave the floor, and as they did, the entire left-hand side of the courtroom arose, with the whooshing sound of coordinated motion. The fifty parents, friends, and relatives of Wee Care children stood at attention out of respect for the panel of sixteen jurors.

∎ ∎
∎ ∎

"I probably won't win this motion, but . . ." That was how Harvey Meltzer opened his remarks.

The floor had been cleared, and Meltzer was addressing the court: "As of this moment, my client is no longer clothed with the presumption of innocence. I would like this court to consider granting my client bail pending appeal."

Harvey Meltzer outlined the dual criteria that needed to be met before Kelly could attain bail. First was the requirement that the individual not present a danger to the community. Meltzer said, "I think that has been very well addressed by the fact that for the past two and a half years she has been out on bail and living with her parents." Additionally, he pointed out that his client had been in court daily throughout her trial and had always been prompt and cooperative.

The second criterion for granting bail was that there be a legitimate appealable issue. Meltzer said, "As far as the issues pending appeal, in my 'umble opinion, the verdict of this jury will be overturned."

Harth asked whether the state had any comment, and Sara addressed Meltzer's points: "First of all, the defendant did not comply with the conditions of bail."

She stated tersely, "The defendant *is* a danger to the community." Sara had done some calculations with her verdict notes, and now she read them into the record: "She stands convicted of thirty-four first-degree offenses, forty second-degree offenses, and forty-one third-degree offenses. This is not a happy day." Sara pulled back, trying to depersonalize the moment. Her request wasn't made out of vindictiveness, just rightness. She said, "The state stands for the revocation of bail."

Though courtroom proceedings couldn't penetrate the walls, the sound of clapping and cheering pulsed out from the jury room.

Judge Harth looked down at Kelly from the bench and concurred with Harvey Meltzer: "Her attendance here, her promptness, *has* been excellent." He paused.

Then he ruled, the ruling concise, complete. Harth said, "A criterion is danger to the community, including children—and I just *cannot* forget the children. Accordingly, bail is revoked."

Mrs. Michaels gasped.

Bob Clark requested that Kelly be accorded ten minutes with her parents before being remanded. Harth agreed to allow the time if the sheriff's officers, who were responsible for safely moving Miss Michaels through the courthouse, also agreed.

An officer moved forward to place the cuffs around Kelly's wrists. Her expression was uncommunicative, sullen.

Leslie, her arm over the wall, jabbed her finger toward Sara's back, repeating the motion convulsively. Mrs. Michaels grunted and lurched forward on the bench, brandishing a finger. "You did it!" she accused, glaring at Sara McArdle, as Sara slowly turned. Mr. Michaels, feeling his wife lunge, threw his arm across her collarbone and held her back against the bench. She was red, puffy, sobbing hysterically.

Leslie muttered to her mother: "Stay together. We *have* to stay together." As the officers walked Kelly by her parents, her arms cuffed in front, Kelly said quickly, "Don't worry, Mom." Clark tried to comfort the distraught Mrs. Michaels, his arm around her: "Come on, come on."

The family followed Kelly as she was being led away. Loudly, Leslie Michaels defied: "It's not over yet! It's not over yet!"

Out in the hallway, sheriff's officers created an aisle for Kelly through the mob, and as she made her way across the eighth-floor hall, through the tearshed of reality, Kelly appeared to be smirking.

．
． ．

When the jurors reentered the courtroom to make their way toward the judge's chambers, all trace of Margaret Kelly Michaels had vanished: the spiral notebooks, the crinkly candy wrappers, the flat handbag slung on the back of the chair, the well-traveled paperback, Kelly herself.

21

·.·

Sara had expected, after thirty-five months on this case, that if the state lost she would go through years of condemnation, and that if it won she would be Queen for a Day. Now everyone wanted interviews, but downstairs in the lobby, the prosecutor, victorious, told reporters: "There are no winners today. From the moment Kelly Michaels walked into that school, there were only losers."

Sara's husband, Kevin, was out of town for the weekend, so Sara sat alone in her empty office, terrified by the magnitude of the conviction, overwhelmed by the seriousness of sending the twenty-six-year-old to prison. Sara called whomever she felt she could draw strength from, talking with Peg Foster for close to an hour. Together they reviewed the most persuasive, unsolicited statements and actions of the children, putting the children's communications back into immediate memory. Sara focused her attention on the children to ease any sense of accountability to Kelly Michaels.

The Child Abuse Unit of the County Prosecutor's Office no longer had to worry about being hit with another such day-care case. The State Attorney General's Office had since taken over the investigation and prosecution of these highly publicized institutional abuse cases. Detective Rich Mastrangelo left Sara McArdle's unit for a position investigating similar kinds of cases at the state level.

Even if the jury had acquitted Kelly, Karen Steadman knew she would never have told her daughter. But now with the victory, Alison gloated, "Kelly's in jail! She's gonna die there!" Some of the children, including Jonathan Moore, felt tremendously empowered when their parents told them that the jury had believed the children. Others, though, were upset by the verdict, feeling guilty and responsible for getting Kelly into trouble. Joey Gardner, empowered, began to improve psychologically, but he still had twinges of guilt for what he'd done to Kelly. And, despite the victory, Lewis Dixon was still rocked by the experience of going to court.

Although the trial was over, the children were still racked with nightmares and terrors and disorders. Peg Foster assured the parents that they held some measure of control over their children's recovery: A parent's acceptance and manner of coping with the disclosure would be the number-one determinant of how well and how quickly a child would recover.

Alison Steadman was still sleeping in her parents' bed. When her mother talked about her daughter's problems, friends seemed to imply that she was overreacting. Karen had to accept the fact that her friends would never understand that trying to get Allie to enter her own bedroom at night was like trying to push her into an oven. The permanent change in Karen's daughter was that she didn't feel safe anymore.

Kelly Michaels's conviction on an overwhelming majority of the charges had not instantaneously created closure.

▪
▪ ▪

When the defense attorneys turned to the Appellate Division requesting bail pending appeal, Wee Care mothers began to make anonymous, silhouette appearances on newscasts. One woman said, "She told them she had the power to break out of a jail cell, and if in fact she is let out on bail, she has that power."

Kelly's two attorneys once again argued that Kelly Michaels's conduct throughout her trial had amply illustrated that she would not be a danger to children while out on bail.

Glenn Goldberg counterattacked that Kelly had been convicted beyond a reasonable doubt of abusing twenty children 115 times virtually under the noses of the teachers, aides, and administrators of the Wee Care Day

Nursery, and that she had demonstrated extraordinary skill in scheduling those activities. He insisted that children in general could not be protected short of her incarceration.

The panel of three appellate judges ruled in favor of the defense and set for Kelly Michaels the requirement of a $1 million bail bond or a $100,000 cash equivalent. Judge William Dreier commented that in his opinion, the level of publicity surrounding the trial ensured that mothers in Pennsylvania and New Jersey would know better than to let Kelly Michaels have access to their children.

But before Kelly could take advantage of this ruling, the prosecutors took the issue up to the New Jersey Supreme Court. For the first time ever, Sara McArdle now uncalmed the Wee Care parents and encouraged them to release their inner outrage. Parents and friends of the children bombarded the Supreme Court justice's office with phone calls and telegrams and sent letters to the Governor.

At the preliminary Supreme Court hearing, Justice Marie Garibaldi heard the motions, then stated, "It seems to me if you accept or give any credence to the jury's conviction, this woman . . . certainly may pose a threat to society." Garibaldi stayed the bail order of the Appellate Division, and when the full Supreme Court subsequently reviewed the issue, the panel of justices ruled to deny Kelly Michaels bail.

. .
. .

Kelly was to be assigned a new attorney by the Public Defender's office: Trial attorneys generally were not involved in their client's appeal, although both Meltzer and Clark had made themselves available for consultation on Kelly's behalf. They fully expected the jury's conviction to be overturned on appeal and for Kelly to be granted a new trial.

The possible appeal issues were numerous. The use of hearsay and the application of the closed-circuit statute were sure to come under fire. The inability of the defense experts to examine the children would likely come up, as would various rulings by the judge and statements by the prosecutors. Any conduct or decision that could be considered at all improper would be taken up at the appellate level.

Even if Kelly Michaels's appeal went nowhere, in a sense the Wee Care families would still have to live with indeterminacy, because the long-frozen civil suit against Wee Care, Arlene Spector, and Margaret Kelly Michaels was now going to resume.

The Wee Care parents continued to contend with their new understanding of raising children, striving to incorporate the advice of the professionals. They taught their children about their bodies and tried to make them comfortable discussing sexual things, creating an open atmosphere without shame or recrimination so that if anything were ever to happen to a child, he or she would feel free to tell someone. The parents also encouraged their children to question the behavior of adults so that adults would hopefully become less intimidating and all-powerful. The children were not expected to say no to a potential abuser; however, they were encouraged to trust their own instincts and to believe that they might know what was right even when an adult told them something different.

As a group, the Wee Care parents now accepted greater personal responsibility for overseeing their children's daily lives. They dropped in unexpectedly at the public and private schools their children now attended; they made a point of meeting other parents and comparing notes on their children's development; and they carefully listened to the things their children told them about their lives. For this particular group of parents, having already lived through trauma, it was necessary to try to offset their already existing concerns with an effort not to overinterpret. These new, involved parents no longer left details of care to fall into place: They were vigilant.

The state's investigators settled back into their post-publicity grinds. Lou Fonolleras continued with the Institutional Abuse Unit, but the soreness from his dealings with the Maplewood children remained close to the surface. George McGrath regretted that they had never been able to help Kelly. He still wished that she had confessed: if not to help herself by accepting treatment, then at least to take the burden of truth off the children.

The Michaels family returned to Pittsburgh and began to appear on television and in the press to publicize their version of the facts: that their daughter had been railroaded.

▪
▪ ▪

The mother of one little boy asked her son, now seven, how long he thought she should tell the judge to lock Kelly away. Pete asked his mother how many children Kelly had hurt, and she told him twenty.

Pete thought for a minute, then he asked, "What's twenty times twenty?"

"Four hundred," replied his mother.

"Four hundred years. Well, she won't live that long. What's twenty times four?"

"Eighty."

"Eighty years. Well, she won't live that long either." He considered for a while, then finally decided, "Tell him fifteen years, Mom."

His mother was curious. "Why fifteen years, Pete?"

Her son answered without hesitation: "'Cause then I'll be big enough to take care of myself."

On August 2, 1988, Kelly Michaels was returned to Newark to be sentenced for her crimes. Before the sentencing, Judge Harth accepted personal pleas, but although Kelly's parents and sisters were present, none of them rose to address the judge.

Kelly looked a little worn and disgusted as she made her own statement to the court.

She was curt: "What I'd like to say is I believe in God. I believe in a just and loving God. I declare my innocence, and I have every confidence that the appellate court will vindicate me." Kelly answered the months of testimony against her simply by saying that she would give "special prayers for those who have known me before and who have borne false witness against me."

Sheriff's officers prowled around the courtroom, looking for someone to pull out by the scruff of their neck, but Juror Eighteen, who had been released immediately upon the rendering of the verdict, finally had not returned to Harth's courtroom.

Angie McMahon's mother stepped through the swinging gates out into open court. The parents had selected her to address the judge on behalf of all the children of Wee Care. She articulated clearly, despite the tears soaking her face: "Our lives have changed over the past three years, and they will never be the same. I would just ask that the maximum sentence be imposed and that there be no eligibility for parole." Mrs. McMahon turned quickly and returned to the gallery.

Judge Harth reviewed his assessment of the aggravating and mitigating factors to be weighed in determining Kelly Michaels's sentence. He said: "The word *teacher* . . . and the word *trust* . . . must be synonymous. If they cease to be, the very nature of our civilization is challenged." Harth added, "If ever a case cried out for deterrence, cried out in anguished cries, this case does."

William Harth sentenced Kelly Michaels to forty-seven years in prison, with a period of parole ineligibility to last fourteen years.

Alison Steadman wanted Kelly to be in jail for 137 years. Alison wanted Kelly to be fed only bread and water, and she wanted Kelly to get so weak that she died in jail. Her mother was shocked by what she considered to be the inadequacy of this sentence.

Years ago, when she had first heard Sara Sencer McArdle speak to a parents' meeting, Karen Steadman hadn't even known the difference between civil and criminal law, but she had forced herself to learn because she believed the criminal justice system would make her prove her case and then, believing her, would take the problem out of her hands. That wasn't how it had turned out. Now, as she saw it, she would have to be an enforcer, returning in fourteen years to the parole board, and if all went well and Kelly was turned down for parole, the year after that, and the next year.

Kelly Michaels was returned to prison, this time to the Clinton Correctional Center. While some of the parents of her victims criticized her sentence, others felt that a fourteen-year minimum was an enormous amount of time taken from a life, particularly that of a young woman: Kelly Michaels would not be able to appear before the parole board until she was forty.

Sara McArdle stated in a news conference: "This was not the substantial sentence we were hoping for." Bob Clark agreed that if his client had been convicted only on three penetrations on three separate children, Kelly could well have received the exact same sentence. And Judge Harth acknowledged: "I felt that though I could have gone higher on parole ineligibility, I am satisfied . . . that should be under the jurisdiction of the parole board."

.
. .

Downstairs in the lobby of the courthouse, television cameramen thronged, vying for a clear shot of any one of the principal characters in the day's sentencing procedure. Leaving behind the chaos in the courthouse, several mothers of victims were descending the steps of the building on their way to their cars when an older woman approached them. She wasn't anyone they knew, and for a moment they didn't think she meant to interact, but the woman walked directly up to them and addressed herself to the group. She said, "You don't know me, but I've been watching this case. You mothers have got to stick together."

The woman was imploring them from a slightly lined face. A man stood a short way off waiting for her.

She finished hurriedly, "I just want you to know. In fourteen years, I'll be there."

Author's Note

I attended the four-day-a-week New Jersey Superior Court trial of Margaret Kelly Michaels from July 1987, through April 1988, as well as the several court proceedings that took place after the jury's verdict.

At the time of writing, the transcripts of trial proceedings were sealed from the public to protect the identities of the alleged victims, so I have relied on the ten volumes of my own notes taken daily. Further information was drawn from extensive interviews of many of the case's principals, including social workers, prosecutors, defense attorneys, investigators, parents, child psychologists, researchers, teachers, members of the press, and various trial witnesses: individuals representing both the state and the defense. The only notable exceptions are the accused, Kelly Michaels, and one of her defense attorneys, Harvey Meltzer, each of whom declined to be interviewed.

The names of all Wee Care students and their parents have been changed. The identities of all other characters are actual. Juror Eighteen is also actual.

All the dialogue is derived from courtroom testimony or drawn directly from interviews. As the examination of the witnesses was often disjointed —a given topic coming up on numerous occasions over the course of several days—I have sometimes grouped the testimony on a given subject into a scene.

The reactions and feelings of the character ''Ellen Gardner'' are based on conversations with many actual mothers, not just one. The events in Ellen's life, however, are not composite, but relate only to ''Joey Gardner'' and his actual mother.

Many people choose not to think about sexual abuse, insisting that (a) it doesn't happen, or (b) it doesn't matter. Crimes against children are dismissed with explanations that children won't remember acts of abuse or aren't damaged by them because they don't comprehend sexual feelings: Sex is an adult activity, and therefore a child victim will endure abuse and move on from it without personal consequences. . . .

When a father throws a lobster in the pot, he'll console his family with, ''Don't worry, this doesn't hurt. A lobster has a shallow nervous system; it doesn't feel much of anything at all.''

How much pain does a child feel? Enough to care about?

A child is at a coping disadvantage as compared to an adult. The child's world is smaller and so, proportionately, more completely impaired by trauma. His ability to counter the trauma of sexual abuse with other things he knows and feels is less, as he knows fewer people, places, ways of life. If anything, a child victim's need for empathy must be overestimated.

We rationalize inflicting pain on lobsters because we have a taste for them. If we rationalize to nothing the pain of children, then we indulge those people who have a taste for the flesh of children.

LISA MANSHEL